Malte Griesse (ed.)
From Mutual Observation to Propaganda War

Histoire | Volume 56

MALTE GRIESSE (ED.)
From Mutual Observation to Propaganda War
Premodern Revolts in Their Transnational Representations

[transcript]

Most articles in this book draw on contributions to a workshop at the Center for interdisciplinary Studies in Bielefeld in June 2009. Both the workshop and the book have been kindly funded by the Fritz Thyssen Foundation, Cologne.

Bibliographic information published by the Deutsche Nationalbibliothek
The Deutsche Nationalbibliothek lists this publication in the Deutsche Nationalbibliografie; detailed bibliographic data are available in the Internet at http://dnb.d-nb.de

© 2014 transcript Verlag, Bielefeld

All rights reserved. No part of this book may be reprinted or reproduced or utilized in any form or by any electronic, mechanical, or other means, now known or hereafter invented, including photocopying and recording, or in any information storage or retrieval system, without permission in writing from the publisher.

Cover layout: Kordula Röckenhaus, Bielefeld
Cover illustration: The cover picture is the frontispiece of the 4th edition of
  Maiolino Bisaccioni's »Historia delle gverre civili di Qvesti Vltimi Tempi«
  (History of civil wars of these latest times), published 1655 in Venetia by
  Storti. The image has been taken from a copy located at the Herzog August
  Bibliothek, Wolfenbüttel, call number: 39.7 Hist (1). A digitalized version
  of the book can be consulted on:
  http://diglib.hab.de/drucke/39-7-hist-1s/start.htm.
Printed by Majuskel Medienproduktion GmbH, Wetzlar
Print-ISBN 978-3-8376-2642-1
PDF-ISBN 978-3-8394-2642-5

Content

Introduction: Representing Revolts
across Boundaries in Pre-Modern Times
Malte Griesse | 7

REPRESENTING REVOLT BEFORE THE ADVENT OF THE GUTENBERG-GALAXY: A QUESTION OF DISSEMINATION?

Cross-Border Representations of Revolt in the Later Middle Ages:
France and England During the Hundred Years' War (1337-1453)
Helmut Hinck, Bettina Bommersbach | 37

Trans-national Representations of Pretenders
in 17th-Century Russian Revolts
Maureen Perrie | 53

TRANSGRESSION OF BOUNDARIES AS A FEAT OF LIBERTY: EARLY MODERN ANTHROPOLOGIES OF REVOLT

Political Vacuum and Interregnum in Early Modern Unrest
Ives-Marie Bercé | 81

Stenka Razin's Rebellion: The Eyewitnesses and their Blind Spot
André Berelowitch | 93

INSURGENTS AS DIPLOMATES: CROSS-BORDER ALLIANCES AND THEIR REPRESENTATIONS

Framing The Borderland: The Image of the Ukrainian Revolt
and Hetman Bohdan Khmel'nyts'kyi in Foreign Travel Accounts
Frank Sysyn | 127

Transnational Representations of Revolt and New Modes of
Communication in the Mid-Seventeenth Century Polish-Lithuanian
Commonwealth: Jerzy Lubomirski's Rebellion against
King Jan Kazimierz
Angela Rustemeyer | 159

GOVERNMENTS STRUGGLING WITH FOREIGN REPRESENTATIONS OF INTERNAL REVOLTS

"Revolts" in the *Kuranty* of March–July 1671
Ingrid Maier, Stepan Shamin | 181

State-Arcanum and European Public Spheres:
Paradigm Shifts in Muscovite Policy towards Foreign
Representations of Russian Revolts
Malte Griesse | 205

REVOLTS AS POLITICAL CRIME: LEGAL CONCEPTS AND PUBLIC REPRESENTATION

Quietis publicae perturbatio: Revolts in the Political and Legal
Treatises of the Sixteenth and Seventeenth Centuries
Fabrizio dal Vera | 273

Early Modern Revolts as Political Crimes
in the Popular Media of Illustrated Broadsheets
Karl Härter | 309

Authors | 351

Introduction: Representing Revolts across Boundaries in Pre-Modern Times

MALTE GRIESSE

Since the heyday of research on late medieval and early modern social unrest in the 1960s-1980s, historians have referred to the fact that contemporaries had already considered the manifold revolts (and revolutions) of their epoch as a phenomenon transcending particular countries and reigns.[1] Stating thus researchers tried to release their own approach from the limitations of 19th century national historiographies. Both Soviet-Marxist and Western historiographies sought to embed early-modern expressions of protest into a broader analysis of historical structures. Accordingly, they examined them as symptoms of a deeply-rooted societal crisis that characterized the problematic process of transition from the middle Ages to modernity.[2] Boris Porshnev and Soviet historiography alongside him interpreted revolts in terms of "class struggles" between peasants and feudal lords, whereas Roland Mousnier and his successors perceived them as an interrelation of "challenge and response" between a modernizing state and the purely reactive, conservative estates, or else the population at large.[3] In spite of the

---

1 Winfried Schulze, "Europäische und deutsche Bauernrevolten der frühen Neuzeit – Probleme der vergleichenden Betrachtung", in *Europäische Bauernrevolten der frühen Neuzeit*, ed. Winfried Schulze (Frankfurt am Main, 1982), 10–60, 12; Wolfgang Reinhard, "Theorie und Empirie bei der Erforschung frühneuzeitlicher Volksaufstände", in ibid., 66–99; John Elliott, "Revolution and continuity in early modern Europe", *Past and Present* 42 (1969): 35–56; Yves-Marie Bercé, "Troubles frumentaires et pouvoir centralisateur. L'émeute de Fermo dans les Marches (1648)", *Mélanges d'archéologie et d'histoire* 73 (1961): 471–505; Andreas Suter, *Der schweizerische Bauernkrieg von 1653: Politische Sozialgeschichte – Sozialgeschichte eines politischen Ereignisses*, Frühneuzeit-Forschungen, ed. Peter Blickle et al., vol. 3 (Tübingen, 1997), 320.
2 Hagen Schulze, *Staat und Nation in der europäischen Geschichte*, Europa bauen (München, 1994).
3 Roland Mousnier, *Fureurs paysannes. Les paysans dans les révoltes du XVIIe siècle: France, Russie, Chine*, (Paris, 1967); Yves-Marie Bercé, *Histoire des Croquants. Etude*

significant differences, however, both interpretations observed a structural similarity between the manifestations of social upheaval in different countries. Nevertheless did the contemporaries' own perceptions and their *cross-border comparisons* – if quoted at all – remain mere illustrations.

HISTORICAL ANTHROPOLOGY AND TRANSNATIONAL HISTORY

Two trends in present day historiography seem to have paved a way for a revaluation by now: 1) the increasing influence of anthropological approaches and 2) the growing awareness of "transnational" dimensions.

Firstly, the turn to cultural history, historical anthropology and renewed political history made the historical agents' views, interpretations and semantics themselves an object of enquiry. Although revolts have become less popular in scholarly research since the fall of the Soviet empire and the concomitant marginalization of Marxism, concepts such as "moral economy", "language of the crowd", or symbolical orders have ousted the prevalence of external structural models. For this reason, the common reference to economic factors and other measurable items shaping the social actors' behavior however unconsciously was given a new framework.[4] Ricoeur characterized such structuralism as an "interpretation of suspicion", thus criticizing a perspective which had devalued the agents' views solely as surface phenomena that would hide deeper and more significant social, economic, psychological etc. mechanisms – mechanisms that were said to be the true determination or at least a profound instigation of human behavior.[5] This shift

---

des soulèvements populaires au XVII siècle dans le sud-ouest de la France (Genève, 1974).

4   On moral economy see Edward Palmer Thompson, "The Moral Economy of the English Crowd in the 18th Century", *Past and Present* 50 (1971): 76–136; on the language of the crowd see especially idem, "Eighteenth Century English Society. Class Struggle without Class?", in *Social History* 3, 2 (1978): 133–165.

5   This includes all interpretations seeking for invisible driving forces behind the phenomena, forces that are considered to be more real than phenomenal reality. In the "interprétations du soupçon" the protagonists' own arguments are mainly rationalisations that they might believe in themselves, but that are superficial for serious observers because they hide more than they reveal. Compared with this, Ricoeur's phenomenological approach pleads for taking seriously the protagonists' statements, similar to what is often championed in historical anthropology. Paul Ricoeur, *Du texte à l'action. Essais d'herméneutique II* (Paris, 1986).

to a more balanced view of contemporary accounts has gradually triggered innovation in the study of social unrest and uprisings, which goes into opposite directions. On the one hand the focus on the contemporaries' voices, representations and "worldviews"[6] has led to an emphasis on the peoples' struggle for the "old right" or the topos of the "good king and his bad councillors", which supported Mousnier's or Charles Tilly's hypotheses on the "backward" role of the peasantry or of the larger population. On the other hand, this new focus has enabled important studies questioning such images of one-sided re-activity in order to claim that the population's protest was in fact the engine of many innovations and a hitherto neglected source of the emergent idea of "human rights". In opposition to Habermas' influential *Theory of communicative action* that had located the genesis of a public sphere in urban (bourgeois) Enlightenment reasoning through the written word, historians of pre-modern revolts observed the subalterns' potential to create such public spheres well before.[7] Andreas Würgler has therfore argued that a recurrent element of revolts had been to insist upon the publication of acts guaranteeing privileges and rights to the population, documents that the authorities systematically tried to conceal. In this light the focus on "old" rights inherent in the insurgents' rhetoric rather seems to be a disguise for change and is in any way superseded by the novelty of the call for publicity.[8]

Secondly, and simultaneously to the cultural turn, historical research has become increasingly attentive to transnational dimensions. This is certainly due to present day entangled world economy as well as the ever growing importance of transnational organisations and agencies while the national ones loose momentum. Probably first and foremost, however, the transnational outlook is due to the process of European integration, which is, unlike the aforementioned phenomena of globalization, (still) regarded as a politically desired aim rather than an automatic process that cannot be halted anyways. For that reason efforts to ideologically and

---

6   Cf. on "moral economy" Edward Palmer Thompson, *Plebeische Kultur und moralische Ökonomie. Aufsätze zur englischen Sozialgeschichte des 18. und 19. Jahrhunderts,* trans. Günther Lottes, intro. Dieter Groh (Frankfurt am Main, 1980).

7   Winfried Schulze, "Der bäuerliche Widerstand und die 'Rechte der Menschheit'", in *Grund- und Freiheitsrechte im Wandel von Gesellschaft und Geschichte,* Veröffentlichungen zur Geschichte der Grund- und Freiheitsrechte, ed. Günter Birtsch, vol. 1 (Göttingen 1981), 41–56.

8   Andreas Würgler, "Das Modernisierungspotential von Unruhen im 18. Jahrhundert. Ein Beitr. zur Entstehung der politischen Öffentlichkeit in Deutschland und der Schweiz", *Geschichte und Gesellschaft* 21 (1995): 195–217. See also David Zaret, *Origins of democratic culture. Printing, petitions, and the public sphere in early-modern England* (Princeton, New Jersey, 2000) for the particularly ample case of the English Civil war.

scientifically foster Europeanization by exploring historical roots of a common European culture often receive privileged funding. Many studies and projects on the closely intertwined European history have thus taken shape. Europe is often conceptualized as an overlapping communicational space. Among other key developments the printing revolution and, even more so, the emergence of regular newspapers during the 17th century are identified as stepping-stones of European integration.[9] For a long time studies on the press have apparently lived in the shadows, and maybe they are still to a certain extent marginalized within the field of historical research; but historians begin to revise their views and to take the wide range of early-modern media more seriously. There has been done considerable work in order to digitalize early-modern newspapers, and this provides new facilities for research.

An important genre that combines both the transnational dimension and the anthropological interest for contemporaries' perceptions and world-views is the travelogue. In literary studies it has been popular for decades, but historians followed suit. The perception and description of foreign and particularly exotic peoples made authors sensitive to what was normally taken for granted in one's own culture. Even if this was not explicitly reflected, the descriptions often focused on what was perceived as unfamiliar. Much profit can be drawn from post-colonial studies that examine the interactions between colonizers and the colonized, for in these circumstances the cultural difference was particularly huge or at least incited strong presentations of contrast and discord. What is sometimes overlooked within the emphasis on difference is that travellers, when comparing and juxtaposing different countries and cultures, also drew parallels. They registered parallels between countries they knew, sometimes referring to home and host country only, but sometimes even reflecting upon a series of countries they had visited consecutively. One example, for instance, was Engelbert Kaempfer (1651-1716), who travelled to India, South-East Asia and Japan via Russia and Persia.[10] In middle and Western Europe whose kingdoms and principalities were certainly less

---

9 *Die Entstehung des Zeitungswesens im 17. Jahrhundert. Ein neues Medium und seine Folgen für das Kommunikationssystem der Frühen Neuzeit*, ed. Volker Bauer and Holger Böning, Presse und Geschichte – neue Beiträge, ed. Holger Böhning et al., vol. 54 (Bremen, 2011); Asa Briggs and Peter Burke, *A social history of the media. From Gutenberg to the Internet* (Cambridge, 2010); *The dissemination of news and the emergence of contemporaneity in early modern Europe*, ed. Brendan M. Dooley (Farnham, 2010).

10 *Engelbert Kaempfer (1651-1716). Ein Gelehrtenleben zwischen Tradition und Innovation*, [Vorträge, gehalten anläßlich eines interdisziplinären Arbeitsgespräches am 20. und 21. September 2001 in der Herzog August Bibliothek], ed. Detlef Haberland (Wiesbaden, 2004).

divided in terms of nationality/ ethnicity than religiously and even more so socially and legally), many parallels simply imposed themselves on the observers (and those who wrote were generally not peasants). Ethnographic alienation and analogy have thus to be seen as complementary forms of representation. Observers pre-selected information more or less consciously when writing down their experience and observations for the reading public at home that generally judged on the basis of what was familiar. But even the very perception of foreign reality was a genuine process of filtering that obeyed patterns of both *identization* and *alterization,* which we might rather call *assimilation* and *dissimilation.*[11]

Maybe the strong (anthropological) focus on *dissimilation* in recent investigation of trans-cultural perception has contributed to the researchers' preference for contemporaries' descriptions of unfamiliar and seemingly strange customs, manners and everyday practice – at the expense of the narration of extraordinary events. Of course, wars have always been treated: and because all of them indisputably involved different countries, mutual perception and depiction have finally lent themselves to transnational approaches.[12]

REGARDING REVOLTS ACROSS BORDERS: FOREIGNERS AS PRIVILEGED OBSERVERS

Events like social unrest and revolts, however, which were seemingly beyond the ordinary and of purely local or regional character, have rather been disregarded. The two underlying assumptions (held by historians) obviously were 1) that revolts were indeed rare events, and 2) that they did not really have an impact on other countries. Our objective is not so much to question these assumptions about what revolts actually were, but to examine how contemporary observers depicted and conceptualized them. If we take metaphors comparing the people (*populus*) to the

---

11 Even though Wolfram Lutterer, Identitäten, Alteritäten – Normativitäten? Die Bedeutung von Normativität für Selbst- und Fremdbilder, in *Normen, Ausgrenzungen, Hybridisierungen und 'Acts of Identity'*, ed. Monika Fludernik and Hans-Joachim Gehrke (Würzburg, 2004), 23–43 already employed the German terms *Identisierung* and *Alterisierung,* they are no current concepts in theoretical debates. But in contrast to the polar opposites *identity/alterity* they emphasize the ascriptional aspect and show to what extent *sameness* and *otherness* are discursively constructed. Even more appropriate seems to be the conceptual duality of *assimilation* and *dissimilation* (although the latter is also used in biology in order to describe metabolic processes).

12 Cf. for instance *Kriegsniederlagen: Erfahrungen und Erinnerungen,* ed. Horst Carl, Hans-Henning Kortüm, et al. (Berlin, 2004).

ocean and defining the task of rule as the (captain's) art of steering the ship of state through tempests into account, this equation of social unrest and bad weather rather implies that revolts were regarded as periodically occurring phenomena. And a didactic poem from as early as the 13th century suggests the same when advising nobles to put up *with their peasants' hate*.[13] It seems as if the etiological question *why* revolts happened, coexisted and often combined with the question *how* they were to be prevented, the latter implying at least a certain degree of normality. Concerning the allegedly local character of revolts, other recurrent metaphors in contemporary writings on seditions might similarly lead to doubts: when revolts were compared to a wildfire, a contagion or epidemic it was clear that they had no reason to come to a halt at borders, at least if their spreading was not actively prevented.

Without any doubt, cases where insurgents themselves referred to foreign models are rather rare; on some occasions rebels would have quoted or tried to imitate the examples of the Swiss Confederacy or the Dutch Republic, for instance.[14] Such cases occurred mainly in the Italian seaports that were nerve centres of a vivid flow of information, with merchants bringing in information from around the Mediterranean. Thus, during the revolts of the mid-17th century in Southern Italy one can find references to the insurgents in Catalonia, Portugal and the Netherlands, all of them having previously rebelled against the Spanish Habsburgs. Especially the successful secession from Spanish rule by the Portuguese and the Dutch nourished hopes when the inhabitants of the Italian seaports saw themselves unjustly overburdened with taxes since they had to pay the bill for the extensive warfare (similar to the subjects of other European monarchies in and

---

13 On representations of the people as "stormy sea" cf. A. Collurafi, *Le Tumultuationi della Plebe in Palermo* (Palermo 1651), 12-20, quoted from Peter Burke, "Some Seventeenth-Century Anatomists of Revolution", in *Storia della Storiografia* 22 (1992): 23–35. In this vein the state is often compared to a ship that has to be steered through the open sea. Cf. for instance Philipp Andreas Oldenburger, *Tractatus iuridico-politicus de rebuspublicis turbidis in tranquillum statum reducendis, in eoque conservandis* (Geneva, 1677), 21, 70, 390. On the didactical poem cf. http://www.litde.com/das-hfische-gesellschaftsideal/das-ritterliche-tugendsystem.php, consulted August 29, 2011.

14 The Swiss model of the *Eidgenossenschaft* (Confederacy) was most notably followed in the German Peasants' war, where the insurgents founded their Upper-Swabian *Eidgenossenschaft*. On the Venetian and the Dutch model see Eco O.G. Haitsma Mulier and Gerard T. Moran, *The Myth of Venice and Dutch Republican Thought in the Seventeenth Century* (Assen, 1980).

around the 30-Years War).[15] When a rebellion reached a certain level and attracted influential and internationally connected groups or individual personalities, insurgents often even forged transnational alliances. This applies to the well-studied case of the English Civil war against Charles I and the ensuing republic whose principal agents entertained diplomatic relations well before the kingdom was abolished. This pattern recurs in many revolts in the Polish-Lithuanian Commonwealth, where both the Ukrainian Cossacks under Khmel'nyts'kyi and the dissenters under Lubomierski relied on foreign partners, not without having some difficulties in justifying these alliances as Frank Sysyn's and Angela Rustemeyer's papers show.

Far more frequent, though, was the explicit or implicit comparison between different revolts by contemporary *observers*. Their search for comprehensive explanations shows to what extent revolts were seen as interrelated and a coherent phenomenon. The contributions of this volume draw on such contemporary observations and subsequently try to combine a general focus on transnational dimensions with the quasi-anthropological attention to historical actors' perceptive and conceptual patterns, their way of seeing and interpreting the world. The volume is a first attempt to examine the "transnational representation" of pre-modern revolts, to explore perceptions and descriptions of revolts across borders. It cannot claim to be systematic as yet. But it shall give a fresh impetus in order to inspire further research in this direction, an undertaking that requires intense cooperation of specialists with different regional, linguistic, disciplinary and methodological competences. The first step has been taken at a conference at the Centre of Interdisciplinary Studies (Bielefeld) in June 2009 and most contributions of the present book are elaborations of what we have discussed there.

To be sure, *explicit* juxtapositions and comparisons of revolts are not innumerable in early modern times.[16] It is, however, not for this reason alone that in the present study *implicit* comparisons have often been privileged. Considering contemporary awareness of the ubiquity of revolts, one of my leading hypotheses is that many descriptions of uprisings in *foreign* countries were at the same time, or at least to some extent, reflections on analogous phenomena *at home*, even more so since revolts were an extremely delicate matter to deal with for a writer. However

---

15 Wayne Te Brake, *Shaping History. Ordinary People in European Politics, 1500 - 1700* (Berkeley, Los Angeles, 1998), 129-137, for quotations see especially 109-110.

16 Burke, Anatomists gives a list of contemporary histories of revolt, many of them explicitly comparative. Focusing mainly on 17th century Italian authors writing on revolts and what they often called revolutions, Burke examines their use of metaphors for describing phenomena of unrest. He claims that these metaphors are more than decorations, but were supposed to contribute substantially to the explanation of contemporary phenomena.

far-reaching or narrow-minded their concrete aims had been, revolts were generally registered as a broadside towards the authorities and treated as *crimen laesae majestatis* in court. Such classifications considerably limited the scope of interpretation for an observer, especially if he himself was subject to the contested authority. He could not but paint the rebels in rather dark colours if he wanted to avoid a serious conflict of loyalties. Intimate knowledge of internal matters was thus outweighed by a somewhat biased view, whereas foreign observers, less familiar with political and cultural specificities of the country they were writing about, were freer in their interpretation and in their quest for explanations.

Therefore did the Muscovite envoy to England in 1645-46, serving at a time when the civil war was in full swing, rather sympathize with Parliament in its conflict with Charles I (1645-46). He was certainly influenced by his English merchant-interlocutors,[17] but he did not in the least bother to conceal this attitude in his report to the ambassadorial office, i.e. for the tsar and the Muscovite governing elite concerned with foreign affairs.[18] Inversely, the foreign residents in Moscow showed much sympathy for the plight of the urban population that rose to rebellion at the same time as in many other European countries. The correspondents did not mince matters in depicting the authorities' corruptive practices and deliberately contrasted them with the rebels' common good-oriented argumentation and their considerable efforts to avoid any exploitation of the general chaos for personal enrichment; and thus they steered clear of bringing into discredit the legitimacy of their actions and objectives.[19] This is even more remarkable for observers who personally suffered from the uprisings, whenever their residences were devastated or further harm was done by the insurgents who seemed to regard them as unduly privileged. Foreigners, indeed, would not dare present the insurgents as heroes, but often they depicted them as pityable victims of misery and abuse, whose actions were at least understandable if not to a certain extent legitimate.

---

17 Cf. M.A. Alpatov and L. V. Cherepnin, *Russkaya istoriceskaya mysl' i Zapadnaya Evropa XII-XVII vv.* (Moskva, 1973), 335-342.

18 The Russian chronicles that relate the extraordinarily ferocious events in Moskau, Pskov and Novgorod (1648-51) are written with big temporal delay. The accounts on Moscow are inexact to a degree, that it is even hard to identify the uprising; the simultaneous uprisings in many other towns are practically not represented at all.

19 See numerous references to sources in *Volksaufstände in Rußland. Von der Zeit der Wirren bis zur "Grünen Revolution" gegen die Sowjetherrschaft*, ed. Heinz-Dietrich Löwe, Forschungen zur osteuropäischen Geschichte, ed. Holm Sundhaussen, vol. 65 (Wiesbaden, 2006), where the insurgents' motives are identified as being oriented towards legality and the reestablishment of the "old law", but the external standpoint of the authors is never considered on the background of their original cultural baggage and experience.

Beyond the tricky question of legitimacy Peter Burke has pointed to the problem of literary genre conventions that many authors of Renaissance and Baroque faced when writing on *popular* rebellions in particular. On the one hand, tragedy seemed the most appropriate genre. On the other hand, were people of low status worthy of being represented in tragedy, the most respected genre of the Antique tradition which had so far been reserved for personalities of high status? Comedy was not a convincing solution, neither. Sometimes writers recurred to tragicomedy. The question remained an object of debate.[20] In any case, foreigners had a larger scope to ponder on the motives and grievances that moved people to rise in rebellion; their quest for explanations of early modern revolts was less limited.

READING CROSS-BORDER ACCOUNTS OF EARLY-MODERN REVOLTS

With respect to the exploitation of such transnational sources Russian studies – frequently labelled as backward as is (labelled) their object of enquiry – can provide new insights. Historians of medieval and early modern Russia have always been obliged to rely heavily on foreigners' accounts, simply because of the scarcity of domestic narrative sources.[21] The writings of Sigismund von Herberstein, Adam Olearius or the above-mentioned Engelbert Kaempfer are only the most famous accounts of Russia in the 16th and 17th centuries, well-known also among non-specialists. The trustworthiness of their testimonies, as well as the prejudices and limitations of their knowledge on Russian culture have been debated at length. But just like the writings of less known foreigners – mercenaries of the Time of Troubles (the civil war at the beginning of the 17th century), physicians at court,

---

20 See Peter Burke, *The renaissance sense of the past*, Documents of modern history (London, 1969).
21 This makes the situation of early modern Russia to some extent comparable to the colonial world that has been authoritatively described and interpreted by the colonizers who thus (by the use of the written word) imposed their own categories of evaluation and made the natives regard themselves with European eyes. In postcolonial theory this epistemological conquest is considered much more profound and long-lasting than political rule and military oppression. To be sure, in the Russian case the story is much more complex. There has been neither military colonialism, nor Western political rule. But the emergent Russian historiography in the 18th and 19th centuries had to draw on foreigners' descriptions. This could actually make Russia the litmus test for the validity of epistemological hypothesis.

diplomats, travellers and others –, their descriptions constitute bedrocks in our record of late medieval and early-modern Russian history in general, and of revolts in particular, be they town uprisings, or large-scale rebellions occurring in the vastness of the Cossack peripheries.[22]

However, a shift of perspective is required in the use of these documents. We should not consider them primarily as sources of facts anymore, as it has been done for ages of historical research. Instead of focusing exclusively on the objects of description, i.e. the revolts on Russian soil, we should have a closer look at the people who put pen to paper and explore their role as transcultural mediators. Their accounts have thus to be read as both 1) representations of the events in the foreign culture they describe, and 2) as more or less implicit reflections of the authors' own cultural backgrounds and often their domestic (direct or indirect) revolt experience. From this point of view these representations are *mediation acts*. The lacking comprehension of Russian culture that is often deplored in historiography of Muscovite revolts can be put to an advantage, if we adopt the idea of the authors as cross-border commuters who (more or less consciously) compared and juxtaposed their two (or sometimes more) cultures of reference. What has traditionally been dealt with as a shortcoming turns out to be a gain when viewed from the perspective of contemporaries' transnational comparisons of revolts or revolt-cultures. The testimonies should accordingly be read on this double ground leading into a connected history or a *histoire croisée* of revolt-perceptions and -representations.[23]

Similar to Russian studies, researchers of West- and central-European revolts suspected representations from abroad to be ignorant of national or regional specificities and therefore less reliable than internal descriptions. And since domestic sources including chronicles, court records and others are abundant despite constraints and conflicts of loyalty, foreign descriptions and interpretations of revolts have hardly been taken into account. Apart from the different level of writing and print culture, this prolificacy might be attributed to the rulers' attempts to rapidly launch their hegemonic interpretations of these challenges wherein they focussed on punishment and the spectacle of suffering; quite on the contrary, the Russian government rather tended to silence revolts and would have them narrated only with considerably hindsight, often decades after they had happened. Furthermore, most of these official chronicles were designed to preserve the medieval style for long, almost until the end of the 17th century. This circumstance

---

22 The classical bibliographical survey of these foreigners' writings on pre-petrine Russia is Friedrich von Adelung, *Kritisch-literärische Übersicht der Reisenden in Russland bis 1700, deren Berichte bekannt sind* (St. Petersburg, Leipzig, 1846).

23 Cf. Michael Werner, Bénédicte Zimmermann, "Penser l'histoire croisée. Entre empirie et réflexivité", *Annales* 58 (2003): 7-36.

of a deliberately continued pre-Gutenberg Age connects the case of Muscovy and the available sources in some respect to medieval France and England, treated by Bettina Bommersbach and Helmut Hinck in this volume.

Winfried Schulze, one of the most distinguished scholars of early modern revolts in the Holy Roman Empire, raised the question whether "revolt and uprising have inspired new and salutary laws", taking up the question posed by the early-modern political scientist Neumair von Ramsla, who specifically dealt with the phenomenon of sedition.[24] Thinking along these lines, one has to consider that the adjustments and learning processes that generally evolved in the long term were hardly ever the result of the immediate revolt experience made by the authorities, but were in fact mediated by complex detours, by multiple forms of reception and representation that must be retraced and examined with respect to their agents and (af)filiations in time and space – including the transnational level. If we think of Schulze's far-reaching hypothesis that a process of increasing legal consolidation (*Verrechtlichung*, "juridicazation") has taken place as a result of the experiences of social upheaval in early modern times[25], the development of legal systems and criminal justice gains particular significance. This development has to be regarded in a process of close transnational interaction. Growing penal awareness often drew on public and secret representations of uprisings, which were generally classified as treason, lèse-majesté or political crime.[26]

It shall not be denied that the governments did everything in their power to monopolize the representation of revolt in support of their official version, which commonly aimed at thoroughly discrediting the insurgents. But from revolt to revolt, or from country to country, this denigration could be launched with very diverging thrusts. If in some cases revolts were politicized as attempted coups and

---

24 Winfried Schulze, "'Geben Aufstand und Aufruhr Anlaß zu neuen, heilsamen Gesetzen'. Beobachtungen über die Wirkungen bäuerlichen Widerstands in der frühen Neuzeit", in *Aufstände, Revolten, Prozesse: Beiträge zu bäuerlichen Widerstandsbewegungen im frühneuzeitlichen Europa*, ed. Winfried Schulze (Geschichte und Gesellschaft, vol. 27, 1983), 261–285.

25 See Peter Blickle, "The Criminalization of Peasant Resistance in the Holy Roman Empire: Toward a History of the Emergence of High Treason in Germany", *Journal of Modern History* 58 suppl. (December 1986): 88-97.

26 Fabrizio Dal Vera's contribution to this volume deals with this question. See also the classical study by Mario Sbriccoli, *Crimen laesae maiestatis. Il problema del reato politico alle soglie della scienza penalistica moderna* (Milano, 1974) and Angela Rustemeyer, *Dissens und Ehre. Majestätsverbrechen in Rußand (1600-1800)*, Forschungen zur osteuropäischen Geschichte, ed. Holm Sundhaussen, vol. 69 (Wiesbaden, 2006), who gives a large comparative view of the criminalization of revolt in different countries.

high treason, the common-good-oriented claims and practices of the insurgents were presented as banditry, lawlessness and pursuit of egoistic self-interest and enrichment in other cases.[27] But the more multifarious and complex the public spaces were, the more fragile was the authorities' representational monopoly. It should not be forgotten, though, that the surviving written records are nothing but the tip of the iceberg, since public spheres were essentially based on oral communication in the pre-modern societies of presence.[28]

CONCERNING THE STRUCTURE OF THIS VOLUME

Cross-border descriptions of social upheaval existed well before print, even though their scope was significantly inferior to what was to come with the printing revolution and especially with the age of regular newspaper-circulation in the 17th century. The **first section "Representing Revolt Before the Advent of the Gutenberg-Galaxy: A question of dissemination?"** therefore deals with revolts that occurred at times and/or in regions where the Gutenberg era had not yet started. This is definitely the case of the Hundred Years War, but also partially applies to early-17th century Muscovy. Bettina Bommersbach and Helmut Hinck focus on the times of the Hundred Years War (1337-1454). As England and France found themselves in an almost constant state of war and contemporary observers were particularly attentive to what was going on in the adversary's realm and took special interest in bigger uprisings that might weaken the ennemy's forces. Even though the evidence is rather scarce, there are some notable exceptions, among them the *Anonimalle Chronicle* in England and Jean Froissart's famous chronicle in

---

27 These reversals have been observed by Bettina Bommersbach, "Gewalt in der Jacquerie von 1358", in *Gewalt im politischen Raum. Fallanalysen vom Spätmittelalter bis ins 20. Jahrhundert*, ed. Neithard Bulst, Ingrid Gilcher-Holtey and Heinz-Gerhard Haupt, Historische Politikforschung, vol. 15 (Frankfurt am Main, New York, 2008), 46–81; Helmut Hinck, "Obrigkeitliche Gewalt bei der Niederschlagung der englischen Erhebung von 1381", in *ibid.*, 82–133 with respect to the French and English uprisings during the Hundred Years' War on the example of the two biggist revolts, the Jacquerie of 1358, and the Peasants' revolt of 1381.

28 Talk and rumour can only be retraced when occurring in files of investigation, generally occasioned by denunciation. See Würgler, Modernisierungspotential, 195-202. On the society of presence see Rudolf Schlögl, "Kommunikation und Vergesellschaftung unter Anwesenden. Formen des Sozialen und ihre Transformation in der Frühen Neuzeit", in *Geschichte und Gesellschaft* 34, 2 (2008): 155–224.

France, which actually do depict the events of the French Jacquerie (1358) and the English Peasants' Revolt (1381) respectively.

On the one hand, the cross-border accounts tend to reproduce internal narrative patterns. This mainly seems to owe to a scarcity of sources. Chroniclers copied their colleagues when they had the possibility to read the manuscript or one of the rare copies. On the other hand, foreign authors appeared to be more sympathetic (or less hostile) to the insurgents than native writers, a tendency that we can observe throughout the whole pre-modern period. The most balanced – or even neutral – account, however, is to be found in Thomas Gray's description of the Jacquerie because he as an English soldier in France was able to collect his evidence on the spot and therefore ignored the French model-narratives. More striking is the example of Thomas Walsingham, a monastic chronicler from St. Albans: while offering one of the most hostile descriptions of the insurgents in his account of the English Peasants' Revolt, he almost takes sides with the rebels in his representation of the Parisian tax revolt of the early 1380s and demonizes the French king for his cruelty.

Nevertheless has most attention been paid to those riots wishing to enforce the election of an Italian pope in Rome; this event clearly outweighed the revolts in the adversary's realms since papal elections were of unquestionable importance to the whole Christian world. For the so-called "cluster of revolts" at the beginning of the 1380s (with the Peasants' Revolt in England, the Parisian tax uprising, the revolts in Flanders and the Ciompi in Italy) contemporaries seemed to assume common causes: Jean Froissart feared that the peoples all over Europe were trying to get rid of their nobility. And a prominent explicative pattern for the accumulation of heavy social unrest was cross-border imitation, which implies the observers' assumption that insurgents in different countries knew of each other – a remarkable observation for the pre-Gutenbergian era.

In Russia the printing revolution arrived only at the turn of the 17th to the 18th century. Many historians hence consider prepetrine Muscovy as a medieval country. And indeed, internally the country had much in common with medieval France and England. But we will see to what extent 17th century Muscovy and the major revolts it experienced were affected by the intrusion of revolt-representations from abroad. In early-modern times, communication at distance through print always overlapped with oral face-to-face communication and participation in print culture was socially limited. If we look at 17th century Muscovy and Ukraine from a transnational perspective, we can realize how pre-Gutenbergian regions were challenged by the printing revolution. Foreign representations of revolt could have an increasing impact on the protagonists of major events of social protest in Muscovy.

Thus Maureen Perrie explores how the First False Dmitrii, who conquered the Muscovite throne in the Russian Time of Troubles in 1605, was portrayed by foreign eyewitnesses, historians and dramatists. She shows to what extent the belief or non-belief in the pretender's royal identity were determined by concrete interest. Since Dmitrii, supported by Polish magnates and their entourage, was believed to have converted to Catholicism, his ascension to the throne was applauded by writers like the Italian Barezzo Barezzi (alias Possevino) or the Spanish *Siglo de oro* dramatist Lope de Vega, who nourished hopes of Russia's conversion to Catholicism. In contrast to that, protestant writers such as the Swedish agent in Muscovy Petrus Petreius, fervently denounced him as an impostor and a puppet mastered by Polish and Vatican interests. Exceptions are British diplomats like William Scott, or the French Huguenot mercenary Jacques Margeret, who served Boris Godunov until the overthrow of 1605 and then became commander of the False Dmitrii's troops. Though Protestants, these writers regarded Dmitrii as the real authentic heir to the throne. As Perrie argues the attitude of the British ambassadors, who actually were merchants, was in the first place pragmatic: they were interested in smooth commercial relations with Muscovy and wanted to conserve privileges for English merchants, i.e. for themselves. Therefore they decided to support whoever detained the throne. For Margeret, if he wanted to be credible, it was even a basic necessity to dispel doubts about his master's legitimacy. It apparently was mainly a question of culture how far the foreigners referred to international precedents of royal imposture. But as soon as they referred to antique examples, and to Tile Kolup, the false Frederick II (in the Holy Roman Empire), Lambert Simnel or Perkin Warbeck in England, or the false Sebastians of Portugal, the foreign authors had a concept of imposture at hand,[29] whereas Russian contemporary sources indiscriminately spoke of the "villain" or the "heretic". So Perrie demonstrates that Dmitrii's back-story, his pretence to have escaped from his murderers by placing a substitute (in 1592), did not draw on internal Russian folktales, as it has formerly been claimed by Soviet historians, but it essentially built on a historical and literary narrative circulating across borders among European elites. Only gradually, through Dmitrii's self-portrayal was it assimilated in Russia where

---

29 The classical book on Sebastianism in Portugal is O sebastianismo. Breve panorama dum mito português. (Colecção Portugal ontem, Portugal hoje.). Lisboa 1978. Yves-Marie Bercé, *Le roi caché. Sauveurs et imposteurs: mythes politiques populaires dans l'Europe moderne* (Paris 1990) has compared royal pretenders in Portugal, France and Russia. Maureen Perrie herself has worked on the phenomenon of tsarish imposture in Muscovy and Russia throughout the early-modern period, see Maureen Perrie, *Pretenders and popular monarchism in early modern Russia. The false tsars of the time of troubles* (Cambridge 2002) and Tobias Hug, *Impostures in early modern England. Representations and perceptions of fraudulent identities* (Manchester 2010) has studied imposture in medieval and early-modern England, not restraining himself to pretenders to the throne, but also including alleged officials and others.

it became a veritable success-story, a major cultural topos often taken for a Russian specificity.

Well beyond Russia and the Time of Troubles the absence of a legitimate heir to the throne was a crucial factor that fuelled major revolts and civil wars. Contemporaries became increasingly aware of this factor. They particularly feared periods of questionable legitimacy and dubious recognition of a sovereign.[30] In the end David Hume acknowledged that "on opinion only" government was founded – and this would become the practical maxime of the founding fathers in the American Revolution where Madison asserted that "all government rests on opinion". This was a "revolutionary" insight against the background of medieval and early-modern concepts of divine right as the source of a sovereign's legitimacy. In political theory this mindset emerged only gradually and over the centuries, going along with the continuously growing importance of the print media. Of course, governments had always depended on their subjects' belief in the legitimacy of their rule, which included amongst others the recognition of a single ruler's divine rights. Beliefs also shaped movements of protest – and this is the focus of the **second section "Transgression of boundaries as a feat of liberty: Early-modern anthropologies of revolt"** that deals with revolts as transgression of customary boundaries and the representation of these transgressions as markers of early-modern or even transhistorical anthropologies of revolt. Beliefs could be rather stable and a purported anthropological constant, as Yves-Marie Bercé shows for the popular ideas of archaic original freedom returning during a vacancy of central power. But they could also be highly dynamic, related to a more or less spontaneous emotional eruption, borne by the enhancement of communicative space and bringing to the fore a particular mass psychology that made social actors take the initiative – and the concomitant high risk – of joint violent action, as André Berelowitch demonstrates.

In this sense Yves-Marie Bercé deals with the vacuum of power as a major trigger of unrest and revolt. The ancient tradition of suspending law and order in times of dynastic uncertainty or transition can be observed in many countries. This is hardly astonishing in regard to elective monarchies like Poland-Lithuania, where succession was reputed to be a source of ferocious struggle between different Szlachta factions and often brought the country to the margin of civil war. At the Holy See succession was defined by the conclave in a highly regulated procedure, but during almost every *sede vacante* the "anthropological utopia of a primitive free status of humanity" broke through in the towns of the Papal State – with

---

30 On early-modern ideas on Fama see Andreas Würgler, „Fama und Rumor. Gerücht, Aufruhr und Presse im Ancien Régime", in *WerkstattGeschichte* 15 (1996): 20–32.

plundering, riots and the expectation of the newly nominated Pope's largesse. In contrast to such examples of riotous freedom and self-rule, the French dynasty seemed to be firmly established after the religious wars had ended and the Bourbons had acceded to the throne. Succession seemed to work smoothly, at least until the Revolution of 1789. But Bercé shows that the minority of Louis XIV has to be interpreted in a similar way as the events in Poland or Rome, as an almost complete eclipse of central power. A closer look reveals how coherent the protest movement actually was and how provincial parliaments as well as local peasant resistance opposing elite- and popular actions in the capital were choreographed by a unique urge of a return to archaic freedom. Once Louis XIV had taken over the reigns his ideologists systematically launched an incoherent and rather ridiculous picture of elite and popular resistance, while preaching the ineluctability of absolutism. This narrative was reproduced approvingly by national historiography that was mainly concerned with depicting the glory and might of the French monarchy and the teleological story of its emergence. The story seems to have been extremely successful as early as in the 1660s when French observers had apparent difficulty understanding the Magnates' rebellion in Poland-Lithuania of 1665-66 (analysed by Angela Rustemeyer). So they did not find a translation for the Polish term *Rokosz* and the concomitant idea of a "legal rebellion". It obviously did not even come to their mind to call the events a Polish "Fronde". Turning a blind eye to the more or less distinct parallels, they *dissimilated* the events in Poland from their own domestic experience.[31]

Like Ingrid Maier and Stepan Shamin, André Berelowitch also deals with the representations of the Razin uprising (1770-71) that affected huge parts of the Cossack periphery and also included other social strata of Muscovy's population. The uprising was a major challenge to the Muscovite state and encountered a huge media response throughout Europe. This was fuelled by Muscovite authorities' propaganda, but also by the rare foreign eye-witnesses such as the Dutchman Ludwig Fabritius, who had fallen into the rebellious Cossacks' hands. Foreign revolt reports often tended to paint rebels in a much more favourable light than the concerned authorities did. To some degree, this is even true of the Ukrainian Cossacks. As Frank Sysyn demonstrates, in the case of most Cossack revolts in Russia during the 17th and 18th centuries *dissimilation* was a leading perceptional

---

31 This might already go along with a sense of cultural superiority that tended to repudiate "the East" as barbarian and backward, and to include Poland into this general notion, although for a long time it had been a topos referring to Russia/Muscovy as a "Northern" (not an Eastern) country. On the shift from a South-North to a West-East civilizational gradient in early-modern mental maps see Larry Wolff, *Inventing Eastern Europe. The map of civilization on the mind of the enlightenment* (Stanford, California 1994).

pattern. Muscovy was generally described as a barbarian (or backward) country. Furthermore, Cossacks and other warrior-populations of the Military Frontier further to the West (Uskoks, Kuruc, etc.) were highly mobile, partly lived on raids and significantly differed from the sedentary norms and moral standards of Middle and Western Europe. Muscovite Cossacks (or the Cossacks in Muscovy) rising up in revolt were thus a favourite projection surface for *dissimilative* representations.

As Berelowitch points out, both in official records and in foreigners' relations Razin and his followers were labelled as "rabble", "riff-raff", "curs", "scoundrels", etc. Even though one can sense some observers' understanding for serfs and slaves who had to suffer their lords' "tyranny", the revolt was unmistakably vilified. The deeply negative judgments generally extended to anybody who would join the movement, notwithstanding particular motives and grievances. Refugees from serfdom in the black-earth regions, who gained the steppes, rapidly adapted to a Cossack way of life; and in major revolts the insurgent Cossacks proclaimed they wanted to impose their own political structures upon the rest of the population. Naturally the revolts with their large-scale military campaigns were particularly brutal. Therefore the revolting Muscovite Cossacks were easily considered as "inhuman", leading a lifestyle marked by looting, plundering and murdering. The foreigners are unanimous in describing the whole Razin movement as an uprising of the "populace" that was associated with the Cossacks. Along with the representations of the insurgents' social appearance Berelowitch is interested in the trigger of revolt, i.e. the crucial moment that made hitherto loyal subjects join the camp of the rebels. People were perfectly conscious of the painful consequences of revolt. Making the decisive step implied taking enormous risks. Both mechanist explanations like the powder-keg-metaphor, and rational-choice arguments of weighing pros and cons seem incongruous. In foreigners' accounts of the Razin uprising, and in representations by the rebels or the authorities themselves, one cannot find a really satisfactory answer to the question what mysterious force had often made thousands of people change sides in only a few minutes or even seconds. "Seduction" and "lure" figure prominently in contemporary representations; and often the observers ascribe irrational conduct or even "madness" to the insurgents. This incites Berelowitch to more global anthropological considerations on the human psyche and the trance-like condition individuals assume when fusing with a rebellious mass. Mass psychology à la Canetti can instantaneously eclipse rationality, which does not prevent people from alleging rational motifs for their acts in retrospective. Early-modern analysts of revolt frequently speak of "contagion" to explain the tremendous speed with which revolt can spread. In this mass psychological fever Berelowitch sees both an ennobling aspect of taking destiny into one's own hands, and an extremely destructive force that was likewise an integral part of these mass-actions: bloodthirstiness and mordlust, as the eye-witnesses describe it. With his ambivalent appraisal Berelowitch is not too far from Ortega y Gasset's ideas as exposed in his *Revolt of the Masses*.

In Poland-Lithuania, where central power was weak, the insurgents were able to mobilize considerable communicative resources. Bigger uprisings were not only a privileged item of representations abroad, insurgents also activated far-ranging contacts and forged international alliances, which played an active role within the very uprisings. The **third section "Insurgents as Diplomates: Cross-border alliances and their Representations"** thus focuses on the Polish-Lithuanian Commonwealth.

Frank Sysyn analyses foreign accounts of the Cossack uprising under the leadership of Hetman Bohdan Khmel'nyts'kyi in Ukraine (1648-1657). The revolt was propelled by one of these classical vacuums of power within the Polish-Lithuanian Commonwealth. Wladislaw IV had more and more retreated from an active regiment and then died in May 1648. This provided fertile terrain for factional struggles among the aristocratic elites of the country – and factional struggle paralyzed the countermeasures against the rebellious Cossacks. Sysyn does not limit himself to rather *dissimilative* standard narratives written by core-European observers. His contribution centres on two clergymen, the Catholic Venetian Alberto Vimina, who visited Ukraine in 1650, and the Syrian Orthodox Paul of Aleppo, who was there twice, in 1654 and 1656, together with his father, Patriarch Makarios III of Antioch. Especially the Syrian perspective is rather new. Both observers, Catholic and Orthodox, embrace the idea of Ukraine as a country of abundance and a realm of liberty, though probably for different reasons. Remarkably enough, they both acknowledge the movement as legitimate. This is not only due to the assumption of a general right to resist against oppression (in this case mainly by Polish nobles), but also to the perception of Ukrainian Cossacks as a nation of its own, an idea that can be traced back to the 16th century, when the Zaporozhians had already been the destination of diplomatic missions. Vimina and Paul of Aleppo came to Khmel'nyts'kyi's Ukraine with diplomatic missions, too. It was both the particular nature of their missions and their cultural and confessional backgrounds (as well as those of their readers) that made their accounts differ. Vimina's confessional sympathy was naturally rather with the Catholic Poles than with the "schismatic" Orthodox Cossacks. Furthermore, to a cultivated Venetian the Eastern European people and their manners might have appeared barbarian. But the Venetian Republic entertained intense intercultural relations. It was in close contact with the Muslim world of the Ottoman Empire, not only through constant warfare, but also through economic competition in the Eastern Mediterranean and in the Indian Ocean. Ottoman power inspired awe to Venitian ambassadors. This respect included cultural aspects, too, but the Muslim Empire was definitely regarded as a place of difference.[32] Orthodox Ukrainian Cossacks were classical allies in the struggle against the awesome Sublime Porte. Vimina was charged with rallying support against the Ottomans from both the Polish king and the Ukrainian Cossacks. This was apparently the main reason why he sought to downplay the Cossacks' religious allegiance as a means of enlisting them in a purported alliance with Catholic powers. At the same time, this has certainly inspired his positive view of the Cossack polity that he likened to antique Sparta. Thus he revaluated what he had sometimes perceived as uncultured crudeness and ascribed native ingenuity and wit to the people. This was, of course, an ambiguous undertaking, since Sparta was associated with both exemplary soldierly discipline and despotism.[33] Paul of Aleppo (with his father) tried to raise funds for the Orthodox Christians in the Ottoman Empire. For him religious purity was a crucial trait of the Cossack realm as a model Orthodox society. He drew a clear dividing line between Cossack freedom and Polish servitude, between the Polish elites' anarchy and Ukrainian justice, thus partly taking over Western European stereotypes about the Polish elites' unruliness and the Commonwealth's decline, and partly contradicting prejudices against Cossack savagery by idealizing Cossack institutions. Curiously enough, he contrasted severe oppression of the Orthodox faith by Poles, Armenians and Jews in pre-revolt Ukraine with the religious tolerance he experienced in his homeland, where the Ottoman rulers would content themselves with extracting taxes. He rather ignored the massacres perpetrated by the Ukrainian Cossacks and peasants against Jews, though. What is even more noteworthy, he also expressed his distinct preference for Ukraine over Orthodox Muscovy where "a padlock had been set on our hearts" during their two-year stay. Whereas Muscovites are described as ignorant subjects deliberately complying with their dull fate of servitude, Cossack Ukraine under Khmel'nyts'kyi is depicted as blossoming, with a whole population striving for literacy and culture. Both, Vimina's and Paul of Aleppo's accounts give a positive image of the Hetman himself, whom the writers have met personally. But if Vimina recommended a military leader as a potential ally to his Venetian

---

32 On the struggle for supremacy in the Indian Ocean see Giancarlo Casale, *The Ottoman age of exploration* (Oxford 2010). On European reverence for Ottoman might before the unsuccessful siege of Vienna (1683) see for England Gerald M. MacLean, *Looking East. English writing and the Ottoman Empire before 1800* (Basingstoke [England], New York 2007), more particularly for Venetian diplomatic staff cf. Palmira Brummett, „Classifying Ottoman Mutiny. The Act and Vision of Rebellion", in *The Turkish Studies Association Bulletin* 22 (1998): 91–107.

33 Cf. Paul Cartledge, "Spartan Traditions and Receptions", *Hermathena* 181 (In honour of George Huxley) (Winter 2006): 41–49.

compatriots and furthermore acknowledged his despotic traits and his penchant to alcohol, Paul of Aleppo praises him also as an irreproachable monarch with unlimited moral qualities.

For the Polish-Lithuanian Commonwealth the Khmel'nyts'kyi Uprising ended with the loss of Left-Bank-Ukraine to the Moscovite tsar, who guaranteed the Cossacks their hard-won privileges. In the following, the depleted kingdom was haunted by further wars, first against Sweden and then against Russia, so that Jan Kazimierz' reign is generally considered as the age of decline for Poland-Lithuania.

Angela Rustemeyer examines the transnational dimensions of Jerzy Lubomirski's aforementioned *rokosz* (1665-66) that divided the nobility (*szlachta*) into supporters and adversaries of the reigning king and thus paralyzed the Diet, where every member had the right to a *liberum veto*. Even though she highlights foreign observers' difficulty understanding the very idea of "legal rebellion", Rustemeyer is not in the first place concerned with representations of the phenomenon abroad. She rather focuses on how the conflicting parties themselves appealed and variously referred to transnational entanglements in the course of their inner confrontations. On the one hand foreign support was an important resource; on the other hand it could eventually be used as a discrediting argument. However, Lubomirski benefited from wide-ranging support, also within the *szlachta*. He was one of the highest-ranking nobles of the realm and could easily have been a candidate to the throne himself. It was merely impossible to accuse him of treason simply because he enjoyed backup from the Brandenburg elector, since at the same time the king drew on support from the elector's adversary, the noble opposition of Brandenburg-Prussia. In the end Jan Kasimierz tried to fight out the conflict on juridical ground and accused his adversary of lèse-majesty. This was not less problematic, since the Sejm had significantly restricted the extension of this major crime in the 16th century. But as Rustemeyer demonstrates, the crucial argument brought to the fore by the king's party was based on a transnational comparison. The anti-centralist oppositional confederation was accused to have planned a regicide and Lubomirski himself to have been aiming at the office of Lord Protector, similar to Cromwell in England. Curiously enough, this allegation echoed major propaganda-battles during the French Fronde, where Mazarin's party accused the Frondeurs of imitating the English Parliament's treason against King Charles. Similarly, in his *History of the Cossack War against Poland* (1663), the Frenchman Pierre Chevalier had compared Khmel'nyts'kyi to Cromwell, i.e. at a moment when the memory of the Fronde was already neatly disentangled from the English civil war. All this shows the enormous impact of the English Revolution on the continent, but as an appalling spectre and a ready-made pattern of accusation rather than as a model for real imitation.[34] Interestingly, Jan Kazimierz' party invoked the spectre of the English regicide even in its propaganda addressed to the peasants of the Podhale region, who were known to be particularly rebellious. This agitation of Polish peasants against Lubomirski shows to what extent transnational motifs apparently mattered (or were believed to matter) even among the rural lower classes, which are generally imagined to have been confined to a narrow local horizon. But the very fact of this risky address to the peasants also drew on the precedent of the fight against Swedish invasion in 1655 and it is not a coincidence that simultaneously the term "civil war" was thrown into public debate. Public debate in the Polish-Lithuanian Commonwealth played a crucial role in the conflict and it included major players abroad: Apart from Lubomirski himself, who acted mostly from his exile in Silesia, Rustemeyer draws attention to the Anti-Trinitarian Lubieniecki who offered a particularly "modern" analysis of what was going on from his Prussian exile. Instead of interpreting the events in terms of conflicts of honour, he emphasized economic aspects and the problem of the Commonwealth's financial dependency upon foreign powers. Sensitive to transnational entanglements, he also distinguished clearly between Cossacks and their Tatar allies, who were often tarred with the same brush by contemporary observers. However, he would not reveal his "heretical" identity: here the "modernity" of the Polish-Lithuanian public spheres would have reached its limits. Taking into account the high degree of publicity channelled by political communication and negotiation, Rustemeyer comes to the conclusion that it was rather its modernity than the frequently quoted anachronism of medieval-style noble prerogatives that weakened the Polish-Lithuanian state in a period where absolutist tendencies were the dominant paradigm in the European environment.

The **forth section "Governments struggling with foreign representations of internal revolts"** introduces a dimension of double reflexivity. Governments were not only concerned with suppression of their internal revolts but also feared the dissemination of news on the events abroad, which might be damaging to their country's image in international relations. This preoccupation is particularly salient in Russia, where the government registered coverage on its internal affairs in

---

34 On the arguments drawn from the English Civil war during the Fronde see Philip A. Knachel, *England and the Fronde. The impact of the English Civil War and Revolution on France*. (Ithaca N.Y. 1967). On Chevalier's comparison of Khmel'nyts'kyi with Cromwell see Christopher Hill, „The English Revolution and the Brotherhood of Man", in *Puritanism and Revolution. Studies in Interpretation of the English Revolution of the 17th Century*, ed. idem (London 2001), 112–138.

Western newspapers and sometimes reacted immediately to representations of major revolts.

Ingrid Maier and Stepan Shamin take the Razin uprising as an initial point. Unlike Berelowitch who examines foreigners' accounts of this uprising as such, they analyse the reflection of Western revolt-reports in Russian *kuranty* of this period, i.e. in translations from mainly German and Dutch newspapers for the Tsar's court.[35] The *kuranty* indicate how the Muscovite government wanted, and how it did not want to have its country presented to a European public in this period of major internal crisis. At the same time the translations mirror a particular interest in contemporary events of contestation abroad. Since the translations for the end of 1670 and the beginning of 1671 are entirely lost, Maier and Shamin focus on the period between March and July 1671, for which the *kuranty* seem to be complete. At that time the uprising had almost come to an end: in April Razin was handed over to the authorities by his closest Cossacks followers. But this did not stop rumours and many Western newspapers continued to report on the movement's alleged successes. Much of the Russian reception of these reports was motivated by a preoccupation with the possible abasement of the Tsar's might. Apparently the Muscovite government specifically collected erroneous foreign reports on Razin, in order to use them as a means of pressure in diplomatic negotiations, particularly towards Sweden. Translators even omitted insertions qualifying the related news-item as "rumours" that were "not believed to be true". Occasionally, though, Maier and Shamin have discovered detailed and astonishingly accurate accounts that betray considerable insider knowledge. Due to the noticeable delay with which the events are reported, they presume that these accounts must have been delivered to the foreign newspapers by Muscovite authorities in order to actively correct current misrepresentations. With regard to revolts abroad, those of concern for Russian foreign policy were apparently the activities of the Ukrainian Cossacks under hetman Doroshenko that figured prominently in translations. Their alliance with the Ottoman Porte was of immediate importance, not only for Poland-Lithuania, but

---

35 Both Ingrid Maier and Stepan Shamin are major specialists in these handwritten translations. Maier has coedited the last published volume to date. In contrast to the preceding ones, it consists of two parts, one with the translations from the Moscow state archives, the other one with the text of the original Western newspapers reports, from which the translations/paraphrases have apparently been drawn from. Since the sources were neither indicated nor conserved together with the translations, she had to search for the original newspapers in innumerable libraries and archives throughout Europe. Thanks to this tremendous work she is able to compare the texts and thus follow the translators' choice, preferences, omissions, errors, biaises. See Ingrid Majer and Sergej I. Kotkov, *Vesti-Kuranty. 1656g., 1660-1662gg., 1664-1670gg.* (Moscow 2009).

also for Muscovy that risked losing Left-Bank Ukraine anew. Further away was the Magnate conspiracy in Hungary against Habsburg rule (1670/71). Since the rebels, however, also tried to mobilize Ottoman support for their aims, the *kuranty* diligently covered the events. Ottoman engagement in Poland-Lithuania and/or in Hungary was likely to deflect military ambitions from Muscovy. Other revolts that were farther away from Muscovite immediate interests showed to be items of curiosity, but were covered in a more stereotyped manner that did not allow a precise conception of what was actually happening. In the case of the Braunschweig citizens' desperate resistance against the Duke of Lüneburg's encroachments against their city's traditional liberties, the kuranty only reproduced the Duke's medial propaganda that presented the commoners as rebelling against their lawful sovereign. According to Maier and Shamin this misconception of the situation in the Reich rather corresponded to the legal status of Muscovite towns since the extinction of Novgorod's and Pskov's autonomy in the late 15th and early 16th century.

In my own contribution I follow up Muscovite/Russian preoccupation with its image abroad and with foreign representation of its internal revolts. I try to view foreign accounts of Russian revolts in a long-term perspective, in order to point out a major shift of paradigms that apparently occurred in the early years of Peter's I reign. The abundance of such accounts of Russian revolts in the 17th century contrasts glaringly with their scarcity in the 18th, which is even more astonishing since in general the Russian Empire of Peter the Great and his successors was much more a focus of Western interest than the pre-Petrine Muscovite state. This observation makes the diplomatic scandal revolving around the publication of Johann Georg Korb's diary in Vienna (1701) a cornerstone of my investigation. Korb depicts the last strel'tsy rebellion and narrates subsequent mass repressions in great detail because he had witnessed them during the embassy's journey to Moscow in 1698/99. As soon as Russian diplomats and Peter I got wind of the book, they tried everything they could to have it prohibited. When diplomatic pressure failed, they staged a book-burning with all the copies they could get hold of. On the one hand I analyse the reasons and context of this harsh reaction. Since central descriptions of the mass repressions had been previously published in newspapers and journals that were systematically screened by the translators of the Foreign office, I argue that the visual representation of torture and mass executions (on a copperplate enclosed in the book) was a major bone of contention. Therefore the conflict also needs to be regarded as a clash of two fundamentally different visual cultures and, in a way, as a cultural misunderstanding, since author, illustrator and publisher were hardly aware of provoking the Muscovite government. On the other hand, the exchange of letters between Russian officials and the head of the imperial embassy (which was held responsible for the book) reveals a considerable revaluation of (foreign) public opinion by the Russian government. From that time on it was not only the foreign policy-makers' image of Russia that mattered, but also the broader public's views. This shift led to a new media policy with the creation of the *Vedomosti* (the first so-called newspaper in Russia) and the installation of Russian agents abroad, whose task was both to intervene against undesirable coverage (at best before publication) and to provide the foreign press with "correct" information about Russia. Even though Emperor Leopold I had not succumbed to diplomatic pressure concerning Korb's book, the scandal and accompanying measures had a long-lasting effect on foreign writings on Russia. Traces of social unrest became scarce and authors tended more and more to distort and minimize the few events they continued to mention. Once threatening and dreadful, revolts were increasingly interpreted as manifestations of backwardness contrasting with the progressive civilizing mission propelled by enlightened tsars.

The depiction of punishment that plays a crucial part in the case of the Korb scandal is also at the heart of the **fifth section "Revolts as political crime: Legal concepts and public representation"**, which analyses representations of revolts from a legal perspective.[36] Therefore Fabrizio Dal Vera's and Karl Härter's contributions deal with the emergent concept of political crime in contemporary legal thinking and with visual representations of retribution as an integral part of legal representation.

Fabrizio Dal Vera investigates the elaboration of the early-modern concept of political crime referring to collective violence against political authorities. Since the escalation of unrests in the late 14th century, we witness an ongoing process of criminalization of seditions that led legal scholars to systematize the legal questions involved. Under the immediate impression of such collective violence, jurists developed the legal tradition in order to define a *crimen seditionis* functional to the actual turbulent situation. Embracing the methodological approach suggested by a legal history based on evolutionary theory, Dal Vera traces the development of the term *seditio* in legal and political treatises and *dissertationes* published on this problem from the beginning of the 16th until the end of the 17th century. During the 16th century jurists elaborated an extensive definition of *crimen seditionis* – strongly

---

36 Another volume on the reactions of legal systems to revolts, going back to a conference at the Max-Planck Institute for legal history in Frankfurt is currently in print. See Revolten und politische Verbrechen vom 12.-19. Jahrhundert. Reaktionen der Rechtssysteme und juristisch-politische Diskurse/ Rivolte e crimini politici tra XII e XIX secolo: Reazioni del sistema giuridico e discorso giuridico-politico. (Studien zur europäischen Rechtsgeschichte.). (Frankfurt am Main forthcoming). I have contributed an article dealing with the thesis of juridicization (*Verrechtlichung*) as a long-term consequence of revolts.

associated with *proditio* and *rebellio* – and understood any form of collective violence as a violation of *maiestas*. In the following century, they developed a more nuanced representation of crime that differentiated between a wider range of violent behaviors in order to classify them with respect to the extent of their dangerousness for inner stability. Consequently, jurists defined different *gradi* of sedition that were not always related to *crimen laesae maiestatis*. They also applied to minor unrests punished as *cimen vis*. The study of legal doctrine shows how the definition of *crimen seditionis* was embedded in more general political conjunctures and closely related to broader political theory. In contrast to that, previous doctrine had provided legal justifications of ad hoc-measures toward ongoing episodes of urban and agrarian unrest. The advent of political realism and new theories on *ratio status* in Machiavelli's footsteps largely influenced the legal understanding of seditions: to prevent disorders jurists made greater efforts to precisely analyse the organization of dissent. For that they built on examples of revolts both at home and abroad. This realist approach partially modified and enriched the definition of crime, which had a long-lasting impact on practical implementation of both repressive and preventive strategies with regard to concrete unrests. The taxonomies of collective violence and the recommended remedies are inscribed in an international development of legal doctrine on political crimes. Jurists in different countries shared a common legal background, used the same concepts and quoted the works of their predecessors, regardless of territorial borders or even confessional allegiances. Moreover, they continuously referred to insurrections all over Europe and their joint efforts produced a common representation of inner turbulences in early-modern times.

If jurists in their academic ivory-towers were able to discuss revolts more or less freely, the authorities concerned were much more reluctant to commemorate the events that challenged their rule. This is reflected in the brutal scenes of public retribution and their dissemination through the print media. Descriptions of punishment tended to eclipse the actual revolt, which was classified as a political crime.

Karl Härter explores the representations of early modern revolts in illustrated broadsheets, a genre that could even be "read" by the illiterate and thereby constituted an important addition to purely textual representations. Both pictures and the accompanying texts focused on punishment, whereas the revolt itself was often ignored or summed up in a very short and distorted version. In this sense the broadsheet-representations are part of a whole juridical arsenal of condemnation. Prosecution of political crime went along with *damnatio memoriae* of the very event of the revolt. Especially the authorities tried to obliterate memory of any just causes of the revolt. Härter studies broadsheet-coverage of exemplary revolts of three different categories and presents the Fettmilch-uprising in Frankfurt/Main in 1614-16 as an implementation of urban revolt. The resistance of the Bohemian nobility against the Emperor in 1621 and the Magnate conspiracy in Hungary are shown as examples of aristocratic revolts; and the Bavarian upheaval of 1705 against the Habsburgs and the uprising led by Horea and Kloska in Hungary in 1785 demonstrate common patterns of peasant revolts. Interestingly, these different social classes and their quite different resources in terms of societal weight and access to public space are hardly reflected in the representation of their crimes in the media. Broadsheet production seems to be dominated by the authorities and their interpretation of the events as political crimes, at least as far as commemoration or retrospective representation is concerned. Often the verdict is related to the accusation of conspiracy and collaboration with foreign powers, in the case of the revolts in the Reich mainly collaboration with France and/or the Ottoman Empire. This important transnational feature in representation of revolts underlined the idea of treason and made brutal execution with loss of personal honor and property an ineluctable consequence that was deemed necessary to re-establish public order and justice. However, representational patterns were not identical: while the revolt was still going on, it was described in a different way than after it had been suppressed and the ringleaders publicly executed. When the rebels themselves managed to issue broadsheets, these prints naturally differed significantly from those issued by the authorities. But in this phase the authorities' broadsheet-propaganda, too, conveyed a certain flexibility that suggested scope for compromise, negotiation and by the same token for reinterpretation of the situation. People were more or less invited to change sides. This changed fundamentally once the revolt had come to an end and ringleaders publicly executed. Now the revolt was being described in black and white: former flexibility was erased. It was exclusively the point of just punishment that was put to the fore. In this sense, the illustrated broadsheets analysed by Karl Härter correspond to Yves-Marie Bercé's observation made for the Fronde in France, where all former attempts to come to an arrangement, also through public representation of what was going on, were ignored after the defeat of the Frondeurs.[37] However, besides authoritarian censorship Härter also hints at the commercial interests of the publishers who had to sell their production and were dependent on the curiosity of the readers and spectators.

This commercial aspect was probably more developed in the Reich than it was in France under Louis XIV, where the political imperative was paramount and printers independent of the state's domain of control could only be found abroad

---

37 Commemoration under Louis XIV.'s reign was paradigmatically symbolized by Gilles Guérin's statue of the king crushing underfoot a Frondeur, or rather the Fronde as such. For a reproduction and interpretation see Peter Burke, The Fabrication of Louis XIV (Yale 1994): 54.

(mainly in the Netherlands and partly in Geneva and Neufchatel). In spite of the emperor's overarching position in the Reich, censorship was mainly exercised on the level of the principalities. For this reason, publishers from cities or realms that had not been struck by a revolt would sometimes depict the events in adjacent territories differently, as it was the case for a broadsheet on the Fettmilch uprising published in Darmstadt, where one of the ringleaders had sought refuge. What broadsheets from Frankfurt depicted as a dangerous revolt spurred by four demonized ringleaders was represented as a quarrel for the true Christian faith elsewhere (the uprising was largely directed against the Frankfurt Jews). In the pro-revolt accounts, the leaders are portrayed as respectable burghers and ordinary sinners.

The cross-border perspective is thus an important dimension which has considerably contributed to the dynamization of revolt-representations and their circulation.

Representing Revolt before the Advent of the Gutenberg-Galaxy: A Question of Dissemination?

Cross-Border Representations of Revolt in the Later Middle Ages: France and England During the Hundred Years' War (1337-1453)

HELMUT HINCK, BETTINA BOMMERSBACH

1) REPORTING FROM ABROAD

Pointing to the Hundred Years' War and its manifold political, social and cultural consequences, one could easily argue for an albeit hostile but nonetheless strong connection between the kingdoms of England and France in the later Middle Ages. Since 1337 English kings were trying to take hold of the French crown and to secure their possessions on the continent, which led to more than a century of interrupted warfare and deeply affected the societies on both sides of the channel. As the war more than once lay at the roots of popular unrest in these countries,[1] there should have been a good deal of cross-border reporting of insurgency in England and France, making the period an ideal field of research for the transnational representation of pre-modern revolts.

The findings, however, are surprisingly few in number. They are almost exclusively restricted to chronicle sources and even there cannot be said to abound.[2]

---

1 This has been pointed out for the Jacquerie, the 1380s' tax rebellions, the Peasants' Revolt and for the rising of Jack Cade and will hold for even more revolts in the period; see, for example, R. W. Kaeuper, *War, Justice, and Public Order. England and France in the Later Middle Ages* (Oxford, 1988), 349-60; L. Mirot, *Les insurrections urbaines au début du règne de Charles VI (1380-1383): Leurs causes, leurs conséquences* (Paris, 1905), 7-9; I. M. W. Harvey, *Jack Cade's Rebellion of 1450* (Oxford, 1991), 53-64.
2 Outside the chronicles we know of only a single case from England or France, namely an allusion to the French Jacquerie in a petition of the English Commons in 1377; see *The*

Combing through more than eighty chronicles from the late fourteenth and early fifteenth century, we have only been able to find some fifteen examples of popular revolt in England and France being reported by authors from the other side of the channel. English accounts have survived for the Jacquerie of 1358,[3] the urban tax revolts of the early 1380s[4] and the risings in Normandy fifty years later;[5] French texts include the Peasants' Revolt of 1381,[6] the risings against the Ricardian Earls in 1400[7] and the disturbances surrounding the Kentish rebellion of 1450.[8] As none of these movements has been recorded by more than three chroniclers from the other country, we can speak of a fairly even distribution of transnational coverage

---

Parliament Rolls of Medieval England 1275-1504, ed. C. Given-Wilson et al., 16 vols. (London, 2005), 6: 47. Further examples are from the German Hanse [two letters reporting the English risings of 1381 and 1450] and from Venice [a decree of the senate concerning the 1450 revolt]; cf. F. Pedersen, "The German Hanse and the Peasants' Revolt of 1381", *BIHR* 57 (1984): 92-98; *Hanserecesse von 1431-1476*, ed. G. von der Ropp, 7 vols. (Leipzig, 1876-1892), 3: 506-10; *Calendar of State Papers, Venice*, 38 vols. (London, 1864-1947), 1: 74.

3 Sir Thomas Gray, *Scalacronica 1272-1363*, ed. A. King (Woodbridge, 2005), 152-5, 164-165, 168-169; *The Anonimalle Chronicle 1333 to 1381*, ed. V. H. Galbraith (Manchester, 1927), 41-43.

4 *The St Albans Chronicle: The Chronica Maiora of Thomas Walsingham*, ed. J. Taylor, W. R. Childs and L. Watkiss, Oxford Medieval Texts, ed. J. W. Binns et al. (Oxford, 2003), 1: 390-395, 652-655; *Historia Vitae et Regni Ricardi Secundi*, ed. G. B. Stow (Philadelphia, 1977), 60; John Capgrave, *The Chronicle of England*, ed. F. C. Hingeston, Rolls Series (London, 1858), 235-236.

5 *Chronicles of London*, ed. C. L. Kingsford (Oxford, 1905), 137-140.

6 *Œuvres de Froissart*, ed. Kervyn de Lettenhove, 26 vols. (Brussels, 1867-1877), 9: 386-424; *Chronique du Religieux de Saint-Denys*, ed. M. L. Bellaguet, 6 vols. (Paris, 1839-1852), 1: 132-135, 256-259; *Nouvelle Collection des Mémoires pour servir à l'histoire de la France*, ed. J. F. Michaud and J. J. F. Poujoulat, 32 vols. (Paris, 1836-1839), 2: 348, 358.

7 *Chronicque de la Traïson et Mort de Richart Deux Roy Dengleterre*, ed. B. Williams (London, 1846), 77-103, 229-261; Religieux de Saint-Denys, 2:734-738; Œuvres de Froissart, 16: 221-219. Jean Creton, "French Metrical History of the Deposition of King Richard the Second", ed. J. Webb, *Archaeologia* 20 (1824): 1-423, 209-216, 400-407 does not mention popular agency here.

8 Thomas Basin, *Histoire de Charles VII*, ed. C. Samaran, 2 vols. (Paris, 1964-1965), 2: 60-64, 166-168; *Histoire de Charles VII. Roy de France*, ed. D. Godefroy (Paris, 1661), 448-449, 602-604.

in our period.[9] Such numbers, to be sure, are quite considerable compared to the reports from or about other countries like Italy or the Empire,[10] but the interest in Flemish insurgency, both in England and in France, appears to have been a good deal higher than any mutual notice of revolt in the two kingdoms.[11] To understand this relative scarcity of findings we first have to consider the conditions of cross-border representation in late medieval chronicles and annals.

Putting aside the traditional distinction between 'chronicles' and 'histories', which had lost most of its strictness by the fourteenth century anyway,[12] a chronicler in the late Middle Ages was primarily concerned with recording events. He usually provided the continuation of an older chronicle and relied on other writers for what happened before living memory, so that his major contribution, apart from collecting the sources, was to relate contemporary history.[13] The focus of medieval historiography varied to a considerable degree, ranging from domestic or urban history to regional and national history, all of which could include passages

---

9   The French accounts, however, outnumber those from England by nine to six.
10 See, for example, *Chronicon Adæ de Usk A.D. 1377-1421*, ed. E. M. Thompson, 2nd edn. (London, 1904), 99-100, 276-277 [Rome 1405]; Capgrave, *Chronicle of England*, 242 [Austria 1386]; Matteo Villani, *Cronica. Con la continuazione di Filippo Villani*, ed. G. Porta, 2 vols. (Parma, 1995), 2: 185, 214-216, 274-275 [Paris 1358]; *Mercanti Scrittori. Ricordi nella Firenze tra Medioevo e Rinascimento*, ed. V. Branca (Milan, 1986), 383-385 [Paris 1381].
11 Thus, a single Flemish rising like the rebellion in Ghent led by Philip de Artevelde could get the attention of at least nine chroniclers from England and France; see Œuvres de Froissart, 9: 158-236, 341-378, 431-445; 10: 1-175; Religieux de Saint-Denys, 1: 108-119, 168-231; *Chronique des quatre premiers Valois*, ed. S. Luce (Paris, 1862), 284-290, 294, 302-308; *Chronique du Mont-Saint-Michel (1343-1468)*, ed. S. Luce, 2 vols. (Paris, 1879-1883), 1: 14; Nouvelle Collection, 2: 346-348, 351-356; St Albans Chronicle, 1: 314-317, 376-379, 604-609, 650-653; Historia Vitae et Regni, 55, 60, 71, 76; *The Westminster Chronicle 1381-1394*, ed. L. C. Hector and B. F. Harvey, Oxford Medieval Texts, ed. C. N. L. Brooke et al. (Oxford, 1982), 24-27; *Eulogium (Historiarum Sive Temporis)*, ed. F. S. Haydon, Rolls Series, 3 vols. (London, 1858-1863), 3: 355.
12 B. Guenée, "Histoire, annales, chroniques. Essai sur les genres historiques au Moyen Age", *Annales ESC* 28 (1973): 997-1016, 1008, 1015; cf. J. Taylor, *English Historical Literature in the Fourteenth Century* (Oxford, 1987), 37-39; N. Bulst, "›Jacquerie‹ und ›Peasants' Revolt‹ in der französischen und englischen Chronistik", in Geschichtsschreibung und Geschichtsbewußtsein im späten Mittelalter, ed. H. Patze (Sigmaringen, 1987), 791-819, 795.
13 Cf. Taylor, Historical Literature, 40-42; C. Given-Wilson, *Chronicles: The Writing of History in Medieval England* (Hambledon & London, 2004), 59-60.

on what may be called "general" or even "international history".[14] Even more versatile in their outlook were biographers and chivalric historians, for they wrote about the deeds of people, and these moved freely through regions and countries. Nevertheless, the internal history of foreign countries was not on top of the list of medieval historiography. With a few notable exceptions, it focused on events at home and only occasionally looked for news from across the borders.

But what made medieval chroniclers write about an incident from abroad? This, it appears, was a question of attention as well as of interest. First of all, the author must have got wind of the event and been sufficiently impressed not to dismiss it without further consideration. The incident, in other words, must have caught his attention. Arguing from the cases in our sample, there often seems to have been some kind of impulse, like first-hand experience or personal shock, which led to the insertion of foreign material into an account. The monk of St. Denis probably would not have noted the rising of 1381, if not for his presence in England at the time of the revolt and the indignation he felt when he learned about the way the insurgents had treated their archbishop's head.[15] Closer still to the revolt he recorded was Adam of Usk, for when in 1405 the people of Rome rose against Pope Innocent VII, he was working for the papal see and therefore barely escaped the public anger himself.[16] Eyewitnesses, then, seem to be the most likely candidates for the cross-border representation of insurgency.

However, attention was not the only condition for a popular revolt to be reported abroad. There had to be interest as well, in those involved in the incident, in its background and consequences, in the implications of the episode. This goes beyond the mere focus of a text, for a chronicler will only be interested in a foreign event if it can be useful for his narrative, if it has entertaining, explanatory or

---

14 Cf. Given-Wilson, Chronicles, 93-97 for the focus of institutional writers. A distinctly universal outlook can be found in universal chronicles, but these were mainly concerned with earlier periods of history; Taylor, Historical Literature, 40.

15 Religieux de Saint-Denys, 1: 134: *"Michi causam ecclesie nostre in hoc regno promoventi, cum indignanter audirem ipsa die per ville bivia illius archiepiscopi capud sacratum plebem pedibus huc illucque projecisset, unusque assistencium diceret: "Scias in regno Francie abhominabiliora futura et in brevi," hoc solum subjunxi: "Absit ut Gallie continuata fidelitas tanto monstro deformetur!"*. For an English translation see S. K. Cohn, Popular Protest in Late Medieval Europe: Italy, France, and Flanders (Manchester, 2004), 277.

16 Chronicon Adæ de Usk, xxv, 99: *"Que dies illa presencium compilatori dies erat ire, calamitatis et miserie, quia, usque ad ligulas spoliatus, vix cum vita, in habitu fratrum predicatorum per octo dies latitans, vix eorum tirannidem evasit."* He was, in fact, a personal friend of the pope.

rhetorical potential. The Jacquerie must have been a "good story" to the compiler of the Anonimalle Chronicle, a story related to the world of chivalry like most of the other foreign accounts he included in his narrative.[17] Thomas Basin had other reasons to write about the English rebellion of 1450, for he regarded the disturbances as a result of the expulsion of the English from Aquitaine and his native Normandy.[18] Of course, the revolts in these examples had also caught the attention of the authors, but it was a combination of attention and interest that was decisive for their transnational representation.

These considerations might help to explain the relative dearth of cross-border representation in our sources. In his study of popular protest in medieval Europe, Sam Cohn has pointed out that there was hardly any international coverage of the now most famous late medieval risings – the Ciompi, the Jacquerie and the Peasants' Revolt. By contrast, at least fourteen non-Roman authors recorded the riots in Rome in 1378 to enforce the election of an Italian pope.[19] As it comes as no surprise that writers all across Europe should be informed of as well as interested in the forced election of a pope, it must have been mainly interest that was lacking for the other risings. A parliamentary petition of 1377 proves that the Jacquerie was well-known in England at the time,[20] but only two English chroniclers bothered to report this event from abroad.[21] Others obviously saw no reason to do so, either because it did not fit in or because it was of no use for their narratives. And this, it appears, will have been primarily due to the fact that the Jacquerie did not affect European politics the same way the Roman rising did, and that the Jacques were not established political players like the Flemish rebels contemporary historians so loved to write about.[22]

However, neither their prevalence in contemporary chronicles nor the conditions for their being included make for the real significance of these cross-border reports of revolt. To fully appreciate their transnational character in our

---

17 Cf. Anonimalle Chronicle, xxxiii, xxxviii; see also A. Gransden, *Historical Writing in England*, 2 vols. (Ithaca, 1974-1982), 2: 112.

18 Basin, Histoire, 2:166: *"Quales autem quantique civiles et domestici tumultus atque motus, postquam Normannia primum deinde Aquitania pulsi fuerunt, inter Anglos in suo regno oborti sint, non ab re fuerit neque impertinens si hoc loco aliquid de rebus hujuscemodi retulerimus."*

19 S. K. Cohn, *Lust for Liberty. The Politics of Social Revolt in Medieval Europe, 1200-1425: Italy, France, and Flanders* (Cambridge, MA, 2006), 2.

20 Parliament Rolls, 6: 47; cf. R. B. Dobson, *The Peasants' Revolt of 1381*, 2nd edn. (London, 1983), 75, 77.

21 Gray, Scalacronica, 152-155; Anonimalle Chronicle, 41-42.

22 Cf. Cohn, Popular Protest, 4, 265-266 for the Flemish rebels and their political standing.

considerations, we have to look at the particularities of their representation of foreign insurgency, both compared to the picture of those risings painted by native chroniclers and to their own depiction of insurgency at home. In this way it should be possible to shed some light on the influence an author's origin had on the way he wrote about popular revolts in another country. And, since in our case the country he was writing about was at war with the country he was coming from, there could well emerge some alternating sympathies for rebels and authorities at home and abroad.

2) ALTERNATING SYMPATHIES

The depiction of popular insurgency in medieval chronicles was usually characterized by a strong hostility towards the rebels and their causes. Most of the authors were coming from – and writing for – the social elite, which held the agitated populace with contempt and greatly feared the frenzy of the insurrectionary crowd. This general attitude was shared by chroniclers all across Europe, and one will hardly find any narrative source openly siding with the insurgents. Nevertheless, there could still be significant differences in the representation of revolt. Comparing the chronicle pictures of the Jacquerie and of the Peasants' Revolt in England and France, Neithard Bulst has pointed to different traditions of perceiving and portraying social conflict in these countries. French chroniclers tended to fall back upon stereotypes and tropes, even denying the rebels any sense of reason in some cases, while their English counterparts gave much more attention to an accurate and detailed description of what they were writing about, and were much more interested in the causes of the events.[23]

These contrasting ways of representing revolt are also reflected in the cross-border reports of the Jacquerie and the Peasants' Revolt. There is one chronicle in each country covering both of them, the *Anonimalle Chronicle* in England and Jean Froissart's *Chroniques* in France. Rather surprisingly, both texts seem to follow the French model for the French revolt and the English pattern for the English rising. Thus, the *Anonimalle Chronicle* has a detailed and fairly balanced account of the

---

23 Cf. Bulst, ›Jacquerie‹ und ›Peasants' Revolt‹, 813-819. For the chronicle representation of these risings see also M.-T. de Medeiros, *Jacques et chroniqueurs: Une étude comparée de récits contemporains relatant la Jacquerie de 1358* (Paris, 1979); Bommersbach, Gewalt in der Jacquerie, 46-81, 71-79; P. Strohm, *Hochon's Arrow: The Social Imagination of Fourteenth-Century* Texts (Princeton, 1992), 34-51; H. Hinck, "Das zeitgenössische Bild der englischen Rebellen von 1381 und ihres aufständischen Handelns" (MA thesis, Bielefeld University, 2005).

Peasants' Revolt, but its report of the Jacquerie is primarily focused on the atrocities of the rebels, showing no interest whatsoever in their motives or in the causes of their rising.[24] With Jean Froissart it is just the same: he offers an albeit prejudiced but nonetheless valuable account of the English rising, but is only concerned with the rebels' cruelty and beastliness in his influential version of the French revolt.[25] However, this curious manner of following the representational conventions of the country written about is not shared by a third cross-border reporter of these risings, the Englishman Sir Thomas Gray. His brief account of the French Jacquerie is an essentially English one: despite reproducing some of the stereotypes it takes a much more sober approach and does not try to vilify the insurgents beyond measure.[26]

But how can we account for these different ways of representing revolt at home and abroad? In the cases at hand it will have been largely a matter of sources. Both Froissart and the author of the *Anonimalle Chronicle* seem to have drawn on sources from abroad for their cross-border reports of revolt, importing the "foreign style" of representation in this way. The account of the Jacquerie included in the *Anonimalle Chronicle* has much in common with the so-called "chivalric version" found in the chronicles of Jean le Bel and Jean Froissart,[27] but it also provides some distinctive new material not known from any other text on the rising. It therefore appears that the English compiler had access to an unknown report of the Jacquerie which was in some way related to the chivalric texts from abroad.[28] Froissart himself, by contrast, relied on oral evidence for his account of the Peasants' Revolt.[29] That he, almost exclusively among the chroniclers, cared to distinguish between an essentially good-hearted majority of insurgents and the "great venom"

---

24 Anonimalle Chronicle, 41-42, 133-151; cf. Bulst, ›Jacquerie‹ und ›Peasants' Revolt‹, 807; Cohn, Popular Protest, 144, 172-173. Cohn's translation, however, has to be approached with caution.

25 Œuvres de Froissart, 6: 44-58; 9: 386-424; cf. Bulst, ›Jacquerie‹ und ›Peasants' Revolt‹, 812-813. Most of the account of the Jacquerie was copied from Jean le Bel, but Froissart introduced some variants in the second and third redactions of his chronicles; cf. Cohn, Popular Protest, 143, 150-158; Gransden, Historical Writing, 2: 89-92.

26 Gray, Scalacronica, 152-155, 168-169; cf. Bulst, ›Jacquerie‹ und ›Peasants' Revolt‹, 815.

27 For the "version chevaleresque" see Medeiros, Jacques et chroniqueurs, 26–27, 45–46.

28 Cf. Anonimalle Chronicle, xxxviii; Bulst, ›Jacquerie‹ und ›Peasants' Revolt‹, 807-808. For the chronicle in general see Gransden, Historical Writing, 2: 110-113; Taylor, Historical Literature, 133-147.

29 Cf. Gransden, Historical Writing, 2: 91; Taylor, Historical Literature, 321; Given-Wilson, Chronicles, 11.

leading the rebel forces,[30] for the most part may have been a literary decision. But it also shows his closeness to the English government, for this had adopted a similar perspective by pardoning all but the "principal leaders and exciters" of the rising.[31]

No such connections were entertained by Thomas Gray, who based his account of the Jacquerie on oral testimony as well. Taking part in an expedition to France just a year after the events, he will have collected his evidence on the spot and thus was able to produce a relatively independent version of the revolt for his chronicle.[32] The independence of his report becomes apparent in the lack of any overstated attempt to scandalize the Jacques or to idealize their opponent, the French nobility. Gray's account is remarkably balanced and favours neither the nobles, who were his peers and shared the chivalric values of his writing, nor the rebels, who had risen against those he was fighting as an English soldier. It must have been his position as an outsider to the conflict that enabled him to maintain such a neutral view. Had he been directly involved in the events, either as a victim of the rising or as a participant in its suppression, the tenor of his report might have turned out quite differently. It is most unfortunate that he did not live to see the English commons rise against their betters in 1381, so that we will never know how Gray would have portrayed the insurgents in his own country.[33]

This we do know in another case, and a comparison of the reports of insurgency at home and abroad reveals some fundamental differences that cannot be explained by the sources. The author in question is Thomas Walsingham, a monastic chronicler from St. Albans, who wrote about the Peasants' Revolt as an eyewitness and is famous for his strong hostility towards the English rebels.[34] What is less well-known, however, is that he also included an account of the Parisian tax disturbances in his chronicle.[35] The difference between these reports could not be more striking. While heaping abuse after abuse on the English rebels, Walsingham

---

30 Œuvres de Froissart, 9: 404-406; for the "great venom" (*li grans venins*) see ibid., 406. Apparently, Froissart even had some sympathy for the simple ones; see ibid., 397, 400. A similar distinction can be found in the Anonimalle Chronicle, 137; cf. Hinck, Das zeitgenössische Bild, 22, 37-38.
31 Cf. Parliament Rolls, 6: 222-224, 240-247; Dobson, Peasants' Revolt, 325-333.
32 Gransden, Historical Writing, 2: 96; Bulst, ›Jacquerie‹ und ›Peasants' Revolt‹, 806-807.
33 For Gray and his work in general see Gransden, Historical Writing, 2: 92-96; Taylor, Historical Literature, 171-174.
34 St Albans Chronicle, 1: 410-563; cf. ibid., lxxxv-xcii; Bulst, ›Jacquerie‹ und ›Peasants' Revolt‹, 809-10.
35 St Albans Chronicle, 1: 390-395, 652-655. Cohn should have included this account in his collection.

completely refrains from judging the insurgents in Paris.[36] He may not be too comfortable with the fury and the violence of the crowd, but this is nothing compared to the indignation he expresses at the attacks occurring in England. The villain of his account, therefore, is not the rebellious people of Paris, it is the King of France, who is "proud and arrogant" after his victory in Flanders and resorts to deceit and cruelty to regain control of the city.[37] The distribution of sympathy in this cross-border report and in the account of the rising at home is completely reversed: Walsingham clearly despises the English rebels but apparently favours the French ones.

Walsingham's account of the Parisian disturbances is significant for yet another reason. The author pays much attention to the grievances of the rebels, the recapitulation of which even dominates his report. Starting with the usual reference to royal taxation, the complaints then move into a rather unexpected direction not to be found in any French version of the events. They focus on the country's defences, for in the eyes of the protesters these had not improved despite all the money collected from the people. Most importantly, the taxes had been wasted on a useless nobility, which, with the English rampant in the kingdom, was shamefully hiding in its castles instead of fighting the enemy.[38] Walsingham's emphasis on the cowardice and futility of the French nobles is curiously misplaced in this context, for it rather belongs to the background of the Jacquerie than to the situation of the early 1380s. And when the author in the end even has his rebels threatening to defect to the English, "whom they knew would rule them more gently than their natural French lords,"[39] it becomes clear that this list of grievances is English war propaganda laid into the mouths of French insurgents.[40]

To indicate that a king had lost the favour of his people was not an uncommon form of propaganda in the Middle Ages. Lancastrian authors also employed it against Richard II, and they did not fail to notice that it was by popular agency that

---

36 For his attacks on the English rebels cf. Hinck, *Das zeitgenössische Bild*, 39-50.
37 St Albans Chronicle, 1: 652-655.
38 St Albans Chronicle, 1: 390-393.
39 St Albans Chronicle, 1: 392: *"quin pocius, relictis suo rege et proceribus, qui continue eorum apporiacioni studebant, ad Anglos se conferrent, quos sciuerunt magis placide dominaturos super eos quam Gallicos suos dominos naturales."*
40 For French and English war propaganda in the 15th century see P. S. Lewis, "War Propaganda and Historiography in Fifteenth-Century France and England", *TRHS* 5.15 (1965): 1-21; N. Pons, "La propagande de guerre française avant l'apparition de Jeanne d'Arc", *Journal des Savants* (1982): 191-214.

the earls trying to restore him were stopped in early 1400.[41] But Richard had been on good terms with the French, and his deposition by Henry of Lancaster was perceived as an outrageous act of treason across the channel.[42] French accounts of the deposition therefore paint a different picture of the Earls' Revolt. They tend to play down the popular element in its failure, one of the texts ignoring it altogether, two others indicating that the commoners involved were primarily acting on orders.[43] Thus, it is the Countess of Hereford who in one of the French reports assembles the country people of Essex to put to death the Earl of Huntingdon. But the rustics are extremely sympathetic to the former king's partisan, and it takes a lot of curses and threats from the countess to make the executioner strike off his head.[44] Lancastrians like Walsingham or Usk, by contrast, do not mention the countess at all and simply state that the earl was captured and beheaded by the common people.[45] Keeping in mind how strongly the same commoners were condemned by Walsingham in 1381, and that French texts sometimes described the English as "evil and foolish people,"[46] it is ironic that elitist writers like these should consider the English populace as a narrative asset useful for propagandistic purposes.

But to minimise popular agency was but one way to treat opposition to the favoured faction in the other country. Another was to emphasise it, and to use the representation of revolt for a general attack against the enemy and his character. The monk of St. Denis actually gives two reports of the Peasants' Revolt in his chronicle, the first expressing his shock at the rebels' atrocities in a short aside to his account of the urban tax disturbances in France,[47] the second recounting the

---

41 *The Chronica Maiora of Thomas Walsingham 1376-1422*, trans. D. Preest (Woodbridge, 2005), 315-317; Chronicon Adæ de Usk, 41-43, 197-203; Historia Vitae et Regni, 163-165.
42 See C. Taylor, "›Weep thou for me in France‹: French Views of the Deposition of Richard II", *Fourteenth Century England* 3 (2004): 207-222.
43 See Creton, Metrical History, 209-216, 400-407; Traïson et Mort, 77-103, 229-61; Religieux de Saint-Denys, 2:734-8. Froissart is less sympathetic to Richard and his followers. For these accounts in general, see J. J. N. Palmer, "The Authorship, Date and Historical Value of the French Chronicles on the Lancastrian Revolution", *BJRL* 61 (1978-1979): 145-181, 398-412.
44 Traïson et Mort, 96-100, 253-256; but cf. Palmer, French Chronicles, 409.
45 Chronica Maiora, 317; Chronicon Adæ de Usk, 42, 198. The Historia Vitae et Regni, 165, however, has a version not unlike the French one: *"Et non multum post dominus Iohannes Holand comes Huntindonn, frater Regis Ricardi ex parte matris, apud Plasch' in Estsex' per comitissam Herford' captus et decollatus est."*
46 See Metrical History, 222, 410: *"gent mauvaise et folle."*
47 Religieux de Saint-Denys, 1: 132-135.

events in retrospect as background to the English expedition into Flanders in 1383.[48] In this latter passage, the author describes the populace of England as being bent on renewing the war and indicates that it had been their efforts to establish a lasting peace that the archbishop and other royal councillors had lost their lives for in the recent rising.[49] Since public opinion was rather concerned with the kingdom's defences in the early 1380s and serious resistance to an agreement did not show up until about a decade after,[50] this reading of the revolt is an essentially anachronistic one and primarily serves to polemicise against the English in general: holding an "inveterate and expiable hatred" for the French, they were "unable to endure peace" and even massacred their own government when this dared to work for reconciliation.[51] The rising of 1381 thus is turned into another proof of English wickedness here and as such appears to foreshadow the deposition of Richard II eighteen years later.

In all the cases of cross-border representation discussed so far we have been dealing with foreign authors writing about revolts of the common people against their own native betters. In Caux and Caen, however, the situation was different, for the risings of 1435 in these Norman regions were directed against an occupying authority, i.e. the English forces holding the duchy since 1415.[52] An English version of the events is included in one of the London Chronicles, but, instead of vilifying the rebels, the text maintains a rather neutral stance. It describes the revolts and their suppression like other military affairs on the continent and only blames the Duke of Burgundy, who is said to have incited the rising in Caux after his

---

48 Religieux de Saint-Denys, 1: 256-259. Cf. also the expanded translation of this in Nouvelle Collection, 2: 358, which curiously omits the reference to retrospectivity and therefore describes an independent rising in 1383 here: *"En l'an mille trois cens quatre-vingt et trois, en Angleterre y eut de grandes séditions et commotions".*

49 Religieux de Saint-Denys, 1: 256: *"archiepiscopum Cantuariensem, virum utique in cunctis commendabilem, regis cancellarium, nonnullosque consiliarios regales ferali rabie agitati nequiter interemerant, occasionem addentes quia pacem perpetuam inter reges componere conabantur."*

50 See E. Searle & R. Burghart, "The Defense of England and the Peasants' Revolt", *Viator* 3 (1972): 365-388; N. Saul, *Richard II* (London, 1997), 205-225.

51 Cf. Religieux de Saint-Denys, 1: 4, 256 (*more suo quietis impacientes*), 290 (*odio inveterato et inexpiabili stimulante*). For the "hatred between nations" in the monk's chronicle see B. Guenée, *L'opinion publique à la fin du Moyen Age d'après la Chronique de Charles VI du Religieux de Saint Denis* (Paris, 2002), 68-70.

52 For the occupation of Normandy in general see C. T. Allmand, *Lancastrian Normandy 1415-1450: The History of a Medieval Occupation* (Oxford, 1983).

betrayal.[53] More passionate than this is the account of Thomas Basin, a prominent Norman bishop much affected by the war and its devastations.[54] Even though he is not viciously hostile towards the English, Basin leaves no doubt that the insurrection was caused by English oppression and that the rebels were fighting for their natural lord, the King of France. The latter's inactivity, therefore, is all the more reprehensible in Basin's eyes, and it is at the French monarch's feet that he lays the ultimate responsibility for the plight of the faithful Norman people.[55] Despite showing different attitudes toward rebels and authorities in this conflict, the English and the Norman account have one thing in common: they put the real blame on a third party – the treacherous Duke of Burgundy in the English case, the indifferent King of France in the Norman one.

The distribution of sympathy certainly is one of the most interesting aspects of the transnational representation of revolt in late medieval England and France. The war had a strong influence on the way authors were reporting from abroad and in several of our cases the insurgents in the other country were used to slander the authorities there or even vilify the enemy in general. Naturally, this partisan approach to foreign insurgency was more interested in the national dynamics of a rising than in possible cross-border connections to other revolts, so that most of the writers betray a rather limited view of revolt in their chronicles. There are, however, some notable exceptions to this, and we will finally turn to the question of how contemporaries were linking insurgency across the borders, either unconsciously or deliberately.

3) Linking the Incidents

To draw connections between historical events was definitely not the main concern of medieval chroniclers. Instead of explaining the incidents to their audience, they usually contented themselves with a simple account of what had happened, trying above all to tell the truth and to present examples, as they themselves frequently asserted.[56] Thus, it is not too surprising that we have found only a few chronicles in our sample that directly link occasions of insurgency in different countries. But such linking did not necessarily have to be explicit. An unconscious form of this

---

53 Chronicles of London, 137-140.
54 For a comprehensive study of Basin's life, work and attitudes see M. Spencer, *Thomas Basin (1412-1490): The History of Charles VII and Louis XI* (Nieuwkoop, 1997).
55 Basin, Histoire, 1: 196-227; cf. Spencer, Thomas Basin, 104-105.
56 Guenée, Genres historiques, 1008, 1010-1012; Bulst, ›Jacquerie‹ und ›Peasants' Revolt‹, 795-796; Given-Wilson, Chronicles, 1, 166.

appears when the description of foreign insurgency is notably shaped by the author's experiences of revolt at home. The Florentine Matteo Villani, for example, portrayed the Jacquerie of 1358 like one of the urban risings he knew from his Italian home town, merging this originally rural revolt with the rebellion of Etienne Marcel in Paris and completely passing over any peasant participation in the movement.[57] Froissart will have been influenced by his personal experiences in Flanders when he ascribed to the Londoners a major part in exciting the rising of the English counties in 1381.[58] The link between different manifestations of revolt is not an open and intentional one in these cases, but it nevertheless indicates that the author perceived something familiar in what he had heard or read about a rising in the other country.

Authors explicitly linking revolt across the borders were few, but there are some examples related to the so-called "cluster of revolts" in the 1380s, involving the rebellion in Flanders, the urban tax revolts in France, the English Peasants' Revolt and in one case even the Florentine rising of the Ciompi. A simple way to connect these revolts was to compare them or their participants. The Florentine writer Pitti, for example, remarks that the commoners rioting in Paris were people just like the Ciompi insurgents in his home town.[59] Froissart compares the French rebels to those in Ghent, pointing out that the very year the latter rose against their lord in Flanders the Parisians did the same in France.[60] More important than such comparisons, however, are connections attributed to the rebels themselves. These could have been inspired or even incited by insurgents from abroad, so that the rebellion in one country had been imported from another and therefore was derived from a "parent rising" there. According to the monk of St. Denis, public opinion had it that the people of France not only had received messengers and letters from Flanders but also was following the example of the English when almost all of it rose against the king in 1382.[61] Froissart even describes how the Parisians decided to await the

---

57 Villani, Cronica, 185, 214-216, 274-275; translated in Cohn, Popular Protest, 173-176. Cf. ibid., 144; Bulst, ›Jacquerie‹ und ›Peasants' Revolt‹, 815.
58 Œuvres de Froissart, 9: 389-390; cf. Dobson, Peasants' Revolt, 7, 137; Hinck, Das zeitgenössische Bild, 67.
59 Mercanti Scrittori, 384: *"Il popolo grasso, ciò è i buoni cittadini che si chiamano borgesi, dubitando che 'l detto minuto popolo che si chiamarono i Maglietti, ch' erano gente tali quali furono i Ciompi che corsono Firenze"*; translated in Cohn, Popular Protest, 303.
60 Œuvres de Froissart, 9: 394: *"cheux de Gand et de Flandres qui se rebelloient contre leur signeur, et en celle propre anée li Parisyen le fissent ossi et trouvèrent à faire les mailles de fier."*
61 Religieux de Saint-Denys, 1: 132: *"Sic temerarium ausum malignandi [...] fere totus populus Francie assumpserat, nec minori agitabatur furia, et ut fama publica referebat,*

outcome of the conflict in Flanders before embarking on further insurrection of their own.[62] As it appears, at least those contemporaries with a broader outlook noticed a wave of insurgency in the early 1380s and tried to make sense of this clustering by ascribing transnational connections to it. Whether these really existed is another question, but it is highly unlikely that the rebels themselves were not aware of popular insurgency in other countries.

Of the writers explicitly linking revolt across the borders, Froissart was the only one to draw a connection across time as well. Thus, he not only linked the French, English and Flemish risings of the 1380s,[63] but also included the Jacquerie of more than twenty years before, comparing it to the English Peasants' Revolt as well as alluding to it in a passage about the rebellion in Flanders.[64] In fact, his chronicle contains more explicit linkings than any other text in our sample, which suggests that he maintained a somewhat specific view of popular insurgency. His general outlook was the most comprehensive to be found in the historiography of his day, for he was writing what amounted to a pan-European history of chivalry and included nearly all of western Europe in its scope.[65] The revolts he was recording therefore were more to him than just incidents occasionally linked to one another: they were part of a transnational phenomenon in his eyes, a "great devilry" which threatened to destroy the nobility in many European countries. This danger first appears in his account of the Jacquerie, and is repeated several times in the further course of the chronicle, arguably being one of the underlying themes of his narrative.[66] But thankfully, he asserts, God had always provided a remedy in time, so that the prospect of an annihilation of the nobility remained just a hypothetical one.[67] Froissart, then, is exceptional among the cross-border reporters of revolt. He had changing patrons and loyalties in England, Flanders and France, but due to his distinctly chivalric outlook he painted an almost universal picture of popular

---

per Flamingos, qui peste similis rebellionis laborabant, nunciis et apicibus excitatus, exemplo quoque Anglorum, qui eodem tempore contra regem et magnates regni rebellantes"; cf. ibid., 230, where the chronicler reports the rumour of a letter sent from Paris to Courtrai proposing an alliance between the cities. For English translations see Cohn, Popular Protest, 277, 287.

62 Œuvres de Froissart, 10: 146-147.
63 Œuvres de Froissart, 9: 394, 449; 10: 146, 185.
64 Œuvres de Froissart, 9: 386; 10: 147.
65 For Froissart's historical perspective see, for example, the different contributions in J. J. N. Palmer, ed., *Froissart: Historian* (Woodbridge, 1981).
66 Œuvres de Froissart, 6: 45, 46, 47; 9: 394, 403; 10: 147, 185. For the "great devilry" (*grant déablie*) see ibid., 9: 449; 10: 147.
67 Œuvres de Froissart, 6: 46, 47, 56; 9: 391; 10: 147.

insurgency in the later Middle Ages. And this proved to be a lasting one still shaping our perception today.

SUMMARY

The Hundred Years' War should have encouraged the mutual cross-border reporting of popular insurgency in England and France, but we have only been able to find some fifteen examples of revolt being reported by chroniclers from the other country. To understand this scarcity of findings it is helpful to consider the conditions of transnational representation in late medieval chronicles: these were not normally concerned with events from abroad, so that an incident had to catch the attention of an author and to be of interest for his narrative to be recorded in another country. Thus, it is not surprising that there was more transnational coverage of events like a riot in Rome to enforce the election of an Italian pope than there was of the ordinary risings of the populace, which for the most part did not affect other countries too much.

The transnational character of cross-border reports becomes apparent in the particularities of their representation of foreign insurgency, both compared to the picture of revolt painted by chroniclers abroad and to their own depiction of disturbances at home. In general, there was little sympathy for popular rebels in medieval historiography, even though the representation of revolt could differ considerably from country to country. Cross-border reporters sometimes imported a foreign style of representation with their sources, but they could also develop an independent approach, maintaining the neutrality of an outsider or even siding with the rebels in the other country. These were ideal to voice propaganda against enemy authorities and served well to question a government's legitimacy, so that insurgents from abroad were more likely to be favoured than their counterparts at home. Violent opposition to a faction rather well-disposed towards the author's country, however, could also be utilized for a cross-border polemic against the enemy in general.

Only a few transnational reporters cared to draw connections between individual incidents of revolt in their narratives. Some did so unconsciously, so that their description of foreign insurgency was shaped by their experiences of revolt at home. An explicit relation was created by comparing revolts or their participants, but more important than this were connections ascribed to the rebels themselves. By pointing out that these were inspired or even incited by insurgents from abroad, some of the authors were trying to make sense of a wave of insurgency in the early 1380s. The most inclusive perspective, however, was adopted by the chivalric historian Jean Froissart: to him, the late medieval uprisings were part of a transnational phenomenon which threatened to destroy the nobility all across Europe.

Trans-national Representations of Pretenders in 17th-Century Russian Revolts

MAUREEN PERRIE

Pretenders (*samozvantsy*) played a part in most of the major popular revolts in early modern Russia that were characterised in Soviet Marxist historiography as "peasant wars".[1] In particular, false descendants of Ivan the Terrible were prominent throughout the "Time of Troubles" of the early 17th century; Sten'ka Razin, who headed the cossack-peasant revolt of 1669-1671, was reportedly accompanied by a false Tsarevich Aleksei Alekseevich; and Emel'ian Pugachev, the leader of the similar uprising of 1773-1774, depicted himself as Peter III, the murdered husband of Catherine the Great. Pretenders were not, of course, an exclusively Russian phenomenon. False claimants to a royal identity can be found in most hereditary monarchical systems. Ancient history provides the examples of the Pseudo-Smerdis

---

1 The only one of the four so-called "peasant wars" which had no trace of pretenderism was the Bulavin revolt of 1707-1708. The term "peasant war" was of course highly misleading, based on a (false) analogy with the Peasant War in Germany of 1525, on which Karl Marx's collaborator Friedrich Engels had written. The revolts led by Razin, Bulavin and Pugachev were primarily cossack (or cossack-led) popular uprisings. The Time of Troubles was a much more complex and heterogeneous series of events, involving foreign military intervention as well as civil war and social conflict. Soviet historians themselves disagreed on whether the whole period described by pre-revolutionary historians as the "Time of Troubles" (*smutnoe vremia, smuta*) constituted a "peasant war", or whether the term should be applied only to the episode of most acute social conflict within it, the Bolotnikov revolt of 1606-1607. The main common factor throughout the period c.1603-1614 was in fact the presence of pretenders claiming to belong to the old Moscow dynasty and thereby challenging the legitimacy of the elected tsars Boris Godunov, Vasilii Shuiskii and Michael Romanov. See Maureen Perrie, *Pretenders and Popular Monarchism in Early Modern Russia. The False Tsars of the Time of Troubles* (Cambridge, 1995).

of Persia and the False Agrippa of Rome; the medieval period offers the False Count Baldwin of Flanders and the False Emperor Frederick II. The closest parallels and the most immediate precedents for the Russian pretenders of the Time of Troubles, however, can be found in early modern Europe. England had known the impostors Lambert Simnel and Perkin Warbeck in the late fifteenth century; and in the last decades of the sixteenth century a number of royal pretenders appeared in Moldavia, as well as a series of impostors claiming to be Don Sebastian, the King of Portugal who had died on the battlefield of Alcazarquivir in 1578.[2] But from the beginning of the seventeenth century the pretender phenomenon is particularly associated with Russia, and with Russian popular revolts.

THE TIME OF TROUBLES

Foreigners' accounts have long been regarded by historians as a valuable source of evidence about the Time of Troubles. In this article, however, I am concerned not so much with the factual information which these contemporary observers provide, or its reliability, but rather with the broader narratives through which they interpret the phenomenon of pretendership. As we shall see, there are two rival narratives concerning pretenders. The first is that of the pretender as impostor, which places the Russian examples in the context of a tradition of such fraudsters, dating back to antiquity. The second is that of the persecuted royal heir who miraculously escapes from death, eventually reveals his true identity and reclaims his ancestral throne. This theme, which was popular in adventure romances in medieval and early modern Europe, recurred in the "back-stories" (fictional autobiographies) of many Russian pretenders. Most foreign observers were sceptical about the pretenders' stories, but some took them at face value, and their accounts of the career of the First False Dmitrii, in particular, often resemble the romances of the age of chivalry.

The First False Dmitrii

The First False Dmitrii was the best known pretender of the Time of Troubles. This man appeared in Lithuania in 1602, claiming to be Ivan the Terrible's youngest son, who had died as a child in mysterious circumstances at Uglich in 1591. The old

---

2   On the Moldavian pretenders, see N.A. Mokhov, *Ocherki istorii moldavsko-russko-ukrainskikh sviazei (s drevneishikh vremen do nachala XIX veka)* (Kishinev, 1961), 40-69; on the False Sebastians see, for example, Yves-Marie Bercé, *Le roi caché. Sauveurs et imposteurs. Mythes politiques populaires dans l'Europe moderne* (Paris, 1990), 17-81.

dynasty of the Moscow rulers came to an end in 1598, with the death of Dmitrii's elder half-brother, Tsar Fedor Ivanovich. The throne passed to Boris Godunov, Tsar Fedor's brother-in-law, who was widely believed to have plotted against the heirs of Ivan the Terrible in order to obtain the throne for himself. The pretender invaded Russia in 1604, defeated Boris's armies and became tsar in 1605. He was overthrown in 1606 by the boyar Prince Vasilii Shuiskii, who acceded to the throne.

Both Russian and foreign accounts provide various versions of the explanation which the pretender offered of his supposed escape from death at Uglich and his subsequent life until he revealed his "true" royal identity to Prince Adam Vishnevetskii (Wiśniowiecki) on his estate at Brahin in Lithuania in 1603.[3] The research of the Jesuit scholar Paul Pierling, published in the early 20th century, has definitively established that the earliest version of the pretender's back-story is the account which Adam Vishnevetskii transmitted to the Polish king, Sigismund III, in October/November 1603. According to Vishnevetskii, the account represented the pretender's own version of his biography, but modern scholars have suggested that Vishnevetskii himself may have played a part in its composition.[4]

The story began with some historical background about Ivan the Terrible, his wives and sons. It then proceeded to the reign of Tsar Fedor, and described how Boris Godunov had plotted to obtain the throne for himself. Having gained power by killing his fellow regents, Boris conspired against Dmitrii's life, and hired assassins to cut his throat while he was asleep in bed at night. One of his tutors, however, intervened. He substituted another boy, a relative of the tsarevich, of a similar age, who was killed in his stead while the tutor helped Dmitrii to escape. In the ensuing tumult a further 30 boys were killed, and the substitute victim's body was so badly bruised that the tsarevich's mother failed to realise that he was not her son. Soon after this the tutor fell gravely ill, but before he died he entrusted Dmitrii to the care of a faithful friend, a nobleman, who brought the boy up. When this protector in turn was about to die, he advised Dmitrii to enter a monastery. The tsarevich became a monk, and wandered from one monastery to another. One day a fellow monk recognised him as Dmitrii, "because of his way of walking and heroic

---

3   For references to these explanations see, for example, K.V. Chistov, *Russkie narodnye sotsial'no-utopicheskie legendy XVII-XIX vv* (Moscow, 1967), 42-46; Maureen Perrie, "'Popular Socio-Utopian Legends' in the Time of Troubles", *Slavonic and East European Review* 60 (1982): 224-33; Perrie, Pretenders and Popular Monarchism, 37-43, 64-69, 79-81.

4   P. Pierling, *La Russie et le Saint-Siège; études diplomatiques*, 5 vols. (Paris, 1897-1912), 3 [1901, reprint The Hague, 1967]: 42; Wacław Sobieski, *Szkice Historyczne* (Warsaw, 1904), 82-86; P. Pirling [Pierling], "Nazvannyi Dimitrii i Adam Vishnevetskii", *Russkaia Starina* 117 (1904): 123-128.

manners". Fearing danger, he fled to Poland, where he eventually came to Prince Vishnevetskii's house, and declared himself to be the Prince of Moscow.[5]

Not surprisingly, when the news of Dmitrii's appearance began to circulate in Poland, some scepticism was expressed about the young man's story. The Polish chancellor, Jan Zamoyski, in response to a letter from Adam Vishnevetskii informing him of Dmitrii's arrival on his estate at Brahin, remarked: "As for the Muscovite staying with Your Lordship, who calls himself the son of the Muscovite Prince Ivan Vasil'evich, then very often such matters turn out to be true, but often also to be inventions."[6] Later, at a session of the Sejm on 1 February [20 January Old Style] 1605, Zamoyski compared the episode in Dmitrii's story in which a substitute victim was killed in his stead to "a comedy by Plautus or Terence". What sort of plotter, he asked, did not check to make sure that the assassin he had hired had killed the right person?[7] Albert Baranowski, the bishop of Płock, in a letter of 6 March 1604 to the king, had also expressed scepticism about elements in Dmitrii's story: "First of all, how did his mother not recognise her murdered son? Secondly, why were another 30 children killed? Thirdly, how could a monk recognise Tsarevich Dmitrii, whom he had never seen?"[8]

Suspicions were soon expressed that Dmitrii was an impostor. In Rome, on receiving his first report about Dmitrii from Claudio Rangoni, the Papal Nuncio in Cracow, Pope Clement VIII wrote in the margin: "Sarà un altro Rè di Portogallo resuscitato".[9] The analogy with the false Don Sebastians was also made in Poland: according to a later report by Rangoni to Rome, the Vice-Chancellor [Piotr Tylicki] had compared Dmitrii to the false Agrippa of ancient Rome and to the false King of Portugal.[10] The bishop of Płock, in the letter to the king which we have already cited, also referred to the precedent of "the adventures of the so-called Sebastian", and to the pretenders who appeared in Wallachia whenever the throne was vacant

---

5   F.K. Nowakowski, ed., *Źródła do dziejów Polski*, 2 vols. (Berlin, 1841), 2: 65-70. Nowakowski wrongly dated the text 1606: see Pierling, La Russie et le Saint-Siège, 3: 42, 399.
6   *Zapiski Getmana Zholkevskogo o Moskovskoi Voine*, ed. P.A. Mukhanovym, 2nd edn. (St Petersburg, 1871), *prilozheniia*, no.3, col.9.
7   *Russkaia Istoricheskaia Biblioteka*, ed. Arkheograficheskaia kommissiia, 39 vols. (St Petersburg, 1872-1927), 1: col.16.
8   P. Pirling [Pierling], *Iz smutnogo vremeni: stat'i i zametki* (St Petersburg, 1902), 6-7.
9   Pierling, La Russie et le Saint-Siège, 41.
10 P. Pierling, *Rome et Démétrius, d'après des documents nouveaux, avec pièces justificatives et facsimile* (Paris, 1878), 12, 178 (Rangoni's despatch of 13 March 1604).

there. The phenomenon of pretence, he added, was even known in Poland, "among the nobility, when an inheritance is divided".[11]

Information about Dmitrii quickly spread throughout Europe, especially after he embarked on his successful campaign to obtain the Russian throne. As a result of his secret conversion to Roman Catholicism in Poland, there was particular interest in his story in the Catholic hierarchy and among the Catholic monarchs of Europe. The Polish Jesuit chaplains Nikolaj Czyrzowski and Andrzej Lawicki, who accompanied the pretender on his march from Poland to Moscow, sent reports back to Cracow, and Rangoni forwarded them to Rome. From Cracow news of Dmitrii also reached Venice, where it was enthusiastically received by the veteran Jesuit Antonio Possevino, who had visited Moscow in 1581 to negotiate the end of the Livonian War, and had engaged in debate about religion with Ivan the Terrible. Possevino in turn passed on the information to his contacts in Florence and Paris. News of Dmitrii was spread through other channels too. The French captain Jean La Blanque, who was based in Cracow, corresponded with Philippe Canaye de Fresnes, the French ambassador to Venice, who reported back to the court of King Henri IV in Paris; while in Prague the Emperor Rudolph II obtained information directly from his agents in Moscow and indirectly from those in Cracow and Venice.[12]

The earliest published version of Dmitrii's story to appear in Western Europe was the account issued in Venice in 1605 by Barezzo Barezzi, and generally attributed to Possevino.[13] The details it contains of Dmitrii's campaign for the throne are based on the letters of Czyrzowski and Lawicki. The earlier chapters, which describe the events at Uglich, the tsarevich's escape from Boris's assassins and his eventual revelation of his true identity in Poland, bear some resemblance to the account in Vishnevetskii's report to the king.[14] This indicated to Pierling that the author was familiar with that document,[15] but there are also some differences

---

11 Pirling, Iz smutnogo vremeni, 7. The analogy with the Wallachian (Moldavian) pretenders was one which was likely to be made in Poland, since these pretenders had been supported not only by the Zaporozhian cossacks but also by the Vishnevetskii family. It is perhaps not surprising that the bishop warned the king that Dmitrii should not be allowed to flee to the cossacks (ibid., 7).

12 Pierling, La Russie et le Saint-Siège, 3: 192-201.

13 Baretstso Baretstsi [Barezzo Barezzi], *Povestvovanie o Dimitrii Samozvantse, sobrannoe Baretstso Baretstsi* [translation of the Florence edition of 1606], Inostrannye sochineniia i akty, otnosiashchiesia do Rossii, comp. K.M. Obolenskii, vol. 4 (Moscow, 1847), iii-iv; Pirling, Iz smutnogo vremeni, 205-220.

14 Baretstsi, Povestvovanie, 5-6, cf. Nowakowski, Źródła do dziejów Polski, 2: 68-70.

15 Pirling, Iz smutnogo vremeni, 208.

which suggest the additional use of unknown independent sources, probably – Pierling suggests – of Jesuit origin.[16]

The author of the Barezzi account accepts that the man who became Tsar Dmitrii in 1605-1606 was the true Tsarevich Dmitrii of Uglich, and he adopts a highly triumphalist attitude towards his hero's success (the account ends with Dmitrii's accession to the throne in Moscow) and the enticing prospects which it presented for the conversion of Russia to Catholicism. Although it has a recognisably historical Russian setting, in many respects the narrative resembles those fictional literary texts in which long-lost royal heroes, after many vicissitudes and adventures, eventually regain their ancestral thrones and punish the usurpers who had unjustly deprived them of their inheritance (see below). But the author's Jesuit perspective also means that the story is presented as the working out of Divine Providence on behalf of Dmitrii and in the interests of the Roman Catholic Church.

There are, however, indications in the Barezzi narrative that Dmitrii was regarded by some as an impostor. The author notes that while Dmitrii was in Poland, Boris sent an envoy to the king, claiming that the self-styled tsarevich was a deceiver, the son of a priest, and demanding that he be returned to Russia, dead or alive. Boris had also spread the rumour in Russia that Dmitrii was a well-known magician.[17] The author adds that subsequently, during Dmitrii's occupation of the town of Putivl' en route to Moscow, his men captured "Grishka Otrep'ev, that notorious magician and wizard, about whom the tyrant [Boris] had spread the rumour that it was not Dmitrii, the son of Ivan Vasil'evich, but this magician, known through all Muscovy as a bad person, who had come with Polish cossacks to take the throne from him." Barezzi then piously observes, "Thus God's just judgment, which always brings down on the heads of slanderers their own slanders, clearly revealed that this magician was a completely different person from Dmitrii the lawful sovereign."[18]

Barezzi's account was phenomenally successful in transmitting news about Dmitrii to the wider public in Western Europe. After the Italian editions of 1605 and 1606, published in Venice and Florence respectively, versions in Latin, French, Spanish, German and Czech were published in Madrid, Munich, Valladolid, Lisbon, Grätz and Prague.[19] Thus the earliest narrative of Dmitrii's story to spread

---

16 Ibid., 211.
17 Baretstsi, Povestvovanie, 8.
18 Ibid., 11. On this incident, which is described in one of the Jesuits' letters, see Perrie, Pretenders and Popular Monarchism, 70.
19 See Baretstsi, Povestvovanie, v-vi; Pierling, La Russie et le Saint-Siège, 3: 196-197. See also the editor's introduction to the Russian translation of the Czech version: "Is-

throughout Europe presented him as the true heir returning to claim his father's throne from the usurper Godunov.

In addition to the first edition of Barezzi, another account published in 1605, i.e. before Dmitrii's death, was the report of the embassy of Sir Thomas Smith, who was sent from James I to Boris Godunov to negotiate new privileges for English merchants. News of Dmitrii's invasion reached the diplomatic party in October 1604, when they were in Moscow. They left Moscow in March 1605, but continued to receive information about events in the capital until their departure for home from the White Sea at the beginning of August. The account mostly takes the form of a chronological report of the embassy, incorporating news of Dmitrii's campaign as it was received in Moscow, often in somewhat garbled form. The final section, however, is a kind of appendix that summarises events in Russia since the death of Ivan IV. This provides a slightly different version of Dmitrii's story from that which the pretender himself had related to his patrons in Poland, and which is reflected in Barezzi's account. According to the English author, the substitution of another child for Dmitrii took place at Uglich long before the fateful night of May 1591.[20] Thus, like Barezzi, the author of the Smith report accepts that Tsar Dmitrii was the real Dmitrii of Uglich, but he provides a new variant of his story.

Dmitrii's own proclamations to his Russian subjects had been notoriously reticent about the details of his supposed escape from death at Uglich,[21] and the English account records a version, evidently current in Moscow at the time of the pretender's first entry into the capital, which is more credible – and more consistent with the real events at Uglich – than the earlier "Poland" version, repeated by Barezzi, in which both the substitution and the murder took place on the same night. In Smith's 'Moscow' version, the substitution took place in advance, and the substituted child was killed by one of his playfellows who cut his throat with a knife when they were "disporting themselves" together, evidently in the daytime.[22] William Scott, another member of the English diplomatic party, provided a variant to this version in a letter to Lord Salisbury (undated, but written before Tsar Dmitrii's death). According to Scott, Dmitrii was "changed" before being sent to Uglich, and another child was "kept and killed in his roome". The real tsarevich was then "conveyed" to Poland by some loyal Russians. Scott is, however, sceptical about whether the new tsar is "the true heire". He hints strongly to Salisbury that

---

toricheskoe i pravdivoe povestvovanie o tom, kak moskovskii kniaz' Dimitrii Ioannovich dostig otsovskogo prestola. Cheshskii tekst 1606 g., s predisloviem i perevodom V.A. Frantseva", *Starina i Novizna* 15 (1911): iii-iv.

20 *Sir Thomas Smithes Voiage and Entertainment in Rushia* (London, 1605), f.M2v-[M3].
21 See Perrie, Pretenders and Popular Monarchism, 64-65.
22 *Sir Thomas Smithes Voiage*, f.M2.

Dmitrii is "Suppositio[u]s and Imposter", but that it is politic to recognise him as the legitimate ruler.[23]

A similar version to Smith's is provided by the mercenary soldier Jacques Margeret in his account published in French in Paris in 1607. Margeret, who had been in service to Boris Godunov, switched his allegiance on Boris's death and became commander of Tsar Dmitrii's palace guard. Margeret remained in Moscow until September 1606: like the author of the English account, he believed that Dmitrii really was the son of Ivan IV. According to the French captain, Dmitrii was saved by his mother and "some of the high nobles", who suspected that Boris was planning to kill him. They substituted another child for the tsarevich and brought Dmitrii up secretly; the "changeling prince" was subsequently murdered in his stead. After Boris succeeded Fedor as tsar, Dmitrii, "in a monk's habit, was sent to Poland", where he revealed his true identity.[24] Margeret, like Barezzi, knows that Boris and others claimed that Dmitrii was the unfrocked monk Grishka Otrep'ev (the English author, however, does not mention this), but Margeret asserts that Grishka was a different person, who had accompanied Dmitrii from Russia to Poland, and then returned with him.[25] Since Margeret, like the English writers, dates the substitution of the tsarevich earlier than the night of 15 May 1591, it seems likely that they are conveying a new variant of Dmitrii's story, devised in 1605 by his Russian backers in Moscow, who realised that the version he had used in Poland was unlikely to withstand scrutiny in Russia, where the events at Uglich were well known.[26]

A very different perspective on the pretender is provided by Petrus Petreius (Peer Persson), a Swedish crown agent in Russia, in his *Relation*, published in Swedish in Stockholm at the end of 1608. Petreius is convinced that the First False Dmitrii was the renegade monk, Grisha Otrep'ev, who fled to Poland and entered the service of Prince Adam Vishnevetskii, where he acquired all kinds of knightly accomplishments. Grisha subsequently came to the attention of the Jesuits, who noticed that he bore a strong physical resemblance to Dmitrii of Uglich, and decided to make use of him for their own purposes. They offered to supply him with everything he needed in order to become tsar, provided that he agreed to marry the Polish noblewoman Marina Mniszech and introduce Catholicism in Russia.

---

23 V.N. Aleksandrenko, comp., "Materialy po Smutnomu vremeni na Rusi XVII v.", *Starina i Novizna* 14 (1911): 246-247.

24 Jacques Margeret, *The Russian Empire and Grand Duchy of Muscovy: a 17th-Century French Account*, trans. Chester S.L. Dunning (Pittsburgh, PA, 1983), 17, 81.

25 Margeret, The Russian Empire, 81-82.

26 Cf. Perrie, Pretenders and Popular Monarchism, 79-81.

Grisha soon acquired the patronage not only of the Jesuits but also of the Papacy and the Polish king.[27]

Petreius was not the first foreign observer to represent Dmitrii as a tool of the Jesuits. William Scott in his letter to Lord Salisbury had stated that when news of Dmitrii's invasion first reached the English envoys in Moscow, they had assumed "this interprise to be a jesuitisme (that broode so swarminge in Polande) likelie to vanishe quickly".[28] A Dutch merchant's account, first published in Dutch and French in 1606 and in English in 1607, claims that the main reason for Dmitrii's overthrow in May 1606 was the influence which he allowed the Poles to have in Moscow, and adds: "but I beleeue that the Pope, with his Seminaries, and Jesuites, were a principal cause of his ruine, and totall subuersion."[29] Even in the Catholic world, similar views were expressed by the enemies of the Jesuits: in August 1606 Francesco Soranzo, the Venetian ambassador to Prague, blamed the Order for provoking Dmitrii's murder by encouraging him to marry a Polish Catholic.[30]

Petreius is, however, the most strongly anti-Catholic of all the contemporary foreign visitors to Russia. His entire account is based on the view that the First

---

27 *Reliatsiia Petra Petreia o Rossii nachala XVII v.*, comp. Iu.A. Limonov (Moscow, 1976), 82-84. Petreius' *Relation* of 1608 was probably based on his reports of 1601-1605 to Charles IX. In his Introduction to the text (ibid., 17-18) Iu.A. Limonov notes that Petreius' information (possibly in the form of his reports to Stockholm) was used by the French historian Jacques-Auguste De Thou (Thuanus), who refers to him as "Peter Paterson of Uppsala", and shares his hostility to the Jesuits. See "Skazaniia De-Tu o Dimitrii Samozvantse", in *Skazaniia sovremennikov o Dmitrii Samozvantse*, ed. N.G. Ustrialov, 3rd corr. edn., 2 vols. (St Petersburg, 1859), 1: 329-331. De Thou's *History*, published in 1619, also made use of the accounts of other foreign observers such as Margeret. In its turn, it was used as a source by others, including Samuel Purchas in his compilation of travel writings, first published in 1625. See, for example, Samuel Purchas, comp., *Hakluytus Posthumus, or Purchas His Pilgrimes. Contayning a History of the World in Sea Voyages and Lande Travells by Englishmen and Others*, 20 vols. (Glasgow, 1905-1907), 14 [1906]: 158-163.

28 Aleksandrenko, Materialy po Smutnomu vremeni, 245.

29 Sonia E. Howe, ed., *The False Dmitri; a Russian Romance and Tragedy, Described by British Eye-Witnesses, 1604-1612* (London, 1916, reprint Cambridge, 1972), 60. For the publication history of this account ("The Reporte of a Bloudie and Terrible Massacre [...]"), see, for example, *Moskovskaia tragediia, ili rasskaz o zhizni i smerti Dimitriia*, trans. from Latin A. Braudo and I. Rostsiusa, ed. S.D. Sheremetev (St Petersburg, 1901), xi-xii.

30 Pierling, La Russie et le Saint-Siège, 3: 330. On accusations about the Jesuits' role in the affair of the First False Dmitrii, see Bercé, Le roi caché, 352-359.

False Dmitrii was the instrument of the Pope, the Jesuits and King Sigismund.³¹ In many ways, it represents an inversion of the Barezzi account. Both authors agree that Dmitrii received important support in his campaign for the throne from the Catholic hierarchy, the Jesuits and the Polish King: Barezzi, however, claims that Tsar Dmitrii was the true Dmitrii of Uglich; whereas Petreius believes him to be an impostor, who was justifiably killed by the Russians because of his patronage of the Poles and the Jesuits.³² The contrasting attitudes of Barezzi and Petreius reflected the religious and great-power divide in East-Central Europe in the early seventeenth century: Catholicism versus Protestantism, Poland versus Sweden. The Protestant Swedish agent Petreius rejected the claims of the pro-Polish Catholic convert Tsar Dmitrii, and wrote approvingly of the pretender's nemesis, Tsar Vasilii Shuiskii, who was later to seek Swedish military aid against the Polish threat.

The Protestant/Catholic divide does not, however, explain the support for Dmitrii's authenticity expressed by the author of the report of Sir Thomas Smith's embassy and by Jacques Margeret – both of whom were apparently Protestants.³³ For the English diplomats, in search of the renewal of their trade concessions in Russia, it was clearly expedient to recognise Tsar Dmitrii's legitimacy, even if some, like William Scott, as we have seen, were privately sceptical.³⁴ The mercenary Margeret, who entered Dmitrii's service, had a personal self-interest in asserting that his new royal master was the true son of Ivan IV. Chester Dunning, in the Introduction to his translation of Margeret's account, suggests that he may have been willing to serve the new tsar well "in part because Dmitrii's career reminded him of King Henri's".³⁵ (Margeret had fought for Henri IV during the French Wars of Religion.) This must remain pure speculation, although it is true that there were some similarities between Dmitrii and Henri, who had to wage war for recognition of the legitimacy of his claim to the French throne. It is also interesting to note that in his argument in favour of Dmitrii's authenticity Margeret states that his personal qualities were such that

---

31 Reliatsiia Petra Petreia, 73.
32 Ibid., 93-97.
33 On Margeret's religion, see Margeret, The Russian Empire, XVI; and Zhak Marzheret [Jacques Margeret], *Sostoianie Rossiiskoi imperii. Zh. Marzheret v dokumentakh i issledovaniiakh (Teksty, kommentarii, stat'i)* ed. An. Berelovicha, V.D. Nazarova and P.Iu. Uvarova (Moscow, 2007), 453-454.
34 On the pragmatic considerations which led the English government to recognise Dmitrii, see Geraldine M. Phipps, *Sir John Merrick: English Merchant-Diplomat in Seventeenth-Century Russia*, Russian Biography Series, vol. 13 (Newtonville, MA, 1983), 57-64.
35 Margeret, The Russian Empire, XVIII.

[...] he could not be less than the son of a great prince. He had an eloquence which charmed all the Russians. There even shone in him a certain inexpressible majesty not seen before among the lords in Russia, much less in one of low quality as he would necessarily have been had he not been the son of Ivan Vasil'evich.[36]

The notion that the legitimacy of a true monarch might be revealed through his personal nobility of spirit was part of the political philosophy of the age,[37] and Margeret may genuinely have held this view. The idea that a true monarch possessed such qualities might also, of course, have been an indirect form of flattery of King Henri, who had commissioned the publication of Margeret's account,[38] and who had taken a keen interest in Dmitrii since he first received news of his campaign for the crown in 1605.

As far as the hostile foreign observers are concerned, it is perhaps surprising that none of their accounts of the career of the First False Dmitrii draws parallels with the Portuguese and Moldavian pretenders, although, as we have seen, these precedents were well known in Poland. As the responses of Pope Clement VIII and the Polish sceptics suggest, invoking the European tradition of pretendership was a convenient weapon to discredit a supposedly long-lost heir. Perhaps the type of foreigners who were in Russia in 1604-1606 (merchants, mercenary soldiers etc.) were not sufficiently familiar with the history of pretenders in Western Europe to recognise these precedents. But it may also be relevant that the early sceptical responses were made in Poland before the Russian government had issued a clear identification of the pretender as Grisha Otrep'ev: thereafter, the issue became more specific: was Dmitrii who he said he was; was he Grisha; or someone else? Starting with Margeret and Petreius, the foreign observers' accounts often included lists of arguments, sometimes in the form of numbered points, why Tsar Dmitrii was or was not Dmitrii of Uglich.[39] As we have already noted, however, the decisions of

---

36 Ibid., 88. On Dmitrii's princely qualities, see also ibid., 70, 91.
37 Bercé, Le roi caché, 379-381.
38 The editors of the recent Russian edition of Margeret's account plausibly suggest that he had drafted his text before returning to France in 1606, so that the king authorised only its publication, rather than its composition, as Margeret claimed in his dedication: Marzheret, Sostoianie Rossiiskoi imperii, 16.
39 Margeret, The Russian Empire, 80-91; Reliatsiia Petra Petreia, 98-102; Petr Petrei de Erlezunda [Petrus Petreius], *Istoriia o Velikom Kniazhestve Moskovskom* (Moscow, 1867 [translation of the German version published in Leipzig in 1620]), 241-244; Conrad Bussow, *The Disturbed State of the Russian Realm*, trans. G. Edward Orchard (Montreal, 1994), 81-83. Much of Bussow's material, which remained unpublished until the 19th cen-

foreign participants in the Time of Troubles whether or not to recognise Dmitrii as the son of Ivan IV were probably based not on logical deductions from the evidence about his identity, but rather on considerations of self-interest – as, indeed, were the attitudes of most Russians.

Two non-Russian writers who had not themselves visited Russia, however, did make comparisons between the First False Dmitrii and earlier pretenders. In the *Muscovite Tragedy* published by Gerhard Grevenbruch in Cologne in 1608, the author concludes that it is still unclear whether Dmitrii was the true tsarevich or not (*Verus an supposititius*). He adds: "I know, it is true, that in history there are several examples of people who have aspired to a kingdom or a throne by similar deceit and lies", and goes on to cite the examples not only of the Sebastians of Portugal but also of Perkin Warbeck. He notes, however, that "these and many others, before attaining the kingdom, were executed when their deceit was detected", and that "few of these people, as is well known, achieved what Dmitrii did".[40] Thus for the author of the *Tragedy*, Dmitrii's relative success distinguished him from his unsuccessful predecessors and, by implication, left open the question of whether or not he was an impostor.[41]

The other writer who invokes earlier pretenders is the Spanish dramatist Lope de Vega in his play, *El Gran Duque de Moscovia y Emperador Perseguido*. Lope places the analogy in the mouth of Boris Godunov, who compares Dmitrii to pretenders of antiquity and to the Portuguese Don Sebastians.[42] Lope himself, however, considers that Dmitrii was the true tsarevich, although the Portuguese Sebastians were false.[43] By attributing the reference to previous pretenders to the villainous Boris, the would-be murderer of Tsarevich Dmitrii, the dramatist undermines the relevance of the parallel.

---

tury, was "borrowed" by Petreius for his *History*, which was first published in Swedish in Stockholm in 1615, and is a distinct work from his *Relation* of 1608.

40 Moskovskaia tragediia, 69-70.

41 Grevenbruch's account is a compilation based largely on Barezzi in its first part, and on the anonymous 'Reporte of a Bloudie and Terrible Massacre [...]' in its second part. The author's information about Perkin Warbeck focuses on the assistance which Perkin obtained from the Scottish king, and is based on [George] Buchanan's 'History of the Scots' – which no doubt explains why he does not mention Warbeck's immediate predecessor, Lambert Simnel.

42 Lope de Vega, *El Gran Duque de Moscovia y Emperador Perseguido* (Alicante, 2002), Acto II, ll.190-198. As far as I am aware, no "real" native Russian sources refer to earlier examples of pretenders elsewhere.

43 Ervin C. Brody, *The Demetrius Legend and its Literary Treatment in the Age of the Baroque* (Rutherford, N.J., 1972), 130-131.

Even if most foreign authors were unaware of specific historical precedents for the phenomenon of pretence, however, they were undoubtedly familiar with the concept of imposture, so that a trans-national perspective is implicit in their accounts: most foreigners had words for an impostor available in their own languages, whereas their Russian contemporaries used more generic terms such as *vor* (villain, criminal) or *eretik* (heretic) to describe the First False Dmitrii.[44]

The foreign authors may also have been familiar with literary and folkloric narratives which incorporated the type of motifs that were found in Dmitrii's back-story. Such narratives may have influenced both the production of Dmitrii's fictional autobiography, and its reception and re-telling by foreign observers.

The distinguished Russian folklorist K.V. Chistov has argued that the rumours and tales about Dmitrii which circulated in early 17th-century Russia constituted a "popular socio-utopian legend about a returning royal deliverer". Chistov considers that these legends existed in Russia from the 17th to the 19th centuries; they included motifs such as the attempted murder of the true tsar or tsarevich, his miraculous escape, lengthy wanderings incognito, eventual recognition and restoration to the throne; and they constituted a genre of folklore.[45] Dmitrii's legend, he suggests, "was not the fruit of an individual's devising, but arose naturally, and was devised by the collective consciousness of the peasant, cossack and urban masses".[46] The accounts of contemporary foreign observers, Chistov claims, convey the legend of Tsarevich Dmitrii "in the form in which it reached them from Russians' accounts".[47] But the foreigners' accounts, as we have seen, can mostly be traced back to the version of Dmitrii's back-story which Adam Vishnevetskii reported to King Sigismund in 1603. Far from originating among the Russian masses, it was devised by Dmitrii himself, or his backers, and it first circulated at the highest levels of the European culture of the day. The Polish king, and princes of the Catholic Church such as Rangoni and Possevino, appear to have taken the pretender's fantastic story quite seriously.

Chistov notes that most of the motifs of the deliverer legends can be found in other genres of folklore, in particular in plots about unjustly persecuted heroes,

---

44 The term *samozvanets* does not seem to be used for a pretender (impostor) until the second half of the 17th century.

45 Chistov, Russkie narodnye sotsial'no-utopicheskie legendy, 24-33. I am sceptical about the extent to which these "legends" can be described as "socio-utopian", in relation to the Time of Troubles, at least. See my critique of Chistov in: Perrie, 'Popular Socio-Utopian Legends' in the Time of Troubles.

46 Chistov, Russkie narodnye sotsial'no-utopicheskie legendy, 40-41.

47 Ibid., 43.

where the motif of a substitute victim is common.[48] These plots and motifs, however, are not exclusive to folklore: they can be found in most genres of world literature at all periods. In many fictional narratives, royal heirs are saved from conspiracies against them, and live incognito for many years before eventually asserting their true identity and regaining their ancestral throne. Such narratives, which were popular in chivalric adventure romances in medieval and early modern Europe, have parallels with the tales told by pretenders such as the First False Dmitrii in order to provide themselves with a fictional autobiography. The very nature of pretence, of course, makes miraculous escapes from death, or concealment or substitution at birth, a necessary ingredient in any pretender's back-story.[49]

If the story which Dmitrii or his sponsors devised at Brahin had fictional influences, they were likely to have been derived not only from folklore but also from the chivalric romances, or even from classical literature (remember Jan Zamoyski's reference to "a comedy by Plautus or Terence").[50] To take one example: the medieval romance later known in Russia as 'Bova korolevich (Prince Bova)' ("Bevis of Hampton" in England, 'Buovo d'Antone' in Italy) had spread eastwards as far as Lithuanian Belorussia by the end of the 16th century: in the earliest Belorussian version of this tale, the young hero's father, King Kgvidon, is deposed and murdered by his mother and her lover; they conspire against Bova, who is saved by the servant girl who was ordered to poison him; Bova travels incognito for many years and has various exciting adventures; eventually he returns to his father's kingdom, kills his mother and the usurper and becomes king himself.[51] There is a marked similarity between the first part of this plot and the

---

48 Ibid., 227.
49 For example, those of Perkin Warbeck and François de La Ramée (the False François de Valois): see Bercé, Le roi caché, 172, 361.
50 A later example of a Russian pretender who was aware of – and was perhaps influenced by – earlier historical and literary precedents is Timofei Ankudinov, the False Ivan Shuiskii, who in his writings of 1646 drew a parallel between his own case and that of Tsar Dmitrii (whom he considered to be the true son of Ivan the Terrible). He also compared himself to two pseudo-historical monarchs who had wandered unrecognised by their subjects: Apollonius of Tyre and the Emperor Ovian (Jovinian) of Rome, both of whom featured in the medieval Gesta Romanorum, which Ankudinov probably knew in its Polish version (Historye Rzymskie). See Iu.B. Simchenko, "Lzhe-Shuiskii II. Pravoslavnyi, musul'manin, katolik, protestant", in *Russkie: Istoriko-etnograficheskie ocherki*, ed. S.V. Cheshko (Moscow, 1997), 36-37, 39; and A.M. Panchenko, ed., *Russkaia sillabicheskaia poeziia XVII-XVIII vv.* (Leningrad, 1970), 88, 366.
51 A.N. Veselovskii, *Iz istorii romana i povesti: materialy i issledovaniia*, 2 vols. (St Petersburg, 1886-8) 2 [suppl./prilozheniia]: 129-172.

story which Dmitrii told in Poland-Lithuania;[52] and the happy ending is echoed in Barezzo Barezzi's account of Dmitrii's triumph.

Dmitrii's career in its turn subsequently served as the subject of literary treatments, notably by Lope de Vega in his play, probably written within a few years of the pretender's death, and based on the Spanish version of the Barezzo Barezzi account.[53] Although Lope undoubtedly knew about Dmitrii's death and official unmasking as an impostor,[54] he ended his drama with the hero's victory over Boris on the battlefield. In Lope's dramatic concept, poetic justice is implemented: the virtuous hero triumphs and the villain is punished.[55] Dmitrii's story on the Spanish stage – unlike historical reality, but in line with the conventions of romances such as Bova – has a happy ending, and the true heir is restored to his rightful throne.[56]

Thus Dmitrii himself, or his patrons, may have been influenced not only by the examples of earlier historical pretenders, but also by literary narratives when producing his back-story. Subsequently, the availability and popularity of such tales in early modern Europe may have influenced the reception and re-telling of his story by foreign writers. It is perhaps because it was so often told like a real-life version of familiar and well-loved fictional tales that the story of Tsarevich Dmitrii became such a fashionable theme in literary and historical writings in early 17th-century Europe.

Sometimes a later author, unsure of the details of Dmitrii's story, improvised parts of the narrative. The Dutchman Elias Herckmans, in an account written in 1625, describes the events at Uglich as follows:

When a boyar who was ordered to kill the tsarevich in a certain way came to the town, Dmitrii learned of his intention (it is not reliably known whether this was because he himself was devoted to Dmitrii, or because this boyar was afraid to carry out his mission and told the

---

52 i.e. in the region in which the story of Bova had been recorded in the late 16th century.
53 Brody, The Demetrius Legend, 54-78. I am unconvinced by Brody's argument (ibid., 141-216) that John Fletcher's play, *The Loyal Subject*, is also based on the Demetrius theme.
54 Brody, The Demetrius Legend, 59-68.
55 Ibid., 68-70.
56 Other versions of Lope's play subsequently appeared in 17th-century Catholic Europe: see Brody, The Demetrius Legend, 131-132, 217, 275. In one of these, published in Cesena in 1651, Dmitrii's murder is shown, but the hero is depicted as a martyr for the Catholic faith: Bercé, Le roi caché, 358. In Germany and Russia, by contrast, from the late 18th century, Dmitrii was invariably depicted on the stage as an impostor: Brody, The Demetrius Legend, 217-273, 275-276.

tsarevich's favourites about it, or because the tsarevich had his spies at the court of Boris Godunov, whose evil disposition was known to the tsarevich).[57]

Thus Herckmans offers his readers a choice of variants to one of the motifs in his plot, no doubt drawing on his own store of knowledge of similar tales involving unsuccessful assassination attempts. Herckmans believes that Dmitrii escaped death not only at Uglich in 1591 but also in Moscow in 1606, in the latter case as the result of temporarily transferring power to a double – an episode which he contrasts with the legend of King Ninus of Babylon, who was killed by his concubine Semiramis when he allowed her to become monarch for a day.[58]

The Second and Third False Dmitriis

The Second False Dmitrii did not appear in Russia until the summer of 1607, but rumours were rife in Moscow from the very day of Tsar Dmitrii's murder that he had escaped death. In many of these rumours, in an echo of the First False Dmitrii's back-story, a substitute victim had been killed, and the tsar had fled from the capital.[59] Jacques Margeret, who was in Moscow at the time of the uprising against Dmitrii, recorded the rumours but expressed doubts about their veracity.[60] Petreius left Russia at the end of 1605, but came back in 1607/1608 on a mission from Charles IX to Vasilii Shuiskii. He assures his readers that on his return to Russia he was informed by "Russians and foreigners who can be believed" that Grishka had indeed died.[61] Petreius is very scathing about those who thought that Dmitrii had again escaped death, a rumour for which he blames the Jesuits, the main villains of his narrative.[62] In his Relation of 1608 Petreius does not provide any specific information about the Second False Dmitrii, but in his History of 1620 he discusses

---

57 *Skazaniia Massy i Gerkmana o smutnom vremeni v Rossii* (St Petersburg, 1874), 264.
58 Skazaniia Massy i Gerkmana, 285-286.
59 One variant of these rumours – that "a German named Artsykalus" had been killed in his stead – was incorporated into the back-story of the Second False Dmitrii: D. Buturlin, *Istoriia smutnogo vremeni v Rossii v nachale XVII veka*, 3 vols. (St Petersburg, 1839-1846), 2 [1841]: Prilozheniia, no.7, p.51.
60 Margeret, The Russian Empire, 75-77. For various versions of the rumours, see Perrie, 'Popular Socio-Utopian Legends' in the Time of Troubles, 239-242; Perrie, Pretenders and Popular Monarchism, 109-115. The accounts of foreigners present in Moscow at the time of Dmitrii's overthrow provide the main evidence of the content of these rumours.
61 Reliatsiia Petra Petreia, 103.
62 Ibid., 73, 97. The Jesuits were also accused of spreading these rumours by Philippe de Canaye, the French ambassador to Venice: see Bercé, Le roi caché, 355.

both the Second and Third False Dmitriis, preceding this part of his account with the comment that, although both Dmitrii of Uglich and Grishka Otrep'ev were really dead,

> other Dmitriis were invented in the very same way, causing much evil and much blood to be shed. The Poles and the cossacks played a big vulgar joke and comedy with the Russians, because as soon as one Dmitrii died, another immediately appeared in his place, so that there was no end to the Dmitriis.[63]

In relation to the Third False Dmitrii, who appeared in north-west Russia in 1611, after the murder of the Second False Dmitrii at Kaluga, Petreius notes sarcastically that "he, like the others, called himself the true son of Ivan Vasil'evich, Dmitrii, who had now three times been subjected to such great mortal danger, first at Uglich, then in Moscow and finally at Kaluga, but had always avoided death".[64]

Other foreign observers, too, subsequently mocked the proliferation of Dmitriis. Samuel Purchas notes that when the body of the First False Dmitrii was burned, the ashes were "throwne into the aire, the seeds, as the sequele seemed to show, of many Demetris after".[65] When the same author reports the appearance of the Second False Dmitrii ("another revived Demetrius") he adds, "yea many pretending that Name and Title did after arise, as out of his dispersed ashes", and later refers to "that Demetrius new risen from the dead (not to mention the others of inferiour note)".[66] Jerome Horsey, in his account written in the 1620s, claims that the Polish crown "had many Dmitriis in store to maintain the same title".[67] Lope de Vega – perhaps thinking of the proliferation of Portuguese Sebastians – attributes to Boris Godunov's ambassador to King Sigismund the idea that the appearance of one pretender was likely to give rise to "a thousand" others.[68]

The appearance of multiple pretenders, however, undermined the credibility of each of them. None of the later pretenders of the Time of Troubles was a plausible claimant to the throne. Unlike the First False Dmitrii, whose authenticity continues

---

63 Petrei, Istoriia, 244.
64 Ibid., 297.
65 Purchas, Hakluytus Posthumus, 14: 197. Howe wrongly attributes the quotation to "Captain Gilbert's report" (The False Dmitri, 63).
66 Purchas, Hakluytus Posthumus, 14: 198; cf. Howe, The False Dmitri, 65, 66.
67 L.E. Berry and R.O. Crummey, eds., *Rude and Barbarous Kingdom: Russia in the Accounts of Sixteenth-Century English Voyagers* (Madison, WI, 1968), 365.
68 Lope de Vega, El Gran Duque de Moscovia, Acto III, l.552; Brody, The Demetrius Legend, 65, 131, 279.

to be considered possible by some credulous historians,[69] the claims of the Second False Dmitrii were accepted by only a few contemporary foreign observers, such as the Poles in his camp at Tushino, who had a vested interest in doing so.[70] Charles IX sent Petreius to Ivangorod to inspect the Third False Dmitrii, but the Swedes were soon disillusioned with this new pretender.[71] As we have seen, the critics of the First False Dmitrii in 1603-1604 had cited the precedents of earlier pretenders such as the Portuguese Sebastians in order to discredit his claims; in its turn, the precedent of Tsar Dmitrii, officially "unmasked" by Shuiskii as an impostor, was used by hostile foreign observers to mock his various reincarnations.

Tsarevich Petr and the Other Cossack Tsareviches

Samuel Purchas, as noted above, had referred to the Second False Dmitrii and other pretenders "of inferiour note": since there was only one other False Dmitrii, we may assume that these included the multitude of cossack "tsareviches" who appeared in 1606-1608, all claiming to be relatives of Tsar Dmitrii. With the exception of "Tsarevich" Petr Fedorovich, who was a major ally of Ivan Bolotnikov in 1606-1607, information about these pretenders is very scarce, in both Russian and foreign sources, but they all seem to have acted in Dmitrii's name, as his supporters against Shuiskii, rather than as his rivals or opponents.[72]

The earliest foreign evidence about Tsarevich Petr is provided by Margeret, who notes that at the end of April 1606 Tsar Dmitrii had received news that about 4000 cossacks had assembled between Kazan' and Astrakhan', and that they

---

69 Philip L. Barbour, *Dimitry, Called the Pretender, Tsar and Great Prince of All Russia, 1605-1606* (Boston, MA, 1966; London, 1967); Chester S.L. Dunning, *Russia's First Civil War. The Time of Troubles and the Founding of the Romanov Dynasty* (University Park, PA, 2001).

70 See, for example, *Dnevnik Mariny Mnishek*, trans. V.N. Kozliakov (St Petersburg, 1995); "Dziennik Jana Piotra Sapiehy (1608-1611)", in *Polska a Moskwa w pierwszej połowie wieku XVII*, ed. Aleksander Hirschberg, (Lwów, 1901), 167-332. Those who believed that the Second False Dmitrii was Tsar Dmitrii generally also continued to believe that Tsar Dmitrii was Dmitrii of Uglich; for this reason, versions of the First False Dmitrii's backstory are particularly common in Polish sources.

71 Petrei, Istoriia, 297-300, 307-308.

72 On these pretenders, see Perrie, Pretenders and Popular Monarchism, 90-97, 131-49, 174-81; Maureen Perrie, "Pretenders in the Name of the Tsar: Cossack 'Tsareviches' in Seventeenth-Century Russia", in *Von Moskau nach St. Petersburg. Das russische Reich im 17. Jahrhundert*, ed. Hans-Joachim Torke, Forschungen zur osteuropäischen Geschichte, vol. 56 (Wiesbaden, 2000), 243-256, 244-249.

"caused harm along the Volga" because they felt that they had not been adequately rewarded by Dmitrii.[73] The cossacks were said to have with them a young prince called Petr, who was supposedly the son of Tsar Fedor Ivanovich and his wife Irina. His back-story was a variant of Dmitrii's: the boy had allegedly been replaced at birth by a girl (the real Tsarevna Feodosiia, who died as an infant). According to Margeret, the cossacks' story was untrue, and "it was well known that this was only a pretext to pillage the land". Dmitrii wrote to Petr inviting him to Moscow, but the tsar was assassinated before the cossacks could reach the capital.[74]

The Dutch merchant's account, however, states (somewhat improbably) that it was Dmitrii who had created the new pretender: that after his murder Dmitrii had been condemned by the new government of Vasilii Shuiskii for inviting Tsarevich Petr to Moscow to help him:

[…] he was accused to haue beene the Authour, and occasion of a great spoyle, and domage, which fell out vppon the riuer of Volga, causing himselfe by false markes to be proclaimed the sonne of Fender Iuanuitz, whom under this pretext he had suborned to come to his succour, with many thousand Cosaques, to be the more secured of the countrey.[75]

Like Margeret, the Dutch author describes the looting committed by Petr's cossacks: "[…] he was the cause of marueilous ruine to the country, for all the Ports of Astracasses were sacked, and all the goodes and marchandize there, robbed, and pilled".[76]

Petreius at the time of writing his Relation knew something of the later history of Tsarevich Petr, since he notes that he was captured at Tula in 1607 and hanged in Moscow in 1608.[77] Like Margeret, he regards Petr as a pretender created by the

---

73 Margeret, The Russian Empire, 70-71, cf. 71: 'These Cossacks were discontented with Dmitrii, reckoning that they had not been recompensed by him as they had hoped to be'.
74 Ibid., 71. For other versions of Tsarevich Petr's back-story, mostly taken from Polish sources, see Perrie, 'Popular Socio-Utopian Legends' in the Time of Troubles, 236-239; Perrie, Pretenders and Popular Monarchism, 140-142.
75 Howe, The False Dmitri, 58-59; cf. Isaac Massa, *A Short History of the Beginnings and Origins of These Present Wars in Moscow under the Reign of Various Sovereigns Down to the Year 1610*, trans. G. Edward Orchard (Toronto, 1982), 148: "[…] they accused him of having provoked the appearance of an impostor who was to come and lend him assistance in case of danger." On the relationship between Massa's work and the anonymous Dutch merchant's 'Reporte', see Massa, A Short History, xxiii. Massa was a Dutch merchant whose contemporary account was first published only in the 19th century.
76 Howe, The False Dmitri, 59.
77 Reliatsiia Petra Petreia, 99.

Cossacks,[78] although his only mention of him is very brief, and it is situated in his list of arguments why Grishka Otrep'ev was not the real Dmitrii of Uglich: "In the fifth place, if Grishka were alive and were the true Dmitrii, the cossacks would not have chosen someone else in his place, as they did with Prince Petr, who claimed to be his relative and cousin".[79] Petreius also knows about two other cossack pretenders: he continues: "In the sixth place, if Grisha were the real Dmitrii, the cossacks and other renegades after the death of Prince Petr would not have chosen two others as their rulers and would not have made them sons of Fedor Ivanovich, whom he never had [...]"[80]

Samuel Purchas also knows about these Cossack tsareviches. He cites a Russian source which states that in addition to the Second False Dmitrii there were other pretenders ("Wors") who "did name and call themselves sonnes of the slaine Emperour, as Ivan, Peter, Pheodor, and by many and divers other names: and under the same names, did consume the State, and shead much blood."[81] Purchas himself describes Russia after the deposition of Shuiskii and death of the Second False Dmitrii as a many-headed monster, which he equates both with the Biblical beast of the Apocalypse and with the Hydra of classical mythology.[82] The image of the many-headed monster to represent the multitude was a commonplace of English conservative political discourse in the mid-16th to mid-17th centuries, when it was deployed in response to popular revolts.[83] Purchas too uses it in this pejorative sense to describe the situation which prevailed in Russia in the later stages of the Time of Troubles: "a popular government happened, or if you will, a Confusion of the multitude bare sway"; "the whole Body became Heads in the worst of tyrannies,

---

78 In his *History*, however, Petreius describes Petr as Tsar Fedor's illegitimate son, who had fled to the cossacks and lived among them for several years in order to avoid an attempt on his life by Boris Godunov, but when his uncle Dmitrii became tsar, Petr had planned to approach him to request a princely remuneration. Petrei, Istoriia, 253. This version of Tsarevich Petr's story appears to have been borrowed by Petreius from Bussow, cf. Bussow, The Disturbed State, 96.
79 Reliatsiia Petra Petreia, 99. In fact Petr claimed to be Tsar Fedor's son, and hence Dmitrii's half-nephew. The logic of Petreius' argument is rather obscure.
80 Reliatsiia Petra Petreia, 99. In his *History* of 1620, however, Petreius does not mention these cossack pretenders, probably because they are not mentioned by Bussow, who is his main source for this part of the *History*.
81 Purchas, Hakluytus Posthumus, 14: 247.
82 Ibid., 14: 230, 252.
83 Christopher Hill, "The Many-Headed Monster in Late Tudor and Early Stuart Political Thinking", in *From the Renaissance to the Counter-Reformation*, ed. Charles H. Carter (London, 1966), 296-324.

a popular (government shall I say? or) confusion."[84] He contrasts the anarchy represented by the many-headed monster with monarchies, which "(how ever excessive and tyrannical)" were depicted "in divine Visions" as "simpler and more uniforme beasts".[85] But Purchas adapts the image of the Hydra to incorporate not only mob rule but also the existence of pretenders: the monster's heads included the "many Wor's after the first and second Demetrius", and Purchas laments the fragmentation to which they contributed.[86] The use of this striking imagery to represent the chaos which pretenders could create indicates the fear which conservative thinkers of the age experienced in the face not only of social unrest but also of multiple sources of political legitimacy.

STEN'KA RAZIN'S TSAREVICH ALEKSEI ALEKSEEVICH

The generally hostile and sceptical attitude which foreign observers expressed towards Tsarevich Petr and the other Cossack pretenders of the Time of Troubles can also be found in foreigners' accounts of the revolt of Sten'ka Razin. Two of these provide unique information about the 'Tsarevich Aleksei Alekseevich' who supposedly accompanied Razin on his voyage up the Volga: the anonymous *Relation*, first published in German and Dutch in 1671 and in English and French in 1672; and the 1674 dissertation, written in Latin, of the German writer Johannes Justus Martius (Merz, Mertz).[87]

The real Tsarevich Aleksei Alekseevich, Tsar Aleksei Mikhailovich's eldest son, had died in January 1670 at the age of 16.[88] According to the *Relation*,

---

84 Purchas, Hakluytus Posthumus, 14: 231, 252.
85 Ibid., 14: 230. Of the Biblical references which Purchas provides, the most relevant for beasts representing monarchies is Daniel 7 and 8. Thomas Hobbes was later to use the image of the Biblical monster Leviathan (cf. Job 41) as a metaphor for his ideal Commonwealth and its monarch. See John M. Steadman, "Leviathan and Renaissance Etymology", *Journal of the History of Ideas* 28 (1967): 575-576.
86 Purchas, Hakluytus Posthumus, 14: 252.
87 *Zapiski inostrantsev o vosstanii Stepana Razina*, ed. A.G. Man'kova (Leningrad, 1968), 84-126; *Inostrannye izvestiia o vosstanii Stepana Razina. Materialy i issledovaniia*, ed. A.G. Man'kova (Leningrad, 1975), 15-79.
88 At an earlier stage in the rising, in his speech to the cossacks at Panshin Gorodok in May 1670, Razin had cited the recent deaths of Tsarevich Aleksei, his younger brother Simeon and their mother, Tsaritsa Mariia Il'inichna Miloslavskaia, as evidence of the treason of the boyars. Martius knows this: he states that Razin initially blamed the boyars and proclaimed himself the avenger for the death of Aleksei Alekseevich (Inostrannye izvestiia,

however, as Sten'ka sailed up the Volga he had two ships, one lined with red and the other with black velvet, in which, he claimed, were Tsarevich Aleksei and the recently deposed Patriarch Nikon, respectively.[89] On the first vessel, Razin kept in the role of Aleksei Alekseevich a young Circassian prince whom he had earlier taken prisoner and whom he "compelled to act such a person". Razin

> spred abroad, that this Lord *Czarawitz* had made an escape from the violent hands of the Bojars and great Lords, and taken his refuge to him; adding, that he, *Stenko*, was come by order of the Great Czar to put to death all the Bojars, Nobles, Senators, and other great ones, (that were too near to his Majesty), as Enemies and Traytors of their Countrey.[90]

Martius repeats and amplifies this version of the Razinites' tale:

> Now they began to assert everywhere, that the son of the tsar had not died after all, but had fled from the plots which were being prepared against him and – safe and sound – was with Razin. The rumour was also spread that the boyars, hatred towards whom was irreconcilable, had tried to take all the power into their hands, had planned to kill the tsarevich [...] and [...] are wickedly causing tumult in the realm.[91]

Razin "persuaded everyone who wanted to have revenge and not to submit to the boyars, to join him and punish them for their lawlessness, recognising that this was the only way to save the realm from its decadent condition and to restore the true heir."[92] Martius notes that Razin displayed both Nikon and Aleksei standing in full

---

67). On the Tsarevich Aleksei affair, see Perrie, Pretenders in the Name of the Tsar, 249-252.

89 Zapiski inostrantsev, 97-98. Martius describes the ships as draped in red and black silk respectively (Inostrannye izvestiia, 70).

90 Zapiski inostrantsev, 98. The wording here is similar to that in the text of Razin's death sentence, reproduced as an Appendix to the *Relation*: "Thou didst also send to many other Towns some of thy villanous Companions, by false Writings bearing them in hand, that the Eldest Son of our Great Czar [...] was yet living, and that thou by Order of his Majesty, wast come to put to death as Traytors, all Bojars, Councellors, Noble-men and Officers, being in his Majesties service" (ibid., 104-105). The death sentence, however, did not accuse Razin of setting up a pretender, but simply of spreading the rumour that Tsarevich Aleksei was still alive.

91 Inostrannye izvestiia, 67.

92 Ibid., 67. Neither account tells us how (or whether) Razin explained the tsarevich's escape from death, but presumably the motif of a substitute victim, familiar from the Time of Troubles, was known in the cossack milieu. The False Simeon Alekseevich, who ap-

view on the ships; Sten'ka claimed that they had both fled to place themselves under his protection, and that they were now quite safe from the conspiracies of the boyars.[93]

Neither Martius nor the author of the *Relation* has any doubt that the "Tsarevich Aleksei" on Razin's red-draped vessel was an impostor. According to the *Relation*, Razin "boldly pretended" that Aleksei was still alive, and "to colour this lye the better" he kept the Circassian prince on board the ship in the role of the tsarevich, and disseminated the story about his escape from death, in order "to ruine the Russian Empire and to seduce the common people". The writer describes the entire scenario in terms such as "mischievous devices" and "Artifices", and concludes that "By these base practises invented and push't on by *Stenko*, the ignorant people was inflamed to fight furiously".[94] Martius too identifies the false Tsarevich Aleksei as the captive Circassian prince, and claims that the vessel on which Nikon was supposedly sailing contained only an image of the patriarch.[95] He describes the business with the two vessels supposedly carrying the tsarevich and the patriarch as a "cunning ploy" (*dolum*) and a "shameless fraud" (*impio simulacro*), which nevertheless succeeded in gaining and retaining support for Razin's enterprise.[96]

Both authors, and the author of the *Relation* in particular, present Razin as a skilful demagogue, who made use of the grievances of the ordinary people in order to further his own aims of revenge for his brother's death and his thirst for power. The author of the *Relation* recognises that the people had grievances and aspirations of their own which might motivate them to rebel, but he does so only implicitly and indirectly. He states, for example, that Razin did "much mischief" by sending out his "Emissaries from Astrakhan", who "stirr'd up the people to insurrection", and

---

peared in Zaporozh'e in 1673 in the company of some of Razin's former cossack supporters, told an elaborate tale in which the courtier who was ordered to poison him had poisoned a choirboy instead, dressed his victim in the tsarevich's clothes, and organised the real Simeon's escape: S.M. Solov'ev, *Istoriia Rossii s drevneishikh vremen*, 15 vols. (Moscow, 1960-65), 6 (1961): 462.

93 Inostrannye izvestiia, 70. These two foreign accounts are the only sources to describe the mystification with the red- and black-draped vessels, and the presence of a false Aleksei aboard the red ship.
94 Zapiski inostrantsev, 97-98.
95 Inostrannye izvestiia, 67, 70.
96 Ibid., 46, 70. Compare the wording of the death sentence, on Razin's claim that Aleksei Alekseevich was still alive: "But *Thou Traytor* didst devise this with a designe to discompose the people, and to occasion the shedding of innocent blood." And on Nikon: "Thou hast also craftily given out, as if the Monk Nikow was with thee" (Zapiski inostrantsev, 105).

adds that: "Every where he promised Liberty, and a redemption from the Yoak (so he call'd it) of the Bojars and Nobles, which he said were the oppressors of the Countrey'. In Moscow, the author continues, "men began to speak openly in his praise, *as if* he were a person that sought the publick good and the liberty of the people [...]".[97]

And Martius states that Razin's agents incited the Russians "to rebellion, on the pretext of fighting for their former freedom against boyar violence". In 1667, "he set out on the road to tyranny, while presenting his vile enterprise as hatred towards it [tyranny]".[98] In terms of his rabble-rousing abilities, Martius compares Razin with Catiline and with Wilhelm von Grumbach, the leader of a 16th-century German rising against the Emperor.[99] Thus the German author brings a trans-national comparative perspective to bear on the Razin revolt, but he does so in relation not to the pretender phenomenon as such, but rather to the leadership of Razin, whose exploitation of the rumour about Tsarevich Aleksei he presents as only one device in his arsenal of demagogic stratagems to attract popular support.

Unlike the Time of Troubles, when the source of political legitimacy itself was contested, the Razin revolt was a more conventional example of an uprising against the established order, and both Martius and the author of the *Relation* condemn Razin as a rebel against a legitimate ruler. The English account concludes with the pious words: "God Almighty give to the great Czar, *Alexis Michaelewitz*, the Victory over all his Enemies",[100] and Martius reflects on Razin's execution that "no other end was deserved by one who betrayed his sovereign and was an enemy and traitor to his fatherland (*desertor sui Imperatoris, et Patriae hostis Preditorque fuit*)".[101] In line with the philosophy which prevailed in Europe in the later seventeenth century, after the experience of civil war and rebellion in England and elsewhere, both writers were hostile to a popular revolt which threatened social and political stability.

Conclusion

The Time of Troubles of the early 17th century was a complex sequence of events, involving foreign invasion as well as dynastic strife, civil war and social unrest. It is

---

97 Zapiski inostrantsev, 97. My emphasis (M.P.).
98 Inostrannye izvestiia, 67.
99 Ibid., 67, 69. His other comparisons, with Ivan Podkova and Philip the Magnanimous of Hesse (ibid., 64-65) are made in terms of their physical strength.
100 Zapiski inostrantsev, 101.
101 Inostrannye izvestiia, 50, 75.

not surprising that contemporary foreigners' accounts focussed on those aspects which had the greatest international significance – the succession to the throne, and the rival interventions of Poland and Sweden – rather than on the socio-economic grievances of lower-class Russians, which are stressed in most modern historians' accounts. The greatest trans-national interest of all, however, was aroused by the pretender phenomenon, and in particular by the extraordinary career and intriguing personality of the First False Dmitrii. Even those foreign observers who regarded him as an impostor mostly found him attractive and impressive as an individual; and the complex representation of the pretender in later literary and historical works owes much to his broadly sympathetic depiction by foreign participants in the Time of Troubles (after May 1606 Russian sources, by contrast, painted a uniformly negative picture of him as the apostate monk Grisha Otrep'ev).

Pretenders have often been seen as a peculiarly Russian phenomenon, but the evidence examined in this article suggests that both the phenomenon itself and the narratives which accompanied it originated outside Muscovy and were brought into the country by the First False Dmitrii. Dmitrii's supporters presented him as the true heir to the throne, returning to overthrow the usurper Boris Godunov. This back-story resonated with (and may have been based on) the plots of chivalric romances which were popular in Western and Central Europe, and some foreign observers depicted Dmitrii as the hero of just such an adventure narrative. Others, however, who were acquainted with the pretender phenomenon elsewhere, saw Dmitrii as an impostor in the tradition of the Portuguese Sebastians and the false claimants to the Moldavian throne. The foreigners' accounts of Dmitrii's career transmitted familiar topoi back to their European audience: either the heroic romance of the persecuted tsarevich providentially restored to his ancestral throne (Barezzo Barezzi, Lope de Vega) or the cautionary tale of a fraudster who obtained his just deserts (Petreius).

If the pretender phenomenon was imported into Russia by the First False Dmitrii, it found there a fertile soil in which it rapidly took root: either providing legitimation for revolt against a reigning monarch such as Vasilii Shuiskii, who, like Boris Godunov, was widely perceived as a usurper; or adding weight to a rebellion in the name of the true tsar (the Cossack campaigns involving Tsarevich Petr and others in support of "Tsar Dmitrii"; and Razin's recruitment of Aleksei Alekseevich to help save his father from the traitor-boyars). After the death of the First False Dmitrii, however, the proliferation of self-styled descendants of Ivan the Terrible discredited the pretender phenomenon in the eyes not only of many upper-class Russians, but also of foreign observers. While Tsar Dmitrii had been depicted by some as the real Dmitrii of Uglich, later Russian pretenders were represented in foreigners' accounts almost exclusively as fraudsters and impostors. Within Russia, the motif of the true heir returning to reclaim his throne persisted in the back-stories of pretenders; and it was also found in the popular rumours and tales which surrounded them. The phenomenon of pretendership moved rapidly down the social scale: the First False Dmitrii had been received at the court of the Polish king and corresponded with the Pope, but by the 18th century Russian pretenders were mostly of lower-class (cossack or peasant) background; and the narrative of the long-lost prince, originating in the chivalric romances of medieval Western Europe, had become folklorised in Russian popular culture. In their Russian manifestation, however, pretenders and their back-stories still had the power to mobilise a major popular revolt, as was the case with Pugachev in 1773-1774.

Transgression of Boundaries as a Feat of Liberty: Early Modern Anthropologies of Revolt

Political Vacuum and Interregnum in Early Modern Unrest

YVES-MARIE BERCÉ

Great European revolts and civil wars were often preceded by a particular institutional aspect that was unintended but more or less inherent in monarchical (or maybe any political) order: the temporary lack of central power. The last episode of the French Wars of Religion, the Russian Time of Troubles, the French Fronde and similar events are only the most visible examples of political and social disorder caused by a vacant throne. Bluntly put, the notion of a void of sovereign power lies in the realm of history; it cannot be acknowledged by the Law schools. I would like to suggest that history tries to tell the events as they were, while legal studies describe them as they should have been. Historians are used to explore episodes of unrest, lawlessness and chaos, while positivistic Law teaches that such a thing should not even come into existence. Indeed, in our contemporary societies, constitutional texts provide rules to be followed on extreme occasions. They establish a collection of successive measures securing the continuation of the state so that the throne or head of state's position can never remain unoccupied. Law is used to argue in terms of structural continuity, as if a change of regime was forever unthinkable. As the primary task of constitutional laws is to argue in favour of a legal and undisputable regime, only History has the capacity to show in retrospect how a regime could become incapacitated and eventually overthrown. At worst, in the light of an extraordinary tragedy or an evident impotence of central power, as, for example, it happened in France in 1814 or again in 1940, lawyers convened to compose an expedient legal text in order to organise transition and thus to re-establish a visible realm of legality. Experience has shown that in case of a regime's collapse, there have always been wise and cunning political survivors who then felt called upon to write a new constitution. To follow the 1814 example, the French senators were summoned by Talleyrand in April of the same year to declare the forfeiture of Napoleon's imperial status. For that purpose, they referred to the old and classical utopia of an original social contract, which Napoleon was accused to have violated when imposing new taxes without the consent of the French people.

What is this notion of a political vacuum, the potential of which we are looking for throughout the early modern age? Let us define it as an accidental interruption of a political regime, an obvious vacuum of central power, the absence of any holder of the sovereign title or, conversely, the competition of several pretenders. It is a structural situation, a classical scheme that ancient dignitaries knew well and feared for very good reasons. They knew that it could happen in any form of regime, at any time, in any country. Let us imagine a village or a town left without relations to the central authority, without news, without help; then the political game would halt accordingly, coming down to its minimum scale, providing structure only to what is nearest and most immediate. Let a region be invaded by enemies or isolated by a catastrophe, such as an earthquake or plague, responsibility and power will be taken by a few local notables, mayor, syndic or landlord. So it happened in many regions and localities during the Second World War, especially in the tragic summer months of 1940 and 1944.

In early modern times, in catholic regions, it was generally the parish vicar or a capuchin friar who was able to receive complaints, organise assistance and negotiate with the enemies, in short, to act as community spokesman.

But in any epoch, the vacuum of power causes a return to primary or traditional authorities. This return may remain only a temporary refuge in a moment of adversity or, on the contrary, become a political challenge to central authority as such, an appeal to major traditional communal rights. Very different situations such as the commotion of a successful riot, the momentary victory of popular violence or an invasion by a foreign enemy may have very similar consequences: the legitimate power is overthrown and hence the power belongs to the street, to anyone able to master the course of events, if it is a dignitary or conversely some obscure chief who emerged in this emergency situation. In ancient rural societies, it could be an innkeeper, a veteran, a village solicitor who could become the precarious leader, the hero of the moment. Nothing except bravery, fair speeches or a feather on his hat was required, so that even hitherto unknown people could almost instantly play key roles.

Such a situation occurred in Naples in June 1647, at the time of the most famous and most widely covered revolt of the early modern age.[1] After some scuffles on the

---

1   Among a numerous bibliography on the Neapolitan crisis, see the recent study by Alain Hugon, *Naples insurgée, 1647-1648. De l'événement à la mémoire* (Rennes, 2011). The limits of a possible subversion of society and politics by the Neaopolitan revolt are shown by the easy restauration of Spanish power, which would last peacefully until 1708. On this topic, see the monumental work of Giuseppe Galasso, *Napoli spagnola, dopo*

market, in the timespan of only a few hours, the Spanish viceroy's authority had vanished. The garrison soldiers had disappeared, having locked themselves in the castles. The big city seemed to have fallen, left for anybody who was capable of taking it. A fishmonger called Masaniello became the central figure in town, even if only for the duration of eight days. His extraordinary political fate stupefied contemporaries and fascinated posterity. In historiography, he occupies a strange and prominent place. He has become the best example of popular insolence, of sudden political promotion; he has become also the best model of the misfortune that awaited those who dared to defy the social order. His story would, for a long time, serve as a lesson of civic morality teaching everyone to respect his limits, and this applies both to the seemingly omnipotent viceroy who was so easily driven out of his palace and to the popular leader who was so pathetically murdered after only a week of his unwonted and cruel way of governing the city like a king, or rather, like the most absurd tyrant.

During the following nine months, the Spaniards' incapacity to reconquer the town perpetuated political uncertainty. In those days, every professional group among the Neapolitan people put forward new grievances, requests and controversial opinions. Censorship had disappeared, speech was free, usual eligibiliies for office became irrelevant, utopia was convenient and power was up for grabs, colloquially speaking. As it would happen in Paris in 1648 (during the Fronde) or again in 1790 (during the first months of Revolution), in 1647 a strange social phenomenon emerged in Naples. Historians have called it an explosion of political expression, a sudden, unusual, mad and chaotic freedom of speech.

Disappearance of authority and proliferating demands were complementary. Uncertain legitimacy was a recurrent political danger in the old elective monarchies, sometimes even an unavoidably perilous period of transition. Two historical examples seem obvious in this logic, the State of the Church and the Kingdom of Poland.

In Rome, after the death of a pope, specific institutions were called upon.[2] This procedure was meticulously organised by the Roman Church. It originated from the first centuries of Christianity, as soon as the Pope, bishop of Rome, had become the undisputed political sovereign of the Eternal City. The assembly of cardinals,

---

Masaniello (Florence, 1972); id., *Il Regno di Napoli. Il Mezzogiorno spagnolo e austriaco, 1622-1734* (Torino, 2006).

2 Roman popular customs following the death of a pope have been examined by Italian medievalist historians. Reinhard Elze, "*Sic transit gloria mundi*. La morte del Papa nel Medioevo", *Annali dell'Istituto storico italo-germanico in Trento* 3 (1977): 23-41; Agostino. Paravicini-Bagliani, *Il corpo del Papa* (Torino, 1994); Yves-Marie Bercé, *A la découverte des trésors cachés* (Paris, 2004), 271-273.

referred to as conclave, had to prepare the election of the next pope. Their travels to Rome, and their subsequent discussions could last several months, forming a long interregnum. During this period, government passed into the hands of the cardinal Camerlengo, who normally was in charge of the Church finances. In theory, nothing changed in the way the offices worked, and neither did anything in the institutional hierarchy. However, everybody knew that dangerous days lay ahead. Prelates and noblemen locked up their palaces and established armed guards to repulse possible attacks or sieges. Indeed, according to an ancient tradition the Roman people had a right to the dead Pope's personal property. Already in the 6th Century, following the death of a bishop, the clerics of his diocese were accustomed to keep tabs on the goods left by the dead prelate. There was a logic in this strange custom. A bishop was supposed to be dedicated to the service of his mission, so that after his death his assets had to be returned to his church. This spurious tradition was claimed by the clerics and servants of the bishopric, particularly by the most rapid and skilful of them. The same rule was applied to pontifical assets in Rome and in all cities of the State of the Church. The origin of this creed seems to go back to a legendary memory of the right of citizenship in ancient Rome; it may also be the anthropological utopia of a primitive free status of humanity. It was in the 14th century, when the control of the large Roman population was a stake disputed between the local tradesmen and the clerics, that the pillaging custom became an institution of sorts. When the Pope returned from Avignon to Rome the ritual plundering was considered as revenge, retaliation for the Pontiff's long absence. In 1378, when Urban VI was elected after Gregory XI's death, a mob awaited him in front of the conclave's doors. The populace had already plundered the last Pope's palace and now they asked the new one to distribute gifts, called *mansilia*, i.e. to throw silver coins to the crowd as a gesture of largesse. The ceremonial was supposed to demonstrate that the Pope served only as a depository of a treasure that belonged to all Christians, as if Christianity was represented by those who turned out to be in the streets, i.e. by those who were lucky to be in the right place at the right time.

During the 16th and 17th centuries the right to plunder was maintained and actually exercised at every *sede vacante*. Usual laws and regulations seemed to have lost their legitimacy during this institutional moment. Sometimes plundering, theft and even murder were escalating to a tremendous degree, so that indignant witnesses hoped that it would soon be outlawed, for in their view it was indeed a disgrace to the Church. Such climaxes occurred in 1559, after the death of Paul III Farnese, in 1590, following the passing of the strong Sixtus Quintus, and finally in 1654 upon the death of Innocent X, whose European policy had provoked much criticism, so that hatred between resident foreigners was exacerbated in Roman streets. Municipal magistrates, knowing all too well the traditional dangers of those days, organised patrols of militia men commanded by captains which had been selected by the trades of each borough. It was a measure of precaution and simultaneously an observance of the strange custom. In some way, the dignitaries themselves respected the anomalous statute of these days. Indeed, they had to open the jails to free all prisoners incarcerated for debts or petty crimes, excepting only blood criminals. They organized guards in front of the dead pope's houses, although in some places the pope's relatives had already taken precautions and evacuated all movables, and in other places the servants had helped themselves and carried away whatever they were able to.

In spite of all rules and precautions, nobody hindered the rabble to rule the city. Guards and foreign soldiers paid by ambassadors and cardinals of opposing nations fought openly in the streets. Mobs attacked the jails and freed popular bandits and murderers. In some provincial towns, where powerful factious families were used to fight for municipal dignities, retaliations and brawls exploded.

The attempt to provide free access to the goods and chattels of the dead sovereign, liberation of the prisoners, general armament of the citizens and rights to open vengeance had reappeared at every *sede vacante* for at least four centuries. After 1654, these phenomena disappeared, either due to the modernisation of the Roman institutions or the decay of the politically high reputation of the Papacy.

These behaviours can be read as a tentative form of subversion, as a return to primitive rights coming from God or from a mythical historical moment. Altogether, they can be looked at as a perspective of recurring renewal, a kind of violent welcome of the new pope, a step towards an expected happy pontifical reign to come.

Another classical example of periodical instability was the Kingdom of Poland. Some elements of the Polish state might have to be recalled.[3] It is well-known that the crown of Poland was elective and after the death of Sigismund Augustus, the last king from the Jagellon dynasty, the electoral assembly, Sejm or Diet, for the first time had an open and free choice. The Diet's experiments well before Sigismund had gradually established a complex and precise governmental procedure that was to be observed during the interregnum. The interregnum consisted of three different assemblies: a diet of convocation (which was the most controversial one), a diet of election and a diet of crowning. During the interregnum, sovereignty was maintained by the archbishop of Gniezno, Primate of Poland, with the title of *interrex*. Public power was attributed to an elected marshal

---

3   The following summary of institutional practices of the Polish interregnums comes from the thesis of Ms. Natacha Leclercq, "Les journaux de la Diète de convocation polonaise de 1764". This first hand work, thesis of the Ecole nationale des chartes in Paris, presented in March 2009, has not yet been published.

who came from Little Poland, Great Poland or the Grand Duchy of Lithuania, according to the territory where the Diet was convened.

All interregnum protocols and rites granted the kingdom its native freedom, which in 18th century was said to be inherited from the legendary Sarmatians. The free Polish people was supposed to be solely and completely embodied by its nobility. Indeed, if high-ranking members of the clergy had seats in the senate, there was actually no representation of burghers or town citizens in the diet, to which all noblemen were called. All noblemen were supposed to be equal, from the lowest landlords without any function up to the highest dignitaries and richest magnates. In addition, since the elections were personal, *viritim,* and since the votes had to be unanimous according to the right of *liberum veto* (from the diet of 1652 onwards), any nobleman could effectively filibuster or even entirely block political decisions at the diet.

Ever since the diet of 1572, a list of measures was written down and presented to the future king. They were called *pacta conventa*. The newly elected monarch had to swear an oath, according to the precept *si non jurabis, non regnabis*. In addition, since the diet of 1587, the first point of deliberation had to be a denunciation of the misdeeds or crimes which the last king was responsible for. This collection of misdeeds was called *exorbitances, gravamina* or *Rei publicae vulnera*; the demands for their rejection were grievances or *"doléances"* in the common vocabulary of other early modern states. All these decisions, the writing of a convention to be sworn by and the composition of grievances, were supposed to renew the mythical original contract which, according to fictional memory, had linked the first king and the family chiefs at the time of the free Sarmatians.

Thanks to this collection of rules, the interregnum looked paradoxically like the most legal and most efficient exertion of power, in contrast to which the actual reign of a king looked like a dangerous anomaly. It seemed that freedom reached its greatest degree only during the interregnum and that this political innocence, leaving the official annals of the kingdom aside, had to be renewed at every royal succession.

Of course, a certain danger of anarchy was inherent to *interregna*. Riots, murders and brawls were commonplace during these extraordinary months. Intrusions of foreign powers during the long diets were patent and scandalous. Witnesses spoke of a "fair of freedom", a time of "golden liberty."[4] It was actually during the 1648 interregnum that the wars known as the Time of Deluge began, and afterwards every diet meeting resulted in further weakening of the Polish kingdom.

---

4 Cf. Francis Dvornik, *The Slavs: Their Early History and Civilization* (Boston, 1956; reprint Boston, 1959); and Norman Davies, *God's Playground. A History of Poland*, 2 vols. [Vol. 1: The Origins to 1795, Vol. 2: 1795 to the Present] (Oxford, 1981).

In both cases, the State of the Church and Poland, the mythical theme of a native situation of freedom can be identified. The major common point of these states was the electivity of their thrones, which therefore brought the frequent return of moments of political uncertainty, of sudden interruptions in the ordinary flow of events.

The kingdom of France, however, represented quite an opposite model. There, royal jurists had precociously affirmed the principle of State continuity. They had established succession rules, which they claimed to be ancient and presented as fundamental laws of the realm. According to these laws, the new king immediately took his crown, without any intervention from the Church, the Parisian Parliament or an assembly of the estates. He became king at the very moment of his predecessor's death, as the saying went: "the king never dies" or "the dead vests the living". However, in spite of such a strong tradition, all periods of royal minority remained dangerous stages with threats of civil war. In contradiction to the learned doctrine emerged the popular idea that all political decisions had to be reconsidered at every new reign. In early modern times, this idea was as strong as ever. It demanded that all institutions had to be created anew, that the last reign's misdeeds, such as taxes and wars, had to be cancelled whenever a young prince ascended to the throne. Here again appears the picture of an original contract between the people and the prince to whom public welfare had been entrusted. For political authors like Jean Bodin, this mythical contract could stand as the original consent of primitive forefathers; for some provincial historians it was a precise historical treaty linked to some legendary episode of the annals of the monarchy. At royal succession, this concept of an original state of freedom was remembered, and kingly prerogatives seemed to become subject to re-examination, as if a complete renegotiation of the state was imminent.

It happened precisely in this manner at the end of Louis XIII's reign. Cardinal Richelieu's unpopularity and impatience towards the fiscal loads rose to the highest pitch. In November 1642, Richelieu's death had boosted hope for political change. This opinion was strongly expressed in the words of the time by the parliament courts and by the assemblies of provincial estates. The importance of these representative institutions has often been ignored or overlooked by historians.[5] So

---

5   To understand the importance of General Estates in Medieval and Early Modern France, see Neithard Bulst, *Die französischen Generalstände von 1468 und 1484* (Sigmaringen, 1992); Yves-Marie Bercé, "Le rôle des Etats-généraux dans le gouvernement du royaume, XVI° et XVII° siècles", *Comptes rendus des séances de l'Académie des inscriptions et belles lettres* 144, 4 (2000): 1221-1240. Of course, the estates were summoned in periods of political weakness, but they were not actually a subversive element. Instead they rather brought timely legal solutions.

far, at the end of the 17th century, a majority of provinces maintained their periodical meetings, which decided about consent to taxation, and took charge of tax assessment and collection. These prerogatives were alive chiefly in the Southern provinces, in the periphery of Auvergne and in little Pyrenean estates. In 1624, a strong offensive of fiscal centralisation had extended to some southern countries' local fiscal offices, the so-called *Bureaux d'élections*, which had already been established in the 1550 in the Northern provinces. These finance offices were created to replace the traditional local estates. This occurred, for instance, in two little provinces surrounding the mountains of Auvergne, i.e. Rouergue and Quercy, This provocative administrative innovation had rapidly caused some local peasant uprisings in the summer of 1624; they were easily crushed, but even later the new institution was never accepted by the country folks. During the first months of 1643, the estates of Rouergue were allowed to convene; they impressively asked for provincial fiscal debt relief, implying their intention to recover their local tax control.[6] At the end of March 1643, the estates sent deputies to Paris to demonstrate the peasants' misery and to plead for a fiscal reduction. Louis XIII died on the 14th of May, but the king's councillors maintained the former political course without the slightest intention to modify the fiscal system. So, the deputies came back on the 26th of May without any promises, bringing with them only the recommendation to confide in the "intendant" of the larger province of Haute Guyenne. This dignitary, commissioner of the king's Council, named Charreton, was by political conviction a resolute adversary of local powers. He had even tried to prevent the Estates' deputation. However, notwithstanding the Council's disappointing answer, popular hope had not weakened, so that on the 2nd of June, a score of country parishes from Lower Rouergue gathered in arms. This kind of country folk troop was at that time scornfully nicknamed "Croquants". They managed to block the intendant himself in the town of Villefranche-de-Rouergue. Charreton, isolated, with only a few guards inside the town hall, was coerced by force to write down an ordinance reducing taxes to the level of the crucial year of 1618, when the young Louis XIII had effectively begun his personal government. This fake ordinance was all at once printed on leaflets and distributed all over the province of Rouergue.

At the same time, the parliament courts of Toulouse (Languedoc) and Bordeaux (Guyenne) seemed to officially approve the claims put forward by the rebels of Rouergue. On the 4th of June, the Toulouse court filed a case against all royal

---

6   Yves-Marie Bercé, "La fin des Etats du Rouergue et les Croquants de 1643", *Etudes aveyronnaises. Recueil des travaux de la Société des lettres, sciences et arts de l'Aveyron, 2008* (Rodez, 2009), 219-230; cf. id. "Voyages et routes des paysans. L'exemple du Rouergue en 1643", in *Les passions d'un historien. Mélanges en l'honneur de Jean-Pierre Poussou*, ed. Reynald Abad et al. (Paris, 2010), 91-106.

commissioners who had been sent to Languedoc during the last ten years. On the 1st of July, the parliament court of Bordeaux, in its turn, relieved the intendants of any function under the threat of prosecution. In their logic, as fathers of the subjects and simultaneously keepers of the crown rights, the parliament councillors thought that it was their duty to repel inappropriate ruling, to make kings remember the fundamental laws on which they had to swear on coronation day. They held that a time of regency with an infant king on the throne put forward the political role of the magistrates. They referred to the free consent of the subjects to taxes, and to the required respect of judiciary procedures by the king. They demanded that the recent increase in duties and tolls would not have to be paid, since they had never been approved by the General Estates or by the Parliaments. They denounced the practice of commissioning intendants to the provinces with escorts of armed guards as an insult to the traditional, legitimate institutions of justice. They argued that all the dreadful decisions of the late king disappeared with him, and that these orders had, at least, to be re-discussed, especially in the event of an infant king's accession to the throne, who was represented by his mother, the Regent Queen. So, the judiciary advice met the popular utopia of a return to the innocence of the "old days"; or, in another metaphor, that moment looked like the beginning of a political spring, a vernal renewal of the realm thanks to the arrival of a young prince. The power vacuum seemed to call for a new way of government. Even nowadays, a newly elected head of state is expected to grant reprieves and amnesties, and cut taxes, maybe, more or less sincere or efficacious.

The intendant of Guyenne laughed at the daring actions of the Bordeaux court:

These gentlemen imagine that with the king's death they have got a general licence, that everything is dead with the king and only they have stayed alive and powerful, that all the army generals have had to flee to their home and to leave their duties at the death news, because, as they say, *mandatum finitur morte,* except for their own one.

But the two subversive parliaments' ordinances were published by the court's printing masters, and sent everywhere. They confirmed the resolution of the Rouergue peasants. They directly instigated the noble estate of another neighbouring region, Gascony (Armagnac), to convene and articulate their grievances. There, a number of furious noblemen did even worse, when they took up arms and mounted their horses in order to expel and actually murder the intendant's horse guards.[7]

In Lower Rouergue, the popular insurgents seemed strongly encouraged by the ordinances of the two provincial courts, so that they could maintain their power in

---

7 Y.-M. Bercé, *Histoire des Croquants*, 2 vols. (Genéve, 1974), 2: 568, 569 and 575.

several smaller cities. They were convinced by the righteousness of their deeds; they believed that the Regent Queen would soon approve of their uprising. Alas for them, as a matter of fact, they were routed in a few days, at the beginning of October, as soon as the king's Council was at last able to gather some five hundred horsemen to crush their disorderly, big troops. The intendant, Charreton captured and disarmed the insurgents; five of them had to die on wheels or gallows, and about one hundred others were sent to the Mediterranean galleys.

I have to insist on my particular interpretation of these events. To say the truth, the fate of this small revolt in Rouergue has never been told in this fashion, i.e. stressing the role of the provincial estates and showing the convergence of peasant uprising and parliamentary ordinances. Local historians telling that story have generally referred to the commonplaces of villages' misery and hopelessness of the popular complaints without mentioning the original institutional situation and the recurrent utopia of political renewal.

It is noticeable that five years later, in the spring of 1648, the first events of the national crisis now called Fronde occurred again according to the same pattern. Once again ordinances were issued by the parliaments of Paris and the provinces, and again this happened simultaneously to gatherings of popular crowds almost everywhere, who expelled the intendants and their armed escorts. An assembly of General Estates was more and more expected. Let us repeat that this presentation of facts is only mine; it is not commonly admitted by historians of this period. Why such discrepancies?

Speaking about revolts, historians tend to look only for social causes, which should be present at the beginning of any type of political violence, and they are right in doing so. But, they tend to forget the mechanisms of already existing institutions, their particular stakes and logics, their contradictions and blind alleys, and they also miss the game of political imagination of past realms of justice and the concomitant distortions of historical reality, which are always at work around institutions. In the French examples of the disorders of the years 1643 and 1648, the political vacuum and the contradictions of institutions played a prominent role, remaining silent yet strong. The local troubles that happened in 1643 after Louis XIII's death may be considered as modest forerunners of the great crisis that was the Fronde. This interpretation has not been acknowledged because most historians actually despise the acuteness of the Fronde crisis, for they do not question the classical teleological narrative of events that presents absolutism, taking shape under the rule of Louis XIV in 1661, as a necessary episode in the history of France. Accordingly, they cannot recognise the coherent alternative program inherent in the claims of Rouergue peasants, or in the proliferating demands during the years of the Fronde.⁸ Their rejection to deal with this political program and their scornful narratives of this major crisis has a long tradition. Indeed, it was conceptualized by Louis XIV himself, who gave order to tear out entire pages in the royal court's registers; it assumed its literary strength with Voltaire and Michelet, who had decided to reduce their narratives of this crisis to ridiculous quarrels between some aristocratic ladies.⁹

According to their way of writing history, institutions were only matters of fact which had nothing to tell about major historical events or great political chronicles. My purpose in this paper has been, on the contrary, to show that the dynamic of revolts comes not only from social rights or wrongs or from the characters of their leaders, mad, foolish, brilliant or charismatic, but also from the compulsion of some recurrent institutional situations.

---

8   For an explanation of the research of immanent trends in the course of history contrasting the naive reading of accomplished facts cf. Alphonse Dupront, *Du sacré. Croisades et pèlerinages. Images et langages* (Paris, 1987), 38-42. See commentaries by Sylvio De Franceschi, "Rythmique événementielle et longue durée selon Alphonse Dupront", *Revue historique* 89 (659), 3 (2011): 611-636.

9   The most pertinent history of the period can be found in Orest Ranum, *La Fronde* (Paris, 1993). For a classical version of the crisis, see Simone Bertière, *Condé, le héros fourvoyé* (Paris, 2011).

Stenka Razin's Rebellion:
The Eyewitnesses and their Blind Spot[*]

ANDRE BERELOWITCH

> Richelieu [...] dit avoir reconnu par expérience que, toutes choses égales d'ailleurs, les rebelles sont toujours moitié moins forts que les défenseurs du pouvoir officiel. Même si l'on pense soutenir une bonne cause, le sentiment d'être en rébellion affaiblit. Sans un mécanisme psychologique de ce genre, il ne pourrait y avoir aucune stabilité dans les sociétés humaines.
>
> SIMONE WEIL (1909-1943), *L'ENRACINEMENT* (PARIS, 1949), 261.

> J'ai toujours pensé que dans les révolutions, et surtout dans les révolutions démocratiques, les fous, non pas ceux à qui l'on donne ce nom par métaphore, mais les véritables, ont joué un rôle politique très considérable. Ce qu'il y a de certain, du moins, c'est qu'une demi-folie ne messied pas dans ces temps-là et sert même souvent au succès.
>
> ALEXIS DE TOCQUEVILLE, *ŒUVRES*, T. XII. *SOUVENIRS*, ED. LUC MONNIER (PARIS, 1964), 138.

---

[*] I wish to thank here the Zentrum für interdisziplinäre Forschung of Bielefeld University for their kind invitation and the Thyssen Stiftung for their generous financial support. I thank for their help Malte Griesse and Marcel Thoene who have kindly accepted to revise the present article.

Revolts are no ordinary events. They subvert the pattern of society, the established order of things, an order which, in pre-modern Europe, was consecrated by Church and, even more perhaps, by informal belief.[1] The very real dangers incurred by rebels added to their involuntary feeling of guilt, arousing in them strong, overwhelming emotions, shared also, although in a different key, by their victims. Fueled by these powerful sentiments, hatred, fear, defiance, enthusiasm, and the sheer joy of rebellion,[2] even a minor revolt soon became known across the borders and stirred trouble, or at least excitement, in far-away countries. Because of the semi-divine nature of Order, still strengthened by the transnational solidarity of monarchs and elites alike, rebellion was resented in neighbouring lands as a scourge to avoid or an example to follow, but in any case as a threat to their usual way of life – all the more so, perhaps, because everyone knew that in given circumstances one might also be tempted to revolt.[3] That is why representations of revolts, whether domestic or transnational, are very seldom neutral: their authors do take sides, explicitly or not, and nearly always, in the early-modern surviving texts at least, against the insurgents.

---

1 Even the authority of petty tyrants of the Long Parliament: "To rule is to be sanctify'd", quoth (ironically) Hudibras' squire Ralph (Samuel Butler, *Hudibras in three parts, written in the Time of the Late Wars* [first published in 1663], part I, canto III, line 1176). Conversely, revolt was condemned by Scripture itself: "For rebellion is as the sin of witchcraft, and stubbornness is as iniquity and idolatry" (first book of Samuel, 15, 23).

2 "She experienced, for the first time, the terrible beauty of a rebellion [...] ; the secrecy, the daring, the anarchic joy of breaking a law, sharpened the excitement of [the] affair ", James Ngugi, *A grain of wheat*, (London [1967], 1974), pp. 44, 59 – a book that was suggested to me by the late Yves Benot. The quotation describes the feelings of a British lady, involved in an extra-marital affair, but is actually meant by the author as a parallel to the Mau-Mau movement in Kenya.

3 In his dissertation, defended in 1674 (see below), Johannes Justus Martius could write: "nec unquam major calamitas fuit, quam cum auctore Stephano Räzino turbæ motusque existerent: nam iis non modo Moscovia metu perculsa, sed etiam tota Europa expectatione futuri eventus aliquandiu suspensa fuit" ["there never was a worse calamity than the riots and rebellion aroused by Stephan Razin, for not only was Muscovy shaking with fear, but the whole of Europe also was for some time in suspense, waiting for the outcome"]. This is confirmed by the reaction of German periodicals: "Zwischen September 1670 und August 1671 ist im Durchschnitt jeder dritten bis vierten Zeitungsnummer eine Meldung über die 'Rebellion in der Moscau' zu entnehmen" (Martin Welke, "Deutsche Zeitungsberichte über den Moskauer Staat im 17. Jahrhundert", *Russen und Russland aus deutscher Sicht 9.-17. Jahrhundert*, M. Keller, ed., (München, 1985), p. 264-286, 279.

The contemporary sources about the Razin rebellion, which has been chosen as a case for study in the present paper, are no exception to the rule. If we put aside a few "enticing letters" [*prelestnye pis'ma*], which were part of the rebels' propaganda, all foreign relations of the revolt, all Russian documents pertaining to it condemn Razin and his followers. Not so the Russian folklore: Razin's legend conveys a belated echo of favourable popular feeling.[4]

Representations may be, and often are, analyzed for their own sake: in order to recapture the point of view of the observer, the historian's attention is focused not on the actual events, but on the arrangements and distortions they are subjected to in the narrative. Radical sceptics even argue that representations are the only source available to us, since any conceivable document, be it manor accounts or a ship's bill of lading, endeavours to present facts in a certain light – in other words, the simple act of writing something down is already, to some extent, tampering with reality.

These objections notwithstanding, and believing that cross-checking sources against one another provides a sufficient degree of probability, I will try to relate representations to known facts so as to throw some light on both phenomena. The very nature of the task restricts the circle of acceptable evidence: second-hand or third-hand accounts are more informative about public opinion, i.e. about the historian's or the compiler's mind, than about the actual features of the rebellion. Only narratives written by eyewitnesses, only documents issued by agents on both sides can answer two questions I would like to put to the test: can we ascribe a social nature to Razin's uprising? What kind of mechanism triggered the revolt at the crucial moment? Before dealing with these topics, I will give, by way of introduction, a survey of the available sources, a summary of the events,[5] and devote some space to a seemingly irrelevant problem: how much did 17th century Muscovites, on both sides, care about representation?

AVAILABLE SOURCES

The bulk of the domestic sources on the Razin rebellion (*razinshchina*) has been published by Soviet historians between 1954 and 1976, under the highly ideological

---

4   Philip Longworth, "The subversive legend of Sten'ka Razin", *Russia/Rossiia. Studi e ricerche a cura di Vittorio Strada*, n° 2, 1975, 17-40.

5   A more detailed account in English: Paul Avrich, *Russian Rebels 1600-1800* (New York, London, 1972), chapter II.

title *Peasant War under the Leadership of Stepan Razin. Documents.*[6] Quite a few additional materials have appeared since 1976. However, these documents will be mainly used to check foreign sources, the only ones that are, strictly speaking, in keeping with our subject.

Not surprisingly, since Russia was at the outskirts of Europe, foreign sources are few, if we put aside second-hand narratives and various compilations, and make use only of reports by eyewitnesses.[7] Four Dutchmen have described the early course of the rebellion. The author of the *Letter written on board* [...] *the* Orel, [...] *September 24th 1669*[8] is unknown, but very probably was a member of the Dutch crew of this first warship, Western fashion, ever built in Muscovy. David Butler, skipper, and Jan Janszoon Struys (ca 1630-1694), sailsmaster on the *Orel*, were ordered to join Astrakhan garrison, when the town was put under siege by Razin's army.[9] All of them took some part in the defense of the city and managed

---

6   *Krest'ianskaia voina pod predvoditel'stvom Stepana Razina. Sbornik dokumentov*, vol. I, II/1-2, III, IV (Moscow, 1954-1976) [hereafter: *Krest'ianskaia voina*]. Nearly all are official documents, the only exceptions being the "enticing letters" mentioned above.

7   Since M. N. Tikhomirov's not very satisfactory and outdated essay "Istochniki po istorii razinshchiny", *Problemy istochnikovedeniia*, I (Moscow-Leningrad, 1933), p. 50-69, no recent study, as far as I know, has dealt with the foreign narratives of Stenka Razin's rebellion as a whole. They have been conveniently put together and published in Leningrad by A. G. Man'kov, in: *Zapiski inostrantsev o vosstanii Stepana Razina* (Leningrad, 1968) [hereafter: *Zapiski*], and *Inostrannye izvestiia o vosstanii Stepana Razina*, 1975 [hereafter: *Inostrannye izvestiia*]. Texts are printed both in the original languages and in Russian translation. The latter book includes extracts from chiefly German, but also French periodicals. Man'kov describes foreign Razin narratives in general (*Zapiski*, 5-13, 84-87), and so does Serge Konovalov in his "Ludvig Fabritius's Account of the Razin Rebellion" *Oxford Slavonic Papers*, VI, 1956, p. 72-94, 72-73 [hereafter: Fabritius], and in "Razin's Execution. Two Contemporary Documents", S. Konovalov, ed., *Oxford Slavonic Papers*, XII, 1965, p. 94-98, 94 [hereafter: *Razin's Execution*].

8   Unless otherwise specified, all dates are given in the Julian calendar. In quotations of English or French texts of the 17th century, spelling has been conserved, punctuation slightly modernized.

9   The anonymous letter, Jan Struys' narrative and a letter written by David Butler from Ispahan, March 6th, 1671, are to be found in: Jan Struys, *Drie aanmerkelijke en seer rampspoedige reysen door Italien, Griekenlandt, Lijflandt, Moscovien, Tartarijen, Meden, Persien, Oost-Indien, Japan* [...] (Amsterdam, 1676). Being unable to use the Dutch original, I have quoted here from the English *The Perillous and most unhappy voyages of John Struys through Italy, Greece, Lifeland, Moscovia, Tartary, Media, Persia, East-India, Japan and other places in Europe, Africa and Asia* [...] to which are

eventually to escape from Razin's camp. So did Ludvig Fabritius (1648-1729), a young foreign officer who had already served nine or ten years in the Russian army, and came with the strong detachment sent up the Volga from Astrakhan against the rebels.[10] His account is the best by far, at the same time simple, clever and unbiased, although written some twenty years after the event. The others rather tend to mingle facts with moral and political considerations.

Another group of foreigners, who were not involved in the events, but lived in Moscow at that time and wrote about Russia, seem to have witnessed the arrival of Stepan Razin in Moscow and his execution. Their accounts are especially valuable since only one report by a Russian eyewitness has been found.[11] The anonymous author, perhaps a Dutchman, of *A Relation concerning the particulars of the Rebellion lately raised in Muscovy by Stenko Razin*, who gave the most accurate account of the whole course of the rebellion, had probably access to official documents as well.[12] Thomas Hebdon, an English merchant, brother of the well-known diplomat John Hebdon the Elder, is the most reliable witness: on the very day of Razin's death, he wrote a letter describing his execution.[13] Johannes Justus Merz, *latine* Martius, (1648-1702), a Lutheran minister who worked from 1668 to 1672 as a school teacher in the Foreign Quarter in Moscow, wrote a dissertation on

---

added 2 narrativs sent from Capt. D. Butler relating to the taking in of Astrachan by the cosacs [...] rendered out of Nether-dutch by John Morrison (London, 1686) and the French translation *Les Voyages de Jean Struys, en Moscovie, en Tartarie, en Perse, aux Indes & en plusieurs autres païs étrangers* (Amsterdam, 1681) [both hereafter: Struys].

10 Fabritius' memoirs have remained manuscript until Konovalov's publication. The original German text is in *Zapiski*, 14-46; quotations in this paper are from Konovalov's English translation, see footnote 9 above.

11 *Krest'ianskaia voina*, IV, n° 66-67, p. 61-62.

12 For conjectures about the author, see: A. L. Gol'dberg, "Soobshchenie o vosstanii Stepana Razina", *Zapiski*, p. 157-165. The *Relation* was first published in Dutch: *Kort Waerdachtigh verhael van de bloedige Rebellye in Moscovien* [...] (Haerlem, 1671) and in German: *Kurtze doch Warhafftige Erzählung von der blutigen Rebellion in der Moscau* [...] (Emden, 1671). The English text was printed in Newcomb, 1672, and is reproduced, with Russian translation, in *Zapiski*, p. 84-126 [Hereafter quoted: *Relation*]. The French version *Relation des particularitez de la rebellion de Stenko Razin contre le grand-duc de Moscovie* (Paris, 1672); repr. by Augustin Golitsyn (Paris, 1856) was translated from the English.

13 His letter, written in Moscow on the 6th of June 1671, to Richard Daniell, an English resident in Riga, in *Razin's Execution*, p. 97-98.

Stepan Razin, defended in July 1674, and published in the same year.[14] His information is partly derived from his readings, but his impressions on the mood of the Moscow crowd are undoubtedly his own.[15] Jacob Reutenfels was a spectator of Razin's "horrible" death.[16] All other accounts may safely be ignored for the purposes of the present paper.[17]

---

14 Merz's biography by A. K. Gavrilov in Inostrannye izvestiia, p. 25-30. His dissertation: Martius, Johann Justus, стенко разинъ донски козакъ изменникъ, id est Stephanus Razin donicus Cosacus perduellis, publica disquisitioni exhibitus, praeside Conrado Samuele Schurzfleisch, respondente Johanne Justo Martio, Mulhusa-Thuringo, d. XXIX Quintil. Anno M DC LXXIV, Wittenbergæ Ex officina Christiani Schröteri. It was reprinted in Leipzig (1679), in Wittenberg (1683) and again in Leipzig (1698). Repr. in Inostrannye izvestiia, p. 31-75 (Latin original and Russian translation). Partial English translation (§ 27-30), Razin's Execution, p. 95-96.

15 "Ita ex commentariis actorum Russicorum didici" (§ 25*, Inostrannye izvestia, p. 48: "So I learnt from russian writings"); "Ipse pro comperto habeo, quam parum omnes ab exitio abfuerint" (§ 22, ibidem, p. 47 : "I hold for certain that we all narrowly escaped being killed").

16 "Horrendum ejus modi inusitatioris supplicii specimen in Stenka, seu Stephano Rasin Cosaco rebelli Moscuæ spectavimus" ["A horrifying instance of this unusual kind of death we have seen in Moscow when Stenka, i. e. Stepan Razin, a rebel Cossack, was executed"], in: Yacobus Reutenfels, *De rebus Moschoviticis ad Serenissimum Magnum Hetruriæ Ducem Cosmum Tertium* (Patavii, 1680); facsimile edition by Marshall Poe: *Early Explorations of Russia*, vol. XI (London, New York, 2003), p. 164; German translation: Yacob Reutenfels, *Das grosse und mächtige Reich Moscoviæ* [...] (Nürnberg, 1687). Reutenfels (actually spelled "Rautenfels") lived in Moscow from 1670 to the spring of 1672, cf. Claudia Jensen, Ingrid Maier, "Orpheus and Pickleherring in the Kremlin", *Scando-Slavica* 59:2, 2013, 145-184, 148-150

17 "A Narrative of the Greatest Victory known in the Memory of Man: Being the total Overthrow of the Great Rebel Stepan Radzin [...]", Inostrannye izvestia, p. 8-10; "Ritratto della Moscovia. Ristretto geografico, historico e genealogico del gran Ducato o sia Impero di Moscovia", A. I. Turgenev, ed, Historica Russiæ Monumenta, II, Petropoli, 1848, p. 249-278 ; Historisch Verhael, of Beschrijving van de Voyagie, gedaen onder de Suite van der Heere K. van Klenk (Amsterdam, 1677), repr. with Russian translation, A. M. Lovjagin, ed., *Posol'stvo Kunraada fan-Klenka* [...], (Saint Petersburg, 1900); Carl Valerius Wickhart, *Moscowitische Reise-Beschreibung* [...] (Vienna, 1675), p. 201-202.

SUMMARY OF THE EVENTS

It is no coincidence if Razin's first expedition (1667) starts at the end of the Thirteen Years, Russian-Polish War (1654-1667), at a moment when Russian taxpayers are at the end of their tether (taxes in grain alone have increased fourteen-fold between 1620 and 1670), the Treasury runs short of money, and military men are no longer needed. All these factors help to understand the difficult position of the semi-independent Don Cossacks, who fought alongside of Muscovite troops when they saw fit, and in return received subsidies from Moscow (grain, powder, cash and arms), yet derived part of their income from plundering raids, chiefly, but not exclusively, directed against Crimean and Ottoman territories.[18] No wonder if the Russian government wanted to curb as much as possible the political freedom of the Cossacks. A particularly sensitive topic was the problem of fugitive peasants, who often joined the Cossack Host. Moscow insisted on having them returned, but the Don Cossacks, many of whom were themselves ex-fugitives, took pride in refusing. Razin would say in 1669: "It is not the custom among Cossacks to hand over runaways."[19]

One way of achieving control over the Cossacks was to reduce, postpone or even cut out the Don subsidies, another – the military colonisation of the South, on the Belgorod Abatis line. Both led to unexpected results: since supplies were lacking, the Cossacks switched to plundering, the only way left to survive. Colonisation, undertaken, of course, to defend Russian territory against Crimean raids, but also to keep an eye on the Host, brought thousands of deserters and fugitive peasants into the Don region, thus creating a situation close to famine.[20] Since economic and social differentiation was already well advanced among the Host, those who suffered most were the poorer Cossacks (*golutvennye ljudi*), as opposed to their well-to-do (*domovitye*) brethren.[21]

---

18 Brian Davies, "Muscovy at war and peace", The Cambridge history of Russia, I: From Early Rus' to 1689, Maureen Perrie, ed. (Cambridge, 2006), p. 486-519, 493. Whenever possible, I have translated Russian terms in accordance with this edition.
19 Maureen Perrie, "Popular Revolts", ibidem, p. 600-617, 605; Viktor Ivanovich Buganov, Krest'ianskie voiny v Rossii XVII-XVIII vv., Moscow, 1976, p. 60, 71, 82 [hereafter: Buganov].
20 Davies, p. 499; Krest'ianskaia voina, I, n° 38, p. 73: according to a report from the governor of Tsaritsyn, 14 March 1667, "fugitive bondsmen [holopy] and peasants from the border, with wives and children, have taken refuge in many villages of the Don region, and because of that there is now a terrible famine on the Don."
21 A view contested by Nikolai Ivanovich Nikitin, "O formatsionnoi prirode rannikh kazach'ikh obshchestv (K postanovke voprosa)", Feodalizm v Rossii [Festschrift for L. V.

A minor, but ominous, episode occurred in June of 1666. A 700 men strong Cossack detachment under Vasilii Us (Basil "Moustache") rode North, allegedly to offer their services as cavalrymen to the tsar. A deputation was indeed sent to Moscow, but met with a flat refusal and was ordered to go back to the Don. Meanwhile, Us and his men had moved their encampment further North to Tula, attracting quite a number of local peasants and bondsmen (see below) and looting noble estates in the vicinity. They withdrew in July only under military coercion. Not surprisingly, Us in time became one of Razin's lieutenants.[22]

The Andrusovo armistice (January 1667) didn't improve the situation in the least. Tsar Alexis said as much in his letter to the shah of Iran[23]: "It has come to our knowledge that after we had made peace with the kingdom of Poland, bandits and fugitives from various places have appeared on the lower Volga" (May 3rd, 1668). A little later, in his message to the governor of Tsaritsyn, Razin provides the explanation: "In the Host, there is nothing left to eat or to drink, whereas the tsar's subsidies in money and grain are sent sparingly. That's why we went to the Volga, to feed ourselves."[24]

During the spring of 1667, small bands of Cossacks made their way to the Volga, where they attacked Russian convoys, and to the Caspian Sea, where their targets were Persian ships. They endangered thereby Russia's good relations, and particularly trade, with Iran. Local governors soon put an end to these first attempts at piracy, but they were less successful against the large-scale expedition led by Stepan Timofeevich Razin.[25]

Razin, born ca. 1630, belonged to the Cossack elite. Up to 1667 his life was in no way remarkable, at least according to the little information available.[26] He took part, in 1658, in a Cossack deputation to Moscow. Three years later, as a Don Cossacks' representative, he was a member of the embassy led by secretary Ivan Savvich Gorohov to meet Kalmyk *tayishis* Daichin and Monchak/Puntsuk.[27] He

---

Cherepnin], Moscow, 1987, p. 236-245, who argues that Cossack society was "pre-feudal" and still primitive, nay regressive, in many ways. His analysis of Cossack way of life (p. 236-239) is remarkably lucid.

22 M. Perrie, loc. cit.; more details in Buganov, p. 62-66.
23 Buganov, p.71.
24 Ibidem, p. 72.
25 The diminutive of Stepan, "Stenka", used in Muscovite official documents, is a pejorative, indicating either young age or a low status in the social hierarchy.
26 Buganov, p.66-70; Ocherki istorii SSSR. Period feodalizma XVII v. (Moscow, 1955), p. 283 [hereafter: Ocherki].
27 About this embassy, see Michael Khodarkovsky, When Two Worlds met. The Russian State and the Kalmyk Nomads, 1600-1771, Cornell UP, Ithaca and London, 1992, p. 95.

then headed a Cossack detachment sent against Crimean Tatars in 1663. Meanwhile, he twice asked permission to make a pilgrimage to the Northern convent of Solovki (1652, 1661).

In 1667, however, he takes the lead of the Cossack bands which are gathering again near the portage between Don and Volga rivers. As soon as the ice breaks on the Don (mid-April 1667), Razin and his 600 followers sail towards Panshin and Kachalinsk, where the river islands are well out of reach for regular forces. There he carefully prepares his campaign, recruiting men among Cossacks and "fugitives from various places", stocking up plundered arms, ammunition, food and equipment. Part of the weaponry is provided by well-to-do Cossacks to individual members of the expedition, on a fifty-fifty (*ispoly*) basis, meaning that the investors would receive half of the expected booty. "It would be wrong", writes Viktor Buganov, "to deny the predatory aspects" of Razin's voyage.[28] We may add that, *mutatis mutandis*, the management of this expedition is in many respects similar to the raids of the freebooters and buccaneers in the West Indies, as described by Exquemelin.[29]

Once ready, Razin enters the Volga with his bands, now 1500 men strong: the flotilla heads South, past Tsaritsyn. Razin dodges or overcomes the detachments sent against him from Astrakhan. He already applies the tactics to which he will stick until the end of the movement: nobles, officers, merchants are put to death, as well as the rank and file who resist him; the rest switch sides and join the Cossacks. At last, between June 3rd and 5th, the Cossacks sail past Astrakhan by night, and enter the Caspian Sea. In July, disguised as pilgrims, they take the fort of Iaitsk by trickery, and there they remain during the winter of 1667-1668. All attempts made by the Russian government first to negotiate with Razin, then to drive him out of his stronghold, have failed.[30]

Very little reliable information about Razin's sea voyage is available to historians, since no research has been as yet conducted in Persian archives.[31] As far as we know, the Cossacks abandoned Iaitsk in March 1668, and sailed southwards,

---

28 Buganov, p.72, 73.
29 Original Dutch edition: Alexander Exquemelin, De Americaensche Zee-Roovers, Amsterdam, 1678, followed by German (Nürnberg, 1679), English (Bucaniers of America, London, 1684) and French (Paris, 1686) translations.
30 Ocherki, p. 286.
31 All accounts are only by hearsay, be it the reports of Russian town governors (in Krest'janskaja vojna), or the narratives of European travellers: Jean Chardin (1643-1713), who was in Persia at the time (Le Journal de voyage du chevalier Chardin en Perse et aux Indes orientales, Amsterdam, 1711), and Engelbert Kaempfer (1651-1716), who arrived in Isfahan in 1683 (his account in Inostrannye izvestiia, p. 152-180).

following the Western coast of the Caspian Sea, plundering ships and even towns (Derbent, Baku) as they went along. They freed Russian captives, and made prisoners among Persian population, to be bartered later or sold into slavery.[32] Alternating success and defeats, they accumulated considerable wealth, periodically divided between the fighters,[33] but often suffered from illness and starvation. In the spring of 1669, Razin decided to offer his services to the shah.[34] But the Persian ruler had Razin's envoys executed, and sent troops against the Cossacks. Taken by surprise near Rasht, they took revenge on the city of Farahābād and, after defeating a Persian flotilla, sailed back towards Astrakhan in July 1669.

Since he had been forbidden to sail into the Caspian Sea, Razin, entrenched in the Four Hills island at the mouth of the Volga, feared new attacks from Astrakhan. He certainly didn't expect the third in command in the city, prince Semen L'vov, escorted by three or four thousand men with artillery, to present him a letter issued by the tsar in 1667, forgiving the Cossacks their faults if they promised to behave in the future.

So it came that Razin and his men, "everyone of them appearing in the most splendid manner he could", scattering gold coins to admiring crowds,[35] made a triumphant entry into the town. Far from acting as repentant sinners, the pirates, while negotiations went on, sold slaves, beautiful cloth and jewellery in the market place, thus making a deep and lasting impression on the local population.[36] The governors were even given generous presents by Razin himself. Finally, the Cossacks were allowed to sail back to their homes on the river Don, where they arrived in October 1669.

---

32 Slavery is present everywhere in this story: Razin wants to free Russian peasants from it, but his Cossacks sell their Persian captives, and the defeated rebels are, in their turn, illegally enslaved by their victors (cf. Krest'ianskaia voina, III, n° 11, p. 12 ; n° 15, p. 15), e. g. by Ivan Bogdanovich Miloslavskii (ibidem, n° 205, p. 230) and many others (ibidem, n° 31, 45, 213).

33 This was called duvanit', from duvan (a derivative of turcic divan), meaning the place where the warriors assemble, or the booty itself, human or otherwise.

34 Kaempfer, Inostrannye izvestiia, p. 158.

35 "For they had rifled many Gentlemens Houses where they found always Apparrel, Jewels and other Plunder for Habit and Ornament", Struys, p. 186 ; "La plupart du peuple & des soldats, qui couroient en foule auprès de lui lorsqu'il paroissoit dans les ruës, & auxquels il jetoit souvent des poignées de ducats", Struys, p. 176.

36 Fabritius, p. 79 : "This human market lasted some six weeks" [...] He [Razin] promised to free them [Astrakhan common people] from the yoke of the boyars ant set the slaves free, so that the people listened to him gladly and promised to help him with all their might as soon as he was ready to begin his attack."

The whole Persian campaign looks very much like a rehearsal of the next, so purposeful were Razin's moves between the autumn of 1669 and the spring of 1670. Contrary to custom, he did not disband his troops, but kept them in a fortified island under strict discipline, while using what was left of the booty to arm and equip his small army, which was steadily growing in numbers: "He began straightaway quietly gathering the common people around him, giving them money, and promises of great riches if they would be loyal to him and help to exterminate the treacherous boyars."[37] By May 1670, Razin had under him four or five thousand men.

Already in March, the Cossacks, assembled in a "ring" (*krug*),[38] had been consulted about the choice of a target for the next expedition. They rejected Azov, as well as the Russian project ("go to Russia and fight the boyars"), and adopted enthusiastically the Volga instead. After killing two nobles sent by the tsar to report on Razin's movements (April), the army arrived, probably on May 13th, in Panshin. Another circle was summoned, which confirmed the previous decision, but with a significant addition. When asked: "Would you all go from the Don to the Volga, and from the Volga into Russia against the sovereign's enemies and traitors, to rid Muscovy of treacherous boyars and *Duma* [conciliar] people, and, in the provinces, of governors and administrators?", the Cossacks answered in the affirmative.[39]

Meanwhile, the authorities, who were kept informed by governors and spies, had sent a thousand musketeers [*strel'tsy*] under Ivan Lopatin down the Volga.[40] Another, much more important force (several thousand men commanded by prince Semen L'vov), was slowly moving up river from Astrakhan. When Razin arrived under Tsaritsyn, both armies were still on their way. The town was given over to the Cossacks by its revolted dwellers, and Razin immediately marched against Lopatin, whom he met and defeated some five miles upstream. The greater part of the musketeers were slaughtered, the rest joined the Cossacks or were pressed into service as oarsmen. Razin then turned around to meet the L'vov army, which he

---

37 Fabritius, p. 79-80.
38 "A Krug is a meeting convened by order of the Ataman [elected chief, A.B.], at which the Cossacks stand in a circle with the standard in the centre ; the Ataman then takes his place beside his best officers, to whom he divulges his wishes, ordering them to make these known to the common brothers and to hear their opinion of the matter : if the proposals of the Ataman please the commoners, they all shout together 'Lyubo, lyubo'" (ibidem, p. 81)
39 Buganov, p. 83-88.
40 A picture designed to entertain and instruct tsar Alexis' children represents the flotilla on its way to Tsaritsyn. Cf. Z. I. Fomicheva, "Redkoe proizvedenie russkogo iskusstva XVII veka", Drevnerusskoe iskusstvo. XVII vek (Moscow, 1964), p. 316-326.

found under Chernyi Yar. This is how Fabritius describes the battle (June 11th, 1670):

The next morning, at 8 o'clock, our look-outs on the water came hurriedly and raised the alarm as the Cossacks were following at their heels. [...] In the meantime Stenka prepared for battle and deployed on a wide front; to all those who had no rifle he gave a long pole, burnt a little at one end, and with a rag or small hook attached. [...] The common soldiers imagined that, since there were so many flags and standards, there must be a host of people. They put their heads together and at once decided that this was the chance for which they had been waiting so long, and with all their flags and drums they ran over to the enemy. They began kissing and embracing one another and swore with life and limb to stand together and to exterminate the treacherous boyars, to throw off the yoke of slavery, and to become free men.

The general with his officers sought refuge in the Chernyi Yar fortress, but the garrison had also mutinied, and all eighty men were taken prisoners.

Murder at once began. Then, however, Stenka Razin ordered that no more officers were to be killed, saying that there must be a few good men among them. [...] A *Krug* was accordingly called and Stenka asked through his lieutenants how the general and his officers had treated the soldiers under their command. Thereupon the unscrupulous curs, *streltsy* as well as soldiers, unanimously called out that there were not one of them who deserved to remain alive, and they all asked their father Stepan Timofeyevich Razin should order them to be cut down. This was granted with the exception of General Knyaz Semen Ivanovich L'vov[41] [...] The officers were now brought in order of rank out of the tower [...], their ropes were cut and they were led outside the gate. When all the bloodthirsty curs had lined up, each was eager to deal his former superior the first blow, one with the sword, another with the lance, another with the scimitar, and other again with martels [...] Indeed, some were cut to pieces and straightaway thrown into the Volga.[42]

The road to Astrakhan was now open. The city was defended by 6.000 soldiers and 500 guns; Razin, however, had not only won over the town people[43], but also the

---

41 In return for Razin's presents, in 1669, L'vov had given him "a beautiful gold-plated image of the Virgin" (Fabritius, p. 79), and the Cossack chief became the prince's sworn brother. That is probably why Razin spared L'vov until his own death on the scaffold (ibidem, p. 83, footnote 1).

42 Fabritius, p. 81-82.

43 "The report of these things [news from Chernyi Yar] [...] gave the Rabble greater Occasion to mutiny than they had before, yea, so far [...] that they publicly reproached the Superiority that they durst not look out of their doors or windows, much less walk the streets

garrison itself. In the night of 21st to 22nd June, the city was easily taken, and the sequence of events in Tsaritsyn or Chernyi Yar, repeated: governors, officers killed along with the loyal soldiers; their goods plundered and divided among the rebels; new recruits rushing into Razin's army and henceforth decreed Cossacks.[44] Astrakhan civilians were, likewise, democratically organized: they discussed their affairs in *krugs*, and elected their own atamans (Vasilii Us a popular winner). All official archives were systematically lacerated, especially indentures, thereby putting into effect Razin's promises about "setting the common people free."

On the 20th of July 1670, Razin departed from Astrakhan with 11 000 men, leaving 2 000 behind. Stopping briefly in Tsaritsyn (4-7 August), he sent two detachments to stir up revolt in Ukraine, and moved up to Saratov, then to Samara, which didn't even resist the rebel army. These were his last victories. He tried in vain to secure Simbirsk, a strategically important point on the Abatis line, defended by Ivan Miloslavskii. Razin took the town, but was unable to capture the citadel (September 5th-6th), which he put under siege for a whole month. This delay proved fatal to the movement. In the beginning of October, Simbirsk was rescued by Iurii Boriatinskii. Razin, wounded, was carried away by devoted followers and disappeared from the scene until his final capture.

This did not stop the rebellion; although the main rebel army had been defeated, Razin's lieutenants did not give up the struggle. Moreover, independent detachments, sometimes several thousand men strong, gathered in different parts of the countryside, mainly in the Middle Volga region. They took a few secondary towns, such as Penza, Temnikov, Alatyr', and even marched on Arzamas, then headquarters of the repression. Here, under Iurii Dolgorukii, were concentrated, summarily judged and executed up to 11 000 insurgents: "The place was terrible to behold, and had the resemblance of the Suburbs of Hell."[45] Razin himself, captured on April 14th, 1671 by the notables among Don Cossacks, was brought to Moscow and executed on June 6th of the same year. The rebel city of Astrakhan surrendered to Ivan Miloslavskii only on the 27th of November. This was the last of the

---

[…], for it was no rare thing now to see the Rabble assemble together in heaps, and before the Doors of the Magistrates, to cry out with infamous and bitter Railings, Now, now, the times begin to alter, it will be our turn next to Lord it, you villains" (Struys, p. 208).

44 After his escape, Fabritius is dressed Cossack fashion : "my [former] orderly […] cut my long hair – detested by the villains – […] and gave me a rough coat made of coarse sacking." (Fabritius, p. 82).

45 Relation, p. 98.

razinshchina, which, according to the *Relation*, had mobilized up to 200 000 men,[46] but not the last of Russian revolts. Just as some of Razin's companions had already taken part in the "Copper sedition" (1662), so did Viktor Buganov find survivors of the 1670-1671 civil war among the revolting musketeers in Moscow (1682), or even the Bulavin's Cossacks (1707-1708).[47]

REAPPRAISING THE EVIDENCE

Such is, by and large, the picture resulting from the foreign narratives of Razin's rebellion, if we exclude the abuse showered on its agents. It does not substantially differ from the standard version of the events approved by Soviet historians, except for rhetorical effects about the ruthless ruling classes and the splendid courage of the exploited. Actually, the obsessive class-struggle motif blocked innovative interpretation of the *razinshchina* for the better part of the last century, roughly from the provocative article by Andrei Kabanov,[48] published in 1917, to the paper by Michael Khodarkovsky in 1994.[49] Although the latter mainly discusses the more general problem of "peasant wars", both analyze in some detail the behaviour of the rebels and of the authorities. I will try to follow in their steps, adding some comments of my own.

Khodarkovsky has shown that, from the point of view of the Moscow government, incursions such as Vasilii Us's foray near Tula, or even the Caspian expedition of Razin were not considered as extraordinary, and certainly not as a revolt: "Like their nomadic neighbours, the Cossacks traditionally displayed their

---

46 "It was of great importance to Russia, and a great Mercy of God, that the Rebels lay here and there divided; as also, that they could not agree among themselves, about the Supream Command. For if this power of the Rebels, consisting of Two hundred thousand Men, had been united and unanimous, it would have been difficult for the Forces of the Czar to have resisted and mastered the same" (ibidem, p. 99).

47 Buganov, p. 106, 112.

48 A. K. Kabanov, "Razintsy v Nizhegorodskom krae (priemy bunta i usmireniia)" ["Razin's followers in the Nizhnii-Novgorod region (ways and means of revolt and repression)"], Sbornik statei v chest' Matveia Kuz'micha Liubavskogo, Petrograd, 1917, p. 413-428. On the tragic fate of Andrei Kiprianovich Kabanov (1876-1922), who was arrested by the Cheka and died while serving a sentence of one year forced labour for counter-revolutionaty activities, cf. A. A. Kuznetsov, A. V. Mel'nikov, B. M. Pudalov, "Novye dannye o sud'be nizhegorodskogo istorika Kabanova", on the site: www.opentextnn.ru.

49 M. Khodarkovsky, "The Stepan Razin Uprising: was it a 'Peasant War' ?", Jahrbücher für Geschichte Osteuropas, Neue Folge, vol. 42/1 (1994), p. 1-19.

ultimate dissatisfaction by turning against Moscow. When requests and complaints failed, military action was usually more effective in attracting the government's attention."[50]

When the Nogays brought horses to sell to Moscow (a vital supply for Russian cavalry),[51] the authorities knew that plundering on the way, sometimes on a major scale, was unavoidable. That was the price to pay if one wanted to have nomads at one's service. The fact that most of the Cossacks were orthodox and, in a very broad sense, considered themselves Russians made no difference in that respect. Like the garrisons on the Ottoman-Habsburg borders, they may be described as "march warriors", "living according to their own rules and codes of conduct."[52] Forced tolerance of nomadic excesses explains why in 1667 Razin, when "only" guilty of piracy on the Volga (he was still on his way to the Caspian Sea), was granted a letter of grace by the tsar, forgiving his past misdeeds, provided he promised to sin no more,[53] and also why, when returning from Persian shores, he was pardoned on the strength of that very same letter, and allowed to go home with his unruly band.

By May of 1670, of course, rebellion became obvious and was named as such in official documents. Even then, forgiveness remained an option if the culprits duly expressed repentance. In the initial stage at least, negotiation was not excluded, and no visible barrier, as yet, separated the rebels from the loyal subjects of the tsar.[54] Both sides, as Kabanov has shown, tried to win over people who were hesitating on the brink of rebellion, and used strikingly similar methods to do so. Both drafted letters and manifestos, written by the tsar, his officials, the patriarch or the commanding officers in the field, or conversely by Razin himself or his lieutenants. Both found means to circulate these letters among the population, and both, when they could, wielded more potent arguments such as axes, swords, muskets or the gallows.

---

50 Ibidem, p. 9.
51 Khodarkovsky, When Two Worlds met, p. 28.
52 Peter F. Sugar, "The Ottoman 'professional prisoner' on the Western Borders of the Empire in the sixteenth and seventeenth centuries", Études balkaniques, 1971/2, p. 82-91, 82.
53 Buganov, p. 75-76.
54 In October 1670, two Chuvash hundredmen, loyal to the tsar, met a Chuvash imam (abyz) who was on the side of the rebels. After both parties had sworn not to shoot at each other, the imam departed, leaving "enticing letters" enclosed in a bark-box (Krest'ianskaia voina, II/1, n° 90, p. 105-106).

CIRCULATING THE WRITTEN WORD: THE REBELS

As a rule, Razin's followers couldn't spell, so finding able writers was something of a problem. They managed, nevertheless, with the help of local *literati*, parish clergymen, sextons, local clerks, and the like,[55] and disseminated the messages as best they could. For instance, in October 1670, the small town of Saransk is stormed by a troop of Simbirsk musketeers and Cossacks, led by a Don Cossack. All the prisoners of the city jail are released, one of them is appointed ataman, who then does the round of the villages, handing out "enticing letters" copied by a clerk in Temnikov.[56] A letter, addressed to the "populace" of the Tsivil'sk district and delivered by Cossack Kildibiakov, bids the peasants to turn the text over to local village sextons to have it copied word for word, and then to distribute the copies in villages and hamlets "so that everybody in the district would be acquainted with it."[57]

For the same reason, *viz.* general illiteracy, the messages were read in public, as e. g. at Unzha (a small town in the Galich district): "the local elder, Tarasko Grigor'ev, in lieu of the town crier, made the announcement on the market place, and the blackguardly letter was read by the town priest of Saint-Makarios, Timofei Andronnikov."[58] Reading messages from loyalists was quite naturally forbidden: in April 1671, a sexton pressed into service by the Cossacks (or so he said) stated that "as I read to the assembled people the letters sent by the nobles from the other side of the river, the rebellious Cossacks forbade the people to listen."[59]

Communication, however, was not achieved purely by means of words. Rebel chiefs were not adverse to some show of ceremony: "the criminal Il'iushka Ivanov [a well-known Razin's lieutenant, A.B.] [...] sent ahead scouts, to make sure that the priest would meet him with icons, and peasants with loaves of bread. And if anyone refused to do so, he would have everybody cut down and our houses

---

55 E.g. in the Shatsk region: "Among the bandits [rebels, AB] it was the sexton, Liubim Selivanov, whose surname I don't know, who wrote the letters" (ibidem, II/1, n° 224, p. 273; November 1670). Sergei Ignat'ev, public writer on oath [ploshchadnoi pod'iachii] in Tambov, "wrote, he says, for the lawless Cossacks all kinds of letters" (ibidem, II/1, n° 285, p. 359; December 1670).

56 Ibidem, II/1, n° 110, p. 128-130; October 1670.

57 Ibidem, II/1, n° 78, p. 91; September 1670.

58 Ibidem, II/1, n° 288, p. 362; December 1670. Similarly, a letter from Razin to his followers in Tsaritsyn is read aloud in the krug (ibidem, I, n° 150, p. 210; July 1670).

59 Ibidem, III, n° 47, p. 55.

destroyed."[60] Since this is an answer to official inquiry, the peasants pretend that they were forced to join the rebellion, which may or may not be true. But some of the few extant "enticing letters" are quite explicit:

We beseech you to show your zeal for the house of the holy Mother of God, and for the great sovereign [tsar Alexis], and for your father [*batiushka*] Stepan Timofeevich [Razin], and for the whole Christian Orthodox Faith. [...] But if you don't come to the assembly for advice, the Great [Cossack] Host will punish you, your wives and children will be cut down, your houses destroyed, and your goods confiscated.[61]

CIRCULATING THE WRITTEN WORD: THE GOVERNMENT

The complex relationship between rebels and loyalists is perhaps best illustrated by the Kadom-Kasimov episode. In November 1670, Kirill Khlopov, an official of Kasimov, sent six monks and two men from the postal service to Kadom, with letters from the tsar urging the people of the district "to keep clear of the blackguards and traitors and make repentance." Unfortunately, the governor of Kasimov, Mihail Dmitriev, deaf to Khlopov's entreaties, decided to execute four peasants from Kadom, presumably suspected of rebellion, while Khlopov's agitators were still in Kadom. Khlopov reports : "Thereupon the Kadom people, hearing this and enraged by the hanging of four peasants of their town [...] lynched four of my envoys."[62] Obviously, in hanging the peasants, the governor had violated an unwritten rule, something akin to diplomatic immunity as long as talks were going on. A letter from four rebel atamans to an officer of musketeers confirms this: "As soon as you receive this note, please release our man, Semen Tatarinov, whom you took yesterday. And yet yesterday we were ready to meet you, to talk together for good counsel, and we sent him to talk to you, hoping [to succeed]."[63]

---

60 A. I. Kopanev, "Nakhodki bibliografa (Neizvestnye materialy o krest'ianskoi voine pod predvoditel'stvom Stepana Razina)", *Trudy biblioteki Akademii Nauk SSSR i fundamental'noi biblioteki obshchestvennykh nauk AN SSSR*, vol. VI (Moscow-Leningrad), 1962, p. 210-216, 212 (date unknown). "Loaves of bread" may be part of the traditional welcome, with bread and salt, or more prosaically food for Ivanov's men.
61 Krest'ianskaia voina, II/1, n° 207, p. 252; November 1670.
62 Ibidem, II/1, n° 237, p. 284-285; one of Khlopov's messengers survived and petitioned the tsar in 1672 (ibidem, III, n° 223, p. 251).
63 Ibidem, II/1, n° 221, p. 270; November 1670. Although the context is somewhat unclear, it seems that the rebels sent Tatarinov in good faith, having perhaps received the oral equivalent of a safe-conduct.

These attempts at coming to terms did not suit at all the tsar's policy. He ordered all his officers in the field to collect rebel papers, which they did,[64] but forbade, of course, his subjects to read them. Even to mention the rebel propaganda was considered a crime: for having said, erroneously or on purpose, that a seditious letter had been found in Kurmysh, a peasant was sentenced to have half of his tongue cut out.[65] Informed that Petr Sheremetev had corresponded with the rebels, Alexis complimented him on his military prowess, but warned him that writing to bandits was not seemly for boyars and officers of the tsar.[66] The general purpose is clear: Alexis deliberately aimed at a clear-cut line between rebellion and loyalty, the better to suppress the former.

The same line was pursued in foreign affairs. Receiving in November 1670 colonel Nicolas von Staden, bearer of Swedish proposals for an alliance, tsar Alexis instructed him to demand from his principals that "the gazetteers be punished who are printing [on Swedish territory] unseemly pieces about the tsar, ex-patriarch Nikon and Stenka Razin."[67]

To understand the aspects of the rebellion which have just been described, one needed a really good knowledge of the language and a still better one of Muscovite society. That is why these features have been overlooked by witnesses from Western Europe. They draw a picture in black and white, where exciting tales of massacre and tortures conceal the off-stage talks and, more generally, the deeper mutual understanding that underlies conflict between the two sides in any civil war. The finer details are usually blurred (Fabritius being a welcome exception) under a thick layer of commonplace explanations.

More surprisingly, because revolting non-Russians must have been conspicuous, none of the authors even mentions the Chuvash, Mari, Mordva, Tatars, Bashkirs, who, according to Michael Khodarkovsky, "constituted by far the most numerous and active part of the movement."[68] But that was true only later, in the Middle Volga stage of the rebellion, which the Dutchmen who had escaped

---

64 E. g., Iourii Dolgorukii writes, in December 1670: "In the current year 179 [1670/71], on different months and days, in different battles, these rebellious letters have been taken from rebellious Cossacks. And these letters we, thy slaves, have sent to you (Krest'ianskaia voina, II/1, n° 323, p. 407).
65 Ibidem, II/1, n° 390, p. 507; January 1671.
66 Ibidem, III, n° 100, p. 109, § 2; June 1671.
67 D. N. Bantysh-Kamenskii, Obzor vneshnih snoshenii Rossii po 1800 god. IV. Prussiia, Frantsiia i Shvetsiia, Moscow, 1902, p. 190-191. Later on, the Russian officials broached the same subject with the Swedish envoy (Krest'ianskaia voina, III, n° 236, p. 285-286; December 1672).
68 Khodarkovsky, "The Stepan Razin Uprising", p. 14.

from Astrakhan did not witness, since they were at that time living precariously as slaves in Persia. When Fabritius came back to Russia, the civil war was over.[69] As to Martius, living in Moscow he was far from the field, and perhaps his Russian sources did not insist much on this aspect of the rebellion.

WHO TOOK PART IN RAZIN'S REVOLT?

Can foreign observers be trusted on the nature of the Razin movement, on its social make-up and, more specifically, on its beginnings? Struys has only witnessed the few days in Astrakhan before the storm of the city walls, and escaped before the town was taken. But Fabritius, as we have seen, has faced Razin's men at Chernyi Yar, and lived among them for a few weeks, at first hidden and in Cossack disguise, then in the open, when he "was taken by everyone for a Cossack", to the point of taking his share of the booty. He has met Razin twice, and the rebel chief apparently felt towards him something like benevolence, perhaps because of his skills as an artillery expert.[70]

Painful memories combining with class prejudice, the general picture given of the rebels is utterly unfavourable: "riff-raff", "Rabble", "gemeine Kanalie", "scoundrels", "leichfertiges Gesindel", "ruffians", "curs", etc. But at closer inspection of the texts, one finds that these pejoratives are not distributed at random. The Cossacks are described as "killing everyone and looting everything that came their way",[71] whereas musketeers and other soldiers who defected to Razin, or revolting townsmen, are called "rascally" or "treacherous *streltsy*", "irresponsible scoundrels", "bloodthirsty curs", and the like. This might be a calque from Russian documents, e. g. a report, dated December 1670, by Avvakum Ievlev, governor of Efremov: "blackguardly Cossacks" (*vorovskie kazaki*) and "Tambov traitors" (*izmenniki tambovtsy*).[72] In any case, it fits the facts, since the Cossacks were clearly the initiators of the movement; it also draws the line between independent "march warriors", who only broke vague pledges of good conduct, and

---

69 Fabritius, p. 90-91.
70 "I too had to take my share, but what my feelings were God only knows" (ibidem, p. 87). He first met Razin when the latter came back from his Caspian campaign (p. 79: "Stenka came with us to Astrakhan"), then when appealing to Razin for his countryman Butler (p. 86-87; "artillery expert": footnote 2).
71 Ibidem, p. 70.
72 Krest'ianskaia voina, IV, n° 24, p. 25; vorovskoi or the corresponding verb vorovat' mean any kind of breach of accepted patterns of behaviour, from forging a testimonial in a law suit to kindling civil war.

regular forces, or town and country people, who had solemnly sworn on the Cross allegiance and loyalty to the tsar.

EVERYONE A COSSACK?

A remarkable feature of the 1670 rebellion, as compared to previous (Bolotnikov, 1606) or subsequent (Pugachev, 1773) movements, is its fidelity to Cossack institutions. There is no attempt at setting up a mock court or an imitation of Muscovite official bureaus: *krug* assemblies and elected atamans are supposed to meet the needs for organization in rebel-controlled areas, since all rebels became, at least in theory, members of the Cossack Host. How deep did this overall identification with the Cossacks go?

When it came to storm Astrakhan, writes Fabritius, "the Cossacks had persuaded the common workers, or *jariski* (as they are called), to attack the quarter where the Dutch sailors had been posted". As this was the most dangerous place, because "these Dutchmen knew how to handle guns", it appears that Cossacks used the poorest townsmen as cannon-fodder.[73] This statement is, to some extent, substantiated by the only published letter written by a rebel ataman to another: "And I'd be glad to come back to you, in Kuzmodem'iansk, only the populace (*chern'*) won't let me go, because here, on the Vetluga, they are shouting for help 'The lords are coming!', and wherever they [the lords] meet the populace, they cut them down."[74] Stenka Razin used the same term, as far as we can judge from the largest message apparently issued directly from him:

This is Stepan Timofeevich adressing all the *populace*. Who will serve God and the tsar and the Great [Cossack] Host and Stepan Timofeevich, I have sent out Cossacks, and together with them you should exterminate traitors and exterminate bloodsuckers out of the community. And as soon as my Cossacks start to fight in earnest, you go to them for advice, and [you,] all indentured and banished men, join the army and my Cossacks.[75]

Although perhaps without derogatory intention, the Cossack leaders freely use the word *chern'*, usually applied to the lower classes of Muscovite society, from the country and the towns. It should be remembered, moreover, that Cossacks were no

---

73 Fabritius, p. 84; jariski (more correctly iaryshki) are unskilled labourers employed on ships, in docks, mills, etc.
74 Krest'ianskaia voina, II/1, n° 169, p. 202; October 1670. The author is Il'iushka [Il'ia] Ivanov, mentioned above.
75 Ibidem, II/1, n° 53, p. 65; before September 14th, 1670.

peasants, and even despised husbandry.[76] At best, they protected peasants in a patronizing way, and admitted them in their midst, but I doubt very much that they ever considered them as their equals. Fabritius, who should know, speaks ironically of these newly hatched Cossacks: "So kamen die neiwe Kosacken, dehnen das Rantson von den armen Leuten versprochen wahr",[77] and so does, when caught in November 1670, Semen Tatarinov: "In the small fort of Lysogorsk, there are [...] six peasants or peasants' sons, who pretend deceitfully to be Don Cossack atamans."[78]

It appears that, whatever their appeal to the rural and urban population, the Cossacks clearly remained the undisputed leaders and organizers of the movement, as well as the nucleus and spearhead of the rebel army. The strategy, such as it was, and the aims of the rebellion were decided by Cossacks alone.[79]

WHAT WERE THE COSSACKS FIGHTING FOR?

The foreign narratives give a somewhat contradictory answer to this question. Being born robbers (or so Fabritius and Struys imply), their first objective obviously was to plunder, a view fully confirmed by the evidence. Russian sources even give some idea of the nature and size of the booty. In 1671, a group of Tatar mirzas [nobles] from Temnikov complain that their houses and estates have been looted: Umriak Dosaev's damages are estimated at 500 roubles in cattle and cloth, not counting the currency and the land deeds; Alei Dolatkozin, whose list of stolen goods resembles very much a milliner's catalogue, evaluates his losses at 217 roubles in furs, bonnets, jewels, cloth and linen; his weapons, pewter and copper ustensils, etc. are also listed as stolen; Aidar son of Tokhtar, prince Shihmamet, declares a round price of 600 roubles, plus the land deeds.[80] The *deti boiarskie* [petty nobles] from a village in Kozlov district petition the tsar in March 1671 for help: many of their "men" (serfs or slaves?) have been killed, their houses

---

76 M. Khodarkovsky, "The Stepan Razin Uprising", p. 4: "In the second half of the 17th century when some of the recent arrivals to the Don attempted to farm, the Cossack administration ordered them beaten and plundered, and instructed them to go back where they came from if they wanted to farm".

77 Zapiski, p. 26.

78 Krest'ianskaia voina, II/1, n° 223, p. 272; about Semen Tatarinov, see footnote 65.

79 I have expressed more or less similar views in: A. Berelowitch, "Une jacquerie moderne : la révolte de Pougatchev, 17 septembre 1773-15 septembre 1774", La Revue russe, n° 27 (2005), p. 37-59, 48-51.

80 Krest'ianskaia voina, IV, n° 41, 43, 44, p. 36-39.

ransacked and burnt, their wives, children and cattle taken away.[81] A minor clerk (*pod'iachii*) in Temnikov explains that his wife has been tortured by rebels to reveal where the money and crockery were.[82] In comparison, the Astrakhan booty seems negligible: when it was divided, since "there were several thousand men more than they had reckoned [...] each fellow's share did not exceed ten Reichstaler."[83]

But even exceptionally bold robbers do not usually try to reform society, to take over entire countries, or even big towns,[84] and neither do they, as a rule, aspire to the throne. According to foreign witnesses, Razin and his followers did just that, almost from the beginning of the second campaign. "Here [in Panshin, May 1670] he began straightaway quietly gathering the common people around him, giving them money, and promises of great riches if they would be loyal to him and help to exterminate the treacherous boyars."[85] A speech in the same vein, allegedly delivered by Razin to his army after Chernyi Yar, and probably pieced together by Struys, incriminates the "tyrants" who had so long oppressed them, and proclaims that he will relieve "his children" of their burden.[86] The most convincing materials are given by the *Relation*, when depicting the final stage of the rebellion:

Every where he promised Liberty, and a redemption from the Yoak (so he call'd it) of the Bojars or Nobles, which he said were the oppressors of the Country [...] He, Stenko, was come by order of the Great Czar to put to death all the Bojars, Nobles, Senators, and other great ones [...] as Enemies and Traytors of their Countrey [...] [Razin's followers] were commonly put upon the Rack, and being examined, what they designed in this Rebellion, they answered, that they intended for *Mosco*, and would have the lives of the Nobles, and other great ones.[87]

---

81   Ibidem, IV, n° 52, p. 46.
82   Ibidem, IV, n° 26, p. 26; December 1670.
83   Fabritius, p. 87. The Reichstaler contained 25.98 g. in pure silver, the rouble represented about 43.7 g.
84   With the exception of Sir Francis Drake, but he was a privateer, tacitly approved by the Queen. Cf. the epigraph by Simone Weil.
85   Fabritius, p. 79-80.
86   The French translator obviously took a hand, too: "Enfin mes amis vous voilà libres, & ce que vous venez de faire vous affranchit du joug des tyrans. Ce joug est si lourd & si rude, qu'il y a de quoi s'étonner que vous l'ayez porté si long-temps sans en être accablés. Mais le juste Ciel ne l'a pas permis ; il a été touché de vos larmes, il vous envoie un Libérateur [...] qui vous aimera comme ses enfants & n'aura pour vous qu'un cœur de père" (Struys, p. 176).
87   Relation, p. 97, 98, 99.

This last statement is amply borne out by numerous Russian questioning minutes. Although the majority of foreign witnesses describe Razin as an autocrat[88] and assume that he coveted the throne, none has more forcefully expressed Razin's ambitions than Martius. After comparing him to Catilina and Wilhelm Grumbach,[89] he writes: "This was a harbinger of terrible trouble to come, since things had come to such a point, that it seemed there was no way to end the disorders but either the tsar, or Razin should die."[90] This fits Michael Khodarkovsky's conclusions perfectly: "Both Razin and the tsar insisted on representing the 'true' tsar and the 'true' church. They were not competing for different conceptions of sovereignty and social values, instead they were vying for the same source of legitimacy."[91]

If true, the fact is indeed puzzling, no more so, but just as much as, the illiterate Pugachev undertaking to impersonate the late emperor Peter III. Struys himself, the most fanciful of our witnesses, is at a loss to explain how what might have been a somewhat protracted plundering foray had grown into a full-fledged crusade, or *jacquerie*, against social order at large. The best he has to offer is that "*Radzin* being arrived to this Pitch of Greatness was so puffed up as if he had conquered all the Empire."[92] Whatever the origin of this alleged bid for the throne was, it would imply that Razin, with utmost cynicism, first involved the Cossacks, then the "common people" in his selfish plans, under the guise of fighting the boyars. Indeed, some foreign observers (Struys, Martius) depict Razin as a cold-blooded murderer, maddened by ambition, and ascribe to him alone the origin and making of the whole rebellion. This does not fit, somehow, the impression gained from the available shreds of evidence, but on that point, as on many others, our

---

88 "L'on ne connoissoit Radzin que par le respect qu'on lui portoit, nul ne l'approchant qu'à genoux & le visage contre terre. Et quand on lui parloit, il étoit défendu de le nommer autrement que Batské, c'est-à-dire Père dans leur langue" (Struys, p. 173).

89 Inostrannye izvestia, p. 45, § 14-15*. W. Grumbach (1503-1567), a noble from Franconia, who tried to fight for prince Johann Friedrich the Younger against Augustus, Elector of Saxony.

90 Inostrannye izvestia, p. 46, § 20 : "Hoc vero demum futuri motus maxime terribilis classicum erat, rebus quippe jam in eum locus deductis, ut tumultus, cujus componendi ratio non appareret, vel Tzaris, vel Razini exitio terminaretur." The "harbinger" was Razin's claim that ex-patriarch Nikon, actually detained in Kirillo-Belozerskii monastery, and tsar Alexis' son Alexis († 17 January, 1670) were among his followers.

91 M. Khodarkovsky, "The Stepan Razin Uprising", p. 17.

92 Struys, p. 192; but the French version goes further : "L'Armée de Radzin croissant tous les jours, il en devint si fier qu'il [...] ne douta pas qu'il ne fût bientôt sur le trône de ses voisins. [...] Dans cet esprit d'orgueil secret, il se mit en tête de s'égaler aux Têtes Couronnées." (Struys, p. 179-180).

documentation is silent or ambiguous, and Razin's personality and ultimate plans remain an enigma.

A better way to approach the problem would be perhaps to start from the other end, from the general state of mind in the Lower and Middle Volga region on the eve of the rebellion. As far as we can see, it was a tangle of resentment, hatred, hope, thirst for justice, perhaps nostalgic yearning for the roving life of yore.[93] All this Razin, being a natural leader, perceived and crystallized, becoming at the same time the focus of and the driving force behind the movement. But we mustn't expect ever to determine how far he intended to use the rebellion for his own ends.

As for the Cossacks, they were no Robin Hoods, and probably did not think so much of redressing the wrongs of Muscovite society as of taking the place of the nobles – a surmise put forward by Aleksandr Stanislavskii regarding the Cossacks of the 1610-1620's. Some of them were given estates during the first half of 17th century, but what they really wanted was to become government-appointed beneficiaries of a regular "feeding" income (*kormlenie* or *pristavstvo*), thereby supplanting the nobles as exploiters of the peasantry.[94] If Cossack society was as primitive as Nikitin says,[95] it is no wonder they closely resemble the Bacaudæ, who "seem to have had no social programme other than an exchange of roles between themselves and the landlords."[96] In so doing, they were certainly extending their usual scope of operation, they didn't transform it. The faithless "common people" is another matter altogether.

WHO JOINED THE COSSACKS?

If asked "who joined the Cossacks?", the Western witnesses answer, as one man, "the common people": "In the Space of 5 days after he had got the *Astrachan* Fleet, his Army was raised from 16 000 to 27 000 Men, being a mixt of Pesants, Slaves, Tatars and *Cossacks*, and men of restless minds from all Parts"[97]; "at this time [1669] Stenka had an opportunity of […] becoming acquainted with the mood of the common people."[98]

---

93 Cf. Boris Chichlo, "Sibérie: mode de colonisation – mode de production", Sibérie II. Questions sibériennes, Paris, 1999, p. 95-118.
94 A. A. Stanislavskii, Grazhdanskaia voina v Rossii v XVII v., Moscow, 1990.
95 See footnote 23.
96 Moses E. Finley, The Ancient Economy, London, 1973, p. 89.
97 Struys, p. 191.
98 Fabritius, p. 79

This is not absolutely accurate. Not all peasants joined the movement,[99] and many who joined did so under duress. Conversely, there was a sizable number of recruits from privileged or semi-privileged classes. In June 1671, the governor of Kadom reports that "city dwellers of Korsun *of all conditions* have mutinied",[100] but there are more specific indications in the documents. To give but a few examples: petty noblemen from Kurmysh, Penza, Kozelsk, Voronezh up to a colonel of Circassians in Ostrogozhsk,[101] a public writer on oath from Lyskovo, a dragoman from Astrakhan, a priest turned ataman who plundered goods to the amount of 2070 roubles and kidnapped a six-month old baby.[102]

Nevertheless, on the whole, Struys, Fabritius, Martius are right: this was a popular revolt, joined by sundry renegades from the upper strata of Muscovite society.

WHY JOIN THE COSSACKS?

Nearly all Western documents mention the deep-rooted, long-suppressed hatred felt by the lower classes for the boyars (which sometimes means not only the highest rank in Russian Court, but other noblemen as well), officials, officers in the army, landlords – their masters and oppressors – as the main cause of the revolt: the common soldiers "at once decided that this was the chance they had been waiting for so long [...] The murderers [who] had so long thirsted after blood" (Fabritius). "Hence a rumour spread that boyars, against whom there was implacable hatred, were trying to take all the power in their hands [...] So that in the year 1667 Stephan Razin aroused minds already prepared for rebellion."[103]

Neither is it contradicted by the events, reflected in Russian as well as in foreign sources. In the Astrakhan region, the rebels

---

99 For instance, Ivan Ovchinnik, a serf of Kharlam Ofrosinov, being asked by rebels to give them bread and sheep, called them "good-for-nothing tramps", and was killed accordingly (Krest'ianskaia voina, III, n° 118, p. 128; July 1671).
100 Ibidem, III, n° 95, p. 101.
101 Ibidem, II/1, n° 126, p. 151, captured in October 1670 (Kurmysh); II/1, n° 155, p. 183-184, hanged on October 21st, 1670 (Penza); III, n° 30, p. 38 (Kozelsk); III, n° 178, p. 199 (Voronezh); II/2, n° 29, p. 38-39, n° 32, p. 41-42 (Ostrogozhsk).
102 Ibidem, II/1, n° 161, p. 190-192; October 1671 (public writer); III, n° 298, p. 375-376 (dragoman); IV, n° 38, p. 34 (ataman-priest).
103 Martius, § 13, p. 43-44: "Inde rumor spargebatur, Bojaros, erga quos implacabile odium erat, omnem potestatem ad se trahere conatos [...] Inde anno MDCLXVII Stephanus Ratzinus præparatos rebellioni animos commovit."

committed many inhuman acts, and murthered the Gentry, who were fain to betake themselves to *Astrachan* disguised in Slaves Apparel. The Pesantry who indeed are very tyrannically dealt throughout all the Emperours Dominions, here found an occasion to be revenged of their Liege-Lords, and to show their Man-hood brought the Heads of their Lords and threw them at the feet of a Provost or Executioner thereto ordained, who gave them a reward for their Pains.[104]

In the Middle Volga, "all the Russian Countrey-men living in this Tract, and belonging to Muscovian Lords, rose up against their Governors killing and hanging them."[105] Revolted peasants themselves confessed afterwards, when put to the question, not the murders, but the looting of noblemen's estates.[106]

Of course, official epistles, full of ponderously compounded platitudes, did very little or nothing to pacify the countryside. They could not compete with the brief, fiery messages of the atamans, which said nothing much, only "Be standfast, stand together with us", but had all the glamour of novelty and excitement. Indeed, the attraction of the Cossack way of life, one could almost say "the Cossack style", was a significant factor of the rebellion. Fabritius mentions a Polish nobleman who took him under his protection in Razin's camp: "Wonsofski [...] had been captured a year before by the Cossacks and in the meantime had come to like loose life [das lose Lehben]"; he now commanded a company.[107] At an earlier date, Russian sources describe in detail an attempt to recruit new Cossacks, thus providing us with a short-range view of Cossack seduction.

On July 20, 1666, four non-commissioned officers and an orderly of colonel Kravkov's regiment gave evidence:

a man, rank and condition unknown, met us at the ferry, and started to invite us to come to the Don Cossacks' settlements. He called himself ataman, and [promised us] 10 roubles, and a horse with saddle, and a sabre apiece. On the morrow, he said, there would be 1700 Cossacks at the Serpukhov ferry. Once on the ferry, he told a girl 'Were you younger and prettier, we'd have use of you in our Cossack *krug*.

---

104 Struys, p. 191-192.
105 Relation, p. 98.
106 Krest'ianskaia voina, II/1, n° 110, p. 129, October 1670, and n° 218, p. 267, November 1670.
107 Fabritius, p. 83.

All this is confirmed by different witnesses, and the man's identity was soon revealed: he was page (*zhilets*) Emel'ian Vasil'ev Naryshkin,[108] but he stoutly denied, not very plausibly, all he was charged with, including his none too tactful attempt at flirting and unsuccessful borrowing of tobacco.[109] He was probably sent by Vasilii Us. The total catch of the tsar's forces in July-August 1666 includes another noble, a run-away slave from Moscow, five peasants "led astray" by an ex-serf of Moscow noble (*moskovskii dvorianin*) prince Ivan Golitsyn, and three domestic slaves (*dvorovye liudi*) of his fellow courtier, Stepan Fedorov Zhdanov.[110]

THE SPARK THEORY

Considering the events in retrospect, it seems that the turning point of the whole rebellion was the defection of prince L'vov's army at Chernyi Yar. Had they stood fast against Razin, the Astrakhan revolt would probably not have occurred, or at least would have remained a local affair. Only moments before the defection, they had "unanimously shouted: 'Yes, we will give our lives for His Majesty the Tsar, and will fight to the last drop of our blood.'"[111] How are we to explain this volte-face? It is true that, according to Struys, in Astrakhan, even before the Chernyi Yar defeat, musketeers "who had not in a long time received Pay [...] found now occasion to grow mutinous".[112] The French translation is even more explicit, with a clear hint at desertion.[113] Other soldiers, in the course of the rebellion, showed their unwillingness to fight by abandoning their posts.[114] To join the rebellion was quite a

---

108 Judging by his subaltern, but nevertheless Court rank, he could belong to the Naryshkin family, who gave tsar Alexis his second wife in February 1671. He isn't to be found in the Naryshkin genealogy (A. B. Lobanov-Rostovskii, Russkaia rodoslovnaia kniga, 2nd ed., II, Saint-Petersburg, 1898, p. 5-18, 463-464), but then he wasn't the sort of man the tsar's in-laws would readily boast about.
109 Krest'ianskaia voina, I, n° 22, p.49-52.
110 Ibidem, I, n° 28, 29, 30, 32, p. 57-58, 60-61, 64. Ivan Golitsyn, *Boiarskaia kniga 1658 goda*, N. M. Rogozhin, V. A. Kadik, ed. (Moscow, 2004), p. 147; Stepan Zhdanov, ibidem, p. 189; the 1658 Court register remained in use up to 1676 (ibidem, p. 5).
111 Fabritius, p. 81.
112 Struys, p. 191.
113 "Les soldats [...] disoient hautement qu'ils alloient quitter le service, qu'il n'y avoit plus de quoi les payer, & que l'argent qu'on leur destinoit étant employé à d'autres usages, il n'étoit pas juste qu'ils continuassent à vouloir exposer leurs vies dont on avoit si peu de soin." (Struys, p. 179).
114 Struys, p. 191.

different, and a much more dangerous, prospect. To understand what happened, we must examine the evidence more closely, after attempting to deal with two popular misconceptions of revolt, all the more pervasive because they are only half-consciously professed.

One of them is of the materialistic persuasion: if enough grievances accumulate within a given social group, it will result, almost mechanically, in an insurrection, because the tension becomes unbearable. A pyrotechnic variation of the same compares popular anger to a powder magazine, which needs only a spark to explode. The other, walrasian, rationalistic approach imagines a potential rebel weighing carefully the pros and cons, and deciding for rebellion if and when the former tip the scale. Both interpretations have something in common: they exclude altogether psychology, and freedom of choice as well.

Revolts, however, do not work that way. The powder keg may be full to the brim, but it still needs, to blow up, a specific operation of what, for want of a better word, we shall call the psyche. Actually, the whole human being is involved; an overwhelming rush of feeling brings every faculty to its highest, feverish level.[115] Since rebellion implies the infringement of sacrosanct Order (see above), this trance-like moment, sometimes bordering on madness, is essential in order to overcome fear. This is not to deny that the final outcome is the result of a long chain of factors, and that rational arguments are still remembered by the subject.[116] But they are suspended at the last second: loyalty, fear of punishment, resentment of past injustice, class-hatred, solidarity and twenty others alternate in his mind at lightning speed, until the leap into the unknown, which is the mark of genuine revolt. In a very short timespan, the decision is made: taking chances, assuming risks, and resolving, if need be, to sacrifice one's life ("They swore with life and limb to stand together"[117] – a stereotype of all rebellions and conspiracies). For death is not only, in such a case, a perfectly realistic expectation, it is also the ultimate proof of commitment.

This timeless quality of revolt has been remarkably expressed by Michel Foucault, speaking about the 1979 revolution in Iran: "Uprisings do belong to history, but somehow they elude it. The gesture of a man alone, a group, a minority or a whole people rising up and saying '*I will obey no more*' [...] can't be reduced

---

115 Which accounts for the extraordinary staunchness of Razin's followers, e. g. the "Nun in Man's habit [who] had commanded Seven thousand Men" (Relation, p. 99).
116 Cf. Jacques Lacan, "Le temps logique et l'assertion de certitude anticipée", id., *Écrits* (Paris, 1966), p. 197-213, 204 : "Le temps de comprendre et le moment de conclure."
117 Fabritius, p. 81.

to anything else [...] because the rising man is ultimately beyond explanation."[118] If we adopt this view, it follows that no investigation, no matter how ingenuous or thorough, can really come within reach of the crucial moment of the "turn-around" – the actual meaning of *rivolta*.

Stepping far beyond the borders of a historian's professional caution, I would like to adduce from 1968 France an example which seems relevant to me, although much less risky for the actors than in the case of revolting Muscovite soldiers. Some day around May 15th, shop stewards of Renault factory in Boulogne-Billancourt had refused access to our group of students and professors. After a while, one of them, partly relenting and talking across the closed gate, told us how the strike had started:

There was no meeting, no instructions from the trade-unions, no leaflets, no talks, nothing. Suddenly, in one of the workshops, a machine-tool stopped, still without a word being spoken. Then another, and another. The workshop went silent, and so did, very soon, the whole plant. The old ones remembered: it had been exactly the same in June 1936.

This "trance" theory was vigorously criticized by several members of the conference. I readily admit that not all rebellions start this way, Swiss peasantry of the 17th century, as studied by Andreas Suter, being a convincing counter-example. I dare say a sentence like "Now, now, the times begin to alter, it will be our turn next to Lord it, you villains" seems to show that plans for rebellion had been laid days, perhaps weeks before.[119] I'll try nevertheless to uphold my surmise, and for lack of direct proof, to find at least some corroboration: does the "trance" hypothesis help to explain the "particulars of the Rebellion" and some features of its representation? Even if it yields only faint, mostly negative, indications, the matter is perhaps worth a try.

---

118 Cf. Michel Foucault, "Inutile de se soulever ?", in *Le Monde*, No. 10661, 1979, p. 1-2: "Les soulèvements appartiennent à l'histoire. Mais, par un certain côté, ils lui échappent. Le mouvement par lequel un homme seul, un groupe, une minorité, ou un peuple tout entier dit : 'Je n'obéis plus' et jette à la face d'un pouvoir qu'il estime injuste le risque de sa vie – ce mouvement me paraît irréductible [...] parce que l'homme qui se lève est finalement sans explication : il faut un arrachement qui interrompt le fil de l'histoire et ses longues chaînes de raisons, pour qu'un homme puisse 'réellement' préférer le risque de sa vie à la certitude d'avoir à obéir". My thanks go to Jean-Christian Dumont, who quoted this text in his *Servus: Rome et l'esclavage sous la République* (Paris, Rome, 1987) and made it available to me.

119 But Struys wrote that in 1676 and may have slightly revised his memories, and anyway there is a quite a gap between conceiving a plan and carrying it out.

The Blind Spot

Let us look anew at Fabritius' narrative; it is the closest we can get to the state of mind of soldiers in the process of turning rebels. Rather oddly, he writes: "The common soldiers [...] put their heads together and *at once* decided that this was the chance for which they had been waiting so long, and with all their flags and drums they ran over to the enemy." He seems to imply that the "villains" had already resolved to defect ("the chance for which they had been waiting so long"), and Struys states it ("no doubt they had reached an understanding beforehand"). In that case, what need did they have to hold a council? Besides, if talks had been going on for some time, the officers would probably have heard, or at the very least would have had an inkling of it. What seems more likely is that the final decision was made on the spot, in only a few minutes or even less ("at once").

From Tsaritsyn to Samara *via* Astrakhan, Razin's rebellion spreads very fast and meets with continuous success. This is consistent with what we know of other rebellions. For some, as yet unclear, reasons, the initial, trance-like outbreak of revolt is electrifying, and therefore tremendously contagious. Its epicenter may be, and often has been, compared to a conflagration, which raises instantly the social temperature to an incredible heat level. It is perceived at once, even from far away, and expands, when the conditions are favourable, with terrifying speed, which makes it well-nigh irresistible. Although remote from the Middle Volga theater, Martius understands perfectly that after the taking of Astrakhan swift movement is Razin's chief asset: "Neither did Razin dally, as a man would, who wished to achieve his aims through rapidity, and endeavoured by every means and plan available to expand his power as broadly as possible."[120]

At Cherny Yar, after the paroxysm, tension slackens: "They began kissing and embracing one another."[121] But not all effusions of the rebels' souls are dictated by brotherly love: "Murder began at once."[122] Why? Of course, human nature being what it is, the worst is hardly surprising. Still, on other occasions, Razin's men, despite their general motto of "exterminating the boyars", have made prisoners members of the ruling class, and the slaughtering of useful gunners could not be really justified by security issues. The explanation by revenge, favoured by Fabritius and Struys, is not completely convincing either. Revenge is individual and cold-blooded. Here we deal with a collective, murderous orgy, such as the one

---

120 Martius, p. 46, § 19 : "Nec cunctatus est Razinus, ut qui rebus suis festinatione consultum cuperet, et omni ope atque consilio niteretur, ut potentiam suam quam latissime propagaret."
121 Fabritius, p. 81.
122 Ibidem.

vividly described by Giovanni Verga in an imaginary Sicilian town: as soon as the town-dwellers see the flag on the city-hall which means "freedom", they start massacring the *galantuomi* (notables) in a truly ghastly way.[123] This is not such a rare occurrence, and fits e. g. the description of the September 1789 massacres in Paris. Faithful as historians try to be to their pledge of objectivity, it is sometimes difficult for them not to sympathize with the victims and enemies of such a rebellion.

In that respect, the adjective "bloodthirsty", often used by Fabritius when referring to the rebels, is perfectly apposite, in its most literal sense, even to the meaning of "maniacal". Besides, bloodthirstiness is apparently contagious. After obtaining the surrender of Astrakhan rebels, Ivan Miloslavskii was relieved by Iakov Nikitich Odoevskii: the latter

had got so used to torturing people that he could not eat in the morning until he had been to the place of torture and had people beaten with the knout, burned, and put on the rack. But then he could eat and drink enough for three. [...] I had to remain behind and live for nearly a year among these barbarians.[124]

Here, the "trance" theory may be helpful: Foucault has stressed the nobler side of revolt, but there is also a dark side to it. Not only political order, but customary (for Muscovites: Christian) norms of behaviour are thrown overboard as well. *Mordlust* is given free rein, since it is supposed to be harnessed in a good cause. More than that, it is possible that murder in this context is used as a language. Jan Dhondt, analyzing the political crisis in XIIth century Flanders, concludes that the choice of a prince "is, actually, a very primitive way, the most primitive imaginable, to influence the general policy of the earldom."[125] Murder could represent an even more primitive level of political thinking: actions speak louder than words.

Fabritius must have felt, if not clearly understood, the outburst of passion, akin to lunacy, he witnessed at Chernyi Yar. If so, he did not think it was worth mentioning. For all the remaining observers, domestic and foreign alike, the central moment of revolt remains a blind spot, like an invisible black hole in the course of events. Unable to justify such a tremendous eruption of violence by its causes, they build up a heap of wrong reasons to conceal the gap: ignorance, stupidity,

---

123 G. Verga (1840-1922), "Libertà", *Cavalleria rusticana e altre novelle* (Milano, 1994), p. 233-240. I thank Andrea Graziosi, who suggested this parallel to me.
124 Fabritius, p. 92.
125 J. Dhondt, *"'Ordres' ou 'puissances'", Estates or Powers. Essays in the Parliamentary history of Southern Netherlands from the XIIth to the XVIIIth Century*, Heule, 1977, p. 25-49.

intemperance, cowardness, xenophobia, greediness, cruelty or general wickedness is what made the soldiers forfeit their pledge of loyalty. Once again, Martius is nearer the mark: he blames the rebellion on the instability, a characteristic feature, he says, of Russians and Cossacks.[126]

One more question remains: given the hopelessly fierce attachment to routine common to all human beings, are not these temporary fits of madness which we call "revolts" the only way to achieve even moderate changes in the fabric of society – the fool's bauble taking the place of "the spirits of the past [...] battle slogans, and costumes in order to present this new scene"?[127] But that is another story.

---

126 Martius, p. 40, § g: "Mirum tamen videri potest, quid sit, quod cum gens ista præter ingenitam erga Tzares suos venerationem, servituti assueta sit, tam subito ad seditionem concitandum impelli possit, nisi cognitum esset, ingenia ejus populi esse mutabilis [...]" [One might wonder how it is that a people who, through their inborn veneration for their Tsars, are used to servitude, could be so suddenly impelled to raise sedition, were it not known that they are of a changeable character]. § h: The Cossacks "genus hominum est instabile, et natura sua quietis impatiens, ac prædandi cupidum" ["are an unsettled race of men, who are by nature impatient of quiet and eager for plunder"].
127 Karl Marx, *The Eighteenth Brumaire of Louis Bonaparte* (1852).

Insurgents as Diplomates: Cross-border Alliances and their Representations

Framing the Borderland: The Image of the Ukrainian Revolt and Hetman Bohdan Khmel'nyts'kyi in Foreign Travel Accounts

FRANK SYSYN

In many ways, Ukraine burst upon the European scene in the mid-seventeenth century. The great revolt of 1648 brought the largest European state, the Polish-Lithuanian Commonwealth, to near disintegration. By the 1650s events in the Cossack capital of Chyhyryn were being closely followed from Stockholm to Constantinople. European newspapers avidly printed reports on the Hetman Bohdan Khmel'nyts'kyi and his armies. Yet for much of Europe "the Ukraine" or the borderland of the Polish state was still a terra incognita about which statesmen and reading publics needed basic information and about which many uncertainties reigned.

Within a few years of the revolt, the thirst for information was answered by publications on Ukraine and accounts of the revolt.[1] The first texts were issued by

---

1 On the accounts of the revolt and reactions to it, see Volodymyr Sichyns'kyi, *Chuzhyntsi pro Ukraïnu* (Kyiv, 1993) (from the 2nd expanded Prague edition of 1942), and the English translation *Ukraine in Foreign Comments and Descriptions from the VIth to XXth Century* (New York, 1953); Mykhailo Hrushevsky, *History of Ukraine-Rus'*, vol. 8, trans. Marta Olynyk, ed. Frank E. Sysyn and Myroslav Iurkevich (Edmonton and Toronto, 2002), See especially Note 5: Sources for the Khmelnytsky Era and its Historical Tradition, 670-676, 678-683; Joel Raba, *Between Remembrance and Denial: The Fate of Jews in the Polish Commonwealth during the Mid-Seventeenth Century as Shown in Contemporary Writings and Historical Research* (Boulder, Colo., 1995); Dmytro Nalyvaiko, "Zakhidnoevropeis'ki istoryko-literaturni dzherela pro vyzvol'nu viinu ukraïns'koho narodu 1648-1654 rr.", *Ukraïns'kyi istorychnyi zhurnal* (1969) 8: 137-144, 9: 137-143, 10: 134-145, 11: 131-136, 12: 128-132, (1970) 1: 138-140; id., *Kozats'ka khrystyians'ka respublika: Zaporiz'ka Sich u zakhidnoievropeis'kykh pam'iatkakh* (Kyiv, 1992) and id.,

the government's supporters, in some cases for internal consumption, but also, especially when victories were proclaimed, to rally support abroad. Latin functioned both as the language of the Commonwealth's learned elite and the international medium for the various cultures of the Commonwealth and the reading public abroad. By 1652, the Silesian Lutheran (for a time an Anti-Trinitarian) Joachim Pastorius published his Latin-language history of the revolt in Gdańsk (Danzig).[2] Like many of his Anti-Trinitarian confreres, he had resided in the Ukrainian lands in the 1630s and 1640s, but had fled the revolt. He was later to be rewarded for his historical writing by the post of court historian in Warsaw (he converted to Catholicism in 1658). Other writers had a targeted public in mind. Another refugee from Volhynia, the Jewish Talmudist and kabbalist Nathan Hannover, issued his account of Jewish suffering and martyrdom during the revolt in Hebrew in Venice in 1653 not only as a commemoration but as a way to collect funds for other refugees.[3]

The first work to take advantage of the need for accurate information on Ukraine in Europe originated from the pen of a French engineer and servitor of the Polish king. In 1651, Guillaume de Beauplan published his *Description* in Rouen, with subsequent editions appearing in 1660 and 1661.[4] His perceptive account of Ukraine and the Cossacks, which was translated in full or in part into Latin, Dutch, Spanish, and English by the early eighteenth century, long served as the source for subsequent writing on the revolt. His maps published in Gdańsk provided the basic information on geography, mapping Ukraine for the European world. Indeed another French eyewitness to events in Ukraine, Pierre Chevalier, was to borrow

---

Ochyma zakhodu. Retseptsiia Ukraïny v Zakhidnii Ievropi XI-XVIII st. (Kyiv, 1998). On the earliest accounts of Kyiv and the surrounding area, see Hennadii Boriak, "Inozemni dzherela pro Kyïv XIII-seredyny XVII st.", *Ukraïns'kyi istorychnyi zhurnal* 25 , 12 (1981): 31-41.

2   J. Pastorius, *Bellum Scythico-Cosacicum seu de coniuratione Tartarorum, Cosacorum et plebis Russicae contra Regnum Poloniae* (Gdańsk, 1652).

3   On the influence of Hannover's work, see Gershon Bacon, "'The House of Hannover': *Gezeirot Tah* in Modern Jewish Historical Writing", *Jewish History* 17, 2 [special issue "*Gezeirot T"ah*: Jews, Cossacks, Poles and Peasants in 1648 Ukraine"] (2003): 179-206.

4   The second expanded edition has been reprinted: Guillaume le Vasseur de Beauplan, *Description d'Ukrainie qui sont plusieurs provinces du Royaume Pologne* (Rouen, 1660, reprint Kyiv and Cambridge, Ma., 1990). For a modern English translation and discussion of the various editions and translations, see id., *A Description of Ukraine*, trans. and ed. Andrew B. Pernal and Dennis F. Essar [with introduction and notes] (Cambridge, Ma., 1993).

liberally from Beauplan in his influential account of the revolt.[5] The seventeenth-century English translator of Chevalier's work, Edward Brown, eloquently expressed the reasons for the European public's interest in the area and the revolt in his preface, which also declared that the English as a maritime nation should have a particular fascination with the Cossacks:

> Although *Ukraine* be one of the most remote regions of *Europe*, and the *Cossackian* name very Modern; yet hath that Countrey been of late the Stage of *Glorious Actions*, and the Inhabitants have acquitted themselves with as great Valour in *Martial Affairs*, as any Nation whatsoever; so that this, and other Motives have made me earnest to put this account of it into English, where it cannot be otherwise then acceptable, since the Description of a Countrey little written of, and the achievments of a daring People, must needs be grateful to those, who of all the World, are the most curious and inquisitive, and the greatest lovers of bold Attempts and Bravery. The Ocean is our delight, and our Engagements upon the Seas, have rendred us considerable to the World. The *Cossacks* do in some measure imitate us, who took their rise from their Victories upon the *Euxine*, and setled themselves by incountring the *Tartars* in those Desert Plains, which do so far resemble the Sea [...] The Actions of *Kmielniski*, General of the *Cossacks*, are very remarkable; and how he raised himself to that greatness, so as to be feared by a Nation [Poland-F.S.], which neither the Power of *Christendom*, nor the *Turks* could shake.

Professional historians and men of letters joined in writing about the Ukrainian revolt, not least because Europe of the 1640s and 1650s was shaken by a whole series of upheavals and civil wars. It was this coincidence that would lead the twentieth-century scholar Roger Bigelow Merriman to pen his famous monograph *Six Contemporaneous Revolutions*, in many ways the pathfinder for the discussions on the Crisis of the Seventeenth Century that gripped the historical profession in the 1950s and 1960s.[6] Yet while Merriman did not examine the Ukrainian revolt against the Polish-Lithuanian state, his seventeenth-century predecessor Maiolino Bisaccioni devoted his second longest essay to this subject in his monograph on

---

5 Pierre Chevalier, *Histoire de la guerre des Cosaques contre Pologne avec un dicours de leur origine, païs, mœurs, gouvernement & religion. Et un autre des Tatars Précopites* (Paris, 1663). His work was published in 1672 in an English translation, without mentioning his authorship, by Edward Brown, *A Discourse of the Original, Countrey, Manners, Government and Religion of the Cossacks, With another of the Perecopian Tartars. And the History of the Wars of the Cossacks against Poland* (London, 1672). A Ukrainian translation of the French original appeared as P'ier Sheval'ie, *Istoriia viiny kozakiv proty Pol' shchi* (Kyiv, 1960).

6 Roger Bigelow Merriman, *Six Contemporaneous Revolutions* (Oxford, 1938).

civil wars first published in Venice in 1653.[7] Many Italian historians followed Bisaccioni's lead in writing on the revolt.[8]

ALBERTO VIMINA AND PAUL OF ALEPPO

The accounts and histories of the revolt have often been mined for the information that they provide on the events described. They have also been looked at as sources for European opinion, not least because as the Ukrainian national movement of the nineteenth and twentieth century sought affirmation of its goals and postulates, its proponents could find them in the foreign accounts. Less attention has been paid to the accounts as sources for the cultural world view and political agendas of the writers'. In this paper attention will focus on two of the most important accounts of seventeenth-century Ukraine and the revolt by Michele Bianchi (Alberto Vimina) and Paul of Aleppo. Both were written by clergymen who travelled to Ukraine on missions and personally met with Hetman Bohdan Khmel'nyts'kyi. One came from the pen of a European, while the other is one of the accounts that came from outside Europe, demonstrating the interest the revolt engendered in the Middle East. The comparison of a non-European, albeit Christian account, with a European account affords us with the opportunity to put in sharper focus the importance of the traveller and his world view and formation in shaping the representation of the revolt.[9]

The first mission was undertaken in June, 1650 by the Venetian clergyman Michele Bianchi (1603-1667), who is better known by the pseudonym Alberto

---

[7] Maiolino Bisaccioni, "Historia delle guerre civili di Polonia", in *Historia delle guerre civili di questi ultimi questi tempi*, 2nd ed. (Venice, 1654), 272-397. On Bisaccioni's sources, see Lorenzo Pompeo, "Maiolino Bissacioni i jego polskie źródla", *Barok* 5, 2 (1998): 109-125.

[8] On Venetian historians, see Teresa Chynczewska Hennel, "Najjaśniejsza o Najjaśniejszej. Rzeczpospolita w weneckiej literaturze historycznej XVII wieku", *Odrodzenie i Reformacja w Polsce* 50 (2006): 191-203.

[9] A comparison for Muscovy, using the writing of Paul of Aleppo and Adam Olearius, has been undertaken by Charles J. Halperin, "In the Eye of the Beholder: Two Views of Seventeenth-Century Muscovy", *Russian History* 24, 4 (Winter 1997): 409-23. Many of his comments on Paul of Aleppo's description of Muscovy apply to his account of Ukraine. There has yet to be a full comparison of Paul of Aleppo's descriptions of Muscovy and Ukraine. On the general question of use of travel accounts in describing Muscovy, see Charles J. Halperin "Sixteenth-Century Foreign Travel Accounts to Muscovy: A Methodological Excursus", *Sixteenth-Century Journal* 6 (1975): 89-111.

Vimina. Born into a burgher family in Belluno, Bianchi had adopted a pseudonym and absented himself from the Italian peninsula because of threats to his person. Finding refuge in Warsaw with the papal nuncio, Giovanni de Torres, Vimina gained protection from the Crown grand chancellor, Jerzy Ossoliński, who stood for the policy of accommodation with the Cossacks. Undertaken by Vimina at the behest of the Venetian resident in Vienna, Nicolo Sagredo, the mission sought to convince the hetman to provide his marine forces to come to the aid of Venice in the war it was fighting against the Turks. This mission, like a subsequent endeavor the Venetians undertook in 1652 to win the Cossacks to their side, did not meet with success, not least because it presumed that the rebels and the Polish-Lithuanian government could come to terms and join the struggle together. Nevertheless, Vimina was to have a long diplomatic career, embarking on missions to Muscovy and Sweden, before he returned to Veneto and a sinecure in Pieve d'Alpago.[10]

Like all Venetian emissaries Vimina had to write reports that fully described the lands that he visited. His report of the 1650 trip was included in part in his history of the civil war in Poland that was published posthumously in 1671. That volume also contained accounts of his missions to Muscovy and Sweden.[11] Vimina's book was largely overlooked by historians of the Khmel'nyts'kyi Uprising, but the account of his 1650 mission found in manuscript form in Ferrara by G. Ferraro and published in Reggio nell'Emilia in 1890 has had considerable impact in historical writing, in part in studies of the mission and the correspondence it engendered.[12]

---

10 On Russian-Venetian relations, see Philip Longworth, "Russian-Venetian Relations in the Reign of Tsar Aleksey Mikhailovich", *Slavonic and East European Review* 64, 3 (July 1986): 380-400.

11 For sections of the account on the Cossacks, see Vimina, *Historia delle guerre civili di Polonia* (Venice, 1671), 7-9.

12 G. Ferraro, *Relazione dell'origine e dei costumi dei Cosacchi fatta l'anno 1656 da Alberto Vimina ambaciatatore dell Republicca di Venezia* (Reggio nell'Emilia, 1890) on the basis of a manuscript in a Ferrara library (page numbers for Vimina refer to this publication). The text was also published on the basis of a manuscript in a Vatican library: L.Alpago Novello, "La relazione intorno ai Cosacchi di Alberto Vimina", *Archivo storico di Belluno, Feltre e Cadore* 6 (1934): 581-586. A third manuscript copy in Venice was used as the basis for the Ukrainian translation by Kseniia Konstantynenko: Al'berto Vimina, "Relatsiia pro pokhodzhennia ta zvychaï kozakiv", trans. Kseniia Konstantynenko, *Kyïvs'ka starovyna* (1999) 5: 69. For the correspondence, see M. Korduba, "Venets'ke posol'stvo do Khmel'nyts'koho (1650)", *Zapysky Naukovogo Tovarystva im. Shevchenka* (1907): 51-89; and D. Caccamo, "Alberto Vimina in Ucraine e nelle 'parti settentrionali'", *Europa Orientalis* 5 (1986): 223-283, 265-283. See also P. Pirling, "Al'berto Vimina:

The account appeared in Russian, Polish and Ukrainian translations, and in fragments in English.[13] It has been valued for its description of everyday life in Ukraine and for the first-hand observations on Hetman Khmel'nyts'kyi.[14]

The account of the second clergyman, the archdeacon Paul of Aleppo (Ar. Bulos al-Halabiyy) (1627-1670), son of Patriarch Makarios III of Antioch (Ibn al-Za'im), has had an even greater resonance in modern historiography. In part this greater resonance can be explained because it is the account of an insider, an Orthodox clergyman, who was at the same time an outsider from the Middle East. As such, it combines privileged access to native informants and intimate knowledge of cultural and religious traditions with the curiosity of a traveller from afar who wished to explain what he saw to readers in the Eastern Mediterranean world.

Paul accompanied Makarios on a journey for alms to shore up the tottering Antiochian patriarchate for which the primary patrons were the Orthodox rulers of Wallachia and Moldavia, and above all the sole independent Orthodox ruler, the Muscovite tsar. Trips by Eastern patriarchs over the preceding seventy-five years to

---

Snosheniia Venetsii s Ukrainoiu i Moskvoiu 1650-1663", *Russkaia starina* 109 (January 1902): 57-70.

13 See the Russian translation by N. Molchanovskii, "Donesenie venetsiantsa Al'berto Vimina o kozakakh i B. Khmel'nitskom (1656 g.)", *Kievskaia starina* 19, 1 (1900): 63-75. For the Polish translation, see Teresa Chynczewska-Hennel and Piotr Salwa, "Alberta Viminy Relacja o pochodzeniu i zwyczajach Kozaków", *Odrodzenie i Reformacja w Polsce* 30 (1985): 207-222. For the Ukrainian translation, see Al'berto Vimina, "Relatsiia pro pokhodzhennia ta zvychaï kozakiv", trans. Konstantynenko , *Kyïvs'ka starovyna* (1999) 5: 64-69. For fragments in Ukrainian see Sichyns'kyi, Chuzhyntsi pro Ukraïnu, 77-81 and in English see Ukraine in Foreign Comments, 89-92. English translations in this text were made by MyroslavYurkevich and this author from a corrected version of the Ferrara text supplied by Teresa Chynczewska-Hennel. We are grateful to Olga Pugliese of the University of Toronto for her careful correction of our text.

14 On Vimina and his writings, see Kseniia Konstantynenko, "'Relatsiia pro pokhodzhennia ta zvychaï kozakiv' Al'berto Viminy: Istoriia, uiavy, real'nist'", *Kyïvs'ka starovyna* 5 (1999) 5: 50-64; Riccardo Picchio, "E.M. Manoleso, A. Vimina e la Polonia", in *Venezia e la Polonia nei secoli dal XVII al XIX*, ed. Luigi Cini (Venice and Rome, 1968), 121-132; Lorenzo Pompeo, "Maiolino Bissacioni i Alberto Vimina: Dwóch historiografów wloskich wobec problemu kozaków w 1648", *Warszawskie Zeszyty Ukrainoznawcze* 4-5 (1997): 494-504; Teresa Chynczewska-Hennel, "Venetian Plans towards Poland and Ukraine in the Middle of the Seventeenth Century. Girolamo Cavazza and Alberto Vimina", in *Tentorium Honorum: Essays Presented to Frank E. Sysyn on His Sixtieth Birthday*, ed. Olga Andriewsky, Zenon E. Kohut, Serhii Plokhy and Larry Wolff (Edmonton and Toronto, 2010), also published in *Journal of Ukrainian Studies* 34 (2009): 105-116.

Moscow through Ukraine had given them considerable experience in Ukrainian and Cossack affairs. Makarios's predecessor, Joakeim V, had confirmed the statute of the Lviv brotherhood in 1586. The Jerusalem Patriarch Theophanes III had restored an Orthodox hierarchy under the protection of the Cossack Hetman Petro Konashevych Sahaidachnyi in 1621, and his successor Paisios had blessed Khmel'nyts'kyi as a prince at Christmas 1648. Makarios's trip was the first to occur after the Cossack Hetmanate had taken shape, and Khmel'nyts'kyi had sworn allegiance to the Muscovite tsar in 1654. Passing through Ukraine in 1654 on his way to Moscow and in 1656 on his road back, Paul penned one of the most ample descriptions of Ukraine at a turning point of its history.

A speaker of Greek who picked up some Romanian in his travels, Paul is thought by some scholars to have learned Slavic vernacular during his long stay in Muscovy from 1654 to 1656, though this would not have given him direct access to his interlocutors in Slavic during his first stay in Ukraine.[15] Written as a diary at the behest of a colleague deacon Gabriel, but with an authorial voice that also addressed a purported reader, the immense Arabic text records the trip from Syria to Moscow and back from 1652 to 1659.[16] The trip included two visits to Ukraine in 1654 and 1656, and Paul was present at meetings with Hetman Khmel'nyts'kyi.[17]

---

15 Hilary Kilpatrick maintains that in addition to these languages, he knew Slavonic ("Between Ibn Baūa and al-Īahāwī: Arabic Travel Accounts of the Early Ottoman Period", *Middle Eastern Literatures* 11, 2 (August 2008): 239). The assertion does not correspond with Paul's own statement at the beginning of his stay in Muscovy that the members of the delegation spoke in Greek or Turkish to an interpreter they had hired in Moldavia, who translated into "Russian [Rus']", "for one and the same is the language of the Cossacks [Ukrainians], and of the Servians [Serbians], of the Bulgarians, and of the Muscovites." Cf. Paul of Aleppo, *The Travels of Macarius: Patriarch of Antioch*, 2 vols., trans. F.C. Belfour (London, 1836), 1: 261. Presumably he referred to Church Slavic, a sacred language in Moldavia and in the Orthodox Slavic countries. Maria Kowalska says that he knew Greek and had freely learned Russian by 1656, the end of his stay in Muscovy (*Ukraina w połowie XVII wieku w relacji arabskiego podróżnika Pawła, syna Makarego z Aleppo*, trans. M. Kowalska (Warsaw, 1985), 7). Charles Halperin rejects this view, though he does muse that his meetings with boyars were unlikely to have occurred through a translator (In the Eye of the Beholder, 413). Although there is no direct evidence of his use of Turkish in Ukraine, the language was one known in Khmel'nyts'kyi's chancellery.

16 Kilpatrick's article situates Paul's account in the Arabic travel literature of the age.

17 The diary survives only in copies, not all of which are complete. The Arabic text was published in a partial English translation from one of the extant manuscripts in the 1830s (*The Travels of Macarius*) and in Russian translations in the late nineteenth century. The

Ukraine as the Classical Borderland

Selection of a Western Christian and an Eastern Christian clergyman corresponds well with the position of Ukraine between West and East.[18] Ukraine was a borderland or a meeting point in many ways. It stood at the point where the vast Eurasian steppe met the forest-steppe zone. Largely Slavic agriculturalists came into contact with Turkic pastoralists. Spheres of influence of the Ottomans, the Muscovites, the Lithuanians, and the Poles overlapped. Frontier societies such as the Crimean Khanate and the Zaporozhian Cossacks carried on raids and trade over a porous, sparsely inhabited zone across which the Tatars hunted for slaves and the Cossacks embarked in their small boats to take booty as far away as the environs of Constantinople. Western Christians and Eastern Christians, including the Uniates who emerged in 1596 when some Orthodox bishops and faithful were accepted into the Church of Rome, dwelled together in a land with an ancient Armenian community and a fast growing Jewish population. The second serfdom and a

---

most authoritative Russian translation is *Puteshestvie Antiokhiiskogo patriarkha Makariia v Rossiiu v polovine XVII veka, opisannoe ego synom, arkhidiakonom Pavlom Aleppskim*, trans. G. Murkos, 5 pts. (Moscow, 1896-1900, reprint Moscow, 2005). The sections on Ukraine have been reprinted as *Puteshesvtie Antiokhiiskogo patriarkha Makariia na Ukrainu v seredine 17 veka* (Kyiv, 1997). A 20th-century edition of most of the Arabic text as well as a partial French translation appeared as "Voyage du patriarche Macaire d'Antioch: Texte Arabe et traduction française", trans. B. Radu, *Patrologia Orientalis* 22, 1 (1930): 3-199; *ibid.* 24, 4 (1933): 443-604; *ibid.* 26, 5 (1949): 603-717; and a Polish one in Kowalska, Ukraina w połowie XVII wieku [translated from the Arabic]; the Ukrainian translations are from the Russian texts: Pavlo Khalebs'kyi, *Kraïna kozakiv: Z podorozhnikh notatok*, comp. M. Riabyi, trans. M. Slyvyns'kyi (Kyiv, 1995) and *Ukraïna-zemlia kozakiv*, comp. and trans. M. Riabyi (Kyiv, 2008). Unless otherwise noted, the English translations of Paul's writings used here are from Belfour's English translation, with supplementary identifications in brackets. Belfour's translations are not always satisfactory. Citations are also given to English translations of Hrushevsky's renderings in Ukrainian of the Murkos edition in Mykhailo Hrushevsky, *History of Ukraine-Rus'*, vol. 9, book 2, part 1, trans. Marta Olynyk, ed. Serhii Plokhy, Frank E. Sysyn and Myroslav Iurkevich (Edmonton and Toronto, 2008), chp. 9. The Polish translation is especially valuable because of the translator's understanding of the material and provision of explanatory notes. For fuller information on the editions, translations and literature on Paul of Aleppo, see Halperin, In the Eye of the Beholder, 411.

18 On Ukraine's intermediary situtation in this period, see Ihor Ševčenko, *Ukraine between East and West: Essays on Cultural History to the Early Eighteenth Century*, 2nd rev. edn. (Edmonton-Toronto, 2009).

society of estates were taking hold in a military frontier that had earlier enjoyed greater equality guaranteed by the brotherhood of arms.[19] The mix of civilizations, social norms, and political systems made Ukraine both familiar and exotic to the surrounding societies. The dissonances in this mix were the flash points for an enduring revolt and an involvement of much of Europe and the Middle East in an uprising launched by a few hundred Cossacks from the sich or stronghold beyond the Rapids of the Dnipro River.

Generally states and courts prevailed in the information and legitimation wars waged with the rebels, especially if the rebels did not belong to established elites. In the main, the Polish-Lithuanian government did as well, employing fear of a bloody uprising of the lower orders and the solidarity of Catholic Europe, above all of the papacy, against schismatic rebels as arguments for securing favor and even assistance. Still the paralysis in the Commonwealth in the early phase of the revolt brought on by the death of the king and the enormous successes of the rebels in the first months undermined the Commonwealth's cause. Other perceptions of the Polish-Lithuanian state also worked to weaken the state's case. The Republic was known for its cavalier treatment of monarchs, and the proponents of absolutism and the power of kings had ample reason to be critical of the Republic.[20] At the same time, most commentators saw the harsh serfdom of the Polish state and the overweening power of the nobility as virtually enslaving the populace and having goaded the peasants into rebellion.[21] In addition, the perceived privileged position

---

19 On military borderlands and revolts, see Yves-Marie Bercé, *Revolt and Revolution in Early Modern Europe: An Essay on the History of Political Violence*, trans. J. Bergin (Manchester, 1987), 130-134, 156-163.

20 Janusz Tazbir, "W oczach obcych," in *Rzeczpospolita i świat: Studia z dziejów kultury XVII wieku*, ed. id. (Wrocław, Warsaw, Cracow, Gdańsk, 1971), 175.

21 For Chevalier's discussion that the peasants were treated like slaves and that one should not wonder why peasant disturbances were so frequent, see *Discourse*, 20-21, *Istoriia*, 45-46. Beauplan, A Description of Ukraine, 15, discussed the ill-treatment of the peasantry as a cause of the revolt in the following manner: "Thus, if it happens that these wretched peasants fall into the bondage of evil lords, they are in a more deplorable state than convicts sentenced to the galleys. It is this slavery which goads many of them to take flight, the more courageous of them fleeing to Zaporozhe, which is an area on the Borystenses to which the Cossacks retreat. After having dwelt there for some time and having been to sea, they are considered to be Zaporozhian Cossacks. Because of such flights, the numbers of the Cossack ranks swell enormously, as is shown with sufficient evidence by the present revolt, in which the Cossacks, having defeated the Poles, rose some 200,000 strong and made themselves masters of an area more than 120 leagues long and sixty wide." (French original: *Description d'Ukrainie*, 8)

of Jews in the Polish-Lithuanian state, including their rights to administer Christian subjects, was viewed as unacceptable in Christian Europe and as having driven the populace to revolt.[22]

The rebels' search for a hearing was also aided by the renown of the revolt's organizing force, the Cossacks. The origin and nature of this phenomenon of the Slavic-Turkic borderland had been discussed by Polish historians of the sixteenth century. They dwelt on issues such as whether the Cossacks were merely a group of outliers of society or whether they represented a particular people or nation.[23] Their discussions were picked up by Western and Central European commentators of the late sixteenth and early seventeenth century who had come to see certain legitimacy for Cossacks as a social group or even a nation.[24] As the revolt made Ukraine the Cossack land in popular imagination, commentators more frequently dealt with the Cossacks as either a military force or the totality of the Ruthenians of the Ukrainian territories. Most important was that from the late sixteenth century when the Emperor Rudolf sent a delegation to the Zaporozhian Cossacks, they had received recognition as a subject of international diplomacy.[25] Indeed the Muscovite state and the Ottoman Empire had dealt with the Ukrainian Cossacks as early as the mid-sixteenth century. This prehistory of the Cossacks in international affairs and as a military-naval force that shook Ottoman control of the Black Sea meant that the Cossacks were not an unknown quantity in international affairs in 1648. In addition, the role of the Cossacks as defenders of the Orthodox faith from the early seventeenth century and the rebels' espousal of the Orthodox cause made the Khmel'nyts'kyi Uprising correspond to the most commonly accepted and

---

22 For Chevalier's discussion of the Jewish leaseholders' severity and cruelty as a cause of the revolt, see *Discourse*, 21, *Istoriia*, 46. The Jewish issue was one of the few about which even Polish Catholic apologists admitted fault on the government's side. See Frank E. Sysyn, "A Curse on Both Their Houses: Catholic Attitudes towards Jews in Father Ruszel's *Fawor Niebieski*", in *Israel and the Nations: Essays Presented in Honor of Shmuel Ettinger* (Jerusalem, 1987), ix-xxiv.

23 On the earliest accounts about the Cossacks, see Marshall Poe, "The Zaporozhian Cossacks in Western Print to 1600", *Harvard Ukrainian Studies* 19 (1995): 531-547.

24 "Nations" might be presumed to have certain rights in the early modern world, including as Khmel'nyts'kyi was to argue the right to resist slavery or tyranny. See Frank E. Sysyn, "The Political Worlds of Bohdan Khmel'nyts'kyi", *Palaeoslavica* 10, 2 (2002): 203-205.

25 On the mission of Erich Lassota in 1594, see the German original *Tagebuch des Erich Lassota von Steblau*, ed. Reinhold Schottin (Halle, 1866) and the English translation, L. Wynar and O. Subtelny, eds., *Habsburgs and Zaporozhian Cossacks: The Diary of Erich von Lassota von Steblau* (Boulder, Co., 1975).

legitimizing explanation of revolts of the period, a religious war.[26] The anti-Catholic nature of the revolt meant that Orthodox powers had a certain sympathy for the revolt, even though this sympathy did not always outweigh their fear of social disorder. Protestants could also see the revolt as undermining the Counter-Reformation, and by the 1650s Sweden and Transylvania could conceive of the Cossack Hetmanate as a component of a Protestant coalition.

MYTHICAL UKRAINE

The great revolt occurred at the time that two of the major myths about Ukraine that were to endure for centuries took shape. This was also the period that the myth of Muscovy as a tyranny/depotism flourished as did that of Poland as a paradise for nobles and a purgatory for peasants and later as an anarchic polity.[27] As Nancy Shields Kollmann has pointed out, Ukraine in contrast was the subject of two positive myths.[28] The first was that Ukraine was a land of unbelievable abundance. This myth had its origin in fifteenth and sixteenth-century Polish writings.[29] Some of that abundance was seen as associated with game and fish, but more important was the image of Ukraine as a virtual Eden, in which grain and produce grew with almost no toil on the part of its inhabitants. The second myth represented Ukraine as a land in which the people cherished liberty. Though its inhabitants might seem

---

26 See Serhii Plokhy, *The Cossacks and Religion in Early Modern Ukraine* (Oxford, 2001); and Frank E. Sysyn, "Orthodoxy and Revolt: The Role of Religion in the Seventeenth-Century Ukrainian Uprising against the Polish-Lithuanian Commonwealth", in *Religion and the Early Modern State: Views from China, Russia, and the West*, ed. James D. Tracy and Marguerite Ragnow (Cambridge, 2004), 154–84.

27 On Muscovy as a tyranny or despotism, see Marshall T. Poe, '*A People Born to Slavery*': *Russia in Early Modern European Ethnography, 1476-1748* (Ithaca, NY and London, 2000). On foreign accounts of the Commonwealth, see Tazbir, W oczach obcych, 170-196. On Poland's treatment of peasants, see Beauplan's comments: "In short, since they must give their masters what the latter choose to ask, it is no wonder that these wretches never accumulate anything, being subjected, as they are, to such harsh circumstances. However, that is still not all, for the lords have absolute power over not only their possessions, but also their lives, so great is the liberty of the Polish nobles (who live as if they were in paradise, and the peasants in purgatory)." (A Description of Ukraine, 14-15; Description d'Ukrainie, 7-8)

28 Nancy Shields Kollmann, "The Deceitful Gaze: Ukraine through the Eyes of Foreign Travelers", in Tentorium Honorum, 293-301.

29 See P. Borek, *Szlakami dawnej Ukrainy. Studia staropolskie* (Cracow, 2002), 15-45.

rude and simple, they were credited with native wit and a striving for freedom. In this way, the revolt could often be conceived as embodying this drive for freedom. As Beauplan put it: "They greatly value their liberty, and would not want to live without it. That is why the Cossacks, when they consider themselves to be kept under too tight a rein, are so inclined to revolt and rebel against the lords of their country."[30]

While our two travellers were not the authors of works that formed the seventeenth-century myths (as did the works of Beauplan and Chevalier), their writings were in accord with these views.[31] The pervasiveness of the account of Ukraine as a land of unparalleled fertility lends credence to assumptions that the newly ploughed black earth and the wildlife of the Dnipro basin were the sources of an abundance of produce and game in comparison to long farmed areas of Central and Western Europe or the more arid lands of the Middle East. The account of the Venetian Vimina could be seen as part of the Western and Central European visions that saw Ukraine as a type of Arcadia in the abundance of its bounty, the limited effort required in working the land, and the simplicity of its folk, though certainly not in its peaceful nature. He assures his superiors that grain needed no cultivation and that dairy products, meat, and fish were no less abundant than grain.[32] He regales the reader with visions of wild asparagus superior to that of the environs of Rome and Naples. But Vimina was a careful observer who commented on the lack of enclosed gardens and cultivation of vines. These observations coincide with his

---

30 A Description of Ukraine, 13; Description d'Ukrainie, 6.

31 On the fertility of the land, see Beauplan, A Description of Ukraine, 12: "The fertile land produces grain in such abundance that often they do not know what to do with it" (Description d'Ukrainie, 5).

32 Vimina writes in his report: "The part of the land called Zaporizhia is so fertile that it can not only compare with the most cultivated areas of Europe but also satisfy the voracity of the most avid farmer.
This land is called *Ukraina,* that is, borders; its fertility is sustained by the abundance of grain that one sees growing uncultivated here and there, sprouting from seeds that the reapers and the wind have shaken to the ground, which are called *padalica* in the Ruthenian language and would be rendered as 'fallen grain' (*caduto*) in ours. Sometimes this grain is harvested, at other times it is neglected, there being such an abundant harvest gathered from the sowing as to make the peasants negligent of the effort required to avail themselves of the gifts bestowed by a generous soil. I would have found it difficult to believe these things had I not seen them with my own eyes, observing that the land yields sheaves so large and laden with grain that in many regions one could not obtain their equivalent despite careful cultivation [...]. Dairy products, meat, and fish are no less abundant there than grain, whether because of the great number of pastures or the abundance of ponds." Relazione, 9, 10.

vision of a populus that did not devote itself to arduous cultivation of the soil. His further comments on the Cossacks' dedication to growing cabbages and cucumbers and conserving them in brine in the German manner give his relation a ring of authenticity.[33]

In contrast to Vimina's rather limited factual account, that of Paul of Aleppo reveals a wonder at the abundance that rings closer to the medieval Arabic accounts of distant and exotic lands. His much more extensive description tells us more of husbandry and cultivation techniques so that he does not see the people as lacking in industry, but his account of plenty seconds Vimina's.[34] Certainly when he describes fowl that lay eggs in the forest that are not collected because of their great numbers he seems to corroborate Vimina's discussion of attitudes in harvesting grain. Still, Paul seems at times to exhibit naiveté in his praise of Ukrainian abundance. He comments on the various types of pigs that breed three times a year.[35] His amazement on the fertility of nature crosses over to his description of the numerous children of the land and the ability to raise army after army despite the great losses in war, so much that he speculates on the pregnancy cycles of the womenfolk before attributing the population growth to universal early marriage of

---

33 Vimina asserts: "Besides all the opulence already described, the bounty of the earth provides the inhabitants with unappreciated delicacies and an abundance of asparagus so large that I believe it can be compared with that most cultivated in Verona. It is very tasty and not bitter, unlike the wild variety with very thin stalks that is gathered in the countryside around Rome and Naples. I wondered at this, and at first sight I thought that they might be broom; in order to satisfy my curiosity I tried them many times, and the excessive quantity consumed then gave me a distaste for asparagus. Onions and garlic also grow wild; I tasted the former, which seemed very sweet to me. One does not see, however, in a country so fertile, any enclosed fruit orchards or gardens of unusual vegetables, melons, artichokes, or celery, except in the vicinity of Kyiv; all the Cossacks' attention is fixed on a single goal –to obtain a harvest of cabbage that they eat raw, or shredded and preserved with salt, as practiced in Germany. Moreover, they sow large quantities of cucumbers, which they also season in brine and eat with bread; they also serve them as a condiment with meat and fish. There are no vineyards, not because it is believed that the soil is unsuitable but because the inhabitants do not bother to plant and cultivate them, as is done in Austria and other regions where winter is very harsh, or perhaps because they are negligent farmers." (Relazione, 11).

34 Paul, The Travels of Macarius, 1: 193-195. Paul also describes well-tended orchards in the vicinity of Kyiv. Hrushevsky, History of Ukraine-Rus', vol. 9, book 2, part 1: 396.

35 Paul, The Travels of Macarius, 1: 193-195; Hrushevsky, History of Ukraine-Rus', vol. 9, book 2, part 1: 386-387.

young girls.[36] Seventeenth-century Ukrainian sources reaffirmed Paul's observation on the vast number of children with the phrase "Fertile is the Cossack Mother", and subsequent historians have speculated that the demographic boom explained the tensions and revolutionary nature of early modern Ukraine.[37] Yet while both Vimina and Paul reflect a similar reality in their description of abundance and fertility, occasional divergences in their accounts may have reflected their differing standards and expectations, as well as their differing goals. It is only in this way that we can square Vimina's comments on the lack of orchards apart from around Kyiv with Paul's comments on arriving at Lysianka that "In the evening we came to a large town, fortified as usual, and with waters and gardens: for this blessed country is like a pomegranate orchard, so great is its beauty and cultivation."[38]

The perspectives of a Venetian and a Middle Eastern clergyman not only affirm the myth of Ukrainian abundance, they also agree on Ukraine as a land of liberty, albeit with differing definitions of what the essence of that liberty was. For Alberto Vimina the Cossacks belonged to a band of lands stretching from Muscovy to the Tatars, and to a degree including Sweden, in which barbarity (*barbarie*), the opposite of civilization (*politia*) reigned.[39] Yet in these distant lands he was aware that the political systems varied. The representative of the Serenissima Republic of Venice was able to appreciate republican structures whether of the noble-controlled Commonwealth or the Cossack Host. While the Commonwealth's nobles disdained the Cossacks, the Venetian clergyman who sought their help was more egalitarian in his world view. Despite their rough and coarse appearance, he found them not lacking in lively ingenuity.[40] Vimina turned to classical models and references to define the form of government of the Cossacks. He saw them as a hodgepodge of uncultivated people from which a Senate was formed, and he praised the Senate's manner of deliberation. Comparing their polity to Sparta (a positive model of government in seventeenth-century terms), he described the Cossacks as only having liberty to boast of since they cared not for the amassing of wealth.[41] Seeing

---

36 Paul, The Travels of Macarius 1: 179; Hrushevsky, History of Ukraine-Rus', vol. 9, book 2, part 1: 380.

37 On the demographic explosion as a cause of revolt, with Ukraine a prime case, see Jack Goldstone, *Revolution and Rebellion in the Early Modern World* (Berkeley, 1991), 344.

38 Paul, The Travels of Macarius, 1: 193

39 Caccamo, Alberto Vimina in Ucraine, 264-265.

40 Here too one can find an echo of Beauplan (A Description of Ukraine, p13; Description d'Ukrainie, 6).

41 "On the basis of these observations one can readily deduce the customs of these people, who have never left their country except to engage in warfare, a school that generally produces men who are worldly, but coarse and rough. By their outward appearance and manners they

merit in this rude republic, Vimina did not however perceive a well developed system of administration and finances within it, a characteristic of more developed lands.[42]

---

appear simple, but they are not stupid or lacking in lively intelligence. This is evident from their conversation and methods of governing. For the history of politics is a complex dance that makes men cut a fine figure at gatherings but disappears at the threshold of government and lays bare their crudeness. From this hodgepodge of uncultivated people a rudimentary senate that assists the general is formed. It should be borne in mind that these people take their hands from the plow and the magistracy in order to apply them to wielding arms. In the Senate they bring matters to fruition; arguing their opinions without ostentation, with the goal of contributing to the public good. And if they find the ideas of others better, they are not embarrassed, nor do they hesitate to abandon their own opinion and embrace the better one. I would therefore say that this republic of the Cossacks might resemble that of Sparta if there were a similar degree of sobriety among them, whereas they can certainly be compared to the Spartans in rigor of training." (Vimina, Relazione, 13-14)

Vimina also writes: "On occasions spent at his table, when glasses were frequently raised, I noted that there was no lack of pleasant and witty conversation. I could quote several witticisms, but, wishing to be brief, I shall recount only one. My servant was at pains to emphasize the grandeur and marvels of the city of Venice, which they were eager to hear about. Having expatiated sufficiently on the location, buildings, and riches, he described the city's great expanse, saying that there were so many alleys that even the residents themselves would get lost. A Cossack replied, 'Oh, do not exalt the city of Venice to me, for I find that the same thing happens to me too in this small room: after sitting for a few hours at this table, I cannot find the door to return home.'" (Relazione, 19)

He asserts: The Cossacks can boast of nothing other than liberty; it seems that they do not prize wealth at all, as they are content with little. This was a teaching articulated but not practiced by Seneca, who, while accumulating treasures, endeavored to stress in his writings that a man does not become rich through the acquisition of riches but through the diminution of greed." (Ibid., 14-15)

42 He maintains: "I believe it would be both interesting and necessary, in order to make a complete report, to say something about the administration, its forces and revenue. I would describe it even in detail if there were any particular order to be discerned in it. I can say, however, that as far as administration is concerned, in the towns mentioned there live certain consuls who adjudicate civil cases and impose light corporal punishment, while matters of importance are reserved to the judgment of the general, and so it appears to me that he is a true despot. The state of the armed forces is revealed by the experience of past campaigns. Who knows the precise number of soldiers that can be gathered? One can say that there are as many soldiers as there are heads, for they all prefer to engage in warfare than to handle a spade. Concerning income I cannot say, observing only that it is

Paul shared with Vimina the conviction that the Cossacks were content with little,[43] though in his almost uniformly positively assessment he saw them as having an excellent financial administration.[44] Here, of course, the difference may be that Vimina saw the Hetmanate at its birth, while Paul observed the Hetmanate five years later. But for Paul the liberty that the revolt had achieved was above all freedom from the accursed Polish servitude, which was envisioned above all as religious bondage. He saw as the Cossacks' great achievement that they, through their revolt, lived in freedom, which for him meant in an Orthodox state and society.

And what a blessed nation it is! What a happy country! This is its greatest merit, that it contains not one inhabitant of any other sect whatever, but is pure, and peopled only with the orthodox, the faithful, and the truly religious. How great is its zeal for purity and holiness of spirit! how clear its principles in the truth of orthodoxy! Blessed be our eyes for what we saw, which we experienced! For this people, from being in captivity and slavery, are now living in mirth and cheerfulness and liberty.[45]

Having charged that the perfidious Poles had poisoned their own king, implicitly justifying the revolt and seconding the voices that saw the Polish elite as anarchic, the Orthodox cleric could exult that the time of Khmel'nyts'kyi was an age of

---

of no great amount or consequence, neither in the public nor the private sphere." (Ibid., 19)

Vimina's use of "true despot" (*vero Despota*) for Khmel'nyts'kyi would seem to conflict with his discussion of the Cossack entity as a republic. It seems that he was reflecting the great power gained by Khmel'nyts'kyi after his victories and not using the term to characterize a political system. *Despota* might better be rendered as master. He may have seen Khmel'nyts'kyi in the tradition of the Italian Renaissance despots.

43 Paul, The Travels of Macarius, 1: 200; Hrushevsky, History of Ukraine-Rus', vol. 9, book 2, part 1: 394.

44 Hrushevsky, History of Ukraine-Rus', vol. 9, book 2, part 1: 381.

45 Paul, The Travels of Macarius, 1: 191. "What a blessed people they are! What a blessed land this is! Its great merit lies in the fact that it has no infidels at all but only pure Orthodox believers, steadfast and pious! Delighted are our eyes with what they have seen, delighted are our ears with what they have heard, and happy are our hearts with the joy and rapture they have experienced. Having once been in bondage, these Cossacks now live in joy, pleasure, and freedom". (Hrushevsky, History of Ukraine-Rus', vol. 9, book 2, part 1: 374)

justice.[46] His concept of justice was not only the right religious order in that he also discussed national and social issues.[47] According to him, the Cossacks had been treated as slaves by the Poles, who had impressed them into arduous tasks, and only after the revolt "those who had laboured and endured all the hardships of the work came into their rightful possession of it".[48] He saw Khmel'nyts'kyi's revolt as releasing the Cossacks from slavery and captivity and the Poles' cruelties.[49]

Paul diverged further from the concept of liberty as referring to Orthodox living in Orthodox states and societies when he contrasted Ukraine with Muscovy in a commentary that, while he may not have been aware of them, fit well in the Western myths of the time. On reaching Ukraine from Muscovy in 1656, he proclaimed

During these two years in Muscovy, a padlock had been set on our hearts, and we were in the extremity of narrowness and compressure of our minds; for in those countries no person can feel any thing of freedom or cheerfulness, unless it be the native population. Any one like ourselves, though he became sovereign of the whole territory, would never cease to have a disturbed mind, and a heart full of anxiety. The country of the Cossacks, on the contrary, was like our own country to us, and its inhabitants were to us boon companions and fellows like ourselves.[50]

---

46 Paul, The Travels of Macarius, 1: 175; Hrushevsky, History of Ukraine-Rus', vol. 9, book 2, part 1: 380.

47 For a nuanced discussion of religious and ethno-national themes in Paul's work, see Charles J. Halperin, "Friend and Foe in Paul of Aleppo's Travels of Patriarch Macarios", *Modern Greek Studies Yearbook* 14/15 (1998/1999): 97-114.

48 Paul, The Travels of Macarius, 1: 182. "obtained all rights and all power over that which had been the object of their labor and their suffering in bondage." (Hrushevsky, History of Ukraine-Rus', vol. 9, book 2, part 1: 382.)

49 Paul, The Travels of Macarius, 1: 172.

50 Paul, The Travels of Macarius, 2: 306-307. "During those two years in Muscovy a lock hung on our hearts, and our minds were constricted and oppressed to the utmost. For in that land no one can feel free or satisfied, except perhaps its native inhabitants. Anyone else, just like us, even were he to become ruler of the whole country, will never cease to be agitated in his spirit and alarmed in his heart. By contrast, the land of the Cossacks was as though it were our own country, and its inhabitants our good friends and people like us:" (Hrushevsky, History of Ukraine-Rus', vol. 9, book 2, part 1: 373-374).

While Paul had written approvingly of the Muscovite state and ruler in the massive sections of his diary on Muscovy,[51] he clearly had been put off by the atmosphere in that Orthodox state and found that of Ukraine more to his liking. His evaluation was formed in the context of foreigners' enforced isolation in Moscow. What he came to, however, may be interpreted as an assumption similar to that of so many Western authors that the Muscovites might be disposed to such a state and society that others, including other Orthodox, found constraining. In Ukraine he had an Orthodox society that he found welcoming and attractive without the pressures and confinement of Muscovy.[52]

THE AUTHORS' MISSIONS AND AUDIENCES

In addition to reflecting the two general myths on Ukraine of the age in his work, each author portrayed Ukraine and the revolt in accordance with his mission and his desire to elicit the appropriate response from his intended reader. Vimina had to square a circle in reconciling the Cossack rebels with the Polish-Lithuanian government in order to obtain both powers´ support in the war against the Ottomans. Hence he had to see the Cossacks as a group worthy to treat with not only by the Venetians, but also by the Polish-Lithuanian authorities. They had come to an uneasy truce with the Cossacks in 1649, when the Crimean khan had been wooed away from the Ukrainian rebels. Therefore Vimina's depiction of the Cossack polity as a rude but militarily powerful entity might be expected. Certainly, he affirmed the wisdom of trying to come to an alliance with the Cossacks when he wrote: "Who knows the precise number of soldiers that can be gathered? One can say that there are as many soldiers as there are heads, for they all prefer to engage in warfare than to handle a spade."[53] For the Venetian authorities he had portrayed the Cossack land as a military republic headed by a powerful general or despot in a wealthy land. His superiors undoubtedly had embarked on their policy because of

---

51 See the discussions of Paul's views in Poe, 'A People Born to Slavery', which curiously does not deal with his comparison of Muscovy and Ukraine.
52 Malte Griesse has suggested that Paul's evaluation should be seen as an indictment of Muscovite treatment of foreigners, a situation of captivity not experienced by the native population. I am thankful to him for posing this possibility. Still, I think the passage that "anyone like us, even though he became sovereign of the whole territory" would still not be able to adjust to Muscovite ways indicate a broader negative evaluation of Muscovy and its inhabitants.
53 Vimina, Relazione, 19.

these assumptions that Vimina had amplified and confirmed. They also had to hope that a way could be found to overcome religious differences.

The concept of the alliance would require Western and Eastern Christians to set aside their divides. Vimina stressed recent progress in bridging differing interpretations of the *Filioque*.[54] His plans could only work if the differences between the churches could be minimized. Therefore, Vimina pointed to a certain indifference of the Cossacks to religion and saw only the clergy as knowledgeable. He maintained: "As for devotions, I have not observed frequent public attendance; they frequent taverns more than churches, making it apparent that the maxims of Romulus are valued here more than those of Numa. They show constancy in maintaining the errors of their schism but are unable to identify them and live mostly according to the faith of their fathers; only their priests know the basic distinctions."[55] Thus, he saw the Cossacks as adepts of Rome's warlike founder and military leader, and not his pious successor Numa Popilius. While he was willing to admit a certain level of learning of the monks in Ukraine, he looked condescendingly on the culture and language of the land. Indeed, his attribution of its Slavonic scriptures to a text associated with Seint Jerome may be seen as part of his view of the superiority of the Western Church.[56] He discussed the religious issues in the revolt from a Catholic point of view, especially those emerging in the heat of the revolt, but the

---

54 "But concerning the procession of the Holy Spirit through the Son and not from the Father, as the Latins believe, they disagree with us, although they cannot say how the schism originated. These errors have already been condemned. The deduction seems clear that the Son did not share the original inspiration with the Father, and since there was a moment's interval between them, there was consequently a difference in degree. But now I understand that when the most recent effort was made by Urban VIII and Władysław IV, the king of Poland, to reunite the churches separated from the Latin church, it was determined that it was all the same whether the Holy Spirit proceeded from the Father by way of the Son, or from the Father and the Son; hence it was acknowledged that the Three Persons were alike in degree, in not having been created, in eternity and equality." (Relazione, 15-16)

55 Ibid., 15.

56 "They have no letters other than vernacular Ruthenian, and few are those who even dedicate themselves to them. Their ritual language is Slavic, into which they have translated the Holy Scripture of Saint Jerome, and they also read the doctrines of the Holy Fathers translated into that language. It is said that their vernacular differs from Slavic as Italian does from Latin. Earlier, only the nobles studied it; hence only a few priests understand it. Nevertheless, some monks, especially those attending the metropolitan, are not ignorant of it. One finds some men of letters who devote all their study to confirming their errors." (Ibid., 12-13)

Catholic priest did not wish to see these as excluding cooperation with the Cossacks.[57]

Paul had set out with his father to find material support for the Orthodox of the Ottoman Empire. He had found that the Orthodox world could now look to a new Orthodox power that had triumphed over the Latin foe. He could also seek to raise his own spirit and the spirit of his flock by seeing in Ukraine a model Orthodox society. These were the aspects of Ukrainian society that Paul emphasized in what is the most comprehensive account of the religious and culture life in mid-seventeenth century Ukraine. In marvelling at what the revolt had wrought and the birth of a new Orthodox power, Paul always put the respect shown to his father the patriarch to the fore in making his judgements.

Paul described a society with a high degree of religious practice and learning. Indeed, he found the rigors of the practice, especially the standing in churches during lengthy services, taxing.[58] In describing the population, he maintained: "We observed in them all a perfect spirit of religion, and abstinence and humility, to the utmost."[59] Paul's account has served as the source for discussions on the high literacy rate in Ukraine, including of women and girls.[60] He maintained that since the liberation of the land by Khmel'nyts'kyi, literacy had increased among the populace. Since Paul undertook his trip four to six years after Vimina, there may

---

57 "Many deny Purgatory, while others profess it, not by means of fire, but as punishment of the senses by other means –an opinion that should not be condemned. They deny particular judgment of the soul, maintaining that there will be neither reward nor punishment until the day of the Last Judgment. For they say that if the body itself has had a part in merit or guilt, having become as it has [after death] foul and insensitive matter, it ought to be denied reward or exempted from punishment, while the soul, because of the consent lent to the flesh, should alone enjoy the glory or suffer the punishment. And there are those who declare that it is necessary to rebaptize the Latins, even though they say that they have not been remiss in substance or form. Recently such confusion has been practiced in the revolts of the Cossacks, who have brought to their baptismal fonts those Catholics who have wished to espouse the error of the Cossack schism. There are even those who believe that transubstantiation does not take place with unleavened bread; hence they call the Latins unleavened heretics" (Ibid., 15-16).

58 Paul, The Travel of Macarius, 1: 186; Hrushevsky, History of Ukraine-Rus', vol. 9, book 2, part 1: 391.

59 Paul, The Travel of Macarius, 1: 186; Hrushevsky, History of Ukraine-Rus', vol. 9, book 2, part 1: 391.

60 Paul, The Travel of Macarius, 1: 164. The translation in Hrushevsky that they "know how to read" appears to be the correct one (Hrushevsky, History of Ukraine-Rus', vol. 9, book 2, part 1: 382). See Kowalska, Ukraina w połowie XVII wieku, 18.

have indeed been a change in Ukraine's religious, intellectual, and cultural life. Paul, who travelled slowly throughout Ukraine and served in numerous church services in dozens of settlements, had more opportunity to observe this aspect of Ukrainian life than Vimina did. Yet it is certain that the standards and expectations of Venice and Ottoman Syria may have differed. Still, in reading Paul's account, which Hrushevsky has called

> a panegyric to a liberated people, which had put its newly won freedom and prosperity, gained at great cost, to such fine use: instead of spending time in leisure and luxury, it curbed its physical needs and devoted everything to cultural weal, as it was then understood, and to the building of new churches, the creation of icons and paintings, the cultivation of church singing, and the development of schools and education,

we must assume, without discounting his extensive evidence, that Paul was predisposed to find this model in the land and society that he praised.[61]

The Eastern patriarchates and the Greek clergy in particular often dreamed of liberation from the Turks and even of the great project, the restoration of the Christian Empire. One can find little of these dreams in Paul's account. Indeed, in recounting the indignities of Polish rule over Ukraine, he even proclaimed:

> And why do I pronounce them accursed? Because they have shewn themselves more debased and wicked than the corrupt worshippers of idols, by their cruel conduct to Christians, thinking to abolish the very name of Orthodox. God perpetuate the Empire of the Turks for ever and ever! for they take their impost, and enter into no account of religion, be their subjects Christians or Nazarines, Jews or Samarians: whereas these accursed Poles were not content with taxes and tithes from the brethren of Christ, though willing to serve them; but, according to the true relation we shall afterwards give of their history, they subjected them to the authority of the enemies of Christ, the tyrannical Jews […] [62]

---

61 Hrushevsky, History of Ukraine-Rus', vol. 9, book 2, part 1: 382.
62 Paul, The Travel of Macarius, 1: 165. "Why do I call them accursed? Because they showed themselves to be more vile and malicious than the evil pagans; they tortured Christians and plotted to destroy the very name of Orthodox. May God preserve the kingdom of the Turks for all eternity, since they take tribute and do not interfere with matters of faith. But these accursed ones were not content to take tribute and a tithe from their brothers in Christ; instead they kept them in bondage and consigned them to the rule of the enemies of Christ, the merciless Jews." (Hrushevsky, History of Ukraine-Rus', vol. 9, book 2, part 1: 377).

Far from rallying to the call of a common Christian cause against the Turks, which was essential for Vimina's project to enlist the Catholic Commonwealth and the Orthodox Cossacks against the Ottoman Empire, Paul saw the Catholics as the main enemy and the Turks as even a form of protection from them. He was, however, clearly uplifted by the appearance of a new Orthodox power and above all its immense army, which he estimated with the usual hyperbole of the age as 500,000 strong.[63] Vimina, who had more concrete plans for the army, had merely said that there were as many soldiers among the Cossacks as there were heads. While Paul may not have had a plan for them, he understood the army's significance for the Orthodox cause as he compared it favorably to the forces of Moldavia and Wallachia, the Orthodox vassals of the Porte to which the patriarchates traditionally appealed for support.

In describing the war, Paul turned to the images that pervaded the religious thinking of the age. For him the deaths on the Ukrainian side were those of martyrs and their enemies had committed numerous bestial acts, including cutting open the wombs of pregnant women.[64] One can indeed find direct parallels with the Hebrew chronicles and the Polish accounts of the period, albeit reversing perpetrators and victims. His emphasis on the position of the Jews as abnormal in a Christian society coincided with many Western Christian discussions. But Paul also brought his own world view as to who the enemies of the Ukrainians were to his account. While one cannot know what his informants told him, one suspects that his emphasis on the revolt's destruction of the Armenians, whom he places on an equal plane with the Jews and mentions almost as frequently, may come more from his antagonism toward the numerous Armenian communities in the Ottoman Empire and their church's challenge to Orthodox dogma than from his informants' accounts.[65] In the same way, his hatred of the Jesuits, which certainly was exuded by the rebels, may also have derived from their machinations against the Orthodox in Constantinople or his attitudes toward them in Syria. His play on the similarity of their name to the

---

63 Paul, The Travel of Macarius, 1: 184; Hrushevsky, History of Ukraine-Rus', vol. 9, book 2, part 1: 375.

64 Paul, The Travel of Macarius, 1: 177, 183; Hrushevsky, History of Ukraine-Rus', vol. 9, book 2, part 1: 378.

65 Paul, The Travel of Macarius, 1: 171, 173, 185; Hrushevsky, History of Ukraine-Rus', vol. 9, book 2, part 1: 376. On Paul's discussions of Armenians, see Halperin, Friend and Foe, 108-109. He points out that Paul devotes relatively little attention to Armenian merchants as playing a negative role. On the fate of Armenians during the Khmel'nyts'kyi Uprising, see Yaroslav Dashkevych, "Armenians in the Ukraine at the Time of Hetman Bohdan Xmel'nyc'kyj (1648-1657)", *Harvard Ukrainian Studies* 3-4 (1979-80): 166-188.

Yazidis, the syncretic sect among the Kurds abominated by Christians and Muslims alike, surely sought to sway his potential reader far from Ukraine.[66]

DEPICTIONS OF THE HETMAN

Both authors met with the fabled leader of the revolt Bohdan Khmel'nyts'kyi, the man about whom all Europe and the Near East sought information and whom subsequent generations have found so enigmatic. The discussions of Khmel'nyts'kyi have always been grounded in an author's position on the revolt and the effect desired on the readers.[67] From the Hebrew chronicles' epithet "May his name be blotted out" to the Polish broadsides depicting him as a crocodile, his enemies sought to demonize him. In the same way his followers and successors sought to glorify him from the time he entered Kyiv on Christmas 1648 to the acclamations that he was "well-named Bohdan, given by God, to free the Ruthenian nation from the Polish servitude."[68]

The antagonistic goals and the conventions of the age must make us wary about all depictions of the hetman. In early eighteenth-century Ukraine, the Cossack officers and clergy knew of Bohdan from Hryhorii Hrabianka's history composed over half a century after the revolt, which circulated in numerous manuscripts.

A man worthy of the name hetman: boldly he was ready to take on any misfortunes, even more diligent was he amidst these very misfortunes; whereby no toils tired his body, and his good spirit could not be subdued by adversaries. He endured cold and heat equally. He ate and drank what nature demanded and was not overcome by sleep at night or during the day. When he lacked time due to affairs and military matters, he rested only a little, and then not

---

66 Paul, The Travel of Macarius, 1:205. Belfour translates the term as "priests of the Devil" a play on the term "devil worshippers" often ascribed to the Yazidis (Hrushevsky, History of Ukraine-Rus', vol. 9, book 2, part 1: 376). Largely based on the work of Robert M. Haddad, *Syrian Christians in Muslim Society: An Interpretation* (Princeton, 1970), Charles Halperin paints a picture of "cooperation, if not respect" of Syrian Orthodox (Melkites) with other Christian groups, including Armenians and Italian Jesuits. This opens up the possibility that Paul came to his antagonism as a result of his travels and contacts (especially of the Jesuits) and now sought to propagate these views. I nevertheless believe he came to Ukraine with these antagonisms and now could take delight that these religious antagonists were now defeated,

67 See Frank E. Sysyn, "The Changing Image of the Hetman", *Jahrbücher für Geschichte Osteuropas* 46, 4 (1998): 531–545.

68 Ibid., 532.

on expensive beds, but on such beddings as a military man ought. Even amid the military din, he slept calmly, in no way concerned. His dress did not stand out at all against the others, only the gear and his horses were somewhat better. He was often seen covered with a military cloak, as he rested among the guards. He went first into battle and was the last to leave it.

Some of those readers, graduates of the Kyiv Academy and other higher schools of the Hetmanate, may have recognized that Khmel'nyts'kyi was being appropriately glorified in the manner and almost the exact words that Livy praised Hannibal, albeit with the negative passages removed, but it took modern scholars over 150 years from the time the work was published in full in the 1840s to make that connection.[69]

Vimina's depiction of the Cossack hetman, so important as that of an emissary who met with him, can also in some ways be seen in the tradition of depicting great military commanders stretching back to Livy.

As for his origin, he descends from a noble father who was banished and deprived of his title of nobility. He is of taller than average height, with a large frame and a sturdy constitution.

---

69 See Marko Antonovych, "Kharakterystyka B. Khmel'nyts'koho u Hrabianky i Liviia (Zamitka)", *Ukraïns'kyi istoryk* 32 (1995): 165-166. These passages are from Livy, *Ab urbe condita*, 21.4. See *Books 21-25: The Second Punic War*, trans. Alfred John churchCand William Hackson Brodribb (London, 1883): 4-5.

"There was no one whom Hasdrubal preferred to put in command, whenever courage and persistency were specially needed, no officer under whom the soldiers were more confident and more daring. Bold in the extreme in incurring peril, he was perfectly cool in its presence. No toil could weary his body or conquer his spirit. Heat and cold he bore with equal endurance; the cravings of nature, not the pleasure of the palate, determined the measure of his food and drink. His waking and sleeping hours were not regulated by day and night. Such time as business left him, he gave to repose; but it was not on a soft couch or in the stillness that he sought it. Many a man often saw him wrapped in his military cloak, lying on the ground amid the sentries and pickets. His dress was not one whit superior to that of his comrades, but his accoutrements and horses were conspicuously splendid. Among the cavalry or the infantry he was by far the first soldier; the first in battle, the last to leave it when once begun."

The passage that follows immediately is removed.

"These great virtues in the man were equaled by monstrous vices, inhuman cruelty, a worse than Punic perfidy. Absolutely false and irreligious, he had no fear of God, no regard for an oath, no scruples. With this combination of virtues and vices, he served three years under the command of Hasdrubal, omitting nothing which a man who was to be a great general ought to do or see."

His speech and manner of governance indicate that he possesses mature judgment and acute intelligence; although it appears that he applies himself excessively to drink, he still does not fail to take care of business. Therefore I believe that two powers can be found in him –one active, sober, and capable in the administration of affairs, the other dormant and mired in intoxication. He behaves in an affable and down-to-earth manner with which he wins the devotion of his soldiers, while maintaining discipline by means of severe punishment. To all who enter his chamber he holds out his hand and has all sit down if they are Cossacks. In this chamber no luxuries are to be found. The walls are bare of any tapestries, the chairs unadorned. There are only some rough benches covered with leather cushions, which I believe the Romans called *subsellia*, and with the legs of which, it seems to me Plutarch writes, the Gracchi were killed when they wished to introduce the agrarian law. A curtain of damask hangs in front of his small bed, at the head of which hang a bow and a saber, the only arms that he is accustomed to bear. Neither is his table more sumptuous. Although they eat without napkins, the only silverware is spoons and goblets; the rest of the service is of tin. He has prudently decorated his house thus in order to remind himself of his status, so that his soul does not swell up with inordinate pride. Perhaps he has followed the example of Agathocles, who, being the son of a potter, but elevated to the status of royal despot, ordered that his table and sideboard be furnished with vessels of clay, whence the verses:

Ausonis fictilibus cenasse ferent agatoclea vasis,
Atque Abachum samio saepe ornasse luto.[70]

While Vimina's short description was neither a panegyric nor a "borrowing" in the manner of Hrabianka, one can wonder if his education affected his depiction of Khmel'nyts'kyi as a man of simple demeanor who wins the hearts of his followers by his affable ways but rules with an iron hand. Indeed, Vimina seems to echo Livy on Hannibal when he sees two natures in the hetman, one sober and capable, the other intoxicated. His vivid portrait of Khmel'nyts'kyi with these two natures coincides with many other contemporary descriptions. But in conveying his impressions, Vimina turned to classical descriptions of the military leader as he did in describing his rooms and his manner of setting a table. His comparisons with Agatocles, the tyrant of Syracuse whom Macchiavelli criticized for brutality and impiety in *The Prince*, is intriguing. Still we assume Vimina turns to the well-known epigram of Ausonis primarily as a means of conveying the mode of Khmel'nyts'kyi's success in gaining the people's support to his elevation as a type

---

70 A badly distorted quotation from the poet and rhetorician Decimus Ausonius Magnus (310–393). The lines, taken from the ninth in Ausonius' series of *Epigrammata*, should read: "Fama est fictilibus cenasse Agathoclea regem / atque abacum Samio saepe onerasse luto" (It is said that Agathocles, when king, dined off earthen plates / and that his sideboard often bore a load of Samian ware). Cf. *The Works of Ausonius*, ed. R. P. H. Green (Oxford, 1991), 68.

of despot and his military prowess rather than echoing the criticisms of *The Prince*. Vimina conveys his fundamentally positive assessment of the Cossack hetman and his followers to the Serenissima in providing them a type of leader and an army that could serve as an ally.

For Vimina, the product of a Western society of corporate orders and estates, his egalitarian praise of the low-born Cossacks and his own origin as a burgher did not erase the importance he attached to high birth. Therefore he immediately turned to Khmel'nyts'kyi's noble father, who had been deprived of his nobility, in explaining the reasons for the revolt. For early modern Europe the noble rebel was always more acceptable: superior noble birth and attributes could go far in explaining a rebel's success.[71] Vimina also tried to give us a portrait of the psychology of the man. He alludes to the personal confrontation over a woman that some subsequent historiography focused on as sparking the revolt when he mentions Khmel'nyts'kyi marrying the wife of Daniel Czapliński in a discussion of matrimony and divorce. He provides us with the appropriate Ciceronian adage (*Quales sunt in Republica principes, tales et sunt reliqui cives*) as demonstrating the effect of Khmel'nyts'kyi's example. He does this while at the same time making the stunning assertion that it was Czapliński and his patron Alexander Koniecpolski who were responsible for instigating the current disorders, shifting blame away from the Cossack hetman and making him more acceptable to those opposed to rebels against lawful authority.[72]

Paul of Aleppo praises Khmel'nyts'kyi unceasingly and wholeheartedly throughout his work. His description of the patriarch's meeting with the hetman is one of the most comprehensive discussions of Khmel'nyts'kyi by an eyewitness. Paul's reference points are not to generals, but to rulers. He informs his reader: "Kings and Emperors are unequal to the contest of magnanimity with him" and later that "[h]is mode of conduct is conformable to that of the greatest of kings,

---

71 The tendency to assume that a complex and successfully executed revolt must have been engineered by social betters can be seen in some of the Polish commentary on the revolt, including discussions that the clergy and bishops must have masterminded it. See Frank E.Sysyn, "Seventeenth-Century Views on the Causes of the Khmel'nyts'kyi Uprising: An Examination of the 'Discourse about the Present Cossack-Peasant War'", *Harvard Ukrainian Studies* 5, 4 (December 1981): 430–66.

72 The General has given an example to all, so that the saying might remain true: "*Quales sunt in Republica principes tales et sunt reliqui cives*". By marrying the wife of Czaplinski, a Polish noble, a favourite of Aleksander Koniecpolski, the Major Standard-Bearer of the Kingdom. The two of them are said to have been the instigators of the recent disorders. (Quales in Republica principes essent, tales reliquos solere esse cives. *Cicero, Epistulae ad familiares*,1.19.2).

Basil the Macedonian, according as it is described in history. Every person who sees him is in admiration of him, and says, 'Is this that Akhmil [Khmel], whose fame is spread over the whole world?' 'In the country of the Franks, as we were informed, they have composed poems in his praise and in celebration of his wars and conquests."[73] The Byzantine emperor Basil and founder of the Macedonian dynasty who had been depicted by his grandson Constantine VII as an ideal ruler serves as a fitting precedent in depicting to his Orthodox Arabic flock the founder of the Cossack Hetmanate.[74]

Paul does not explain from which historians he took his view of Basil and whether he accepted Constantine's version of royal descent or other historians' attribution of humble origin, but if indeed the latter was the case, he had one more reason to see Basil as the model for Khmel'nyts'kyi. Certainly he describes Khmel'nyts'kyi's simplicity in dress and manner as a virtue akin to Basil's. Thereby, one sees in the frequent praise of this simplicity by Paul a means of glorifying Khmel'nyts'kyi such as when he says: "'It was delightful to witness the beauty of the Khatman's [Hetman's] language, his placid demeanour, his humility and condescension, and his tears of joy'", that "[t]here is no affair in which he is engaged to which he does not himself attend; and he is moderate in his eating and drinking and clothing," that

At this moment he approached from the gate of the city with a numerous troop, in the midst of whom it was impossible for any one to distinguish him, otherwise than by observing that they were all clothed in handsome garments, accoutred with valuable arms; whereas he wore mean and scanty clothing, and was provided with armour of no price.

and that, "so great is the blessing of God upon him, and so entirely overlooked is the meanness of his person."

In praising Khmel'nyts'kyi as a ruler in the tradition of Basil, Paul had obvious foils in the hospodars of Moldavia and Wallachia, especially Vasile Lupu of Moldavia. He maintained: "Where are your eyes, ye Begs[Hospodars] of Moldavia and Wallachia? And where is now your grandeur, where your haughtiness? Each of

---

73 Paul, The Travel of Macarius, 1: 197-198. The statements that follow about Khmel'nyts'kyi are on pages 196-199 unless otherwise indicated.
74 On Basil's origin, see Norman Tobias, *Basil I Founder of the Macedonian Dynasty: A Study of the Political and Military History of the Byzantine Empire in the Ninth Century* (Lewiston, Queenston, Lampeter, 2007), chp.1. On Constantine's portrayal of his ancestor, see the German translation of Basil's life, *Vom Bauernhof auf den Kaiserthron: Leben des Kaiseros Basileos I*, trans. and ed. Leopold Breyer, Byzantinische Geschichtsschreiber, ed. Johannes Koder, vol. 14 (Graz, 1981).

you is inferior in value to any Prokonikos [polkovnyk-colonel] of the Khatman's [Hetman's] suite, and in justice and moderation infinitely below him". He contrasted Khmel'nyts'kyi's qualities with the Moldavian's stern demeanor, ostentation, and arrogance and Khmel'nyts'kyi's victories with Vasile's defeats.

Now Vasili Beg [Hospodar Vasile] of Moldavia was perfect in the majesty of his stature, and in fierce command of his countenance, and was renowned throughout the universe for his wealth and treasures; and yet all this availed him nothing; but in his first battle, and in his second and third, and many times more, he was defeated, and put to flight.

The two men also differed in the degree of respect they had shown the patriarch, a crucial determinant for Paul's evaluation of a ruler. "In respect to his manner of sitting at table, let it be observed, that he placed himself in a lower seat, and our Lord the Patriarch in the seat of eminence, according to the reverence due to him in every assembly." "He was not like the Begs[Hospodars] of Moldavia and Wallachia, who seated themselves in the centre, and placed the Head of the Clergy below them."[75] Vasile had clearly not demonstrated the respect that Khmel'nyts'kyi had shown the patriarch and the humility that Khmel'nyts'kyi accorded the churchman weighed greatly in Paul's praise of him.

Paul continued the tradition that had begun during Patriarch Paisios's visit at the end of 1648-49 of comparing the hetman to Moses liberating his people from a bondage worse than the Egyptian, that of the Poles.

Truly God is with thee; and it is He who has raised thee to deliver his peculiar people from their bondage to the nations; as Moses formerly delivered the Israelites from the servitude of Pharaoh, whom, with his followers, he overwhelmed in the Red Sea: but thou hast destroyed them, the filthy Poles, with thy depopulating sword - glory to God, who has done in thee all these great works!

---

75 "As soon as he beheld our Lord the Patriarch at a distance, he alighted from his horse, with all his attendants; and came and knelt down, and kissed the hem of the Patriarch's train, a first and a second time; then the cross, and his right-hand. And our Lord the Patriarch kissed the Khatman's [Hetman's] forehead." "Then they brought upon the table some bowls of spirits, which they drank out of noggins; and the liquor was hot: but for Akhmil [Khmel] they set a silver cup of a particular kind of spirit. Having first made the Patriarch drink, the Khatman [Hetman] was the second to drink himself; and then he sent down the cup to each of us, for we were standing before him. How admirable this humility of a soul, which may the Almighty preserve still long on earth!" Paul, The Trave of Macarius, I: 199, 198, 199.

In resorting to the comparison with Moses, so commonly used for Byzantine and other rulers, Paul elevated the person of Khmel'nyts'kyi to royal heights.[76] He praised his having been chosen by his fellows when he said; "This Akhmil [Khmel] is an old man, of those who have been most prospered by the blessing of God: in possession of every quality to be a leader – and of the most important of all, secrecy – he is spontaneously chosen of his fellow-men." Yet it was God's elevation of him as a Moses to his people that had raised him to the level of Emperor Basil.

In elevating his subject in his Syrian Christian readers' eyes, Paul both interpreted and approved of the very different society and mores of the Ukrainian borderland. For his Orthodox flock, he described beardless and mustachioed Cossacks who did not fulfill usual Orthodox prescriptions to be bearded. He did so by maintaining that their very name Cazak contained this meaning, a curious etymology for a Turkic word usually thought to mean free man or nomad.[77] That poems were written to Khmel'nyts'kyi in the lands of the Franks was seen as a positive, just as Paul of Aleppo praised the realistic icons of Ukraine and the Western-influenced choral singing.[78] In part, the alms-seeking churchman was impressed with the state of Orthodoxy he found in Ukraine, where the revolt had made the church dominant and the wealth of a society was directed toward the Orthodox culture. In part, his life under Muslim rule and wandering among various northern lands made him more flexible than, for example, were his coreligionists in the Tsardom of Muscovy. In part, he may have been open to the accomplishments of the West, just as his coreligionists in Crete long under Venetian rule had been in evolving new schools of painting. While he condemned the Latins and the Poles, he willingly accepted many of their influences on the Orthodox Ukrainians. What is clear is his joy in finding a new Orthodox power that might serve as a support and inspiration for the beleaguered Orthodox Christians of the Middle East. He chose to paint that polity and its leader in the brightest of hues.

The accounts of Alberto Vimina and Paul of Aleppo do indeed provide invaluable information on Ukraine at the time of the revolt and the court of Hetman Bohdan Khmel'nyts'kyi. Anyone who has read Vimina's description of the hetman's table will be well prepared for Paul's account:

---

76 On the epithet "New Moses" of the Byzantine emperors and "Second Moses" for St.Volodymyr of Kyiv, see Ševčenko, Ukraine between East and West, 192.
77 "All of them wore, as they are accustomed, their chins shaven: and the meaning of the word Cazak, or Cossack, is this, viz. "beard-shorn", but nourishing the whiskers."
78 On singing, see Hrushevsky, History of Ukraine-Rus', vol. 9, book 2, part 1: 390; on painting, see Paul, The Travel of Macarius, 1: 201.

Then they brought upon the table some bowls of spirits, which they drank out of noggins; and the liquor was hot: but for Akhmil [Khmel] they set a silver cup of a particular kind of spirit. Having first made the Patriarch drink, the Khatman [Hetman] was the second to drink himself; and then he sent down the cup to each of us, for we were standing before him. How admirable this humility of a soul, which may the Almighty preserve still long on earth! He had no cup-bearers, nor any officers to cover up and guard the vessels of his meat or drink, as is the fashion of Princes, and even of subordinate Governors. Next they served up earthenware dishes of salt-fish boiled, and other eatables, in a plain way. There were no silver plates, nor forks, nor spoons, nor any thing of the kind: and yet every one of the servants of his servants had numerous chests full of bowls and cups and spoons of silver and gold, with other treasure, gained from the Poles; which none of them desired or cared for here, being out on a military expedition: but when they are at home, in their own native places, it is a different thing.

Indeed, the two constitute the major sources that we have on that table, and they in many ways corroborate each other. One may also say that one finds similar correspondence on the simplicity of Khmel'nyts'kyi's dress and the approachable nature of his person.

Yet however important the comparative evidence we draw from the two travelers, we must always take care to filter in the models by which they formed their narratives and the goals which they sought to obtain through their texts. Frequently, these are easily discerned such as when Vimina ever anxious to provide context through classical allusions turns to Ausonius to give context to Khmel'nyts'kyi's table.[79] For Vimina the models of understanding were based in the Classical world, the teachings of Catholic dogmatics, and the diplomacy of Venice, just as Paul's world was shaped by Orthodoxy, the Byzantine past, the humiliation of the Antiochian present, and the Ottoman structures (so that hospodars are explained as Begs). Frequently, their comments reflect the cultural world views to which they belonged. Vimina, the product of the world of humanist learning and *questione della lingua*, tells us that the Ruthenian vernacular differs from Slavonic as Italian differs from Latin, while the Orthodox cleric, a product of Eastern Christian thought, informs us that the Serbs, Bulgarians, Cossacks, and Muscovites shared one Rus' language, which was clearly the liturgical Slavonic. Fortunately we have both foreign and domestic sources, above all the voluminous primarily Polish correspondence, that discuss politics, personalities, and plans in a way so largely lacking for sources of Muscovy in the same period. Therefore a

---

79 Yet even here one must take care to see if the mention of Agactocles was meant to resonate with his audience when he was describing a general who had reached despotic powers.

comparison of the travelers' accounts with other sources may frequently expose our travelers' goals and distortions. When Paul describes Khmel'nyts'kyi as abstemious in drink, we may assume that this quality had to apply to his ideal ruler and that Vimina and many other contemporary sources are a more reliable source on Khmel'nyts'kyi's drinking habits.[80] What we must recognize, however, is that the sober Khmel'nyts'kyi and Paul's representation are as important a field for study as our attempts to penetrate what they depicted.

A Western Christian clergyman and an Eastern Christian clergyman travelled at about the same time from the old civilizations of the Mediterranean to the north. They visited the once great city of Kyiv that had been part of the greater Mediterranean world around the year 1000. Their goal was the new polity created by the Cossacks whom they sought to integrate into their plans for their respective southern worlds. Their differing cultures of West and East, albeit stemming from the same roots and frequently interacting, shaped the way they portrayed what they saw. Their accounts are not only of great value for understanding what they perceived. They also tell us much about the observers and their worlds.

---

80 Paul, The Travels of Macarius, I: 199.

Transnational Representations of Revolt and New Modes of Communication in the mid-Seventeenth century Polish-Lithuanian Commonwealth: Jerzy Lubomirski's Rebellion against King Jan Kazimierz

ANGELA RUSTEMEYER

During the last decades, religion on the one hand, and the slow but steady move towards modern nationalism on the other hand have been considered as the most important factors in early-modern conflicts. The use conflicting parties made of transnational motives in their propaganda, mostly allusions to foreign powers taking sides with their domestic rival, should corroborate this accentuation. So should also a closer look at the seventeenth-century Polish-Lithuanian Commonwealth, a place of armed conflict and counter-reformation. However, an analysis of transnational motives in the contemporary representation of a seventeenth-century major rebellion in this country, led by the magnate Jerzy Lubomirski, demonstrates the importance of factors other than religion and an emerging national consciousness, namely the structuring of the public sphere through the perception of the actors and the pressure of a political order providing legitimacy for protest: That order demanded radical figures of argumentation to combat the growing protest, for which allusions to the actors' relations to foreign powers provided. Still, transnational positions in the network of communication dealing with the revolt also provided for moderate assessments, which broke with traditional conventions of discourse.

Scepticism about the exclusive role of religion and emerging nationalism in early modern conflicts in Eastern Europe has been provoked by historian Natal'ia Yakovenko. She has convincingly demonstrated that revolts in the seventeenth century were also shaped by the development of subcultures in a society prone to make these categories look less significant than nineteenth and twentieth-century ideologists wanted them to be. Iakovenko discusses the mid-seventeenth century Khmelnytsky uprising with its numerous victims from all nations and confessions in the concerned areas of the Polish-Lithuanian Commonwealth. What undermined central categories such as confession and nation, was a subculture that could be found in all conflicting parties, i.e. the professional identity of soldiers who, independently of their allegiance, shared mutual respect, the desire to make booty, and the contempt for the lives of civilians.[1] The question asked in this book is whether the (self)-positioning of the agents in a transnational context can also be considered as an orientating factor which fashioned modes of action and discourse in early-modern revolts. In this manner, we are studying transnationality as a resource that guided behaviour in a similar way than the subculture analysed by Iakovenko did.

How did transnational motives influence the basic contemporary categories of conflict? The interaction (and maybe alteration) of concepts interpreting conflicts "vertically", that is, as individuals' attacks against authorities perceived as revolt by the attacked, on the one hand and of concepts describing a conflict as ubiquitous and horizontal, that is, as "civil war", on the other is of particular interest here. Both "revolt" and "civil war" partially transformed medieval concepts, notably the right to resistance and the definitions of peace and of the violation of peace. But the concept of "civil war" was more subtle and more hegemonic as to the still unregulated spaces in which social and political action had taken place before the beginning of the modern era. The term "civil war", designating violent conflict not only between subjects and authorities, but also among subjects, came close to contemporaries' experience as depicted above. Yet the topic of civil war is also well-known to have been elaborated by a contemporary of the events described here, Thomas Hobbes, into an apocalyptic vision of universal warfare to be tamed only by a strong state.[2]

The interlinked construction of revolt and civil war which I am interested in can be considered as a part of a large-scale process in the history of communication. Broadly speaking, face-to-face communication as norm and practice, which provoked the interpretation of conflict as a matter of honour between agents identified and represented as persons, was being transformed. More mediated and less personalised communication encouraged the idea of a plurality of opinions

---

1 N. Iakovenko, Paralel'nyi svit. Doslidzhennia z istoriï uiavlen' ta idei v Ukraïni XVI-XVII st. Kyiv 2002, 189-228.

2 Cf. Bernhard Kroener, "Krieg", in *Enzyklopädie der Neuzeit* (7), ed. Friedrich Jaeger (Stuttgart, 2008), col. 137-162.

being natural.[3] The result could theoretically have been the decrease of discursive pressure towards solutions by battle – unless no new means were used to provoke a conflict.

This view of the development of communication may be elaborated to envisage the front lines in early modern conflict. Persons and parties in conflict on all levels of the social hierarchy were profiled by complex processes of construction and distribution of honour titles. In this sense "revolt" was perceived as an asymmetric interpersonal conflict about honour, with a ruler's honour being attacked by subjects' disobedience. As to the transnational aspect of conflict discussed here, it is clear that there were modes of attributing honour which transcended the increasingly fixed borders between early modern states and also the borders sometimes arising within these states. These modes could be, for example, ideals of military honour both in its traditional knightly and its new soldier's version mentioned above. However, titles equal by name did not equally provide their owners with honour, authority and power. The best example of this is the position of kings. Protected by legal acts that were at least similar in criminalising attacks on the person bearing the title of king, the positions of monarchs nevertheless strongly differed. The king's extent of power and the degree to which his position was rooted in an enduring dynasty influenced the variety of means to represent him as a person – and, thus, also the degree to which both royal and anti-royal propaganda sought these means in a transnational context.

The early modern period was characterized by a rapidly increasing exchange of people, goods and information. Transnational motives, which were not always confined to what had actually happened, but to the needs to provide or confirm legitimacy in the very moment when it was being contested, were thus within the reach of the European political elites. Borrowing was facilitated by basic processes marking the period, even if the final result of these processes was a stronger demarcation between countries and cultures. These processes, namely the profiling of confessions, nation building and military reform, were charged with ideology. Insofar, they stood in sharp contrast to the lived experience, which often strikingly contradicted ideologically based promises and expectations. Given these contradictions, it could be useful for agents to extrapolate the conflict by alluding to "foreign" influence or to their adversaries in the conflict, said to be seeking help from abroad. Such motives were conceived and diffused in expectation of their political use or even their juridical dimension, as they could make the adversaries' actions look like conspiracy and treason in the sense of penal law.

---

3   R. Schlögl, "Kommunikation und Vergesellschaftung unter Anwesenden. Formen des Sozialen und ihre Transformation in der frühen Neuzeit", *Geschichte und Gesellschaft* 24 (2008): 155-224, especially 176, 209, 216-217.

Allusions to foreign influence in propaganda diffused by the different parties in a conflict classified as a revolt are one of two aspects of transnationality in protest movements which I would like to discuss. The other aspect is the structure of the public sphere. A comprehensive discussion of the involvement of European political orders with a transnational space of exchange of information and discourse is out of the scope of this article. But I am going to cite a few examples of how transnationality and extraterritoriality in the seventeenth century provided for an enlargement of the public sphere and for a new perspective on king and rebel, offering an interpretation that transcends the traditional view of revolts as conflicts about honour depicted above.

My topic is a high-ranking noble's mid-seventeenth century rebellion against Jan Kazimierz, king of Poland and grand prince of Lithuania. Due to the lack of a comprehensive study of the public sphere in early-modern Poland-Lithuania, I can only make some preliminary remarks on representation in that rebellion.[4] But I can rely on a number of studies of the factual history of the rebellion, its social background and its political implications. As mentioned above, I also rely on works about conflicts in the Commonwealth which revise the topoi of national historiographies.

The case discussed on the following pages might in still another respect be helpful to continue the revision of stereotypes disseminated by national historiographies. Periods of upheaval in early modern Eastern Europe have been used to establish topoi of vitality or decay. As to the seventeenth century, a somewhat optimistic approach has been applied to Russia, the historical "winner" of that century: Even before the more and more "absolute autocracy" coped with a number of uprisings, the social forces at the very beginning of the century already managed to interpret and present what was in fact mainly a civil war as a conflict with foreign powers, and thus to establish the basis of national statehood.[5] In the case of Poland-Lithuania, historians have stated exactly the opposite: Revolts of the seventeenth century made visible patterns of behaviour that finally led to the fall of the Republic of nobles. Reluctance to reform a political order, which could easily be used for intervention from abroad, was accompanied by the loss of tolerance and the rise of xenophobia, all of which contributed to destabilising and discrediting the

---

4 Such a study, which would include the transnational dimension of the public sphere in early-modern Poland-Lithuania, could recur to the classical works by Janusz Tazbir, notably Janusz Tazbir, *Rzeczpospolita i świat. Studia z dziejów kultury XVII wieku* (Wrocław, 1971). Tazbir, however, does not explicitly deal with the public sphere.

5 V. Kljuchevskii's interpretation of the growth of national consciousness at the end of the Time of troubles can be understood that way (V. Kljuchevskii, *Sochineniia v deviati tomakh*, 9 vols. (Moskow, 1988), 3: 64.

Commonwealth's political order.[6] But does a political order indeed suffer from xenophobic attitudes of its actors? If this had been the case, there would have been a lot more failed states in history. To be sure, when dealing with the last two centuries preceding the divisions of Poland, one cannot help but pay attention to the making of the fatal stigma of Polish anarchy. Still, in order to properly locate the Polish-Lithuanian case in the current discussion about early-modern communication and the public sphere, the focus of interest should be replaced: The way revolts, the climax of disorder, and their transnational dimension were dealt with might have been less due to a direct orientation on (proto-)national values than to the set of references defining what was "public".

What exactly was this particular revolt about? The Commonwealth of Poland-Lithuania had a political order based on far-reaching rights of the nobility, with the assembly of nobles electing the king. In the period under consideration, candidates usually came not from within the Commonwealth, but from abroad. King Jan Kazimierz, himself from the Swedish dynasty of the Vasa, intended to change the political order of the Commonwealth by having his successor elected while he himself was still alive (vivente rege). It was clear that this would be a successor according to the king's choice. Jerzy Lubomirski, a powerful magnate, Great Marshall of the Commonwealth and himself a possible candidate for the throne, acted against these plans, referring to the rights and the freedom of the nobility.

During the mid-seventeenth century, the Commonwealth was permanently at war with its neighbouring countries. Discontent was not only nourished by the king's plans concerning his successor, but also by the crown's incapacity to pay the troops. The king tried to cope with Lubomirski as the head of resistance by political, military and judicial means. But it was not easy to use criminal law against a noble in a Republic of nobles. Having Lubomirski finally condemned for lèse-majesty, the king drove him into outright military resistance. Lubomirski and his adherents called their military actions a "rokosz", that is, military resistance against a king violating the rights of the nobility. The nobles of the Commonwealth considered this form of resistance against the king not only as legitimate, but also as legal. For them, the *rokosz* was based on their right to organize in confederations not only during an interregnum, but also during a reign when it came to fulfil tasks the monarch would not or could not manage, such as the defence of the Commonwealth's endangered borders or the defence of nobility rights.[7]

---

6   M. Nagielski, *Rokosz Jerzego Lubomirskiego w 1665 roku* (Warszawa 1994), 242, referring to Tazbir, Rzeczpospolita.

7   J. Bardach, *Historia państwa i prawa Polski*, 5 vols. (Warszawa, 1957), 2 [Od połowy XV wieku do r. 1795]: 244.

Although lead by a magnate, the Lubomirski rebellion was less far away from mass revolt than it might initially appear. A matter of elite politics, it was also linked to a military revolt, and it was a reason for the top players to turn to the most humble subjects for support. Some aspects of the rebellion thus touch the problem of mass revolt both as it has been associated by historians with what used to be called "antifeudal protest" and as it has been identified as the "language of the crowd" ever since the eighteenth century. Still, the revolt first and foremost has to be considered in the scope of the public space in the Republic of nobles. The way this public space and its legal foundations were perceived within the Commonwealth and beyond the borders influenced the status of the country in international relations.

1. Public Procedure and Informal Politics: The Republic's Open Flank

The notion of *rokosz*, an armed uprising against the king considered legal, concretized the Commonwealth's nobles right to resistance. It is significant that a seventeenth-century French observer of Lubomirski's rebellion found it impossible to translate "rokosz" into French and therefore simply left it as it was.[8]

The French observer's failure to translate the term is significant. Authors like him, writing for external readers, developed a political ethnography of the Republic of nobles, taking an alienated position as referring to what they knew about that political formation. To indicate the uniqueness of certain traits in the Polish political landscape – like the *rokosz* – was a means to make it exotic. Another means to express the author's distance to the subject was the description of the Commonwealth's political procedures in terms of parody.[9] To parody procedure

---

8   Nagielski, Rokosz, 91.

9   An example is the French historian de Bizardière's description of what can be called the epilogue of the Lubomirski rebellion. In 1668, two years after the rebel's death, his main enemy, King Jan Kazimierz, finally abdicated the throne. The nobility was to elect a new king. Having shown how the most insolent tricks used by foreign candidates failed with the assembled nobles, Bizardière is also highly ironic about the final election procedure and its result: the election of a new king from within the nobility of the Commonwealth after a great number of monarchs from foreign dynasties: see Michel de Bizardière, *Neuligst eröffnetes Polnisches Staats-Cabinet Oder Eigentliche Beschreibung der Merckwürdigkeiten/so sich von langen Zeiten her in diesem Königreich zugetragen* (Cölln, 1698) (original text in French, Paris, 1697). I here refer to the text as printed in

was to parody a crucial element in Poland-Lithuania's political order. Procedure in the sense of a formalized process claiming openness concerning its results was certainly not always observed in practice. Nevertheless, it symbolized and guaranteed the public status of the nobility and, thus, its political legitimacy. Notably the formal observation of the rules for convoking and carrying out the assembly of nobles was all the more important because, particularly in times of crisis, political and juridical functions of the assembly of nobles overlapped, with the Sejm also being the Republic's highest court.[10] The qualifications of "public" and "private" mattered concretely as to what was considered as debatable at the assembly of nobles in an open and mediated discussion about matters of common interest.[11]

Of course the reach of the distinction of public and private as well as the reach of the claim to politics being public could not but be limited in real life. There were large areas of informal power dominated by forms of communication far from the procedures of public political communication. For example, the Lithuanian aristocracy participated in the institutions of the Commonwealth, but its influence was mainly organized as informal power based on sociability. Lithuania was dominated by a few aristocratic clans. Surveying the postal traffic, one of them even organized a specific means of controlling communication.[12] The Lubomirski rebellion shows clearly how much informal politics mattered in this context. In order to gain the Lithuanian aristocrats' support, both the royal party and the rebel extensively made use of personal persuasion outside of formal political representation, which meant that the king, the queen as well as a monk charged by Lubomirski travelled to see the Lithuanian magnates and convince them of their cause, with the king promising important offices in order to get military support.[13]

The highly-developed and extensively used vocabulary denoting public institutions and hinting at their assumed commitment to public interest made the contrast between an ideal order and a much less ideal practice visible. Moreover, the understanding of *rokosz* as legal resistance implied that the rebel institutions were ascribed the same public quality as the original ones. As we shall see,

---

Die gelehrte Welt des 17. Jahrhunderts über Polen. Zeitgenössische Texte, ed. E. Szarota (Wien, 1972), 342-348.

10 About the Republic's highest court: Bardach, Historia państwa i prawa, 2: 153-155.

11 Comp. Nagielski, Rokosz, 149.

12 A.Rachuba, "Litwa wobec sądu nad Jerzym Lubomirskim", *Kwartalnik historyczny* 93 (1987): 679-707; A. Rachuba, "Zabiegi dworu i Jerzego Lubomirskiego o pozyskanie Litwy w 1664 roku", *Przegląd historyczny* 78 (1987): 1-17. About the control of the mail traffic: Nagielski, Rokosz, 149.

13 Rachuba, Zabiegi dworu i Jerzego Lubomirskiego, 1-17.

formations belonging to the constitutional order – notably the army – could organize within the frame of legality to articulate their needs as a social group. In case of the army, this concerned the crucial matter of pay. But the more profiled such formations were as public organs, the more could the articulation of limited interests discredit the Republic's political order to the (willingly) unaccustomed eye. It was easy for a French diplomat to declare, for example, in an alarming tone that the unpaid royal army of the Commonwealth "is for sale"[14] – a situation not extraordinary in that period, but of greater public visibility in Poland-Lithuania than elsewhere. The high degree of structured public institutions, that is, modern, not archaic elements, made the Republic of nobles as a political order rather vulnerable. In this sense, the role of crises such as the Lubomirski rebellion in a transnational interplay discrediting the Republic of nobles on the long run has to be investigated further. Given the delicacy of the wide-spread and highly elaborate public quality of institutions in the Commonwealth, my thesis is that the modernisation of the modes of communication about internal conflicts rather accelerated than slowed down this process.

As to the long-term development of the Commonwealth's inner situation as well as its international position, I suppose that these modes of communication certainly played a more important role than xenophobic attitudes or the agents' relations to foreign powers in the Lubomirski movement.

2. Lubomirski in Historical Context: Transnational Elements in Related Revolts

Historians consider resistance against foreigners in the royal army as one of several factors that made up the reasons for the uprisings in 1606-1609. King and rebel alike built up their respective international network in close rivalry to each other, with Lubomirski being supported, for instance, by the Elector of Brandenburg-Prussia, while his rival, the king, was in close relation with the noble opposition in this neighbour monarchy.[15] But neither xenophobia nor appeals to foreign support were specific characteristics of Lubomirski's rebellion, as a look at comparable seventeenth-century revolts inside and outside of the Commonwealth demonstrates.

Lubomirski's rebellion may be compared to another major rebellion in seventeenth-century Poland-Lithuania, and also to the French Fronde.

A major conflict between the crown and a noble rebel in the Commonwealth had already marked the years from 1606 to 1609. That confrontation between the

---

14 Nagielski, Rokosz, 83.
15 Ibid., 43.

crown and part of the nobility was in many respects similar to the conflict between the king and Lubomirski more than half a century later. Both conflicts were centred around the nobles' and the king's prerogatives in their mutual relationship. In both conflicts the issue of confessional freedom as well as noble resistance against the secular power of the church played a role.[16] Contemporaries themselves compared the two rebellions. King Jan Kazimierz's astronomer believed that the Lubomirski rebellion was worse than the older one because of the simultaneous uprisings in the Ukraine and the Muscovite danger.[17] Resistance against the presence of foreigners in the royal army is mentioned as one of several factors that made up the reasons for the uprising in 1606-1609.[18] As to the Lubomirski rebellion, it may have resulted in growing resistance against a king from a foreign dynasty: In fact, the nobles elected their next king from among the Commonwealth's domestic elite. But it would be difficult to prove that the mid-seventeenth century revolt itself was more marked by xenophobia than the one in the first decade of the 17th century.

Compared to the Fronde in France, the Lubomirski rebellion shows important differences, but also reveals parallels. One difference lay in the medial representation of the monarchy, which was, of course, closely linked to the hereditary position of the king in France on the one hand and the position of an elected king in the Commonwealth on the other hand. Relations of the agents to foreign powers played a role in both revolts. This was in part because one of the main motives for these movements was the disappointment of high-ranking office holders with the crown.[19] Needless to say, high-level office holders were also transnational agents. Another similarity is the disastrous financial situation of the crown, that is, its difficulties to pay for its military forces – with the difference that the French monarchy recurred to what has been called an inner "système fisco-financier", while the Polish king had to rely on subsidies paid for by or intermediated by the French court.[20] Yet in general, the use of foreign support by the opponents was by no means unique to the Lubomirski movement and Poland-

---

16 On the conflict about the representatives of the church and their secular power in the Lubomirski rebellion: W. Kłaczewski, *Jerzy Sebastian Lubomirski* (Wrocław, Warszawa, Kraków, 2002), 240. About the early 17th-century Zebrzydowski rebellion: H. Wisner, *Rokosz Zebrzydowskiego* (Kraków, 1989), especially 1-9.
17 Kłaczewski, Jerzy Sebastian Lubomirski, 229.
18 Wisner, Rokosz Zebrzydowskiego, 16, 18.
19 As mentioned above, Lubomirski himself held high offices in the Commonwealth. For the French case: A. James, *The Origins of French Absolutism 1598-1661* (Harlow et al., 2006), 56.
20 Quotation: James, Origins of French Absolutism, 53; Nagielski, Rokosz, 27.

Lithuania: One of the principal actors of the age of the Fronde, the Prince de Condé, tried to achieve military invasion from abroad for his cause.[21]

A transnational context of agency in revolts was thus not exceptional – at least if the revolt was a rebellion of nobles. Dealing with the representation of the Lubomirski revolt on the following pages, we have to consider that its transnational motives reflected a real and quite common state of things. However, propaganda presented the facts in an original way.

3. LUBOMIRSKI'S REBELLION IN DOMESTIC JURISDICTION

At first sight, one of the most prominent representations of the revolt – its staging as a juridical drama - was a purely internal one. Both the king and Lubomirski made abundant use of formalized legal procedures and their written representations to win their case. In practice, legal procedure was, of course, by no means independent of the power of sociability. It was easier to judge those who socially and culturally did not belong to the core of the Republic than those who did.

The king's jurists had a large choice of accusations against Lubomirski to present to the assembly of nobles – and yet a restricted one. These restrictions concerned precisely the magnate's relations to foreign powers in the conflict about the future of the Polish throne. It is significant that there were cases of accusation of political crime in 17th-century Poland in which foreign relations of the defendant played an important role. In the mid-seventeenth century, a former Cossack hetman, Ivan Vyhovs'kyi, was judged mainly for his relations with the Ottoman Empire. At the same period the leader of a peasant uprising, Aleksander Leon Kostka-Napierski, was condemned for talking about his alleged relations with external enemies of the Commonwealth.[22] But in our case, the accused belonged to the inner circle of the formally and informally powerful; he was both in the centre and on the top of the noble stratum, sociable both to the nobles, many of whom felt he shared their cause, and to the king himself. This cut short the field of possible accusations. Lubomirski's acts might easily be compared to the very similar modes of action of the monarch himself. Therefore, the magnate's secret correspondence with the emperor and the elector was no explicit matter of accusation.

So what was left to the king to accuse the rebel of? Fortunately for the royal party, the accusers found it possible to charge him with breaking a law which, in order to promote formal equality among the nobles, forbade the use of particular

---

21 James, Origins of French Absolutism, 70-71.
22 A. Lityński, *Przestępstwa polityczne w polskim prawie karnym XVI-XVII wieku* (Katowice, 1976), 62.

titles hinting at the superior position of the concerned nobles within their estate.[23] This point in the accusation was a tribute to the szlachta as a social formation. The main crimes Lubomirski was charged with and then judged for at a dramatic assembly of the nobles in 1665 were, however, actions against the king. As I will discuss later, Lubomirski was, for instance, accused of having tried to establish himself as a counterweight to royal power by establishing a "protectorate" over the Republic and to have stirred up public opinion against the ruler.[24] In the sense of what has been said above about the early-modern understanding of revolts, lèse-majesty, the legal formula used by the king in the conflict with Lubomirski, was a representation of the sovereign's honour. In the 16th century, Polish nobles had fought against the use of lèse-majesty by their monarchs. In 1539, they had achieved that lèse-majesty referred only to crimes directly against the person of the king. At least as far as Polish (but not Lithuanian) law was concerned, they thus had successfully banned the large understanding of that crime in Roman law, which they considered as "law for unfree peoples".[25] In this tradition a law of 1588 made sure that accusations of lèse-majesty should not hinder a noble in his legal political activity.[26] The concept of *rokosz*, a legalized, far-going form of resistance against the crown, demonstrates that this was a notion wide-open to interpretation. Insofar the 1588 law on lèse-majesty was clearly pro-noble. On the other hand, that law was a relatively fresh basis of reference for accusations of political crime for mid-seventeenth century actors, a legal source which possessed the legitimacy of law made by the Republic of nobles itself. This was important, as the noblemen of the Commonwealth considered foreign law as an instrument for installing the much-feared *dominium absolutum* of a king assuming more and more power.

King Jan Kazimierz and his jurists finally managed to persuade the Assembly of nobles to condemn Lubomirski for lèse-majesty. Some years later, another assembly of nobles – ironically the Sejm following the abdication of Lubomirski's royal adversary – rehabilitated the then late magnate. Thus, so far, the case looks like a series of events within the frame of the domestic noble public sphere. In fact, it transcended this frame. The transnational elements in the discourses about Lubomirski provided for this enlarged scope.

---

23 Kłaczewski, Jerzy Sebastian Lubomirski, 225-226.
24 See below and annotation 28.
25 Lityński, Przestępstwa polityczne, 21, 171.
26 St. Salmonowicz, "La noblesse polonaise contre l'arbitraire du pouvoir royal: les privilèges judiciaires de la noblesse", *Revue du droit français et étranger* 72 (1994): 21-29, 27.

4. ENLARGING THE SCOPE: TRANSNATIONAL MOTIVES IN THE PROPAGANDISTIC REPRESENTATION OF THE REBELLION

The problem with the accusation of lèse-majesty in the Polish-Lithuanian Commonwealth was its very nature: a king-centred crime in a non-king-centred, mixed political order. It is therefore logical that in the eyes of the king and his advisors, the mere declaration of Lubomirski's condemnation, which was sent to all towns of the Commonwealth, did not suffice. To convince the many discontented people, more efforts were needed. Printers worked night and day to immediately produce a large documentation of the Lubomirski case from the king's point of view.[27] This work, "Processus iudiciarius",[28] suggests through its documentary character that there was a well-informed reading public to discuss and judge the case. The text did not do without allusions to foreign princes' influence on Lubomirski's actions, but its polemic elements concentrated on the negative effect of Lubomirski's activity for Poland's position in the conflict with the Tatars and the Cossacks. Yet, most remarkable in our context is a reference to the English regicide of 1649 and the following period of Oliver Cromwell's rule as "protector". According to the "Processus", Lubomirski's adherents had even made an axe for him as symbol of his new function as a "protector". One of these adherents explicitly announced that it was time to cut off the heads first of the king and then of high court officials. The "Processus" underlines that the expression for "cut off the heads" was pronounced in Tatar language! The text further tells us that several other supporters of the rebels agreed to this, referring to the English example and stating that they themselves, the nobles of the Polish-Lithuanian Commonwealth, had more reason to cut off their king's head than the English had had. Some high-ranking nobles were shocked about what they heard and immediately made an effort to install a trial against those who pronounced such "blasphemy". Not so Lubomirski, who did everything to downplay the crime and thus, the text suggests, showed his approbation.[29] Of course, Lubomirski rejected these reproaches in his printed answer to the "Processus", denying any ambitions to become a "Protector" of the Commonwealth.[30]

---

27 St. Szczotka, "Zabiegi o pozyskanie chłopów w okresie rokoszu Lubomirskiego", *Przegląd historyczny* 43 (1952): 319-337.

28 Georgius Lubomierski, *Processus iudiciarius in causa illustri et magnifico Georgio comiti in Wisnicz et Iaroslaw Lubomierski* (Varsaviæ, 1664), E.

29 Ibid.

30 Jerzy Lubomirski, Publicæ Innocentiæ Manifestum Deo Mundo Patriæ (s.l., 1666), 84.

So, the English regicide took a prominent place in the royal propaganda for the reading public. It is remarkable that it reoccurs in the risky propaganda efforts to gain the support of a group traditionally outside of the system of political representation: the peasants. To agitate peasants to rise against nobles was to play with fire and, thus, it was done only when the struggling parties felt that their cause was at stake. The arguments used in the addresses to the peasants are therefore worthy of attention.

Trying to agitate peasants against Lubomirski and his noble followers, the royal side acted according to patterns established during the Swedish invention into the Commonwealth a decade before the events (in 1655): The Swedish king had then tried to rise the peasants against their noble lords, and King Jan Kazimierz, for his part, had tried to make the mountaineers of the Podhale region, the most rebellious element among catholic peasants in Poland, rise against the Swedish invaders. Taking this into account, the king's analogous action in 1665, the appeal to the peasants' support in the struggle against Lubomirski,[31] can be considered as a kind of declaration of war against this domestic enemy. Yet the royal address to the peasants also explicitly raised the topic of civil war,[32] and thus transcended the scope of arguments that had so far been tied to the interpretation of the conflict as a revolt. To be sure, during Lubomirski's rebellion, the idea of civil war had already emerged, but only privately, for instance, in the correspondence of Jan Sobieski's, the future king and the victor of Vienna in 1683, who mentioned robberies by Lithuanian troops on Polish territory.[33] Yet in the king's *uniwersały* (manifestos) to the Podhale peasants the civil war motif was developed *in public*.

The king was the first to address to the Podhale peasants. Lubomirski, for his part, also wrote to them, recommending himself not only as the defender of a just cause, but also as a victorious warrior. The king did not hesitate to contradict this version, stating that Lubomirski's victories had been bought by the blood of the peasants.[34] This is in fact to say that the magnate had not made war against the Swedish troops, but that his war had been a domestic one!

In their manifestos to the Podhale peasants, both the king and Lubomirski accused each other of having exposed the people to Tatar raids.[35] Yet the most remarkable element in the propaganda for peasants is once more the mentioning of the English regicide. Supporting the king's cause, an anonymous adherent of the king's side stated in his appeal to the peasants that Lubomirski had even sent a

---

31 Szczotka, Zabiegi o pozyskanie chłopów, 321-322.
32 Ibid., 319-337.
33 Nagielski, Rokosz, 97.
34 Szczotka, Zabiegi o pozyskanie chłopów, 321, 328-329, 333.
35 Ibid., 332.

person to England to get to know how to proceed. The "Processus" was cited as a proof that these accusations against Lubomirski were true, that is, the authority of the printed text was referred to. The king's supporter justified the fact that this Latin text was incomprehensible for peasants by the need to inform other countries about Lubomirski's evil-doing.[36] The reference to the English regicide, for its part, shows that the author assumed events that mattered for the European public to matter also for peasants in a Polish mountain region. The domestic public (i.e., the whole Commonwealth, including at least a part of its peasant population) was thus consequently thought of as complementary to an international public and vice versa. Yet the regicide motif also fulfils the same function as the other conspicuous transnational motives in the pro- and anti-Lubomirski propaganda, the allusion to the Tatar or Tatar-Cossack danger. Poland-Lithuania's electoral monarchy was a political order rationalised in the sense of not leaving much room for the sacralisation of the king. There was no room for anything analogous to the famous French leaflets of the period – the Mazarinades – with their conspicuous images of the king between heaven and hell.[37] Transnational motifs – the Tatars and, most notably, the English regicide – took the place of apocalyptic motifs which developed along the long-term presence of hereditary kingdom in other political orders. In other words: when it came to constructing radicalism under the given circumstances, transnationality was an indispensable source to recur to. A closer study of the background of the regicide motive and the protector motive shows how this worked.

5. THE ENGLISH REGICIDE AND OLIVER CROMWELL AGAINST A POLISH BACKGROUND

There were good conditions in the Commonwealth for receiving information about developments in England, but the allusions to the English regicide and the Protectorate cannot be considered as a mere reflex of fresh news: In 1664 Cromwell, "Lord Protector of the Realm of England" from 1653 to 1659, had been dead for five years, and the Stuart monarchy had been restored. These new circumstances might have enhanced the Polish king's hope to successfully discredit his adversary in the eyes of an international public by alluding to his alleged

---

36 Ibid.
37 A. Pietsch, "Zwischen Gottesähnlichkeit und Höllensturz. Das Bild des französischen Königs in Zeiten der Fronde", in *Die Bibel als politisches Argument,* ed. A. Pečar and K. Trampedach, Beihefte der Historischen Zeitschrift, ed. Lothar Gall, vol. 43 (München, 2007), 333-348.

ambitions to become Protector himself, as monarchy now seemed to be victorious at the very spot where it recently had been most dangerously been attacked. The argument also corresponded to internal demands. Restricted by the Commonwealth's minimalist law on lèse-majesty, Lubomirski's accusers were to find both arguments for the Marshall's evil intention concerning the king in person and for his treacherous intentions, for his being prepared to collaborate with anyone and to borrow from anyone in order to achieve his aims. England, Oliver Cromwell and the Protectorate offered such opportunities. Yet apart from alleged sympathy with the king-murderers fitting very well into the conditions an accusation of political crime had to fulfil, there were also other reasons why the English case as cited in royal propaganda was suitable.

The strong English presence in several sectors of the Commonwealth's society makes it probable that recent English events were known and that therefore allusions to them would be understood. England's quickly modernising economy, which was heading towards the beginnings of industrialisation, was an important complementary partner for the Commonwealth, which provided England with grain and with raw material for the English textile production.[38] Moreover, due to the fact that in an age of confessional conflict, the Commonwealth had long been receiving persons from many confessions, including those persecuted at home, the British catholics in Poland-Lithuania were quite numerous.[39] They were particularly strong in the army. Jan Kazimierz even had special Irish units.[40] It is significant that not only Polish propaganda presented England (or, better, England in a certain, recent period) as a hotbed of subversion, but in a way also vice-versa: In England, Poland was perceived as a potential *place d'armes* for Irish insurgents who could be recruited from the Irish units in the Polish military.[41]

During the Protectorate, England had become more deeply involved with politics in Poland-Lithuania's sphere of interest than before. Cromwell had ambitious aims as to common strategies of protestant countries, but the interests of English merchants also had to be taken into account. This was especially the case when the Protector, whose original basis of power had been the army, at a later stage tried to gain larger support. He could then count on the London merchants'

---

38 Edward Alfred Mierzwa, *Anglia a Polska w pierwszej połowie XVII w.* (Warszawa, 1986), passim.
39 Antoni Krawczyk, "The British in Poland in the Seventeenth Century", *The Seventeenth Century* 37 (2002): 254-271, especially 254.
40 Krawczyk, The British in Poland, 260.
41 Ibid.

and money lenders' interest in a stable government,[42] but this even more bound him to a balanced strategy in the Baltic region. As a result, the government restricted the number of English soldiers to be recruited for the Swedish wars against the Commonwealth.[43]

The Protector himself was a highly conspicuous figure in England. He had been shaped in this way by adversary English royalist propaganda even at a stage when his actual power did not yet justify such a strong image.[44] Two contradictory symbols, the axe symbolizing his responsibility for the regicide of 1649 and the knightly sword, were attributed to him on printed pictures.[45] The martial qualities he was accorded mirrored his military identity and the military basis of his rule. This martial image was ambiguous in the context of mid-seventeenth century debates about legitimate power. Cromwell's strong connection to the military made him vulnerable to sharp criticism not only in England. "Both Florentine and Venetian ambassadors saw Cromwell as a tyrant because he ruled with the support of the army".[46] In England, a similar argument arose when the question of the Protector's follower and thus the options to extend the Protectorate or to restore monarchy became acute. Cromwell, though probably waiting to be offered the crown himself, had declared hereditary monarchy (but democracy as well!) a negative extreme in 1655.[47] However, it soon became evident that Cromwell's contemporaries stuck to hereditary monarchy, which they considered as a natural order in spite of the 1649 execution of the Stuart king then considered a tyrant. The arguments of the 1649 anti-royalists were now turned upside down: It was no longer the hereditary monarch, but the potentially elected king who was supposed to become a tyrant, and the military men surrounding Cromwell were considered as a danger.[48]

As object to a fierce debate about hereditary monarchy and the influence of the military on politics, Cromwell and the Protectorate were a valuable point of reference in the Polish context. Hereditary monarchy was the central matter of

---

42 Eric Porter, "A Cloak for Knavery: Kingship, the Army and Parliament, 1654-1655", *The Seventeenth Century* 17 (2002): 187-205, especially 192.
43 Barry Coward, *The Cromwellian Protectorate* (Manchester and New York, 2002), 130.
44 Laura Knoppers, *Constructing Cromwell: Ceremony, Portrait, and Print, 1645-1661* (Cambridge et al., 2000), 30.
45 Knoppers, Constructing Cromwell, 50.
46 Marco Barducci, "Oliver Cromwell, European Historical Myth? The Case of the Italian States in Seventeenth-Century Representations of Cromwell", *The Seventeenth Century* 23, 1 (2008): 57.
47 Porter, A Cloak for Knavery, 188.
48 Ibid., 197-198.

conflict between Lubomirski and his supporters on the one hand and the royal party on the other. The military question was a crucial one, too, in the mid-seventeenth century Commonwealth. Citing the historian Iakovenko, I have hinted at the significance of professional soldiers' mentality for the experience of internal violence that large parts of the Commonwealth's population underwent in that period. Military men had not yet been profiled as a social group in the first half of the century, but wars and invasions of the mid-century pushed forward a professional conscience of both the officers and the soldiers. In permanent military conflict both with external and internal adversaries, the rulers of the Commonwealth felt pressure from many sides to make the army more efficient. Trying to do so, they copied what was considered as useful from Habsburg, Swedish, Turkish, Persian, and Tatar troops.[49] The core of the Commonwealth's military forces had been a royal army of mercenaries, which was transformed into a standing formation in the course of the 17th century. This army had differed from the beginning from other European mercenary armies in so far as it was not the product of "private" military entrepreneurship: It was recruited in the name of the king, its leaders were installed by the monarch, and it was to be paid by state means.[50]

Funding is well-known to have been the vulnerable point of army modernisation, especially in the Polish-Lithuanian Commonwealth with its high degree of political participation by all layers of the nobility, since this participation included questions of state finance. A part of the Commonwealth's army, the light cavalry, was "seldom paid except out of booty".[51] Yet the core of the army expected the king to pay the soldiers. If he did not, the army formed one more institution of self-defence legitimated by custom, which could not easily be declared illegal because it was a variation of the noble confederation described above: the *Związek*. This formation was supposed to exert pressure on the king to fulfil his financial obligations. In contrast to the confederation, the *Związek* was no exclusively noble institution: it included non-noble soldiers.[52] Thus it was a sworn association of military men, a *Männerbund*, and in a way a public institution of what Iakovenko calls the military subculture of the Commonwealth.

---

49 Henryk Wisner, "Polska sztuka wojenna pierwszej połowy XVII wieku. Wątpliwości i hipotezy", *Kwartalnyk historyczny* 84 (1977): 405-415; Alfred P. Brainard, "Polish-Lithuanian Cavalry in the Late Seventeenth Century", *The Polish Review* 36 (1991): 69-82, especially 74.
50 Bardach, Historia państwa i prawa, 2: 250, 137.
51 Brainard, Polish-Lithuanian Cavalry, 76.
52 Bardach, Historia państwa i prawa, 2: 244.

To be sure, it was not before the end of the seventeenth century that such a *Związek* tried to pursue political aims beyond pressing for payment.[53] But the formation of two of these formations within a few years – in 1659 and 1661 – was an important political fact even if both restricted themselves to the issue of payment. This is all the more true as it was Jan Kazimierz's major adversary to come, Lubomirski, who took the lead of the 1661 *Związek*. It was this dimension of Lubomirski's military leadership which the mentioning of Cromwell and the Protectorate in royal propaganda alluded to.

Considering transnational representation in Lubomirski's rebellion, we thus have to conclude that this rebellion was not just an act of resistance by nobles fearing a royal *dominium absolutum*. It rather reflected the float of information and the differentiated concepts of legitimate rule in contemporary Europe. Cromwell and the Protectorate as points of reference in royal propaganda against Lubomirski bear witness to the strong presence of people from abroad (the British in this case) in the Commonwealth, but also of the power of military men, whose self-organization made them agents of their own. Thus, the rebellion stood for the manifold subcultures that made up the Commonwealth and which the attribute "Republic of nobles" describes only partially.

6. AN ALTERNATIVE VOICE FROM EXILE

When Lubomirski died in 1667 in Silesia, his legal status was that of a political criminal in exile. He was not alone. The legal categories treating revolt as a crime, which were accepted in all European monarchies under consideration in this article, created not only the option to use European revolts for propaganda purposes, they also created a truly transnational group of people with a common fate: that of persons condemned for major political crimes living in exile. A voice from abroad commenting on the Lubomirski revolt in a way which significantly differed from the king's and the rebel's propaganda was that of the Anti-Trinitarian Stanisław Lubieniecki, whom Janusz Tazbir drew historians' attention to.[54] Lubieniecki was among the Polish nobility living in Prussian exile. He offered a thorough reflection of the transnational character of the conflict, including the topic of money and the relation between want of money, inflation and the dependence of the Republic's political forces on foreign courts. He distinguished Tatars and Cossacks, who for other authors were but one, pleading for the Cossack's reintegration into the

---

53 Ibid.
54 Janusz Tazbir, "Głos ariański w polemice rokoszu Lubomirskiego", *Przegląd historyczny* 60 (1959): 62-80, especially 72.

Commonwealth through religious tolerance. Even the French-born queen's manoeuvres were described with an appeal to human understanding: the Queen's position was explained to be dependent on family loyalty and insofar (considering female nature in its contemporary construction, one may add) natural.[55] Compared to the king's and Lubomirski's propaganda, this author's arguments shifted from describing a conflict of honour to the more "modern" analysis of positions and opinions as described in ideal typology by historians of communication.

For our story, it is important to remark that the cited author did not deem it possible to confront his presumed readers in the Commonwealth with his real identity as an exiled Anti-Trinitarian. The confessional conflict, but, possibly, also a presumed effect of the official dishonouring of the condemned as infamous may have incited Lubieniecki to hide his identity behind a fictional catholic author.[56] He thus assumed an authorship qualifying for legitimate claims to authority in the Commonwealth as it was in the mid-seventeenth century: that of the average catholic nobleman. Voices of the exiled were certainly not supposed to successfully claim such authority. The rules of noble public status and of public discursive authority largely overlapped: This made the way out of the mid-seventeenth century crisis more difficult.

Many elements in Lubieniecki's position were not new. They mirrored traditional views and coalitions of the confessional age. The author's peace vision might have been enrooted in the Anti-Trinitarians' irenical views. The understanding for the cause of the Cossacks might have recurred to the good relations between Protestants and Orthodox in the Commonwealth before the Khmel'nyc'kyj uprising of 1648.

Nevertheless, the alternativeness of that voice might also hint at the specific character of the communicative context it emerged from. The juridical procedure to which their cases had been subjected gave the banished a public status and established a durable, though negatively defined, relation to the political formation they came from. This was also the case with the banished rebel Lubomirski himself, who wrote and printed his propaganda in Silesia, while the Polish crown claimed in vain that the Holy Roman Empire should cease giving him exile. This public status distinguished them ‚from those whom the mass exoduses caused by religious persecution drove abroad. When studying the transnational representation of revolts, the transnational spaces of communication inhabited by the exiled of European monarchies in defence against unruly subjects should be considered.

Lubieniecki's more modern, pluralistic vision of things broke with the view of the conflict as a legitimate or non-legitimate revolt. This vision tended towards the

---

55 Tazbir, Głos ariański, 72.
56 On Lubieniecki hiding his authorship: Ibid., 74.

civil war interpretation, but without the call for a strong monarch most prominently deduced from a vision of civil war by Thomas Hobbes. Ironically, such a broad view on foreign dependence and multiply motivated dissent gave more material to discredit Poland-Lithuania's political order as a façade or even a mere back-drop to "anarchy" than the representation of resistance as revolt could ever provide. The modernisation of communication was not to the Commonwealth's advantage.

Governments Struggling with Foreign Representations of Internal Revolts

"Revolts" in the *Kuranty* of March–July 1671

INGRID MAIER, STEPAN SHAMIN

INTRODUCTION

The *kuranty* are the surveys of the foreign press prepared for the Tsar and Boyar Council starting in the middle of the 17th century. It is impossible to determine when the practice of their compilation began, since it developed gradually over many years. The kuranty began to be compiled on a regular basis in 1665, when a contract was concluded between the foreigner Jan van Sweeden and the Chancery of Privy Affairs (the organ concerned with questions of personal interest to Tsar Aleksei Mikhailovich) for the organization of the Riga post, which was to supply Moscow on a bi-weekly basis with foreign newspapers.[1] Starting in September 1668, the Riga post arrived weekly, and beginning in March 1669 a second post, located in Vilna, also began to operate weekly.[2] The kuranty were read to the Tsar and members of the Boyar Council. In the second half of the 17th century, they were the basic source of operative information for the Russian government about the political situation in Europe.[3] The kuranty used in this manner were filed in the archive of the Diplomatic Chancery. Today, the main collection of them is preserved in the Russian State Archive of Ancient Acts (RGADA, f. 155).

The main aim of our essay is to show which articles in the European press concerning social conflicts such as disorders, plots, revolts, uprisings and popular

---

1 *Russkaia istoricheskaia biblioteka*, ed. Imperatorskoi Arkheograficheskoi komissiei, t. 21. Dela Tainogo prikaza, kn. 1 (Sankt Peterburg, 1907), stb. 1065.
2 I. P. Kozlovskii, *Pervye pochty i pervye pochtmeistery v Moskovskom gosudarstve*, 2 toma (Varshava, 1913), 2: 36–37.
3 E. I. Kobzareva, "Izvestiia o sobytiiakh v Zapadnoi Evrope v dokumentakh Posol'skogo prikaza XVII veka" (Dissertatsiia na soiskanie uchenoi stepeni kand. ist. nauk, Moskva, 1988 [unpublished]), 178.

movements attracted attention from the Russian government during a specified period, viz. from March to the beginning of July 1671.[4]

Previous research has touched upon representations of revolts in the kuranty on more than one occasion. The first translated news items studied by Russian scholars were reports about the uprising of Stepan Razin. As early as 1857, A. Popov commented on the Russian authorities' attempts to prompt Sweden to punish those who spread rumours about the uprising of Stepan Razin and the dispute between Aleksei Mikhailovich and Patriarch Nikon in the European newspapers.[5] Subsequently, N. N. Bantysh-Kamenskii and G. Forsten explored this subject.[6] A significant part of the kuranty containing news about the Razin uprising has been published.[7] Other social conflicts were less elaborately examined. The American scholar D. C. Waugh in his dissertation noted the kuranty reports of the 1660s, which described disturbances in the Ottoman Empire.[8] The materials of the kuranty featuring news about various social conflicts in England have been studied in detail. The Russian scholar E. I. Kobzareva examined the information about England received and translated in Russia from 1642 to 1688 in her (unpublished) doctoral dissertation.[9] S. M. Shamin analysed the reports in the kuranty concerning the uprising in Moscow in 1682.[10] However, no one has yet undertaken to analyse all of the news in the kuranty about social conflicts for a particular period.

For our analysis we have chosen the kuranty ranging from March through the beginning of July 1671. We selected this period because at that time Russia was shaken by a major revolt led by Stepan Razin. The European press reported about

---

4   The relevant documents are kept in RGADA, f. 155, op. 1, 1671, ed. khr. 7 (most documents); ibid., 1665 [!], ed. khr. 12 (just one set of kuranty that ended up in the archive in the wrong chronological order).

5   A. Popov, *Istoriia vozmushcheniia Stenki Razina* (Moskva, 1857), 81–82.

6   N. N. Bantysh-Kamenskii, *Obzor vneshnikh snoshenii Rossii (po 1800 god)*, ch. 4 (Moskva, 1902), 190–191; G. Forsten, "Snosheniia Shvetsii i Rossii vo vtoroi polovine XVII v. 1648–1700" [chast' 4], *Zhurnal Ministerstva narodnogo prosveshcheniia* (June 1899): 278–339.

7   A. G. Man'kov, ed., *Inostrannye izvestiia o vosstanii Stepana Razina. Materialy i issledovaniia* (Leningrad, 1975), 80–151.

8   Daniel C. Waugh, "Seventeenth-Century Muscovite Pamphlets with Turkish Themes: Toward a Study of Muscovite Literary Culture in its European Setting" (Unpublished Ph.D. diss., Harvard University, Cambridge, Mass., 1972).

9   Kobzareva, *Izvestiia*, 145–199.

10 S. M. Shamin, "Kuranty kak istochnik po istorii Moskovskogo vosstaniia 1682 g." (to appear).

the Razin uprising from the very beginning, but no kuranty for the last months of 1670 and the first two months of 1671 have been preserved (the kuranty compiled between July 6 and the beginning of September 1671 are also missing). According to the German press historian Martin Welke, the Razin revolt was one of the most frequently reported events in the German newspapers of 1670–1671.[11] The translators of the kuranty usually did not leave out these reports in their news bulletins for the Tsar and boyars.

Our primary inquiry is not so much concerned with reports about revolts in Europe in general, but rather the way in which European news about events in Russia came back to their starting point. The existence of published studies on the given theme has substantially facilitated our work. In the first part of our paper we examine kuranty materials about social conflicts in Poland / Ukraine and in Western Europe; the second part is devoted to the uprising of Stepan Razin.

The translations in the kuranty of reports written in German were derived for the most part from Berlin newspapers: *B. Einkommende Ordinari und Postzeitungen*[12] and *Mittwochischer / Sonntagischer Mercurius*.[13] In all likelihood, the compilers of the kuranty used the Königsberg newspaper *Königsb. Sontags / Donnerstags Ordinari PostZeitung* as well, but only five complete issues and one fragment of that paper have been preserved in Moscow for all of 1671.[14] Only one of them relates to the period we examined,[15] and that issue was not used as a source for any of the translations. However, since the Königsberg paper was very popular in the Diplomatic Chancery in the 1660s,[16] there is no reason to think that the

---

11 Martin Welke, "Rußland in der deutschen Publizistik des 17. Jahrhunderts (1613–1689)", in *Forschungen zur osteuropäischen Geschichte*, Historische Veröffentlichungen, ed. Osteuropa-Institut an der Freien Universität Berlin, vol. 23 (Wiesbaden, 1976), 105–275, 203.

12 RGADA, f. 155, op. 1, 1671, ed. khr. 2.

13 RGADA, f. 155, op. 1, 1671, ed. khr. 3.

14 One of the six complete copies that have been preserved, No. 104, is in duplicate (RGADA, f. 155, op. 1, 1671, ed. khr. 1). No. 102 is not complete; only pp. 1–2 and 7–8 are preserved. This fragment is bound in together with newspapers from Berlin; see RGADA, f. 155, op. 1, 1671, ed. khr. 2, fol. 141–142. For a detailed survey of all printed German newspapers from the 17th century in RGADA see V. I. Simonov, "Deutsche Zeitungen des 17. Jahrhunderts im Zentralen Staatsarchiv für alte Akten (CGADA), Moskau", *Gutenberg-Jahrbuch* (1979), 210–220.

15 *Königsb. Sontags Ordinari PostZeitung* No. 14 (RGADA, f. 155, op. 1, 1671, ed. khr. 1).

16 See *Vesti-Kuranty 1656 g., 1660–1662 gg., 1664–1670 gg. Ch. 2: Inostrannye originaly k russkim tekstam. Issledovanie i podgotovka tekstov Ingrid Majer* (Moskva, 2008), 78–79.

situation changed significantly in 1671. Due to the poor preservation of the newspaper, we probably did not identify any "Königsberg originals".[17] As for the Dutch kuranty originals for 1671, we could identify Russian translations from newspapers printed in Amsterdam, Haarlem (near Amsterdam) and The Hague. Unfortunately, not many editions printed during the period under consideration are still preserved in Moscow.[18] Since so many 17th-century newspaper issues have been lost forever (not only in Russia, but also in other countries), we could trace the foreign originals for less than 50% of the kuranty texts quoted in this article.

In order to understand which news about revolts attracted the interest of the Muscovite government, it is necessary to establish which of the newspapers that arrived in Moscow were translated and which were not. We can be most confident about this in those cases when translations of articles from specific issues of a European paper are found in the kuranty. In these cases we can surmise that the omitted publications were irrelevant to the translators.[19] The matter is more complicated in the cases when there is no translation in the kuranty from an issue of a newspaper that was nevertheless received in Moscow. Then it is necessary to decide whether the articles of that issue were omitted because they were of no interest to Russian diplomats or whether the file of the kuranty in which they were found has been lost.

In this context we analysed the degree of preservation of the kuranty for the relevant period, viz. March – July 1671. The schedule of the Riga and Vilna posts meant that foreign newspapers for the compilation of the kuranty were obtained about eight times a month (four times each via the Riga and the Vilna postal line).

---

17 No copies have been preserved in other repositories either; see Else Bogel & Elger Blühm, *Die deutschen Zeitungen des 17. Jahrhunderts. Ein Bestandsverzeichnis mit historischen und bibliographischen Angaben*, Studien zur Publizistik. Bremer Reihe. Band 17:III (München etc., 1985), 109.

18 For an exact survey of all printed Dutch 17th-century newspapers still preserved in RGADA see Ingrid Maier, "Niederländische Zeitungen ('Couranten') des 17. Jahrhunderts im Russischen Staatsarchiv für alte Akten (RGADA), Moskau", *Gutenberg-Jahrbuch* (2004), 191–218. Moreover, two (probably unique) issues – which we saw only after the 2004 article was printed – can be found in RGADA, f. 155, op. 2, ed. khr. 45 and 46: *Oprechte Haerlemse Dingsdaegse Courant* No. 14 and *Amsterdamsche Dingsdaegse Courant* No. 15, both printed April 8, 1681.

19 It is possible that in cases when the quantity of information was large, the translators might omit also those materials which would have been included in the kuranty in other circumstances, where there was a smaller amount of pertinent information. In any event, the compilers of the kuranty did not omit new information about subjects which directly touched upon Russian interests.

However, in practice, for the period of the 1670s–1690s the kuranty were compiled less frequently. The reasons for this might vary, although in the first instance they relate to the shortcomings of the postal service. Since the European newspapers passed through several postal stations on the road to Russia, a delay at any of those stations meant that several issues of one and the same newspaper might arrive in Moscow on the same day, and therefore could be translated on the same occasion. Moreover, it cannot be ruled out that the kuranty were not compiled in cases where the newspapers did not contain any new information of interest to the Russian government. In the period of interest to us, March to July of 1671, there are four to nine "issues" of the kuranty compiled each month (see Table I).

Table I. Kuranty compilations from March to the beginning of July 1671

	March	April	May	June
via Riga post	2	2	2	4
via Vilna post	3	2	5	5
Total	5	4	7	9

From Table I we can conclude that the kuranty for May and June – seven and nine compilations, respectively – have most likely been preserved in their entirety. It might even be that all sets compiled during March and April have been preserved to our time. In those months, on account of the melting of the snow and the spring "roadlessness", the mail always functioned significantly worse than in other months; hence, the kuranty were compiled less frequently.

Let us turn now to the analysis of the kuranty texts.

SOCIAL CONFLICTS IN EUROPE

The political elite in Moscow was extremely interested in the European press reports about the struggle of the Cossacks in Western Ukraine under Hetman P. D. Doroshenko against Polish rule. Doroshenko, who could not hope to deal single-handedly with the Polish army and those Cossacks who sympathized with Poland, placed Ukraine under the control of the Turkish sultan. This provoked a war between Poland and the Ottoman Empire along with its subject, the Crimean Tatars. In a letter from July 21, 1667, Sultan Mehmed IV had informed the Polish King Jan Kazimierz that if he wished to preserve peace with the Ottoman Empire, he should refrain from any attempt to bring the Cossacks under his control.[20] Poland had no wish to lose the Ukrainian territories which remained under its rule. The start of the inevitable war was delayed by the fact that until September 1669 the Turkish army was occupied in the war over Crete.

It is no exaggeration to conclude that the events on the eastern borders of the Polish state attracted more attention on part of the Russian government than did any other matter of foreign affairs. In fact, Russia and Poland were obligated by a treaty of alliance to help one another in the event of an invasion by the Turks or Tatars;[21] hence, Russia was directly involved in the events. It is difficult to determine the entire number of publications on "Ukrainian popular movements" in the kuranty on account of the fact that Doroshenko's actions resulted in war between Poland and the Ottoman Empire. In many instances, it is impossible to separate these events. As a whole, the news about the situation in Ukraine, the diplomatic negotiations between Poland and its enemies (Turkey, the Crimea and the Cossacks), articles on the mustering of armies and their funding, and descriptions of military actions constituted no less than 27–28% of the contents of the kuranty for the given period.[22] These reports permitted the readers or listeners to follow the events in all their details. In the European press, the "Ukrainian problem" received significantly less attention. Only in rare cases could a quarter of any issue of a German newspaper be devoted to this subject, whereas news about the Ukraine in Dutch newspapers was still more limited.

The news in the kuranty about Poland allows us to follow the gradual exacerbation of relations between the Polish King and the Ukrainian Cossacks (who were under his rule), an accelerating conflict that became more complicated because of external interference by Turks and Tatars. During the winter of 1670–1671, there was still a serious chance to preserve peace. This becomes evident from a news item sent from Warsaw on January 23, 1671, and translated for the

---

20 B. N. Floria, "Nachalo otkrytoi osmanskoi ekspansii v Vostochnoi Evrope (1667–1671 gg.)", in *Osmanskaia imperiia i strany Tsentral'noi, Vostochnoi i Iugo-Vostochnoi Evropy v XVII v.*, ch. 2 (Moskva, 2001), 78.

21 Floria, Nachalo, 77.

22 The following method of calculation has been used: all the kuranty of the period under study have been copied into the computer, and the total number of characters taken to equal 100%. Then all information not connected with the given theme has been excluded and the number of characters in the remaining text calculated. The given method has some minor faults. For instance, in articles which as a rule contain information on several topics it is not always possible to separate them from one another. Moreover, sometimes difficulties arise in interpreting the text of reports. This problem is especially severe in the analysis of the numerous reports about the course of the Polish sejms.

kuranty.[23] It said, among other things, that the Polish ambassador Karvovskii, who had been in the Crimean khanate for some time, had received the khan's promise that he would preserve peace, at least under certain conditions. Karvovskii was also said to carry with him original letters written by the Cossack leaders Khanenko and Doroshenko, "from which their unsteadiness becomes evident". Since the Warsaw message undoubtedly was written by a correspondent whose sympathies were with the Polish King, the above mentioned "unsteadiness" can be understood as the rival Cossack leaders' lacking the will to subordinate themselves to the Polish King.

In mid-spring there was still hope for peace, as becomes clear from a correspondence under the headline L'vov (= Lemberg), March 6.[24] An envoy from the Ukrainian Cossack hetman Doroshenko to the Polish King had been killed in Podolia. Although the Polish Field Crown Hetman (from 1668), Prince Dymitr Jerzy Wiśniowiecki (1631–1682), wanted to see the supposed killer sentenced to death, further development of the "Ukrainian matters" showed that this did not contribute to the improving Polish-Ukrainian relations. The newspaper article and its Russian translation end with a sentence regarding huge troop contingents in Turkey and the worthless statement "but what their intentions are we do not know".

Later on, toward the end of March, the threat of war became apparent and the news that reached the Russian readers was not only about sabre-rattling, but it also contained reports about minor encounters. In April it was clear that a serious war was imminent. A news item in the kuranty datelined Warsaw, April 11, reads as follows:

There is bad news from the borders with the Tatar, Cossack and Turkish territories. Not long ago Tatars and Cossacks have caused this state [i.e., Poland] huge devastation. It is reported that the Tatars have gathered 4000 men, the Cossacks 2000 [...] Moscow's ambassador was dismissed. He is very dissatisfied, since he received the king's charter[25] not from the king's hand, but from the chancellor's.[26]

---

23 RGADA, f. 155, op. 1, 1671, ed. khr. 7, fol. 5v–6. The Russian text was translated from a Dutch newspaper, *Oprechte Haerlemse Dingsdaegse Courant* No. 6, 1671, p. [2] (RGADA, f. 155, op. 1, 1671, ed. khr. 6, fol. 4v).

24 RGADA, f. 155, op. 1, 1671, ed. khr. 7, fol. 47–47v. We have identified the original article for the Russian translation in the Berlin newspaper *Mittwochischer Mercurius* No. 12, 1671, p. [1] (RGADA, f. 155, op. 1, 1671, ed. khr. 3, fol. 27).

25 In the Dutch original the Russian word *gramota* is used (in the slightly distorted form *Ramotta*).

26 RGADA, f. 155, op. 1, 1671, ed. khr. 7, fol. 89v–90. The translation is made from a Dutch newspaper, *Amsteldamsche Dingsdaegse Courant* No. 17, 1671, p. [1].

The threat of an upcoming war might have been diminished by a constructive agreement with Russia, but apparently such a settlement was not achieved. Another article, under the headline Warsaw, May 1, clearly shows that the absence of internal accord in Poland was an extremely serious obstacle when it came to the organization of any successful resistance against the aggressor. When the fortress Kamenets Podol'skii (which played a key role in controlling Podolia) already was in serious danger of being besieged, the Polish government was unable to collect the necessary troops or to pay the German mercenaries, as the Russian political elite could read in this news item from Warsaw:

This crown is under great danger on the part of the Cossacks, Tatars and Turks, since their [i.e., the Cossacks'] highest hetman Doroshenko has united his forces with some thousand Tatars against Kamenets Podol'skii. His majesty the King has ordered a general mobilization of the Republic, but this will not be possible to get through before the wedding of Prince Dmitrii [i.e., Dymitr Wiśniowiecki, the Field Hetman of the Crown]. Meanwhile much harm will be done to this state. Two days ago an envoy arrived from Moscow; his intentions are not known. In Radom the Polish soldiers have received their pay, but not the German ones. The latter say that they are going to take this matter into their own hands.[27]

The defeat of the Polish troops and the conquest of Kamenets Podol'skii by the Turkish sultan one year later, in 1672, became a natural consequence of this situation. However, these events are already beyond the chronological limits of our study.

Another national liberation movement whose successes were followed attentively in Moscow was the conflict between the Holy Roman Emperor and the Hungarian conspirators – in particular counts Péter Zrínyi (in the printed newspapers and in the kuranty usually called *Serini / Sirini*), Kristóf Frangepán, and Ferenc Nádasdy – who requested military aid from the Ottoman Empire in their struggle to re-establish the rights and freedoms of the Hungarian nobility. This made the Holy Roman Empire a potential ally of Russia and Poland. Furthermore, if the Turkish army moved against the Empire, not against Poland, then Russia would be spared the immediate prospect of a conflict with one of the most powerful armies in Europe at that time. Against this background it is no surprise that reports about the relations between the Emperor and the Hungarian conspirators occupied nearly 6.5% (22 entries) of the contents of the kuranty in the given period. That number of translated reports made it possible for a Russian reader or listener to

---

27 RGADA, f. 155, op. 1, 1671, ed. khr. 7, fol. 112–112v. The original could be located in the Berlin newspaper *Mittwochischer Mercurius* No. 1671/18, p. [2] (RGADA, f. 155, op. 1, 1671, ed. khr. 3, fol. 35v).

follow in some detail the emerging events. In particular the reports included in the kuranty tended to conclude that the Turks did not want to support the Hungarian conspirators: it was too important for them to maintain the relatively good relations with the Empire following the Truce of Vasvár concluded on August 10, 1664. Reports sent from Vienna at the beginning of February spoke of the Turks' unwillingness to support the Hungarian nobles:

From Vienna February 1. Our courier, who has already been expected for three days, has returned from Turkey bringing news that the Turks will not accept the Hungarians as their subjects and do not wish to quarrel with us about that. Thus it is anticipated that there will be no conflict with the Turks.[28]

Later, there was news about how the Turks were handing over to the Emperor his subjects which had fled to them, or were ordering the Prince of Transylvania Michael Apafi to execute them:

From Vienna April 21. From Upper Hungary is news that prince Obavti [= Apafi], on the orders of the Sultan, decreed that several of the Hungarian traitors who wished to flee to Transylvania be beheaded. Also the border pashas have written to the Imperial border commanders of their hope that they would not admit any Imperial traitors and give them refuge.[29]

From the Empire, from Vienna May 9. One of Prince Michael Apafi's men came to us in Vienna from Hungary and informed us that the Turks wish to hand over all Imperial traitors, and several Imperial regiments have been sent to receive these fugitives. But the French ambassador to the Sultan has insistently requested that the Sultan not order the Imperial traitors to be handed over. However, the Sultan has not listened to him and ordered that all the traitors be given back.[30]

Very rarely did the translators in the Diplomatic Chancery omit any articles about the planned (and later carried out) execution of the Hungarian conspirators:

From Vienna April 15 [...] The main conspirators were sentenced as follows: Count Nadasty first is to have his hand cut off and then his head; so likewise Franshipalni [= Frangepán], but Count Sirinii's sentence may be reduced because he willingly confessed his guilt, to wit that

---

28 RGADA, f. 155, op. 1, 1671, ed. khr. 7, fol. 6v. The original is in *Oprechte Haerlemse Saterdaegse Courant* No.1671/7, p. [2] (ibid., ed. khr. 6, fol. 6v).
29 RGADA, f. 155, op. 1, 1671, ed. khr. 7, fol. 104v.
30 RGADA, f. 155, op. 1, 1671, ed. khr. 7, fol. 134–134v.

he wanted to catch the Emperor and hand him over to the Turks. So it is expected that he will be sentenced to imprisonment for life. But others expect that he too will be executed, because after admitting his guilt he conspired with Nadasty about betrayal. Among them no one committed as great an evil as Count Nadasty, because he killed his wife for refusing to poison the Emperor.[31]

This, incidentally, seems highly unlikely – that Count Ferenc Nádasdy, who had been the High Judge of the Crown Court, ordered his own wife to poison the Emperor and then killed her for refusing to do so.[32]

From Vienna May 3. Now the Hungarian traitors have been executed: Count Nadasty and both Counts Francipani and Sirini have been beheaded after their profound expressions of repentance. Before his execution, Count Nadasty wrote to the Emperor and abjectly petitioned for his benevolence, especially regarding his innocent children, that they not be tainted by his treachery. And Count Serini before his death removed his golden chain decorated with diamonds and containing holy relics and handed it over to the Imperial commissioner in order that he give it to his son. And Count Francipani wrote a book while in prison from his deep intellect, and now they wish to publish the book. And the Emperor decreed that 2000 requiems be performed for those executed. Also, in the city of Pressburg, they executed by sword the gentleman Hanov and his companion, and those who are still in custody will soon meet the same fate. The Turkish pasha in the city of Großwardein has captured 17 fugitive Hungarians, and the Sultan has ordered him to hand over to the Imperial Commissioner those individuals and others who fled from Transylvania to the Ottomans, because the Turkish Sultan did not wish to place those fugitives under his protection.[33]

All these reports would not leave any doubt in the minds of Russian kuranty readers that the Turks would not support the uprising in Hungary in the near future and thus would have their army free to campaign against Poland. If one compares the

---

31 RGADA, f. 155, op. 1, 1671, ed. khr. 7, fol. 100v–101.
32 The information about the planned poisoning of the Emperor (that should have taken place in 1666) was also printed in a contemporary pamphlet, albeit with some reservation about the reason of the death of Nadasty's wife: "[...] (deßwegen Sie selbst/ wie man glaubt/ hernach mit Gifft hingerichtet worden) [...]". See: *Warhafftige und ausführliche Relation, Wie die Ungarischen Rebellen Zu Wien in Oesterreich/ Als auch Zur Wienischen Neu-Stadt Und zu Preßburg Am 30. Aprilis Anno 1671. Zur verdienten Straffe gezogen worden*. P. [3]. Six pages of this pamphlet are accessible on www.vd17.de (VD 17 No. 14:002279R; accessed June 23, 2009).
33 RGADA, f. 155, op. 1, 1671, ed. khr. 7, fol. 116v–117v; the original is in *B. Einkommende Ordinari und Postzeitungen* No. 1671/74 (ibid., ed. khr. 2, fol. 56v).

relative quantity of news in the kuranty to that in the European newspapers about Hungarian events, it turns out that the German newspapers were contained more, but the Dutch less than in the kuranty.

News about disorder in the Ottoman Empire was related to what, for Russia, was the critical problem of Turkish expansion in Eastern Europe. Such reports constituted about 2% (10 articles) in the kuranty of the period under examination. If some substantial internal political crisis were to begin in Turkey, then the Turkish army would be unable to embark on an invasion. Reports concerning unrest of local inhabitants of various regions of the Ottoman Empire and concerning the attempts of the Sultan's mother to arouse the janissaries against her son gave the Russian government reason to hope for such a turn of events. Here are two of the most characteristic reports:

From Venice February 28. They write us from Constantinople that the Sultan's mother is diligently trying to depose the Sultan himself and all his officials. On account of that, she has been haranguing all the janissaries. Moreover, we are told that in the city of Kaschau, the local inhabitants have begun a revolt and attacked the pasha's chambers with a great shout and wanted to kill the pasha on account of his having imposed on them high taxes and even more fiscal exactions for the Sultan, and for his arbitrary rule. And the pasha, upon seeing them, ordered all their money to be tossed out the window. And that barely pacified them. Likewise in Macedonia a revolt against the pasha has broken out which he managed to quell with money.[34]

From Venice March 21. Letters to us from all places are in agreement that all efforts to reconcile the Sultan with his mother have failed, and his mother with particular zeal has enlisted the Constantinople janissaries on her side. As a result, disorders are expected which will mean that the Sultan will not attack any Christian monarch.[35]

There is no doubt that the articles on disorders in Turkey were of great interest to Russian diplomats, just as they were to the readers of the European press. The relatively small number of such news items can be explained by the fact that the events reported in those articles had no serious consequences. The proportions of reports in this thematic group in the kuranty and in the European newspapers are roughly identical.

The remaining conspiracies and uprisings in (Western) Europe in the period under examination were of secondary significance to the authorities in Moscow,

---

34 RGADA, f. 155, op. 1, 1671, ed. khr. 7, fol. 38v–39.

35 RGADA, f. 155, op. 1, 1671, ed. khr. 7, fol. 59v. The original is in *Oprechte Haerlemse Dingsdaegse Courant* No. 1671/7 (National Archives, Kew, SP 119/61/42).

since they did not affect Russian interests directly. In the kuranty, they appeared merely as part of the general panorama of European political life. The quantity of information about these events did not exceed one per cent of the surviving documents. On the basis of this evidence, it was impossible to understand the substance of the conflicts noted in the kuranty and figure out their causes. On four occasions, for instance, the kuranty included correspondence concerning the struggle of the free city Braunschweig against the Princes of Lüneburg (House of Guelph). Braunschweig had received its city status back in the 15th century. In 1671, the Prince of Lüneburg annexed it, but in the articles included in the kuranty, the matter was presented as though the inhabitants of the city had rebelled against their ruler.

In actual fact, Duke Rudolf August (1666–1704),[36] after a long siege by an army of 20,000 (commanded by Count von Waldeck) and some 80 cannon, had seized/conquered the city and deprived it of its traditional independence.[37] The city's independence had been defended by about 3,000 individuals (using 137 cannon) – effectively, there was no way Braunschweig could maintain its position as a free city without outside military assistance. The fact that part of the inhabitants of Braunschweig sympathized with the Duke weakened the city's defences and helped the Duke achieve his goals. On June 11, Braunschweig submitted to the Duke's demands, and on June 12, the city gates were opened to his army of some 5,000 men (the rest of the Duke's army left). On June 16 there was a ceremony of taking the oath of fealty to Duke Rudolf August and his brother Anton Ulrich. The city had to pay 3,000 thalers (later 4,000) per month in addition to providing grain, money for the officers and quarters for more than 3,000 men. All of the city's arms, military supplies, and silver were confiscated. The previous city statute was annulled; the autonomy of this formerly free Hanseatic city came to an end.

In the articles selected from European newspapers for the kuranty, there is unqualified sympathy with the policies of the Duke. The defenders of the city's freedoms are described in negative colours: the lower classes revolted; they killed the commandant; drunks are wandering around […] One must suppose that the Duke himself provided the information about the conflict:

From Hamburg May 30. We have been informed from the camp outside Braunschweig that the inhabitants of that city have asked their rightful Lüneburg princes for a respite of one day.

---

36 The son of the famous Duke August, the book collector and founder of the Wolfenbüttel library, Herzog August Bibliothek.

37 See Richard Moderhack, *Braunschweiger Stadtgeschichte. Mit Zeittafel und Bibliographie* (Braunschweig, 1997), 119–122.

And they have proposed the following terms: 1. that they wish to be as before under administration of the Lüneburg princes; 2. that all their villages will be handed over to those princes; 3. that in compensation for their guilt they will give those princes 6 barrels of gold and accept that the princes' troops be quartered at city expense. And in the city the lower classes rebelled and killed their commandant, and wander around all the time drunk, and the Burghers and Councilmen are frightened of them.[38]

From Lüneburg June 3. The Army of the Prince of Braunschweig is besieging the city of Braunschweig and bombarding it with large artillery. And peasants have brought more cannon to the camp on 4,000 horses. And those of the city inhabitants who begin to speak about making peace are threatened with death by the rabble.[39]

From Stockholm May 14. [...] The city of Braunschweig is under siege and two colonels and a major have been killed. And Brandenburg emissaries have gone to the city and persuaded the burghers that they should throw their lot in with the Braunschweig princes. Also emissaries from Lübeck, Hamburg and Bremen have come. The outcome of all this will soon be known. May the Lord bring about a good result.[40]

From Wolfenbüttel May 30. Our Braunschweig and Lüneburg troops with artillery have arrived outside the city of Braunschweig and invested it with force. From within the city they can inflict no damage on the besiegers even though they fire on them constantly. It is anticipated that we will begin to bombard the city with fire bombs. To the great regret of our Prince they are opposing him with arms and fire; and hence yesterday a herald was sent to them in the city demanding that they abandon their evil thoughts. The leading people in the city are inclined to do that, but the rabble will not listen to them, and whoever talks of peace they call a traitor and beat.[41]

One can imagine that it would have been impossible for those who heard such news – i.e., the Tsar and boyars – to make sense of the reasons for the conflict or the course of the military actions. Out of the mass of correspondence printed in the Western newspapers on the subject (in some German as well as in Dutch issues there were as many as five different articles on the Braunschweig conflict), the Russian translators selected either irregular publications[42] or, more probably, those

---

38 RGADA, f. 155, op. 1, 1671, ed. khr. 7, fol. 147v.
39 RGADA, f. 155, op. 1, 1671, ed. khr. 7, fol. 152v.
40 RGADA, f. 155, op. 1, 1671, ed. khr. 7, fol. 159–159v.
41 RGADA, f. 155, op. 1, 1671, ed. khr. 7, fol. 159v–160.
42 Thus, for example, from the Berlin newspaper *Mittwochischer Mercurius*, Week 25, was translated a newsletter from Warsaw of June 19 (fol. 156–157; in the kuranty this article

in which the conflict was described precisely as a revolt of Braunschweig against the city's lawful ruler. Such a strange selection of news is easy to understand in the context of Russian realities during the reign of Tsar Aleksei Mikhailovich. By the 1670s, Russian rulers had not had to deal with independent or politically autonomous cities for over a century, even though the inhabitants of various Russian cities often rebelled against the exactions of royal administrators. For example, in 1650, Pskov and Novgorod revolted. The government's troops were forced to lay siege to them. However, during the revolt there were conflicts between the more radically inclined "masses" and the city elite in both cases. Thus, the compilers of the kuranty selected for translation not the more precise information but that which more readily fitted into the accepted structure of social relations.

It also would have been difficult for a Russian audience to understand the only report in the kuranty for the period under study concerning a conspiracy in Spain. Here, the matter concerned the struggle between the natural son of Philip IV, Juan Jose of Austria and his opponents for influence over the King of Spain, Carlos II, who was still a minor:

From Spain, from the city of Madrid April 3. In recent days in this city they have found a letter containing the discharge of lord Dekardov,[43] who was recently executed. The letter says that he was not guilty in the disputes which arose between the Queen and lord Juan of Austria regarding the Queen's confessor lord Eberhard.[44] And when the King's halberdiers by royal

---

was combined without a new heading into another Warsaw communication of the same date whose original we have not located). In the same issue are four articles about the conflict between the city of Braunschweig and the Dukes of Lüneburg under the following headings: Wolfenbüttel vom 13./23. dito (Junii); Hannover/ vom 13.23. dito (Junii); Hamburg/ vom 16.26. dito; Ein anders/ vom vorigen. The last article contains extremely important information about the events in Braunschweig, but this article is not in the kuranty: "Gleich itzo kömmt der Braunschweigische Bote aus selbiger Stadt/ berichtet/ daß am verwichenen Dienstage Ihre Hochfürstl. Durchl. von Wolffenbüttel/ in Begleitung des Printzen von Oranien und anderer Fürsten und Herren/ daselbst eingezogen. In ermeldter Stadt sind 6000. Mann zu Fuß/ und 100. zu Pferde/ ligen alle auf den Wällen. Die Huldigung ist am Freytage geschehen/ und *imputiret* der Pöbel alles dem Rath/ der ihnen nicht von Ihro Hochfürstl. Durchl. *Postulatis* fürgebracht. Die Herren und dero Völcker sind schon voneinander."

43 "Dekardov" is a transliteration of *Antonio de Cordoue* in the original (see footnote 45); apparently, the Spanish family name *Córdoba* (Italian form: *di Cordova*).

44 Johann Eberhard Nidhard / Neidhardt, 1607–1681, later (from 1672) Cardinal Nidhard. The Queen's advisor after the death of King Philip IV, forced by Juan of Austria to leave Spain in 1669.

decree had been sent to the residence of the executed [i.e., "Dekardov"] in order to look for that letter, they found there another letter, in which he ["Dekardov"] indicated that he planned to poison the lord Juan of Austria. In addition he wanted to place gunpowder under the royal chambers. On account of this report the king and queen wish to leave those chambers for the time being until the gunpowder be found.[45]

The article does not permit drawing any kind of intelligible picture of the situation at the Spanish court. It is possible that the compiler of the kuranty was attracted by the fact of the supposed mining of the royal palace.

A month later the kuranty included one more report concerning a planned attempt on a certain king's life – this time, true, the planned attack concerned a period which antedated the newspaper entry by some 65 years:

From Rome May 9. Last week the Jesuits informed the Roman Pope about 40 individuals of their order whom they termed martyrs and brought him their portraits in order that he enrol them in the list of martyrs. And afterwards the Pope learned the truth: that the English King had executed those Jesuits because they had tunnelled under his palace and placed there a barrel of gunpowder, and the Pope thus turned down the petition citing the fact that they had been punished for criminal activity and not because of their Christian faith.[46]

Certainly not all readers of this news article understood that it deals with the "Gunpowder Plot" of 1605, when English Catholics (among others, the Jesuit Father Henry Garnet)[47] organized an unsuccessful assassination attempt on the life of the English King James I. Apparently the compilers of the kuranty took that information to be "current". A plot aiming to kill the King of England was in and of itself a sufficiently noteworthy event to attract attention. In this instance, the information was doubly interesting for the Russian government, because the assassination attempt was organized by the Jesuits. The Russian government was very suspicious of that order, since they were active in spreading Catholicism among the Orthodox population of those parts of Ukraine and Belorussia which

---

45 RGADA, f. 155, op. 1, 1671, ed. khr. 7, fol. 110–110v. The original is in the Hamburg newspaper *Europæische Sambstägige Zeitung* No. 16 (State Archives Stralsund, E4O 511o).
46 RGADA, f. 155, op. 1, 1671, ed. khr. 7, fol. 150v–151.
47 Born 1555, executed on May 3, 1606.

were under Polish rule. News about Jesuit activity was regularly included in the kuranty.[48]

THE RAZIN UPRISING

A significant part of the kuranty in the period studied (6.7% of the total volume or 32 entries) consists of news about the uprising initiated by Stepan Razin.[49] A larger part of the materials, both in the quantity of text and the number of entries, was given over only to the "Ukrainian" subject matter. Also, in the European press – especially in the German newspapers – the Razin rebellion played an important part, although it probably occupied less space than in the kuranty, especially in the Dutch newspapers, which were printed at quite a temporal distance from the events (as opposed to German newspapers from the relevant period), from the corpus of which every third or fourth issue contained news about the uprising in the Volga region.[50]

Of course, the Russian government possessed much more information about this uprising than the compilers of the European newspapers. Therefore, the inclusion of such news in the kuranty could not broaden the knowledge of Russian diplomats about the activities of the rebels. The reason for the interest in the event lay elsewhere: the translations showed what was being written about the Russian state in Europe, that is, they enabled the Russian leaders to learn something about the image of Russia abroad.

This interest in Russia's image was not purely theoretical. The success or failure of Russian embassies depended on how Russia was perceived in Europe. Moreover, the Russian government actively undertook to attract to Russian service foreign specialists – soldiers, doctors, mining specialists, artists, musicians, etc. Negative press about Russia either made the hiring of such specialists more costly or even impossible. News about victories by Razin also might have forced European merchants involved in long-distance international trade (especially that through Arkhangelsk) to refuse travelling to Russia. This is the key to why the picture

---

48 S. M. Shamin, "K voprosu o vliianii inostrannoi pressy na dukhovnuiu zhizn' russkikh liudei v XVII – nachale XVIII vv.", *Vestnik tserkovnoi istorii* (2007), No. 2, 139–149, 140.

49 RGADA, f. 155, op. 1, 1671, ed. khr. 7, fol. 6v–7, 9v, 14, 20v–21, 23, 24–26, 30, 40v–41, 49v–50, 51–51v, 55–58v, 70, 70v, 88, 101–101v, 102v, 103, 113–113v, 118–118v, 122v, 128, 134, 158v, 166.

50 Approximately 640 German newspapers from that time are preserved, containing more than 180 news items about the Razin uprising. See Welke, Rußland, 203.

painted by the kuranty could not please either the Tsar or the boyars. Even though there were quite varied publications in the press, many articles substantially exaggerated the successes of the rebels and understated the victories of the Tsar's armies. For instance, the Hamburg newspaper *Nordischer Mercurius* wrote about the fact that especially news sent by correspondents in Riga could not be trusted at all; in their newsletters, people who had never been in the army, who were no longer in active service and even people who had already died could be named as having been taken captive, etc.[51]

In fact, at the time when the kuranty we are discussing were compiled, the peak of the rebellion had already passed. On the 1st–3rd of October 1670, Razin had been severely wounded and his army crushed in a decisive battle near Simbirsk. On April 14, 1671, the Cossacks captured Razin and handed him over to the authorities. The leader of the rebellion was executed in Moscow on June 6, 1671. While the unrest continued yet for some time, it no longer presented a threat to the state. Nonetheless, the European press right up to the summer of 1671 continued to publish "news" about the victories of Razin. The translation of a newsletter from Hamburg (dated June 6 – the day of Razin's execution) reads as follows: "Couriers report from Livonia and from Moscow that the traitor Razin is again gathering his forces and seizing cities".[52] Other articles reported about the political isolation of Russia and its actual collapse. News items of this kind were fraught with very serious image problems for the Russian authorities and substantially weakened the position of Russian diplomats in international negotiations. Here are the most striking examples:

From Warsaw January 31. There is news from Moscow that the disorders there are still going on and that Razin has taken Astrakhan' and Kazan' as well as about 50 other places. He is said to have with him about 200,000 men. A Swedish emissary is said to have arrived there to negotiate a treaty, calling him the Tsar of Astrakhan. Allegedly the Persian shah also is interfering in this unrest on account of differences [with Russia] over the Caspian Sea.[53]

From Vilna February 26. Here there is definite news that plenipotentiary ambassadors from the Muscovite state have been sent to his Majesty the King in order to seek assistance against Stenka Razin. And in exchange they wish to offer the Poles Smolensk and all of Ukraine. And Stenka Razin wishes to send his emissaries to the King, so that he will not aid Moscow.

---

51 Welke, Rußland, 204.
52 RGADA, f. 155, op. 1, 1671, ed. khr. 7, fol. 158.
53 RGADA, f. 155, op. 1, 1671, ed. khr. 7, fol. 6v–7. The original is in *Haeghse Dynsdaeghse Post-tydinge* No. 14, from The Hague (ibid., ed. khr. 5, fol. 8).

And this gives the Polish crown hope that all which Moscow had seized from it will be returned.[54]

From Prussia March 3. They report from Vilna that they are awaiting the return of their envoy from Moscow, and it is expected that he will bring news as to whether the Russians will surrender Smolensk, Bykhov and Kiev or wish to fight. The latest letters from Riga indicate that the Tsar ordered the removal of the largest artillery detachment from Smolensk on account of the news that Stenka Razin has submitted to the Poles and Swedes.[55]

From Wismar March 27. From Riga they report that several regiments of cavalry have been ordered from Sweden to Riga, but it is not known for what purpose, whether to help his Majesty the Tsar or because they wish to obtain some compensation. With regard to the troops of his Majesty the Tsar, the letters affirm that they have all been defeated, and the rebel has sent to his Majesty the Tsar six demands that must be agreed to by his Majesty the Tsar if the rebel is to desist from attacking in the future, i.e.: 1. that the Tsar shall name him Tsar of Astrakhan' and Kazan'; 2. that the former Patriarch be restored to his place in Moscow; 3. that the rebel be given 20 millions in gold; 4. that ten princes be handed over to him; 5. that an image of him is to be painted and erected; 6. that he receive tribute on an annual basis.[56]

It is impossible to see a communication of actual information in the last of these texts. There are no documents confirming that such negotiations should have taken place. Much later, in 1672, Russian diplomats told their Swedish colleagues: "[…] it is not true that the bandit Stenka Razin should have sought opportunities to communicate with his Majesty the Tsar and submitted demands concerning the above-mentioned points."[57]

The text with the six alleged demands by Razin has to be seen as a composition of an inflammatory nature, similar in function to the fabricated "letters of the Turkish Sultan", rather curious examples of anti-Turkish propaganda.[58] The authentic letters of Stepan Razin and his cohorts have been thoroughly studied. In them, Razin always presents himself as the ally of the Tsar or of his son Aleksei Alekseevich (already deceased at that time). The leader of the rebellion purports to be carrying out their instructions – to decimate the boyars and other "evil perverters" of the Tsar's will.[59] Such an attitude toward the powers was called

---

54 RGADA, f. 155, op. 1, 1671, ed. khr. 7, fols. 24v–25.
55 RGADA, f. 155, op. 1, 1671, ed. khr. 7, fols. 25–25v.
56 RGADA, f. 155, op. 1, 1671, ed. khr. 7, fols. 56–57.
57 Popov, Istoriia, 82.
58 See Daniel C. Waugh, *The Great Turkes Defiance: On the History of the Apocryphal Correspondence of Ottoman Sultan in its Muscovite and Russian Variants* (Columbus, Ohio, 1978).
59 V. I. Buganov, *Razin i razinitsy* (Moskva, 1995), 12–45 and *passim*.

"naive monarchism" in Soviet historiography. It was common to all peasant movements in the Middle Ages. In any event, we cannot see in the "ultimatum of Stepan Razin" a work by a Russian author. The European newspapers, however, identify for us the source of its spread, the city of Riga in Sweden's Baltic provinces.

Why did bogus newsletters about the weakness of the Russian state appear in the European press? The Soviet historians A. L. Gol'dberg, A. G. Man'kov and S. Ia. Marlinskii suggested that "no occasion was missed to distort specifically and intentionally information about the situation in Russia and compound the horrors in order to prepare popular attitudes abroad for the event of an intervention in the internal affairs of Russia by a European state."[60] However, we disagree with this viewpoint. There are no facts attesting any preparation by the governments of Poland or Sweden, Russia's European neighbours, for an incursion into its territory, so it would not be necessary to "prepare" the European public opinion for such an incursion. The reason for spreading such reports must be sought elsewhere. In the 1650s and 1660s, Russia engaged in wars with Poland and Sweden. The inhabitants of Poland and the Swedish Baltic provinces feared their eastern neighbour and disliked her. This was fertile soil for the fabrication of reports that could be damaging to the Russian government, since news about Russia's impoverished situation might discourage the entrepreneurs of Holland, England and Hamburg from trading with her, and thus automatically give an advantage to their Polish and Baltic colleagues.

The Russian government reacted fiercely to such publications. At the end of 1670, the foreigner von Staden (who was in the service of Tsar Aleksei Mikhailovich) was commanded by the Russian government to induce the Swedish side to punish "gazetteers" who printed unseemly talk about the Tsar himself, about the former Patriarch Nikon and about Stenka Razin. As an example of such a publication, the Russian diplomats adduced a text about

how the former Moscow Patriarch gathered a large army and intended to march against his Muscovite Tsarish Majesty, the reason being that the Tsar had dishonoured him and removed him from the Patriarchal rank for no reason at all, and without considering that he, the Patriarch, was a wise and learned man and in every regard better and more worthy than the Tsar himself. And the reason for the Patriarch's removal was that he had allowed Lutherans, Calvinists and also Roman Catholics to enter the Russian churches, something that in earlier times had been looked upon as unchristian acts. Moreover, from the borders of Russia this news has come, that his Majesty the Tsar is seeking to make peace with Stenka Razin, something which Razin is inclined to do only on the following conditions: 1) that the Russian

---

60 Man'kov, Inostrannye izvestiia, 88.

ruler honour him as Tsar of Kazan' and Astrakhan'; 2) give him from the royal treasury 20 barrels of gold for his army; 3) hand over to him, Stenka, eight of the Tsar's closest boyars, whom he intended to execute for their misdeeds; 4) that Patriarch Nikon, who was now with him, be restored to his rank.[61]

According to the Russian diplomats, this text was printed in the "Riga newspapers" from November 19, 1670.[62] Obviously this is another variant of the report cited above (from Wismar on March 27, 1671), about the "ultimatum of Stepan Razin"; the report had in fact been received in Wismar from Riga (see above, "From Riga they report [...]").

On December 29, 1672, during negotiations in the Diplomatic Chancery in Moscow with the Swedish envoy A. Eberschildt, it was asserted that

other faults have been committed on the side of his Royal Majesty, concerning which the above-named Colonel of the Tsar's, Nikolai von Staden, declared in Riga to the subjects of his Royal Majesty, who control the printing houses and print newspapers and write falsely and much that impugns the honour of our Great Sovereign, his Majesty the Tsar. They print and write and thus by means of their publications and letters foster disputes, and hostility and vexation between our Great Sovereign and their most powerful sovereign, his Royal Majesty. And an excerpt from some newspapers was shown the envoy to indicate which were the articles in question [...].

The envoy responded: "Those news letters are printed near Riga in Königsberg; in Riga there are no news letters in German ordered to be printed by the subjects of his Royal Majesty, but only ones in Swedish."[63]

As we can see, the Swedish diplomats re-directed the complaint to the publishers in Königsberg.

The subject of the Riga publications about Razin was raised many years later by Russian diplomats. In 1676, during the Russo-Swedish negotiations on the River Meuzitsa (the border between the Russian and Swedish possessions in the Baltic

---

61 Bantysh-Kamenskii, Obzor, 190–191.
62 A newspaper printed in Riga as early as 1670 is not known. The oldest preserved issue of any newspaper printed in Riga dates from January 1681; see: V. I. Simonov, "Aus der Geschichte der periodischen Zeitung in Riga im 17. Jahrhundert", *Gutenberg-Jahrbuch* (1984), 172–179 (reproduction of the title page on p. 173); Bogel/Blühm, Die deutschen Zeitungen des 17. Jahrhunderts, 140–141. Probably a newspaper from another city had printed the incriminating text under the headline "From Riga [date]".
63 *Krest'ianskaia voina pod predvoditel'stvom Stepana Razina*, t. 3 (Moskva, 1962), 285–286.

region), the Swedish diplomats were again put on notice that during the rebellion of Stepan Razin, in Riga and other Swedish cities, newspapers in which the honour of the Tsar was impugned were published: "[...] and such papers filled with falsehoods were spread throughout Europe."[64] The last time this accusation was aired in Russo-Swedish negotiations was in 1684.[65] By then, the uprising of Stepan Razin was already history. Mentioning him was not an actual offense, but a means of putting pressure on the Swedish negotiation partners.

It is not impossible that the Russian government devoted particular attention to publications impugning the Tsar's and the country's honour in order to put forward complaints concerning these publications in diplomatic negotiations later on. A hint in this direction might be attributed to the fact that some articles about the defeat of the rebels were not translated. Thus, three articles (the first three in the newspaper) were selected for the kuranty from No. 12 of the Berlin newspaper *Sonntagischer Mercurius*: from Lemberg (today L'viv, Ukraine) March 6, from Warsaw March 13, and from Prussia March 21. All these articles concerned events in Ukraine (in particular, the activities of the Cossacks) and in connection with that the activities of the members of the Polish sejm. The translators ignored the remaining articles printed in that issue of the newspaper – with news from The Hague, Nürnberg, from the Lower Rhine, from Hamburg and Brussels. A brief report about the rebellion of Stepan Razin on the fourth page of the newspaper (contained in a second communication from Hamburg dated 14/24 March) was among the omitted ones. It stated that Stepan Razin had been defeated, and 100,000 of his men had been killed.[66]

Quite curious is also the way in which a report from Danzig was treated. The Russian kuranty version states: "From Gdansk February 4. They write in various letters that the traitor Razin calls himself king of Astrakhan' and Kazan'."[67] The Dutch original for this article has been located. It is longer than the Russian translation; the author here adds his doubts as to whether this is accurate

---

64 Forsten, Snosheniia Shvetsii i Rossii, p. 321.

65 K. A. Kochegarov, *Rech' Pospolitaia i Rossiia v 1680–1686 godakh. Zakliuchenie dogovora o Vechnom mire* (Moskva, 2008), 270.

66 The "Russian" information in that newspaper issue reads as follows: "[...] Die grosse Theurung in Moßkau sol nun meist von dar ab- und nach Wolgada und Archangel kommen seyn/ da doch vor diesem von selbigen Orten eine grosse Quantität von Korn nach Moßkau gebracht worden. Daß der Rebell Roharzin [sic! = Razin] geschlagen/ und das Landvolck/ welches ihm in der Länge von 200. Meilen/ zwischen der Stadt Moßkau und Wolgada/ zugefallen/ von der Moßkowitischen Armee bey 100000. niedergesäbelt worden/ davon wird von einigen Moßkowitisch-gesinneten viel gesprochen [...]."

67 RGADA, f. 155, op. 1, 1671, ed. khr. 7, fol. 6v.

information: "[…] but this is not believed to be true"[68] – however, these doubts were not translated into Russian. Thus only the part which could have been adduced as a complaint in negotiations with Dutch diplomats was translated.

In all likelihood, the Russian government not only protested against such publications through diplomatic channels but sent its own information about the situation to the European press. The following kuranty item supports such a hypothesis:

Translation from Dutch newspapers.

From Moscow January 26. Here there are letters from the regiments of his Majesty the Tsar which write how the bandit Stenka Razin has arrived at the city of Simbirsk with 20,000 men. And from the 4th of September through the 3rd of October they launched 15 terrible assaults on the city. But thanks to the zeal of the defenders and the manly boldness of the general Ivan Bogdanovich Miloslavskii all of these assaults were turned back. And when the general prince Iurii Nikitich Boriatinskii arrived from Kazan' and joined forces with the besieging soldiers, the bandit was clobbered and himself wounded and barely escaped in a boat. And only a few people escaped with him. 500 people were taken alive who were executed on the spot, and for this service his Majesty the Tsar rewarded that lord Ivan Bogdanovich Miloslavskii with a high rank. Afterwards the military forces of his Majesty the Tsar defeated the bandits in many places and took back from them the places they had seized. And this disorder has now completely ended. And the merchants can once again set out for this state.[69]

The article contains many precise details. It encompasses a whole month of military actions at Simbirsk (from September 4 through October 3). Moreover, the compiler of the information knows not only of the victory over Razin but about the fact that general Miloslavskii was rewarded for that victory. This latter fact does not allow us to see in the article a letter sent after the raising of the siege of Simbirsk directly from the battlefield. Rather, the article is based upon an official communication of the Russian authorities.

---

68 "Dantzich den 4 Februarij. Met eenighe brieven heeft men, dat den Rebel Stephanus Ratzin, den Titul van Koningh over Astracan en Casan, sich soude toegeeyghent hebben: maer het selfde wert niet voor seecker aenghenomen […]." *Amsterdamse Dingsdaegse Courant* No. 1671/7, p. 1. The original is in RGADA, f. 155, op. 1, 1671, ed. khr. 4, fol. 6. We cannot be absolutely sure that the Russian version is made exactly from this Amsterdam newspaper, since there is only one overlapping news item; of course, the same (or a very similar) report could also have been published in another issue of a Dutch newspaper.

69 RGADA, f. 155, op. 1, 1671, ed. khr. 7, fol. 40v.

The peculiarity in the dating of the report is also consistent with this hypothesis. It was sent from Moscow approximately three months after the battle, when the "news", to put it mildly, was already dated. If we suppose that here we do not have "fresh news" but the refutation of false reports about the victories of Razin, then such a delay in no way seems strange. One can see in the text of the report the purpose for which it was compiled: in the last line its author declares "merchants can once again set out for this state", that is, merchants can again ply their trade. If our hypothesis is correct, then the placing of such a publication in a Dutch newspaper at the end of January, when the merchants trading with Moscow were deciding whether or not to go to Arkhangelsk during the current year, was completely appropriate.

CONCLUSIONS

The analysis of the kuranty compilations shows that the Russian government was very interested in conspiracies, revolts and uprisings in various European countries. This interest was fed both by the needs of foreign policy and by simple curiosity. All of the European social conflicts, which were widely reported in the European press, were also registered in the kuranty. However, the interest of the compilers of the kuranty in such events was unbalanced. Even in those cases where the events greatly interested the Russian government, material which was repetitive and of secondary importance was omitted.

The closer to the borders of Russia the event, the greater the attention it drew. In those instances, when the events touched Russian interests, the kuranty included a sufficient number of publications to allow the Russian authorities to understand the details of what had happened. In the remaining cases the compilers of the kuranty merely described the event. In these instances, the kuranty could seriously distort the substance of what was happening, as was the case with the taking of Braunschweig.

The inclusion in the kuranty of news about the rebellion of Stepan Razin was connected with the fact that the Russian government was concerned about its image in Europe. The Muscovite authorities fought the dissemination of negative publications by two means: they registered complaints to the publishers through diplomatic channels and they sent letters to the publishers of newspapers with their own description of the events.[70]

---

70 The authors are very grateful to Daniel Clarke Waugh (Seattle) for his valuable help in translating an earlier version of this paper from the Russian.

State-Arcanum and European Public Spheres: Paradigm Shifts in Muscovite Policy towards Foreign Representations of Russian Revolts

MALTE GRIESSE

In the 16th and 17th centuries, public interest in social unrest was steadily growing. Contemporaries perceived revolts increasingly across state borders. The development of newspapers played an important role in the dissemination of such representations. European governments challenged by domestic revolt often tried to influence and, if possible, monopolize revolt representations.[1] These efforts were generally limited to the internal spheres of debate. There seemed to be no point in trying to exert concrete influence on foreign representations. But the internal interpretation of the events was decisive for the definition and adjustment of the relationship between rulers and subjects. We know little about the extent to which the concerned governments saw to international coverage. Probably they cared about their reputation abroad, and this contributed to a certain parallelism of the development and normative shifts in dealing with rebellious subjects. Questions of legitimacy were debated in an international context. Manuals of statecraft and works of political philosophy addressed to a larger reading public and tackled political and ethical problems on a more general scale.[2]

---

1 Cf. Andreas Würgler, Unruhen und Öffentlichkeit. Städtische und ländliche Protestbewegungen im 18. Jahrhundert (Tübingen, 1995).
2 This did not necessarily mean that violence against subjects was branded as illegitimate. Clemency towards internal rebels could also be regarded as a token of weakness and thus diminish a government's weight in the eyes of its diplomatic or military allies and/or adversaries. It seemed not always compatible with the idea of absolutist rule and a strong sovereign, and consequently it could have a negative impact on a country's position within the larger constellation of powers.

In general, governments could influence foreign interpretations of revolts in their realm only insofar as they adjusted their policies and sometimes tried to conform to more or less universally accepted standards of legitimacy. However, in the case of the Russian Empire we can observe a gradual shift to more particular and increasingly systematic attempts at moulding foreign perceptions. Certainly this is true not only for representations of revolts: the claim to self-representational monopoly also extends to other spheres concerning the image of the Russian government and state. But I argue that the Tsarist government was particularly sensitive to foreign descriptions of revolts in Russia – and of the way it handled them. It was the preoccupation with such descriptions and the rather successful attempt to muzzle foreign coverage that contributed to a dynamical process of estrangement that ran counter to the simultaneous efforts at Europeanization.

A major shift can be observed in the aftermath of the second and last uprising of the strel'tsy (musketeers) in 1698, which ended up in the complete abolition of this particular military (and social) estate of the Muscovite empire.[3] Nevertheless, this shift was not an abrupt one. It was preceded by a gradual development of what we could call a particular representational policy, but it was also accompanied – and maybe even triggered – by noteworthy changes in foreign patterns of depicting Russian revolts in general. An isolated snapshot of the echo of the strel'tsy uprising would not be sufficient. The dynamic it engendered has to be put into a long-term perspective, which can be done here only in a very cursory way.

In this article, I will therefore try to tell two stories, which are intimately linked together and at the same time oddly detached from each other. The *first one* is that of foreign representations of Russian revolts: it traces some European perceptions of social unrest and uprisings in Russia and explores the underlying paradigms that shaped the narratives based on the observers' and their (potential) readers' cultural and experiential backgrounds. As the material is abundant, this story can be told in more detail than the *second one* that deals with the Russian government's policy towards these foreign depictions, i.e. with its explicit or implicit reactions to the foreign literary and journalistic treatments of these most delicate issues of Russian domestic politics. Explicit evidence is scarce. These issues of representational policy were rarely raised in written form. Apparently, they were a matter of taboo in Russia. That's why we can often only guess about the motives of the government's

---

3   The abolition of the strel'tsy helped complete military reform that had been underway since about the 1630s. For the history of military reform in the 17th century see Carol Belkin-Stevens, Soldiers on the steppe. Army reform and social change in early modern Russia (DeKalb, 1995), who regards the process as being triggered from the steppe frontier, where besides the Cossacks in the open fields the strel'tsy regiments stuffed the fortresses.

representational policy. Where we can find articulate reference to content, it was expressed in terms of "true" and "false": foreign authors were accused of lying, but generally it remains vague what exactly was the bone of contention. Of course, there is distortion in these foreigners' reports, probably much of it involuntary, based on inadequate information and misunderstandings. But the Russian government's negative reactions are far from being limited to actual deformations of historical facts; and on top of that certain deformations seem to be more than welcome. This vagueness is the reason why the two stories may occasionally appear as detached from each other.

Without excluding other sources my main focus will be on German accounts. The German newspaper-system of the 17th century was the most substantial in terms of diversification, editions, print run and reception.[4] German papers were highly commercialized and disposed of a whole network of correspondents, among whom one can even find non-German residents or travellers to Russia. Still more important than the overall significance of German-language journalism in early modern Europe is the fact that since at least the first half of the 17th century the Muscovite ambassadorial office (*posol'skii prikaz*) acquired mainly German newspapers and translated relevant parts of them that were read to the Tsar and his diplomatic staff. Many of these readers' digests (called kuranty) have survived.[5] Muscovite politicians thus used Western (mainly German) newspapers as a source of information on international affairs, but also to learn what foreign powers thought about Russia. This makes German accounts particularly relevant for an enquiry on what we might call the Russian government's representational policy.

In a *first* part I will present paradigms of the foreign depiction of revolts in Russia and sketch some directions of their development until the end of the 17th century. The material is well exploited: internal sources on Russian revolts are scarce and scholars of social unrest in Muscovy have largely relied on foreign accounts such as diplomatic records, travelogues, leaflets and even newspapers, to reconstruct the course of such events. My focus is a different one. Rather than in the actual events of revolt, I am interested in recurring patterns that allow for conclusions on experiential backgrounds, implicit understandings and interpretative frameworks employed by the eye-witnesses and second-hand disseminators, who were themselves not entirely familiar with Russian culture, and who were writing for an almost ignorant audience. From this angle, stereotypes and distortions are not

---

[4] 400 Jahre Zeitung. Die Entwicklung der Tagespresse im internationalen Kontext, ed. Martin Welke (Bremen, 2008).

[5] In second place after the German papers were the Dutch ones. All other languages were rather rarely translated. See Vesti-kuranty. 1656g., 1660-1662gg., 1664-1670gg., ed. Ingrid Maier and Sergei I. Kotkov (Moskva, 2009).

a problem. On the contrary, they are often even more revealing than descriptions that stick closely to historical facts (although it is often hard to distinguish between myth and reality when the same documents inevitably serve as cornerstones for an allegedly factual reconstruction by historians).[6]

For the above-mentioned reasons, it is probably not a coincidence that it was a German text that caused a scandal: Johann Georg Korb's diary. The author was secretary of an imperial embassy to Moscow (1698/9) and had witnessed the brutal mass repressions staged against the strel'tsy accused of large-scale rebellion upon Peter's I return from his great embassy to the West. The diary was published about two years later (in 1700 or 1701) with emperor Leopold's I privilege. This book, dealing (amongst other aspects) with the strel'tsy uprising of 1698, encountered severest diplomatic reactions in Muscovy and entailed a far-ranging and long-lasting shift in Russian representational policy, which in turn had considerable consequences on subsequent foreign representations of Russian revolts. The conflict, however indirectly, reveals much about the Muscovite government's shifting conceptions of Arcanum and of what was sayable in (different) public realms. In the *second* part of this paper, I therefore analyse Korb's description and interpretations of the strel'tsy revolt and of the ensuing waves of governmental repression. His interpretation is regarded in the light of its continuity with former foreign accounts on earlier Russian revolts rather than in terms of rupture.

In contrast to that, the Russian diplomatic reaction, the pressure the Muscovite government exerted on the imperial court in Vienna to obtain a revocation of the book, and the measures it would undertake with regard to future representations of Russia, reveal, if not complete discontinuity, at least a new quality and intensity of interference into foreign representations of Russia. In the *third* part of this article, I therefore turn to the Russian government's point of view. I try to explore its motives and describe the practical consequences that Russian foreign-policy makers have drawn from the scandal. I will argue that the consequences were not limited to the response to Korb's book and to diplomatic relations with Vienna, but that they were more long-lasting and gave birth to what I would call a new proactive foreign-media policy. The prohibitive impact of this policy can be seen from the representation or rather non-representation of the revolts of the early 18th century, mainly the Astrakhan rebellion and the Bulavin uprising. Here the grip of Russian media policy seems to have already been quite palpable. In the 18th century large-scale revolts became rarer in Russia as well as in the rest of Europe. But the memory and apprehension of such events was still vivid. This might be one reason

---

6 For a revaluation of stereotypes in mutual perceptions as a source of cultural history see Gabriele Scheidegger, Perverses Abendland - barbarisches Russland. Begegnungen des 16. und 17. Jahrhunderts im Schatten kultureller Missverständnisse (Zürich, 1993).

for revolts being increasingly debated as threatening potentials that had to be prevented. At the same time, the interpretation of revolts as a phenomenon of backwardness became more and more prominent. Since at least the 16th century Muscovy had the reputation of a barbarian and savage country. Now a developmental factor was brought into play. This was immediately related to a revaluation of the monarch in the person of Peter I, who was regarded as the promoter of Enlightenment. This strengthened an interpretation of revolts as a manifestation of backward resistance against progressive projects of reform and civilizational missions, which I deal with in the *fourth* and concluding part.

FOREIGN REPRESENTATIONAL PATTERNS OF MUSCOVITE REVOLTS IN THE 17TH CENTURY

There is no need to emphasize that the 17th century was rich in revolts. This is true for Muscovy as well as for most European countries, and well beyond Europe.[7] Observers were familiar with manifestations of social unrest and sometimes even engaged in explicit cross-country comparisons. In spite of all regional differences, observers apparently considered the situation in middle and Western European countries to be comparable. Was this also the case for Russia, independently of all exotic (or barbarian) flavour it had for most Europeans? To a large extent the country was still a *terra incognita*. Interestingly, in his voluminous history of civil wars (*guerre civili*), written in the early 1650s and referring to most recent events, the Italian Maiolino Bisaccioni did include chapters on the Ottoman Empire and Poland/Ukraine, but not on Muscovy, although the country was haunted by revolts no less than others at the time.[8] By contrast, in 1689/90 the Hamburgian Kern-Chronik, an annual journal giving a month-by-month discussion of current events, published an "Appendix concerning the most noteworthy and outstanding revolutions and changes of the state, from 1600-1690, through all kingdoms and estates of the whole world" that includes, after the most familiar European countries, a chapter on Muscovy, then, in order: on Hungary, Persia, India, China, even Japan and on what the editors call a "barbarian revolution" in Morocco.[9] If the

---

7   For the discussion of a general crisis of the 17th century see The general crisis of the seventeenth century, ed. Geoffrey Parker and Lesley M Smith (London, 1997).
8   Maiolino Bisaccioni, Historia delle gverre civili di qvesti vltimi tempi (Venetia, 1655).
9   Appendix zu dieser Kern-Chronica: Betreffend die fürnehmsten und sonderbahresten Revolutiones oder Staats-Veränderungen dieses itzigen Seculi, von Anno 1600 biß 1690. Durch alle Königreiche und Stände der gantzen Welt. In: Historischer Kern oder kurtze Chronica Der merckwürdigsten Zeit- und Wunder-Geschichte/ so sich im Jahr 1689 zuge-

extension to "all" countries indicates a process of representational globalization, but would not necessarily mean an increased familiarity with Russia in particular, it is remarkable that in the succession of the chapters Muscovy figures before Hungary. It shows an increased sense of Russia's belonging to a European community of states.[10]

Most foreigners travelling to, or even permanently living in, Muscovy resided in the capital. Some traders also lived in the Northern commercial centres like Novgorod and Pskov. Their depictions of Muscovite revolts have to be differentiated. Urban riots, such as the town rebellions of 1648-50 were fairly familiar to many of them. So they often qualified the actors of urban unrest as "commoners", "*die Gemeine*" or "*der Gemeine Mann*", expressions that establish terminological equivalence with European models. That dwellers of Russian towns were far from enjoying privileges and rights comparable to other European ones was not a problem, and in Western countries, terms like *der gemeine Mann* were not limited to townspeople. The huge uprisings in the periphery were much further away from the foreigners' mental and cultural universe. These revolts – quite misleadingly labelled as "peasant wars" in Soviet historiography – were generally led by Cossacks, a social stratum (or even estate) that did not correspond to Western standards.[11] The Cossack revolts were also far away in a literal sense. Whereas foreigners often became immediate eyewitnesses of the town rebellions they wrote about, this was hardly ever the case for the rebellions in the periphery.[12] This naturally had an impact on their judgment. They mainly had to rely on government information and propaganda. Often their personal contacts were quite limited to representatives of the Muscovite elites, so that they had little access to rumours circulating among the "commoners". This resulted in relatively gloomy portraits of the actors, who were often depicted as scoundrels or traitors, conforming to their undiscriminating qualification as *vory* [criminals or traitors] by Russian authorities.

---

tragen. Mit den vornehmsten Conterfaiten der itzo im Krieg befindlichen Potentaten/ und sonst vielen Abrissen der merckwürdigsten Belagerungen. (Hamburg, 1690).

10 Such synopses have apparently been written by authors who had not visited Russia and compiled their information from the accounts in regular newspapers and from travelogues written by eye-witnesses.

11 This was true for Ukraine as well and it would thus be interesting to compare Western Europeans' perceptions of Russia and Ukraine.

12 A notable exception is Fabritius for the Razin uprising. See Arkadii G. Man'kov (ed), Zapiski inostrantsev o vosstanii Stepana [Timofeevicha] Razina (Leningrad, 1968): 14-83, 132-156 (German original with Russian translation).

In contrast to this negative pattern, in descriptions of town rebellions such as those of 1648, 1662 and partly even 1682, many foreigners tried to go beyond the one-sided interpretational schemes offered by proclamations of the authorities. They asked for the reasons for the insurgency, described the misery of the people and did not even refrain from explaining the observed resistance as more or less legitimate, because it was directed against the ubiquitous abuse of power and systematic embezzlement practiced by high-ranking government officials at the public expense.[13] Even more so, in such narratives the corrupt behaviour of government officials is often contrasted with the actions of the insurgents, who are depicted as explicitly avoiding selfish behaviour in their own ranks. Looting was a matter of revenge, not of robbery. Luxury items pillaged from the detested targets of violence were ostentatiously destroyed, not stolen. Much emphasis was put on just and impartial distribution of goods or money according to actual or imagined rights or privileges and, of course, on the constant appeal to the Tsar, who was at rare critical moments even obliged to engage into direct negotiations with the insurgents. Lawful conduct was of paramount importance for the protestors, and those who violated their basic ideas of justice were often tried and severely punished, especially if they came from the insurgents' ranks or pretended to do so.[14] To be sure, foreigners did not explicitly justify the insurgents' violence – and revolts in Russia tended to be much more violent than in Western Europe, where the subjects had more legal channels at their disposition. But they manifested understanding. This understanding and relative sympathy towards the urban insurgents is even more noteworthy, as foreigners had often become themselves targets of revolt. What historians often attribute to people's ingrained xenophobia was not necessarily seen as such by the foreigners immediately concerned. In contrast, many of them were well aware of their trading privileges that put Russian urban dwellers at a disadvantage. For instance, the Swedish ambassador Pommerening, whose residence burnt down completely in the Moscow uprising of 1648, even asserted in his account to Queen Christina that it was not the insurgents, but the people of the Tsar's odious favourite Morozov, who put fire to almost the

---

13 This was the way how foreigners painted officials such as Pleshcheev, Trakhaniotov Morozov in 1648, or the strel'tsy officers like Griboedov and others in 1682.

14 This aspect is also emphasized in a recent study on revolts in Russia, Volksaufstände in Rußland. Von der Zeit der Wirren bis zur "Grünen Revolution" gegen die Sowjetherrschaft, ed. Heinz-Dietrich Löwe (Wiesbaden, 2006). The evaluation is largely based on foreigners' accounts, particularly for the town uprisings. However, this foreign perspective is not reflected as such here.

whole town because their master hoped to take advantage of the chaos to better escape from the people's anger.[15]

For the mighty revolts on the periphery, the picture is different. Foreigners, who had rarely seen the insurgents with their own eyes, describe them as bad characters with basically evil intentions, devoid of any sense of justice and order. But still another explicative pattern is noteworthy: the emphasis on the multinational character of the Empire. Incontestably, Russian revolts in the periphery enjoyed significant support from many non-Russian peoples, both peasants and nomads, whose territories had been more or less recently incorporated into the Muscovite state. Especially at the beginning of Russian rule, these movements were often separatist and seemed to aim for a *status quo ante* of independence, but more often they fought for inherited (or imagined as such) privileges under the Tsar's rule,[16] similar to the claims of their Cossacks allies. The multinational dimension became an increasingly important motive in many accounts of revolts by foreigners. This is apparently due to a particular European interest in this dimension. Several factors seem to be important:

1) Many, but by far not all, of these non-Russians were Muslims: Tartars, Bashkirs, Kalmyks, etc.), and their participation in Muscovite revolts was somehow related by some to European aspirations to win Muscovite support for the struggle against the Ottoman Empire.
2) Especially in newspapers we can observe an increasing sensibility to the idea of "nations". The term had not yet acquired our modern-day all-inclusive meaning and the non-Russian ethnic groups of the Muscovite empire could certainly not be equated to what German-speaking contemporaries dubbed "Nationen".[17] But observers of Russia seemed to draw at least parallels.
3) The multinational dimension inspired some Europeans' imagination and attracted their taste for exotic flavour. Perhaps except for the Tartars, heirs of

---

15 Report to Queen Christine, June 6, 1648. In: Gorodskie vosstaniia v Moskovskom gosudarstve XVII v. Sbornik dokumentov, ed. K. V. Bazilevich (Moskva, 2003): 36-39.
16 For a very instructive overview of the non-Russian nationalities of the Middle Volga, including their insurgent activity from the 16th to the 18th century cf. Andreas Kappeler, Russlands erste Nationalitäten. Das Zarenreich und die Völker der mittleren Wolga vom 16. bis 19. Jahrhundert (Köln, 1982). For the nomad Bashkirs of the Ural region, who were much later incorporated into the Russian Empire, cf. Irek G. Akmanov, Bashkirskie vosstaniia (Ufa, 1993).
17 On the emergence of the idea of nationhood in late Middle ages and early modern times see Caspar Hirschi, Wettkampf der Nationen. Konstruktionen einer deutschen Ehrgemeinschaft an der Wende vom Mittelalter zur Neuzeit (Göttingen, 2005).

the Mongols that had once terrified Europe, these people were almost unknown to Europeans. They seemed so radically different – much more than the Russians who were at least Christians –, that their ethnonyms alone opened fertile grounds for the imaginary, for spine-chilling stories as well as for more benign associations.

During the enormous revolts stirred up from the Cossack periphery – those of the Time of Troubles (1604-1615) and those relating to the Razin uprising (1667-1671) – the non-Russian peoples incontestably played an important role. Abroad, one was well aware of Muscovite expansion and the increasingly multinational character of the emerging empire. Corresponding to the significance of the event, the narrative of the conquest of Kazan' and Astrakhan figured prominently in the historical narratives of most Western travellers' accounts. But they did not necessarily give attention to the multinational dimension of revolts. Numerous observers, for instance, hardly took note of the insurgent activity of the non-Russian peoples of the Middle-Volga region during the Time of Troubles.[18] These commotions in the periphery were completely overshadowed by the events in the centre, where the False Dmitriis and their numerous supporters aimed for the Kremlin. Foreign interference, particularly open Polish and Swedish intervention and their sovereigns' claims to the Muscovite throne, were deemed much more important, especially from a Western point of view. And, interestingly, the neglect of the non-Russian periphery in Western accounts like Margeret's and Petreius', published shortly after the events, was often perpetuated in Russian chronicles composed from the 1630 on.[19]

---

18 The Dutch merchant Isaac Massa (1586-1643) is an exception. See Isaak Massa, Kratkoe izvestie o Moskovii v nachale XVII v. (Moskva, 1936). But whereas he relates at length the history of the conquest of the Khanates of Kazan' and Astrakhan under Ivan IV. (in the early 1550s), he only cursorily mentions joint actions of the "Nogais, Chermis Tartars together with the Mordvins" in the Time of troubles, during which he was in Moscow almost until the end of Vasilii Shuiskii's reign. Massa was well informed about the multi-ethnic dimension of the emerging Russian empire. He managed to publish two articles on Siberia at his lifetime, whereas his major account on the Smuta remained unpublished and would only be edited in the 19th century. I thank Andreas Kappeler for drawing my attention to Massa's reference to the events in the Middle-Volga-region.

19 Only the Novyi letopisets mentions for 1606/07 that "Mordvins, apiculturists, Boyar kholopy and peasants" and for 1608-11 that "people from downstream, Mordvins and Cheremisy" besieged Nizhnii Novgorod. Then it mentions the clerk Nikanor Shul'gin in Kazan', who refused to participate in the Opolchenie (the people's volunteer militia set out to liberate Moscow from the Poles) and then (in 1613) to kiss the cross for the new

In contrast to the events of the Time of Troubles the Razin rebellion (1667-1671) did not have a real international dimension – except for Razin's Persian campaign and for the participation of some Zaporozhian Cossacks. But the growing dissemination of newspapers throughout Europe already made it a media-event and, as the contemporary Justus Martius' put it in his doctoral dissertation in 1674: "the whole Europe lived for some time in anxious expectation of its outcome".[20] An Ottoman dimension was pitched high by foreign observers. The *Northern Mercurius*, a newspaper published in Hamburg that obtained information on Muscovy via Riga, emphasized the significance of the Tartars, who are even mentioned in the first place, before the Don-Cossacks, as the instigators of the revolt.[21] Furthermore, the correspondent suggests a strong implication of the Ottoman Empire. He calls Razin "Prince Stephan Razin Ottoman" and presents him either as an ally, or as an instrument of the Sultan. As to the Tartars, this connection seems self-evident to him. In many German accounts "the Tartars" make their appearance as odious brutes raping government officials' wives and daughters after their husbands were executed by Razin. This "big tyrant"[22] would have been particularly fond of having these wives bound naked on horseback to hand them over to the Kalmyks "who are the ugliest among the Tartars".[23]

Tsar Mikhail Romanov. According to the chronicle he tried to rally the people of Kazan' and then of Arzamas, because he wanted to rule in Kazan'. The chronicler suggests that these attempts were rather unsuccessful. Khroniki smutnogo vremeni. Bussov, Konrad; Elassonskii, Arsenii; Gerkman, Elias, ed. A. Liberman (Moskva 1998): 312, 328, 366, 369, 378, 381.

20 "[...] domi periculum adiit, nec unquam major calamitas fuit, quam cum auctore Stephano Räzino turbae motusque existerent (g): nam iis non modo Moscovia metu perculsa, sed etiam tota Europa expectatione futuri eventus aliquandiu suspensa fuit." Zapiski inostrantsev o vosstanii Stepana Razina, 39.

21 Ibid., 92-96. At the beginning, in a correspondence dating from August 20, 1670, published Sept. 6, the fall of Astrakhan is even exclusively attributed to a Tartar rebellion. 100.000 Tartars were said have conquered the town, the Cossacks and Razin are not even mentioned.

22 The term indicates that Razin is recognized as a sovereign, although a bad one who abuses his power.

23 Relationis historicae semestralis autumnalis continuatio. Historische Beschreibung der denckwurdigsten Geschichten, so sich [...] vor und zwischen jüngst verflossenen Franckfurter Fasten biß an und in die Herbst-Meß dieses lauffenden 1671. Jahrs [...] zugetragen. Franckfurt-am-Mayn, 1671. In ibid., p.98-99. It is conspicuous that in English accounts Razin gives the wives simply to "his soldiers" for rape. "A Relation concerning the Particulars of the Rebellion raised in Muscovy by Stenka Razin. Its Rise, Progress, and Stop:

Although Razin allegedly aimed for Moscow and the Kremlin, the main message of the accounts from Riga focuses on his activity in the south-eastern periphery, especially on the non-Russian territories around the former Khanats of Astrakhan and Kazan'. The most imminent threat to the Muscovite state, they said, was thus to be thrown back to its territorial status of 1554, i.e. to the time before the annexation of Astrakhan and probably even Kazan' (1552). This would entail the loss of Siberia and its rich natural resources. Access to Siberia would be barred by something comparable to a new important Ottoman outpost ranging from the Khanat of the Crimean Tartars through the southern Russian steppe far into the black-earth agricultural region of the Middle-Volga.[24] In the same light, another German account from Frankfurt (Main) asserts that Razin had negotiated with the Muscovite crown and presented a whole catalogue of claims, among them to be recognized as king of Kazan' and Astrakhan.[25] In fact, such negotiations had never taken place. Razin probably had offered his services to the Persian Shah in the first phase of his campaign (1667-1669). But he did not seek an alliance with the Sublime Porte or the Crimean Tartars – nor were the non-Russian participants of his movement. This "misinterpretation" figures mainly in the accounts originating from the Holy Roman Empire that was actively seeking for the inclusion of Muscovy into a Christian military alliance against the Turks.

And these newspaper accounts made their way (back) to Moscow. They were translated for the foreign office and read to the Tsar. Of course, Moscow was shocked by the Razin revolt. But the German interpretations in terms of cooperation between Cossacks and non-Russian nationalities under Muscovite rule with the Sultan might have had a particular impact on the Tsar. And Russian foreign policy indeed underwent a radical turn after A.L. Ordin-Nashchokin's dismissal from the foreign department (1671). Whereas this latter's ultimate priority had been prevalent against Sweden in the Baltic Sea, his successor A.A. Matveev abandoned North-Western aspirations to finally put into practice the anti-Turkish alliance that

---

together with the manner of taking that Rebel, the Sentence of Death passed upon him, and the Execution of the same." See: Ibid., 91-106, 96.

24 The correspondents do not hint at the Ural population, mainly nomadic Bashkirs, Muslims like the Tartars, whose resistance to Muscovite rule was ferocious throughout the 17th (and still during parts of the 18th Century). It is true that their territory was hardly touched by the Razin uprising, but they had initiated a big and long-lasting revolt only some six years earlier (1662-64), it would have been easy to include them into this supposed Turk-inspired campaign of conquest. But apparently the Bashkirs were still completely out of sight for European observers. On the Bashkir revolts see Akmanov, Bashkirskie vosstaniia.

25 Relationis historicae... Zapiski inostrantsev o vosstanii Stepana Razina, 99.

the middle-European powers had desired for such a long time. Of course it would be exaggerated to attribute the fundamental shift exclusively to the foreign representation that related the Razin revolt to the Ottoman Empire, but it apparently did play a certain role.

We can also find emphases on the actions of non-Russian peoples in foreign accounts of the strel'tsy revolt in 1682, which was so entangled with the fight of the different court factions for the succession to the throne after Fedor Alekseevich's death in April 1682, that the spectre of a second Time of Troubles (Smuta) began to haunt Moscow. This revolt, during which the strel'tsy temporarily took hold of the Kremlin and killed many high-ranking boyars on May 15-17, 1682, was in fact an urban uprising and it took place in the capital. There was no link to a simultaneous Bashkir uprising against Russian rule and colonisation in the Ural region, which had been going on since 1681. References to the Bashkirs can be found in a letter to the Apostolic Nuncio in Poland Cardinal Cybo. The representative of the Curia was well informed, as he attributed the rebellion to the attempts under Tsar Fedor Alekseevich to convert the Muslim Bashkirs to Christianity.[26] In contrast to earlier guarantees to respect the religion of the non-Orthodox, the Tsarist government had started in 1680-81 to foster Christianization. It resorted to draconian measures, such as the confiscation of the land of non-Russian nobles who refused to convert. As a corollary, their peasants' were enserfed. The new policies aimed mainly at the sedentary peoples of the Middle Volga (Muslim and pagan), but the nomad Bashkirs were well aware of what was happening to their Muslim neighbours: they reacted with alarm and violent revolt, when in November 1681 the decision was taken to establish a new eparchy in Ufa, which heralded a new intensity of Orthodox encroachments upon the nomadic Muslims' religious self-determination.[27]

Naturally, the Curia was particularly sensitive to religious matters in Russia. Given Moscow's reluctant opening towards Western influence, the Vatican did not abandon hopes to win over the country to the Roman Catholic Church. It was certainly an attractive idea (and illusion) to overcome the schism with what had been the most important branch of Eastern Christianity since the fall of Constantinople. But apart from that, in an age of reformation and counter-reformation and after the devastations of the Thirty Years' War, religious conflict was a major explanation for the era's violent social conflicts in general. Therefore it is all the more astonishing that the foreign observers, including the Vatican,

---

26 Letter dated 21 October 1682. In: Monuments historiques relatifs aux règnes d'Alexis Michaélowitch, Féodor III et Pierre le Grand czars de Russie. Extraits des archives du Vatican et de Naples, ed. Augustin Theiner (Rome, 1859): 238.
27 Akmanov, Bashkirskie vosstanija, 83-85.

completely neglected the intra-Orthodox conflict that fuelled the uprising, especially in its later phase. They did not even mention the rebel leader Khovanskii's attempt to rehabilitate Old Belief.[28] This apparently had to do with their profound misunderstanding of what Nikon's church reforms and the Old Believers' resistance to them really meant for Russian Orthodoxy. Certainly the continuation of the reforms and the simultaneous dismissal of the Patriarch (1666) had contributed to this confusion. (The reason for his destitution was not liturgical reform but dissension about the primacy of worldly or ecclesiastic power, a dissension that was never fully acknowledged).[29]

Whereas the representatives of the Vatican were quite accurate in making a clear distinction between the events in Moscow and what happened in the Ural and Volga regions, it is again the Kern-Chronik published in Hamburg that relates the strel'tsy's movement to both the Bashkir uprising and the first Russo-Turkish war that had in fact already been brought to an end in the truce of Bahçesaray in 1681:

In Moscow things looked quite badly. Some restless people abused the musketeers' uprising to arm themselves and to fish in troubled waters. The Turks and the Tartars took hold of many islands in the black sea and in the Dnepr, to the great harm of the Cossacks, as the rightful masters of these. The Bashkir Tartars who are subjected to the crown of Moscow, rebelled and went into battle with a huge force, in order to relieve themselves of the Muscovite yoke; a militia was sent to steer this rebellious people, and [the Bashkirs] were defeated twice, but thereupon they [the Bashkirs] withdrew to their neighbours, the Kalmyk Tartars, whose king, himself on horseback, and with considerable auxiliary troops, came to the assistance of the Bashkirs, so that they gathered an army of 50.000 men, and went directly for the main town Kazan.[30]

Indeed, Bashkirs and Kalmyks, both Muslim nomads, were acting in concert. The Kalmyks in the Southern steppe beyond the Jaik, were not yet subjected to Muscovite rule, but their raids for booty onto the adjacent Muscovite territories were a quite common practice. But sedentary non-Russians also joined the Bashkirs, which, in this case, consisted mainly of the indigenous peoples of the Middle Volga region, namely Tartars and Mari (Cheremisy), who could still profit

---

28 Ivan Khovanskii was a high-ranking boyar, who took sides with the insurgents. The uprising lead to his promotion to the top of the streletskii prikaz (musketeer's office) and he became the most popular leader of the rebellious strel'tsy. For this reason the revolt is often called Khovanshchina – also in Musorgskii's famous opera (1883).
29 Foreigners' perceptions of Nikon's church reforms and Old Belief have been examined by Aleksandr Lavrov's in his presentation at the workshop this volume is based on.
30 Kern-Chronik (August 1682): 90-91.

from their former revolt-experience during the Razin uprising. It was not least due to the chaos in the capital that the regional authorities were not able to cope with the situation. The auxiliary forces they demanded from Moscow did not come and they were forced to employ a mixed strategy of stick and carrot: as usual the Don and Jaik Cossacks were mobilized to fight against the Kalmyks, and at the same time regional officials in Ufa and Kazan' tried to persuade the Bashkirs to surrender voluntarily and thus be sure of the Tsar's grace and the guarantee of their privileges. But the Bashkirs remained suspicious. Previous experience had shown them that it might be naïve to rely on Moscow's promises. In its Bashkir epicentre the revolt thus continued until 1684. The emphasis on conflicts with the Turks and the Crimean Tartars in the Black sea area and on the territories of the Zaporozhian Cossacks, and the implicit assumption that all these Muslim activities must be related, have to be ascribed to the apprehension that after the first Turkish war the Russians had again made their peace with the Ottoman Empire. Invoking and exaggerating the Turkish danger and relating it to multi-national and internal revolts imbued with religious conflict, was time and again an attempt to win over Moscow for a crusade alliance against the Sublime Porte (and in 1686, with Moscow joining the Holy League, this seems to have been successful).

Of course, most attention was attracted to the events in the capital. Here, foreigners were on the scene. And here the dynastic succession itself was at stake. All accounts connect the strel'tsy's insurrection against their superiors to the power void that was due to the fact that after Tsar Fedor's death on April 27, 1682, his two potential successors were minors and would be unfit for rule at least for a few years. Ivan was 16 and mentally insane; his half-brother Peter was only ten. This opposed the family clans of their respective mothers: the Miloslavskiis for Ivan and the Naryshkins for Peter.[31] The final decision to crown both, which was taken in the heat of the strel'tsy revolt, was at least a temporary victory for the Miloslavskiis with Ivan's sister Sofiia emerging as the new regent. Subsequent Russian memoir literature under Peter I (after his accession to power in 1689) cited Sofiia as instigator of the strel'tsy's murderous enterprise, a view that has often been reproduced in historiography. But in contrast to that, the foreigners did not demonize Sofiia and regarded the outbreak of the strel'tsy uprising as largely independent from the factional struggle within the high nobility. According to the established narrative of the town revolt, they recognized the strel'tsy's claims as

---

31 And indeed, the revolt broke out only a few days after Fedor's death. The question of succession was disputed; and the highest nobility was divided between the elder but insane Ivan and the younger but healthy Peter. The final decision to crown the two of them was a novelty in Russian and European history. Their sister Sofiia was victorious: she managed to get the regency.

legitimate: the commanders had misappropriated the pay for the troop and had forced their subordinates to work on their private estates. Tsar Fedor's initiatives to redress these abuses had been cut short by his death. His death thus triggered two parallel but separate phenomena: the boyars' fight for succession and influence, and the strel'tsy's protest against their superiors' abuses, against their regime of egoism and narrow self-interest.[32]

Foreign accounts often depicted this arena of court-struggle in terms of conspiracy and palace revolution, at the time a common master narrative for denouncing revolts, especially in England, where regicide had a certain tradition. However, in the overall-framework of this narrative the *London Gazette*, which turned out to be relatively uninformed in those days, drops a keyword that will become increasingly important during the following years:

Our Letters from Moscow give the following account: That the late Czar Alexis [sic! in reality Tsar Fedor is meant] who Married with a Polish Lady, having by her means taken a great Affection to the manners and customs of this Nation, and designed to introduce them among his own Subjects, the more *to civilize them*, had thereby raised a great hatred in the Boyars, and other great Men against him, who resolved to Poyson him and his Queen, and effected it by the means of a Jew.[33]

The regicide attributed to "a Jew" is not so astonishing here, as anti-Judaism was widespread all over Europe: during the chaotic May days the strel'tsy indeed made a chase on foreign (including Jewish) physicians who were suspected of having

---

32 See the accounts and correspondences of the Danish commercial agent Heinrich Butenant in Petr N. Krekšin, Peters des Grossen Jugendjahre. "Kurze Beschreibung der gesegneten Taten des grossen Gosudars, des Kaisers Peters des Grossen, Selbstherrschers von ganz Russland" ; nebst einem Anhange aus zeitgenössischen Stimmen, nämlich Heinrich Butenant, Patrick Gordon und Otto Pleyer, zu den geschilderten Ereignissen (Stuttgart 1989), of the Danish diplomat Hildebrandt van Horn, Hildebrandt von Horn, "Doneseniia koroliu Danii. Moskovskoe vosstanie 682g. glazami datskogo posla", Voprosy istorii 1986, no.3 and of the Dutch resident van Keller in M. I. Belov, "Pis'ma Ioanna fan Kellera v sobranii niderlandskich dokumentov", in Issledovaniia po otechestvennomu istochnikovedeniiu. Sbornik statei posviashennyi 75 letiiu S.N.Valka (Moskva, Leningrad, 1964), 374-383. Cf. also Aleksandr S. Lavrov, "Politicheskaya bor'ba v Rossii 1680-kh godov v doneseniiakh Khil'debrandta fon Gorna. (istochnikovedcheskie zametki)", Vestnik S.-Peterburgskogo universiteta Seriia 2 (istoriia) 16, 3 (1999).

33 London Gazette, Monday August 14 to Thursday 17, 1682, headed: Warsaw, July 25.

provided the boyars with poison to murder the Tsar.[34] It is rather remarkable that "the Boyars" are globally identified as the culprits, which even adds to the legitimacy of the strel'tsy's preoccupation with settling accounts with the "traitors". According to this narrative, the boyars wanted to get rid of the Tsar – for a noteworthy reason: they opposed his Westernization policies. But the spectre of Westernization is not connected here to religion and to fears of Western attempts to introduce Catholicism[35] as it was the case in earlier foreign accounts of the Time of troubles: Here the issue is the goal of "civilizing" Russia and Russian subjects, including the boyars themselves. This aspiration is mainly ascribed to Fedor's first Polish wife, Agaf'ja Grushetskaya, who was indeed the first Tsaritsa to appear in public at all, even in Western clothes. And, with the Tsar's approval, she was the first to summon the boyars to cut their beards, a measure of Westernization that would be taken up in a ruder and more coercive way by Peter I after his return from the first great Embassy to Western Europe in 1698.[36]

The discourse about recalcitrant, backward subjects roused up by a modernizing and civilizing Tsar, would become prevalent in the following years under the impact of early Enlightenment. This changed the face of revolts in foreign representations. More and more foreign accounts depicted revolts as manifestations of backward resistance to the civilizing efforts of a centralizing state.

The leading circles in Russia seemed to be aware of an ever increasing European interest in the exotic "tribes" and "backward" ethnic groups of the Empire. Apparently they also tried to exploit such Western curiosity, which can be seen from a strange news item in the kuranty (the translations from Western newspapers for the Tsar and his diplomatic staff) from the same troubled period of 1682. It purports a revolt of the Siberian "Irgen' tribe". These "savages" would have rebelled "for the sake of the sable fur" (apparently questions of hunting rights, trading privileges, tributes, taxes, etc.). Stepan Shamin, who has discovered this item in a dossier of kuranty dated 1st May, assumes that the report had been launched by Yazykov, a supporter of the Naryshkin clan, who tried to use Western newspaper coverage (real or fake) as an instrument in the factional struggle. The report says that "the important Man, Sir Kholopov, was sent to the Enisei with troops, in order to extinguish the fire" of the rebellion. Apparently Yazykov wanted

---

34 A vivid account of that is supplied by Heinrich Butenant, who was suspected to shelter a physician, because he was his neighbour and friend. See Wahrhaftige Relation der traurigen undt Schrecklichen Tragedy hier in der Stadt Moscau furgefallen auff Montag, Dienstag undt Mitwochen, den 15, 16 undt 17 May jetzigen 1682-ten Jahres. In: Krekšin, Peters des Grossen Jugendjahre, 160–76.
35 Here the whole question of Old Belief is again completely ignored. See above.
36 Hans-Joachim Torke, Die russischen Zaren. 1547 - 1917 (München, 1995): 137.

to get a rival out of the way. According to a later complaint by Kholopov, it was on Yazykov's initiative that Tsar Fedor had assigned to him this Siberian mission. But after Fedor's death the order had fallen into oblivion. Therefore Yazykov tried to remind Fedor's successor(s) of the decision *through foreign newspapers*, i.e. through publicity in the West. Once the message was printed in Western newspapers, he could be sure that it would soon figure in the *kuranty*, since virtually any message relating to Russia was translated. It was more difficult *to persuade Western correspondents* of the relevance of Kholopov's nomination into the Trans-Baikal region. Why should it be of any interest to Western readers? Why should a newspaper print such a message? Here the combination of wild tribes of the Far East with the issue of revolt was suitable bait.[37]

We don't know exactly whether this revolt of the Irgen' tribe in the Trans-Baikal region had really taken place or if it was made up as a news item. But be that as it may, the case highlights a conscious gamble with the Europeans' attention to the multi-ethnic dimension of the Muscovite Empire.[38] The news item corresponded to an emerging paradigm in foreign accounts that ascribed a close relationship between backwardness and revolts. Backwardness was seen particularly in the exotic tribes of the Russian Wild East that seemed to prompt European fantasies in a similar way to perceptions of the various peoples in the overseas colonial world.[39]

JOHANN GEORG KORB'S DIARY AND THE SECOND REVOLT OF THE STREL'TSY, 1698

When the second strel'tsy revolt took place (in June 1689) and Emperor Leopold's delegation under F.A. v. Guarient und Rääl sojourned in Moscow (from April 1698 to July 1699), Peter's reign was consolidated. Nine years earlier he had taken over the regency from his half-sister Sofiia – after she had waged a complot against

---

37 S.M. Shamin, "Kuranty kak istochnik po istorii Moskovskogo vosstaniia 1682 g.", in Problemy istochnikovedeniia, ed. S. M. Kashtanov (Moskva, in press).

38 Ibid. finds the case particularly noteworthy, because in his eyes this information on the far-away Siberian ethnic groups had not been of any interest for European readers – this in order to emphasize the aspect of instrumentalization. But in fact, if this was true, the message would have hardly been published. In my view, the occurrence indicates to what degree the ethnographical interest had increased and how Russian elite members were sufficiently aware of this European trend to be able to make use of it.

39 The topos of (European) civilization as opposed to Asiatic barbarism can be found in many foreigners' accounts on Russia. See for instance Jenkin's account who outlined the struggle of civilization with the Timurian Mongol barbaric heritage.

him.[40] His nominal co-regent and half-brother Ivan V was dead (since 1696), and so was his mother (since 1694), who had influenced his government in the first years of his reign. Peter was on his first journey abroad ("incognito") to study the European navies. He only returned after the message of the strel'tsy's mutiny had reached him in Vienna. This came when he had realized during negotiations with Leopold I. that his plans to activate the Holy League for his struggle against the Crimean Tartars and the Ottoman Empire were thwarted.[41]

The strel'tsy's revolt of 1698 was a far-ranging event, not so much because of the size and amplitude of the uprising itself, but because of its aftermath: the complete abolition of the old Muscovite military estate that helped to accomplish the army reform initiated under the first Romanov Tsar, as well as the diplomatic scandal caused by the publication of the diary that Johann Georg Korb, the imperial delegation's secretary, had held during the stay in Moscow and that I will analyze in what follows. The artistic echo of the uprising is considerable, partly because it became intimately interwoven with Peter's legendary cutting of his boyars' beards and the introduction of Western garments at court: a symbol of Peter's break with Old-Moscow.[42] Apparently, the mutiny itself was relatively small-scale in comparison to the following requital. Recently historians have even doubted

---

40 On the confrontation between the regent Sofiia and her half-brother Peter in 1689 and the alleged conspiracy see Lindsey Hughes, Sophia, Regent of Russia. 1657-1704 (New Haven, 1990): 221-241; Aleksandr S. Lavrov, Regentstvo tsarevny Sof'i Alekseevny. Sluzhiloe obshchestvo i bor'ba za vlast' v verkhach Russkogo gosudarstva v 1682-1689gg. (Moskva, 1999): 157-190.

41 Handbuch der Geschichte Rußlands, Band 2 Vom Randstaat zur Hegemonialmacht, 1613-1856, ed. Manfred Hellmann and Gottfried Schramm (Stuttgart 1986), 243-244. The Reich was absorbed by the controversy over the Spanish succession. This was an inversion of the situation earlier in the 17th century, when the Reich tried unsuccessfully to win Russia for an anti-Ottoman coalition. The Reich's refusal to engage in a common war against the Turks would contribute to Peter's I reorientation towards the North, to his concentration on the access to the ice-free Baltic Sea, by which he picked up the thread of A.L. Ordin-Nashchokin's foreign policy of the 1660. This would lead to the Great Northern War (1700-1721).

42 Cf. for instance Albert Lortzing's popular opera "Tsar and carpenter", first performed in 1837 in Leipzig. The break with Old-Moscow is the central motive in Olaf Brockmann, "Der Bruch Peters mit Alt-Moskau. Korbs Diarium und Diplomatenberichte aus Moskau zu den Ereignissen der Jahre 1698 und 1699", Jahrbücher für Geschichte Osteuropas 38, 4 (1990): 481-503, who interprets Korb's diary in this light.

whether it merited the appellation of a revolt at all.[43] Four strel'tsy regiments had been directly transferred from Azov to the Polish-Lithuanian border, where they had to serve as guards under extremely miserable conditions. The situation still aggravated as a consequence of crop failure and delayed in kind wages. In spring 1698 they thus sent some 175 representatives to Moscow. There Peter had established a temporary boyar government for the time of his absence. Suspicious of the strel'tsy, he had instructed this government to keep the regiments at any rate away from Moscow.[44] Accordingly, the government reacted with nervousness, but in the end it satisfied the strel'tsy's claims and they returned to their garrisons at the border.[45]

Only when Peter branded the boyars' softness in a letter from abroad and ordered a transfer of the regiments to other garrisons and exemplary punishments of the "deserters", the boyar government revised its former measures and put Peter's orders into practice. The strel'tsy refused to hand over the "deserters", but they set off to their new garrisons. Only on the way they apparently decided to take in Moscow along the way to visit their wives and families whom they had not seen for more than 18 months. – Home leave had already been a major request of their preceding petition. When their commanders refused, the strel'tsy deposed them and elected new ones. Now the boyar government set out an army detachment against them. The encounter took place at the New Jerusalem Monastery, some 60 km to the North-West from Moscow. Patrick Gordon, Peter's Scottish favourite, was among the military commanders and led the negotiations with the strel'tsy. He described the events in his diary (that remained unpublished at the time): The strel'tsy handed over a petition in which they asked for a permission to come to Moscow in order to "visit their houses, wives and children" and "to petition for their necessityes".[46] When this was not granted they persisted. After further unsuccessful negotiations, the government forces opened fire; the mutineers were

---

43 On the course of the events cf. Alexander Moutchnik, "Der 'Strelitzen-Aufstand' von 1698", in Volksaufstände in Rußland, 197-222; Sarah Schiffmann, Aufruhr der Strelitzen im Jahre 1698. Ursachen, Verlauf, Unterdrückung, Folgen (PhD diss., University of Vienna, 1932); Brockmann, Der Bruch Peters mit Alt-Moskau.

44 In 1697 there had been a conspiracy, into which some strel'tsy were accused to be involved. On the 1697 Tsykler affair see Hughes, Sophia, Regent of Russia, 248-249.

45 For a detailed historiographical account see Moutchnik, Der "Strelitzen-Aufstand" von 1698.

46 Tagebuch des Generals Patrick Gordon, während seiner Kriegsdienste unter den Schweden und Polen vom Jahre 1655 bis 1661 und seines Aufenthaltes in Rußland vom Jahre 1661 bis 1699, ed. M. A. Obolenski and Moritz Conrad Posselt (Leizig, 1853): 195. The entry refers to June 17.

apparently reluctant to launch an offensive, and it came to a very short skirmish, in which they were rapidly defeated. Requital and investigation followed immediately.[47] But only in autumn, when Peter hastily returned to Moscow from Vienna and took the investigations into his own hands, was the decisive link to Sofiia as instigator of the "conspiracy" finally "established": allegedly she had summoned the strel'tsy to the capital in order to be restored to the throne.

Peter did not conceal his massive application of torture: the innumerable executions were staged publicly and apparently foreign ambassadors, including the members of the imperial delegation, were even invited to assist. That's why Korb could give an eye-witness account of the punishments. Although the requital seemed particularly ferocious, neither torture, nor the publicity of repression was much at odds with contemporary "European standards".[48] Although he did not spare the lurid details of Peter's crackdown on the strel'tsy, Korb therefore did not expect to provoke a scandal with the publication of his diary. And he had some reason not to expect such a ferocious reaction. His diary appeared only at the end of 1700 or in 1701, although previously, in 1698 and 1699, right after the events, several reports on the executions had been published in German newspapers and journals. These reports astonishingly resembled Korb's later diary-publication and maybe even stemmed from his quill.[49] As in the diary, cruel details were not withheld. For example, the accounts described at great length how imperial Ambassador Guarient was invited to the Kremlin for three consecutive dinners: the opulent meals were accompanied by executions. According to one report of the *Kern Chronik*, 1.300 persons were beheaded on the first day, 700 on the second, and on the third day, the hangman cut off noses and ears of 400 more insurgents who were then exiled to forced labour in Siberia, all this in presence of the Tsar and the ambassador who were virtually at table.

The Tsar ordered a considerable number of the rebels to be hanged on girders that were fixed in the embrasures in the city wall. Many of them got a brand on their cheeks and many of them were sent to Siberia into eternal misery. The Tsar's blood brother and many boyars had their hands sawed off or had to suffer other humiliations.[50]

---

47 This account is based on Ibid., 192ff.
48 On repression standards cf. Karl Härter's contribution to this volume.
49 I am grateful to Martin Welke for having drawn attention to this circumstance and for having shared his source-findings with me.
50 Die gestraffte Revolten, Kern-Chronik (November 1698). "Ein groß Theil der Rebellen ließ der Czaar an Balcken hengen/ welche er rings der Stadt-Mauer aus denen Schieß-Löchern stecken lassen. Viele wurden auff denen Backen gebrandmahlet/ und eine große

Interestingly enough, these reports *did not cause any scandal* in Russia. But they were widely read abroad. Leibniz, for instance, an avid reader of newspapers and journals, had already manifested a particular interest in Russia. Already in 1698 he commented on the repressions of the strel'tsy in a letter to his Swedish correspondent: "One could imagine that the Tsar has done that in order to tacitly reproach Emperor Leopold I that he is not absolute enough to do similar things. [...] It's a pity that this grand duke who has so many laudable qualities is not yet able to get rid of his penchant for cruelty." And as his correspondent had already expressed apprehension that Russian military priority might shift from the Black Sea towards the Baltic and notably to Sweden, Leibniz added ambiguously:

> But instead of quarrelling with Sweden, which might become bad for him [i.e. for Peter I], I would recommend him to turn his weaponry against the Levant and to subjugate the barbarians, the Kalmyks for instance, who don't yet recognize him [as their sovereign]. It is true that the conquests he could make in this direction would render him still more formidable. But as he does not seem to remain with his arms folded, it would be better for Christianity, if he was occupied further away from us.[51]

In a letter to Nicolaas Witsen, the mayor of Amsterdam, Leibnitz is less critical and refers to the domestic disorder that forced the Tsar to re-establish internal peace by such atavistic means, "a custom originating still from the Scythes."[52] The ambivalence of Leibniz's evaluation of Peter I, an enormous admiration for his reforms in general coupled with certain bewilderment about these cruel acts, corresponds more or less to the general tone of Korb's diary. Admiration for the reform-Tsar was definitely prevailing, although Peter had so far done little that made him stand out from his predecessors – apart from his appearance abroad that indeed earned him the most sympathy from the European *hommes de lettres*.

Menge nach Syberien in das ewige Elend geschicket. Der Zaarin leiblicher Bruder und viele Bojaren mußten sich die Hände absägen/ oder eine andere Schmach anthun lassen."

51 Draft of a Letter to Sparvenfeld, December 27, 1698 in French, quoted in Woldemar Guerrier, Leibniz in seinen Beziehungen zu Russland und Peter dem Grossen. Eine geschichtliche Darstellung dieses Verhältnisses nebst den darauf bezüglichen Briefen und Denkschriften (Hildesheim, 1975): 39.

52 Letter of March 14/24, 1699. Quoted from Mechthild Keller, "Wegbereiter der Aufklärung. Gottfried Wilhelm Leibniz' Wirken für Peter den Großen und sein Reich", in West-östliche Spiegelungen. Russen und Rußland aus deutscher Sicht und Deutsche und Deutschland aus russischer Sicht von den Anfängen bis zum 20. Jahrhundert, ed. Mechthild Keller, Ursula Dettbarn and Lev Zinov'evich Kopelev (München, 1985), 400.

What distinguished Korb's diary from formerly published German newspaper records on the retaliation against rebellious strel'tsy? What was it that provoked the scandal? Certainly, the bone of contention has to be searched for in the author's *description* of events rather than in his attempts to *explain* why things happened as they did. However, in coherence with our cursory look at the paradigms of preceding foreigners' approaches to interpreting revolts in Russia, I will start with Korb's "aetiology", his search for adequate interpretations and explanations of what happened. Probably the scope and cruelty of the retaliation seemed excessive to him, at least in comparison to the seeming harmlessness of the mutiny itself. Indeed, normally even in cases of much fiercer insurrection, as in 1682, the Tsarist government contented itself with executing the ringleaders to set a warning example, and to grant an amnesty to the rest. It seems as if Korb was rather puzzled by the sudden cruelty that, on the first glance, hardly fit with his positive image of the enlightened monarch. In his attempt to justify the cruelty of repression he thus tends to enlarge the rebellion and the depravity of its underlying motives.

How to Reconcile the Russians' "Inborn Servitude" with the Occurrence of Revolt

Korb's diary with its regular entries for almost every day of the embassy's stay in Moscow contains not only information on the mutiny and its aftermath. The author covers various topics, jumping erratically from one to another. Only the first part of the published book is the actual diary. It seems not to have been considerably reworked for literary purposes, although Korb translated his originally German entries into Latin. This actual diary is less prone to interpretation and explication than thematic second part that starts with a coherent narrative of the strel'tsy's rebellion. Certain points mentioned before in the diary reoccur here, but Korb also added new aspects and attempts at interpretation. In subsequent chapters Korb portrays court-life, customs and traditions based on what he has seen and experienced in Moscow and its environment.[53]

In this sense this two-part book is much more comprehensive than the newspaper reports. And although many depictions seem to be quite well-balanced and far from a simple black-and-white-scheme, Korb generally sticks to a

---

53 The most detailed study on Korb's diary is Friedrich Dukmeyer, Korbs Diarium itineris in Moscoviam und Quellen, die es ergänzen. Beiträge zur moskowiisch-russischen, österreichisch-kaiserlichen und brandenburgisch-preussischen Geschichte aus der Zeit Peters des Grossen (Vaduz, 1965), a doctoral dissertation that was originally published in 1909-1910.

widespread Western view of the Russians' barbarianism,[54] superstition,[55] excessive cruelty, penchant for tyranny, the leading circles' inclination to corruption and embellishing military defeats,[56] as well as to the ubiquitous habit of lying. In a chapter on the "Russian character" Korb also reproduced existing Western stereotypes of the Russians' almost natural servitude and inborn servility. He explicitly and affirmatively quotes John Barclay's *Icon animorum* with his comments on

> this race, born for slavery [that] becomes ferocious at the least trace of liberty; placid if oppressed, and not refusing the yoke, they of their own accord confess themselves slaves of their prince. He has the right to their wealth, their bodies, and their lives. Humility more sordidly crouching the very Turks entertain not for their Ottoman sceptre.[57]

It is the idea of "tyranny without a tyrant" – an Aristotelian response to an apparent conceptual dilemma. In the categorisation of the different forms of government, tyranny was understood as a short-lived, illegitimate form characterized by the ruler abandoning the common good for the sake of his private benefit. This form of rule sooner or later provoked the resistance of the subjects, whose inborn sense of liberty would urge them to remove the illegitimate monarch. However, what was perceived as tyranny in Russia seemed astonishingly permanent and stable, similar to what Aristotle at his time observed in the Empires of the Orient. Aristotle's solution of the problem was simple: the "barbarian" subjects lacked the sense of freedom that was so fundamental to the Greeks. Government of the state was assimilated to the despotic rule of the household, where private interest was (quite

---

54 For the theme of barbarianism in European ethnographical accounts of Russia see Marshall T. Poe, 'A people born to slavery'. Russia in early modern European ethnography, 1476-1748 (Ithaca, NY, 2000).

55 Cf. the entry for August 10 and 11, 1698. Johann Georg Korb, Diary of an Austrian secretary of legation at the court of Czar Peter the Great, trans. Marshall Poe (London, 2003), 165-167.

56 See the entry for August 19, 1698. Ibid., 168-169.

57 Ibid., 516. Korb has taken the quotation from John Barclay's (1582-1621) Icon animorum (8th chapter on the Russians' national character): "servituti gens nata, ad omne libertatis vestigium ferox est; placida, si prematur, neque abnuunt jugum; ultro fatentur Principi se servire. Illi in suas opes, in corpora, vitamque jus esse. Sordidioris reverentiae humilitas Turcis non est in suorum. Ottomanorum sceptrum [...] Magnatibus, licet ipsi serviant, in minores suos & plebejos, quos per contemptum nigros homines, & Christianos [in the sense of krestiane, peasants] communiter appellant intolerabilis fastus est, & vulgus horum maxime supercilium timet." Cf. Dukmeyer, Korbs Diarium itineris, 2: 49.

naturally) paramount. Instead of striving for freedom the subjects loved their servitude, so that tyranny became a permanent institution and even functioned as such without an explicit tyrant at the head of the state.[58]

Korb seemed to see the Russians more or less in this light. He thus describes episodes from Moscow in the Tsar's absence, that illustrate the idea of *tyrannis sine tyranno*: for instance the fate of a woman who had shown compassion towards a strelets in the pillory. When passing she let slip a sigh: "Alas! Which mortal knows whether you were guilty or innocent"? This was enough for another passerby to denounce her exclamation "to the Boyars as an indubitable indication of treason." Korb was bewildered:

A woman's pity for condemned and public criminals was deemed dangerous. So she was forthwith dragged up, along with her husband, to an examination. Now, when it was proved that there was nothing more in question than unreflecting and womanly compassion for the unfortunate, and that there was no trace of deliberate malice, they were indeed exempted from the penalty of death, but nevertheless condemned to exile. Thus thoughtless and guileless liberty of the tongue is chastised where subjects are coerced to obey through fear alone.[59]

This fits with Korb's depictions of the leading Boyars' tyrannical behaviour. Even B.A. Golitsyn, Peter's former educator and head of the government in the Tsar's absence, who was often visited by the Ambassador Guarient, Korb's superior, boasted in the presence of his foreign guests of his despotic regime at home towards his servants and family.[60]

The Muscovites' compliance with this sort of arbitrariness seemed to be rather at odds with the very possibility of rebellion and revolt. And like many other foreigners who subscribed to the idea of Russian servility, Korb had some problems classifying the uprising. He was aware of this contradiction, although he did not explicitly address it. In his chapter on "the Russian character" he thus sketches a situation of general depravity and falsehood:

Devoid of honest education, they esteem deceit to be the height of wisdom. They have no shame of lying, no blush for a detected fraud: to such a degree are the seeds of true virtue proscribed from that region, that vice itself obtains the reputation of virtue.[61]

---

58 Poe, A people born to slavery.
59 Korb, Diary of an Austrian secretary, 156-157 (Entry of July 24, 1698).
60 Ibid., 158-160 (Entry of July 25 and 26, 1698).
61 Ibid., 517.

This habit of lying is illustrated in a description of a scuffle that took place between German ambassadorial servants and some Muscovites. It ended with the interference of a contingent of soldiers who brought the Germans to the military guard, where the officers (also mainly Germans) considered them innocent and released them all. However, the following day the Russians scufflers wrongfully accused Guarient's servants of having made use of weapons in the brawl:

> One of the Muscovites went about showing his wounds, and having suborned witnesses at a cheap rate, contended that he bore the marks of a sword that had been drawn against him: the falsehood of which being evident to our eyes, we could not but marvel prodigiously at the corrupt morals of this people, and how their abominable custom of lying and perjury is allowed to go unpunished. Search for false witnesses where you will among the Muscovites, and you will find them. For fate hath instituted such a universal perversity of reason in Muscovy, that it is very nearly the index of a superior intellect to be able to cheat.[62]

But rebellions and revolt do not necessarily ensue from lying, fraud and ubiquitous crime. Even if these deviant practices turn out to be extremely widespread, they remain individual rather than collective.[63] Fraud and other criminal acts aim at small egoist benefit, whereas in their descriptions of 17th century Russian town rebellions many foreign observers point at the circumstance that collective agency was accompanied by an orientation towards a common good, which implicitly challenged the authorities, especially when a tyrannical ruler or more often his evil councillors lacked precisely this such a dedication to the common good.[64]

Reasons for the Revolt as Suggested by Korb's Account

On these premises Korb felt compelled to speculate as to possible reasons for the strel'tsy revolt. Why such an act of resistance, and resistance against what, if the Muscovite subjects were "natural slaves", who had no idea of freedom and actually

---

62 Ibid., 155-156 (entry July 24, 1698).
63 On criminality in Moscow see Christoph Schmidt, Sozialkontrolle in Moskau: Justiz, Kriminalität und Leibeigenschaft 1649-1785, Quellen und Studien zur Geschichte des östlichen Europas 44 (Stuttgart, 1996). Foreign images of criminality and deviant behaviour are quoted in the Introduction. The separation between criminality and rebellion was in reality not as strict as this conceptualization suggests. Robber gangs sometimes linked the two phenomena and fitted more or less to Hobsbawm's paradigm of the Social bandits. At least vaguely they often defended a notion of social justice. But this dimension is ignored in representations by foreigners, differently from their depictions of town revolts.
64 See above.

loved their servitude? Korb's explanatory attempts go in different directions that are not always reconcilable with each other: he refers a) to celestial constellations; b) to the major "ringleader" Sofiia; c) to an "infection" from Polish unrest; d) to the multi-ethnic character of the empire and finally, and apparently related to this multi-ethnic dimension, e) to the circumstance that in Russia people would not fight against, but to retain a servitude that seemed endangered by Peter's enlightenment policies.[65]

a) Comets as Harbingers of War and Revolt

The link between ignorance and servility was almost classical, but Korb relates this *topos* to astrological questions:

In their schools positively the only labour of the schoolmasters is to teach the children how to write and shape letters. The height of learning consists in committing to memory some articles of their creed. They despise liberal arts as useless torments of youth, they prohibit philosophy, and they have often publicly outraged astronomy with the opprobrious name of magic. It is criminal to introduce the calendar of Vo[i]gt the astronomer into Muscovy, because this general proposition, Moscau wird seinem Ungluck auch nicht entgehen (neither will Moscow escape her ill-fortune), he presaged rebellion to the Muscovites.[66]

J. H. Voigt (1613-91) was at the time one of the most popular German mathematicians and astronomers (and astrologists) writing on comets. He regarded them as harbingers of disaster. This general assumption since Antiquity had been made an object of new scientific enquiry by outstanding scientists such as J. Kepler and H. Cardanus. Given the appearance of comets immediately before the Thirty Years' War (1618), the plague in Hamburg, along with the numerous revolts and civil wars in the mid-17th century this idea had become particularly widespread.[67]

---

65 Curiously, Korb did not even evoke one of the most widespread explanations in foreign records on the events: an interpretation of Peter's absence in the light of his alleged attempt to reunite rally the Orthodox Church to Rome and thus to betray the Muscovite religion of his fathers and of the population at large. Many reports that go along with this idea combine it with a social differentiation, saying that the Boyars' and many representatives of the clergy stirred up the population against the Tsar by propagating that he aimed at converting his country to Catholicism. For a synopsis of these accounts see Dukmeyer, Korbs Diarium itineris, 1: 179-184.

66 Korb, Diary of an Austrian secretary, 518-519.

67 Already Cardanus (1501-1576) was convinced that comets stirred up the human bile. In this sense Johannes Kepler ascribed the Portuguese King Sebastian's impulsive and imprudent military campaign of 1577 in North Africa (that ended up in a defeat and finally

Voigt's prognostics of earthly events based on stellar phenomena were quite detailed, and in this sense he had predicted uproar in Moscow. Korb enumerates Voigt's calendar among other Western scientific achievements. In Russia, such calendars were highly popular. This made their predictions extremely dangerous in the eyes of the government. Therefore, Sofiia's government forbade them shortly after the 1682 strel'tsy uprising.[68] According to Korb the Russian authorities said "that evil spirits, at whose suggestion and showing astronomers may sometimes guess about the future what is beyond mortal ken, must have helped him [Voigt] in this black art."[69]

The Russian authorities apparently feared unrest, not least because such announcements risked frightening and stirring up the population. In our eyes, this seems rather rational: superstition and popular beliefs were perceived as a mighty force that was able to foment uproar and should therefore be bridled.[70] But for Korb (and his well-read European contemporaries) proscribing such calendars meant rejection of *scientific knowledge* and was a clear indicator of superstitious obscurity, absolutely equivalent to the rejection of fine arts and many other

---

cost the king's life) to the apparition of a comet. The impact on royal blood was particularly high, so that Sebastian did not want to listen to his soberer counsellors' warnings. Bisaccioni, Historia delle gverre civili di qvesti vltimi tempi, the contemporary "historian" of the transnational political crises around 1650 explicitly relates the numerous revolts of the mid-17th century to comets. Not only were scientific observers prone to such explanations of human behaviour. Politicians also recurred to these scientific insights. At the negotiations for the Westphalian Peace of 1648 the Swedish delegate Salvius referred to "the disposition of the stars" that might have been the reason why "in the whole world one hears about the people's revolt against their sovereigns: for instance in France, England, Germany, Poland, Muscovy and in Turkey." Georges Livet, La guerre de trente ans (Paris, 1966): 121.

68 See S.M Shamin, "Evropeiskaia astrologiia i russkoe pravitel'stvo v XVII stoletii", in Estestvennonauchnaia knizhnost' v kul'ture Rusi, ed. A.Iu. Samarin (Moskva, 2005).
69 Korb, Diary of an Austrian secretary, 519.
70 Repercussion of astrological beliefs on actual human behaviour could really be a catalyst of revolt. For instance in the wake of the Swiss peasant war (1653) the fire-tail of a comet was interpreted as the symbol of a sword announcing imminent war. Andreas Suter, Der schweizerische Bauernkrieg von 1653. Politische Sozialgeschichte - Sozialgeschichte eines politischen Ereignisses (Tübingen 1997), 94-95 affirms that the ensuing excitement and apprehension has contributed to heated atmosphere that led into the confrontation.

achievements of the Enlightenment.[71] And in spite of all interdictions, Moscow still had not escaped uproar. Concerning the paradox of inborn slaves revolting against servitude, natural (or astronomical) law was thus an explanation of revolt that did not need people's striving for justice or freedom.

However, stars and comets were only causes of causes and most of Korb's explicative efforts involved deliberate human agency, although in an inverse sense. Well informed by Patrick Gordon and other military commanders, Korb listed the strel'tsy's grievances: their lack of adequate rations and consecutive half-starvation, as well as the long separation from their families in Moscow. But these limited motives did not seem sufficient to him. The unspoken question he tried to answer was: If the strel'tsy revolt had such a limited and presumably rather easily remedied cause, would Peter's retaliation have been so ferocious? As an admirer of Peter as an enlightened monarch Korb was convinced that there must have been much more at stake.

b) Ringleaders – Sofiia as the Clandestine Instigator

Revolts could not develop without ringleaders: this was *opinio communis* in early modern Europe and maybe until now. And the more important the ringleaders, the more dangerous a revolt could become.[72] In Sofiia, the revolt had a high-ranking ringleader who strove for nothing less than the crown. Korb subscribed to Peter's indictment against his half-sister and reproduced the official scenario of her alleged secret correspondence with the strel'tsy from her ecclesiastical imprisonment. Through a beggar woman, Sofiia would have transmitted her instructions in a loaf of bread.[73] Probably Korb still doubted if this scenario was sufficient to convey to his readers the dangerousness of the situation that alone would legitimize Peter's brutal reprisal. So he awkwardly introduced a flashback to the 1682 uprising that served to outline the whole potential of the 1698 events. His description of the 1682 events was certainly influenced by Heinrich Butenant's narrative. The German merchant and commercial agent of the Danish crown had been an eyewitness and almost a victim of the uprising: his description had circulated in German publications for years. But Korb did not adopt the Butenant's rather positive evaluation of Sofiia. Rather he made her image conform to the negative view propagated by Peter's government. Korb thus tried to show how the strel'tsy had been Sofiia's puppets in 1682, with the cruel slaughters of a considerable part of the

---

71 The same argument can be found in Olearius' account that strongly influenced Grimmelshausen's Simplicissimus. Cf. Mechthild Keller, "Simplizianische Moskowienfahrt. Hans Jacob Christoffel von Grimmelshausen", in West-östliche Spiegelungen, 377-378.
72 Cf. Karl Härter's contribution to this volume.
73 Korb, Diary of an Austrian secretary, 413-418.

highest court-elite[74] as a result. The impending repetition of this scenario in 1698 called for severest counter-measures.

However, this "historically informed" picture seems not to avoid perplexity about the causes, especially given the premises that Korb was convinced of Peter's outstanding qualities and presented the Tsar as a sovereign who wanted and did the best for his people and who acted for the sake of the common good, different from the tyrannical type of rulers. Korb wanted to go beyond a simple designation of a culprit and tried to explore more profound motives for resistance. He apparently wanted to explain *why* the strel'tsy could have stood up for the power-hungry Sofiia and, principally, why they assisted her *against the enlightened Tsar Peter*, in whose policies Korb saw the burgeoning of far-reaching reform.

c) Revolt as an Epidemic that does not Stop at State Borders

Korb's introduction to his chapter on the strel'tsy revolt is an attempt to find and explore deeper reasons for the uprising. Apparently, Korb identified revolts as *trans-border-phenomena*, something similar an infection that could spread like a wildfire, even across state-frontiers, and even if (as in the given case) the subjects on both sides of the frontiers lived under different political systems with different social structures and with monarchs who were far from equal in terms of their actual powers.

By a common sport of fortune it very often happens that when a friend would extinguish the houses of his neighbours which the flames are devouring, his own is involved in the same peril. And so it is not without reason that we deplore a calamity that may befall ourselves as often as Ukalegon hard-by is on fire.[75]

Everybody knows that when the Poles were about to proceed to the vote for the election of a monarch to the throne of their widowed Republic, their struggles were divided between two candidates. These wild gusts bursting beyond the narrow limits of the Diet, among this fiery people [lit. lively/ vivid tribes/peoples (lat. apud vividas gentes)], burning as they are with subtle and active intrigue, menaced a tempest fraught with universal danger.[76]

---

74 Ibid., 436-443.
75 Ucalegon was one of the Elders of Troy, whose house was set on fire by the Achaeans when they sacked the city. His name in Greek is translated as "who doesn't worry" and has become synonymous for a "neighbor whose house is on fire."
76 "Quae procellae ex Comitiorum freto exaestuantes, apud vividas gentes, subtilique, & exerto ambitu ferventes, funestam omnium discrimini minitabantur tempestatem."

The Czar of Muscovy, roused by the proximity of the peril, ordered a strong body of troops under the command of General Knes Michael Gregorowicz Romodanowski, to lie in observation upon the frontiers of Lithuania, so as to be able, should public disorders arise out of the strife of private individuals, to settle them promptly and repress with strong succours the disturbers of the public peace, and force them the more efficaciously into the reverence due to their lawfully elected king.

But how wonderful are the vicissitudes of fortune and of human affairs! The flood burst in wild rage upon him, who rashly thought to brave the unruly inundation that menaced the quiet of a neighbouring nation. Four regiments of Strelitz, which lay upon the frontier of Lithuania [inspired by the Polish neighbours], had nefariously plotted to change the sovereignty.[77]

Korb's account evoked serious troubles, almost civil war in the terminology of natural catastrophe: wildfire, storm on the sea, tempest, inundation, etc.[78] Of course, Peter stationed his strel'tsy garrisons at the border, not out of human kindness towards his Polish neighbours, but as a supporting measure for his active interference into the Polish struggle over succession to the throne. Peter had his candidate, August of Saxony (the "lawfully elected king"), and succeeded in imposing him on his neighbours, and that with the aid of military threat. The strel'tsy regiments at the frontier played an important role in this menacing scenario.[79] But it is not likely that Korb's introduction on Poland was meant as an ironic criticism of Peter's interventionism. Such intervention was perceived as rather normal and, beyond that, Peter's engagement corresponded to the general interests of the Reich that favoured: August to keep out the French-backed candidate Prince Conti, who would have dissociated Poland-Lithuania from the anti-Ottoman front in Eastern Europe.[80] In any way, the Polish-Lithuanian republic and its political system with its powerful aristocracy and its weak elected king was not viewed as an enlightened model. By contemporaries it was rather seen as an

---

77 Ibid., 391-392.
78 These metaphors, modes of explanation, were widespread in 17th century literature on revolts. See Peter Burke, "Some Seventeenth-Century Anatomists of Revolution", in Storia della Storiografia 22 (1992): 23-35 on the mainly Italian historians writing on the uprisings and civil wars of the mid 17 century crisis.
79 K. Piwarski, "Das Interregnum 1696/97 in Polen und die politische Lage in Europa", in Um die polnische Krone. Sachsen und Polen während des Nordischen Krieges 1700-1721, ed. J. Kalisch and J. G. Gierowski (Berlin, 1962), L. R. Lewitter, "Russia, Poland and the Baltic 1697-1721", The Historical Journal 11, 1 (1968).
80 Even though the Germans were busy with the debate over Spanish succession and therefore did not engage in a coalition with Russia to wage war against the Turks, the Reich remained interested in an eastern-European anti-Ottoman stronghold.

appalling example of chaos and inability to act (due to the magnates' *liberum veto*), which was a strong argument for absolutism as the most rational and progressive form of government.[81]

d) The Multi-National Dimension as a Fermenter of Extreme Violence

According to Korb "political fermentation" came from those "tribes" or "peoples" who were "seething with rage". The multi-"tribal" dimension of the Polish "inundation" seemed particularly prone to spill onto Russian territory, for the Empire was to an even greater extent multi-national. For this reason, it is important to take into account *how* Korb introduced his clumsy digression on the 1682 events:

> Others have already stated that the Russians are sprung from the Roxolanes, the name being only slightly altered. More recently the river Moskva, which flows past the metropolis of Muscovy has given rise to their name of Muscovites. Nor have there been wanting men of genius to describe the times when this race, whom some will have it came from beyond seas, grew to their mighty strength from small beginnings, from their first royal feat in Novgorod and Kiew, the Wlodimir, and lastly Moscow. By the tyranny of Ivan Basilowicz which served him to subdue to himself so many vast neighbouring regions, the kingdoms of Casan and Astracan, either by the death of their rulers or their imprisonment, Muscovy grew to its present immensity of empire, the very hugeness of which has often already proved a source of misery, and the incurable wounds of which the restless minds of the people are constantly tearing open before the heal.[82]

Only after this focus on territorial expansion into the terrains of wild peoples, and on the perils of separatist stirrings, did Korb come to the "1682 civil dissensions" and the accompanying "fearful internecine cruelties in rapine, and slaughter, and pillage".[83] When reading Korb's account, one feels slightly bewildered by his sudden historical flashback to the "Roxolanes" and the annexation of Kazan' and

---

81 For foreign views of the political system in Poland see Elida Maria Szarota and Adam Kersten, Die gelehrte Welt des 17. Jahrhunderts über Polen. Zeitgenössische Texte (Wien, 1972).

82 Korb, Diary of an Austrian secretary, 436. The Latin text reads: "Joannis Basilidis tyrannide, qua tot amplissimas vicinas Provincias Casani, Astrachanique regna Principum morte, aut captivitate sibi subjugaverat, i eam, quae nunc est, amplissimi Dominatûs magnitudinem adolevit, quam hucusque sua moles saepe afflixit, cujus insanabilia vulnera inquietae subditorum mentes periculissima sui avulsione nec dum passa sunt ducere cicatricem."

83 Korb, Diary of an Austrian secretary, 436-437.

Astrakhan. This seems rather awkward and out of context. But apparently it was meant to stress the general potential for conflict of the Muscovite Empire's multi-ethnic composition. For Korb this should help explain the amplitude of the 1682 uprising, although the events themselves were not related to any multi-ethnic dimension and Korb was not able to establish such a link.

e) Resistance to Enlightenment – Struggle for the Maintenance of Servitude

The significance of the non-Russian peoples seemed to be at the core of Korb's (mostly implicit) aetiology. It is the reading of revolts as manifestations of retrograde resistance against the civilizing process imposed from above. We have seen an earlier glimpse of such an interpretation in the *London Gazette* that tried to explain the upheavals of 1682 as a response against Tsar Fedor's inclination to Western, notably Polish, habits and his attempts to "civilize" his people.

In Korb's eyes revolt in Russia could also not be explained by a misled fight against servitude, as it had often been done in accounts of European revolts.[84] "Inborn slaves" could certainly not be seduced by the fallacious prospect of freedom and justice. Rather he believed the Russians to love their servitude and to struggle against those who wanted to deliver them from tyranny, who vouched for progress and enlightenment (like Peter). Korb could build on many earlier travelogues, whose authors had noted with stupefaction how Russians deliberately sold themselves into serfdom, when he wrote:

The slavery laws are in vigour among the Muscovites. Some become slaves by captivity, others are so by birth, many from being sold by their fathers, or by themselves: for if they be manumitted by their dying masters, so accustomed are they to slavery, that they make themselves over as slaves to other masters, bind themselves slaves for a sum of money.[85]

Korb actually reverted to a well-established stereotype, when he underlined that in Russia a father could sell his son into bondage four times.[86] Only Peter I had

---

84 For this pattern of a fight against servitude see for instance the following treatise: Wahrhafftig-Abbildender Auffruhr- und Empörungs-Spiegel. In welchem Alle unruhige und verwegene Köpffe gahr leicht und eigentlich zu erkennen seyn/ beydes Ihnen selbst zu nöthiger Betrachtung/ und allen redlichen/ Gottfürchtenden/ ihr Vaterland liebenden/ ... Gemüthern zu nützlichem Gebrauche vorgestellet (Friedberg [i.e. Hamburg], 1687).

85 Korb, Diary of an Austrian secretary, 522.

86 This assertion comes from Herberstein and has since be repeated in many travellers' accounts, but also in political philosophy. Still in the 16th century Bodin has taken it up in his major work, Les six livres de la République. See Poe, A people born to slavery, 173.

attacked these evils, Korb noted admiringly, but at the same time these efforts on behalf of his people's freedom and maturity incurred hatred against him:

However [...], now that Muscovy possesses a monarch whose intellect is so highly gifted by nature, and who is urged on by the wonderful stimulus of glory, people opine that a milder statute will be substituted for this very crude authority of parents over their sons. Though, in truth, the nation itself has such a dislike of liberty, that it seems to exclaim against a happiness for which it was not created, and is so inured to its slavish condition that it will scarcely endure the prudent and kindly solicitude of the Prince for his dominations and his subjects to be carried out to the full extent.[87]

Korb assumed that these objections to "happiness" could get extremely violent. According to the manifestations of this sort of violence could already be observed in the revolt of 1682. In retrospect Korb thus presented the 1682 events as a revolt against Peter's accession to the throne, since initially Peter alone had been nominated Tsar. Therefore he interprets the strel'tsy's refusal to take an oath on Peter in 1682 as an act of resistance against the breakthrough of enlightenment. As we have seen, this is rather at odds with the representation of that time, since Peter had been a child and the party of his family (the Naryshkins) stood rather for tradition and for the rejection of foreign influence, whereas the Miloslavskiis (with Ivan as their candidate) had proved to be open reform-oriented. Many reform projects had been initiated under Fedor and under Sofiia's regency (until 1689). The early years of Peter's actual reign, i.e. the first half of the 1690s, witnessed in reality a revocation of many of these reform initiatives. The government ordered the eviction of the Jesuits from Moscow, the persecution of the Kievian Uniates and even the suppression of the "regiments of the new order" [polki novogo stroia]. This made the initial phase of Peter's regency a period of Orthodox and xenophobe intolerance, with notable setbacks on the reform process, even in the military domain, which would later be at heart of the Tsar's reform efforts.[88]

But whereas for Herberstein this was a sign of Russian despotism, Bodin quoted such passages approvingly, since he made Muscovy a model for his idea of sovereignty.

87 Korb, Diary of an Austrian secretary, 523-524.

88 For de la Neuville, apparently a French diplomat in Polish service, Peter is the embodiment of cruelty and Asiatic backwardness, whereas Sofiia and especially her lover and policymaker Golitsyn are the guarantors of progress. This is even more noteworthy as he was on a diplomatic mission in Moscow at the time of the coup d'état of 1689 that led to the end of Sofiia's regency. In his account that has apparently been written up at the beginning of the 1690s (first published in 1698) Neuville well purports Sofiia's assassina-

All this seemed now to be forgotten, and Korb described Peter as if he was born as the enlightened reform Tsar. In contrast to him, all his predecessors appeared to Korb as the obscure representatives of a tyrannical and unenlightened past:

> The Czar is endeavouring, by means of various arts and sciences, to frame a better state of things in his kingdom. If success should crown the prudent efforts of good counsel, people shall shortly be astonished at the fair edifice that will stand where there was nothing but huts before; unless some misfortune should happen or a *defection of the people*, or perhaps even simply the very barbarity of their inclinations should render them incapable of bearing their own good fortune, or make them grudge to their posterity a lot so happy, and envy the labours of the present for the profit of future generations.[89]

Thus Korb considered even the people's jealousy towards the future, towards their own children and grandchildren's generation, as a motive for opposition to Peter. The events of 1698 bore a similar potential as the 1682 revolt, and apparently Peter's wrathful reprisals were necessary, all the more so as the boyars subscribed to the same tradition of tyranny as the commoners.

The Ignominious Role of the Elites: Boyars and Clergy

Korb made clear that Peter often could not rely on his boyars, who also resisted his reform measures – not only the cutting of beards, which Korb regarded as symptomatic, but also more profound changes. General corruption and depravity forced Peter to take ruthless steps. Returning from abroad, he learned at a banquet that his commander-in-chief, A.S. Sheyn, had promoted colonels and other officers for money, regardless of their merits. This was a major infringement of one of Peter's principal reform aims, the establishment of a meritocracy, as well as the struggle against corruption and haggling for positions. Following Korb's account, Peter's

> wrath had grown to such a pitch that he drew his sword, and facing the general-in-chief, horrified the guests with this threat: "By striking thus, I will mar thy malgovernment." Boiling over with well-grounded anger, he appealed to Prince Romodanowski, and to the Dumnoi Mikitim Mosciwicz; but finding them excuse the general-in-chief, he grew so hot that he startled all the guests by striking right and left, he knew not where, with his drawn sword. Knes [Prince] Romodanowski had to complain of a cut finger, and another of a slight

---

tion attempt on Peter's live. See Foy de La Neuville, Zapiski o Moskovii (Moskva, 1996) with Aleksandr Lavrov's informative introduction.
89 Korb, Diary of an Austrian secretary, 519.

wound on the head. Mikitim Moscivicz was hurt in the hand as the sword was returning from a stroke. A blow far more deadly was aiming at the general-in-chief, who beyond a doubt would have been stretched in his gore by the Czar's right hand, had not General Lefort (who was almost the only one that might have ventured it), catching the Czar in his arms, drawn back his hand from the stroke.[90]

However choleric Peter behaved in this episode, Korb considered his outburst of rage justified: corruption was so ingrained among the Muscovite elites that extraordinary action was indispensable to have any chance of making them grasp to what extent they acted wrongly and, in the long run, of uprooting this evil.

Representatives of the clergy were presented as equally or even more untrustworthy. The clergy had been given custody of Peter's half-sister Sofiia, an issue of highest delicacy directly related to the 1698 uprising:

The Patriarch cast upon others the blame that the Czarine was not yet shut up in a monastery, and the consequent contempt of the Czar's commands: his Majesty the Czar's indignation at which was so fiery that he ordered the archimandrite and four popes, to whose charge the Patriarch imputed it, to be set upon little carts (sboseck) by soldiers, and dragged to Bebraschentsko [Preobrazhenskoe, a village near Moscow, where executions were staged] by night.[91]

In Korb's record these scenes were Peter's first confrontations after his return to Russia that predicted the brutal reprisals that would follow. But on top of that, Korb contended that priests had pronounced their benediction over the insurgents' deeds and were ready to carry icons in order to get commoners of the capital to join the uprising. Thus the clergy were not spared in the executions, even though this meant breach of a taboo:

The ignominious gibbet cross awaited the popes, by way of reward in suit with the thousands of signs of the cross they had made, and as their fee for all the benedictions they had given to the refractory troops. The court jester, in the mimic attire of a pope, made the halter ready, and adjusted it, as it was held to be wrong to subject a pope to the hands of the common hangman.[92]

The Tsar's dissatisfaction with some Orthodox Church clergy must have attracted the attention of Guarient's delegation, as Rome, the Emperor, Jesuit circles and

---

90 Ibid., 184-185 (Entry of September 14, 1698).
91 Ibid., 192 (Entry of September 19, 20, 1698).
92 Ibid., 431 (7th execution, October 27).

others still hoped for Russia's conversion to Roman Catholicism.[93] Korb refrained from any speculation about this point. Moreover, in a conflict where the patriarch reproached the Tsar for his heavy use of torture in the interrogations of the rebels, the chronicler clearly took sides with the Tsar, although otherwise he was reluctant to admit the necessity of such cruel measures. Korb saw the unreliability of major representatives of the court-elites as the main reason why Peter personally interfered in the interrogations of the strel'tsy's:

The very Grand Duke himself, in consequence of the distrust he had conceived of his subjects, performed the office of inquisitor. He put the interrogation, he examined the criminals, he urged those that were more pertinaciously silent, to be subjected to more cruel tortures; those that had already confessed about many things were questioned about more; those who were bereft of strength and reason, and almost of their senses, by excess of torment, were handed over to the skill of the doctors, who were compelled to restore them to strength, in order that they might be broken down by fresh excruciations.[94]

The same mistrust seemed to be the reason why Peter compelled his boyars to carry out numerous death sentences and closely observed their performances. "[A]ll the Boyars, Senators of the realm, Dumnoi, Diaks, and so forth, that were present at the council constituted against the rebel Strelitz, had been summoned by the Czar's command to Bebraschentsko, and enjoined to take upon themselves the hangman's office."[95] Serving as executioner was extremely disgraceful and degrading for the members of the aristocracy. They could have refused to obey in this matter, if the Tsar himself had not assumed this odious job on the very first day: "Five rebel heads had been cut off in that spot by an axe that was swung by the noblest arm of all Muscovy."[96] The summons of the boyars to take an active part in the execution became both an act of humiliation and a test of loyalty.

Foreigners as Peter's only Trustworthy Support

In the diarist's eyes, the Tsar's well-founded mistrust of his boyar entourage and of representatives of the Orthodox high clergy helped to explain why *foreign servitors* had become Peter's main allies in the struggle against ubiquitous depravation. In his separate chapter on the strel'tsy's revolt, Korb emphasized that Patrick Gordon's diplomatic skills had prevented a worse outcome of the confrontation between

---

93 Dukmeyer, Korbs Diarium itineris, 1: 167-214.
94 Korb, Diary of an Austrian secretary, 409.
95 Ibid., 429-430 (5th execution: 23rd October, 1698).
96 Ibid., 424 (The First Execution, 10th October, 1698).

rebellious strel'tsy and his loyal Muscovite troops at the New Jerusalem Monastery. Korb singled out German Lieutenant-Colonel von Grage, whose accuracy and precision would have broken the rebels' resistance immediately: "The Strelitz saw safety nowhere; arms could not protect them; nothing was more appalling to them than the ceaseless flash and roar of the artillery showering its deadly bolts upon them from the German right."[97] Similarly the diarist describes a banquet at this same von Grage's residence, where the Tsar himself deigned to be present (in spite of swollen cheeks by toothache): "The Czar never showed himself more frankly gay; perhaps because none of the Boyars or anybody else was present to trouble the sensations of joy with evil eye."[98]

Such comments were not devoid of patriotic pride on Korb's part, but they also remind us of the dreams of leading Enlightenment thinkers in Germany about their close collaboration with the Tsar for the sake of civilizing Russia. However, as Korb and others before him depicted the situation, the Russian people were far from being a *tabula rasa*, onto which it would be easy to inscribe a new progressive and enlightened code that would henceforth determine their thinking and behaviour.[99] Deep-rooted evils tended to make the Russian people not only less receptive to Enlightenment ideas, but foreign observers made them out as the principal cause of stubborn resistance against anything progressive. The Tsar favoured "progressive foreigners", whereas the Russian people hated them for their "progressiveness". Foreign accounts quoted this among the central motives of the rebellion. Korb referred to an interrogation of Sofiia's ladies-in-waiting, one of whom

---

97 Ibid., 401. Probably these two armies were also his main informants on this encounter in which he had naturally not assisted. For the similarities with Gordon's account of the suppression of the uprising at Novoerusalimskii, cf. Brockmann, Der Bruch Peters mit Alt-Moskau; Dukmeyer, Korbs Diarium itineris, 2: 100.

98 Korb, Diary of an Austrian secretary, 191 (Entry September 18, 1698). "Liberius nunquam animi fui alacritatem Tzarus ostendit; forte quod Bojamen aliorumque, nemo aderat, qui inviso aspectu gaudii sensum turbaret."

99 This was Leibniz's idea as he expressed it in his memorandum of 1708 that he addressed to Tsar Peter. He emphasized the hugeness and thus the importance of the empire reigned by Peter that "encompassed almost the whole North of our hemisphere". And "since most of it is still tabula rasa and the new pot that has not yet assumed foreign taste in studies, many mistakes that have invaded [our sciences] can be avoided and improved, especially because everything is canalized by the mind of a sage ruler". Tat'iana Anatol'evna Oparina, Inozemtsy v Rossii XVI - XVII vv. [ocherki istoricheskoi biografii i genealogii] (Moskva 2007): 402.

after threats and a few strokes with the knout, confessed that the hatred which all Muscovites bear to General Lefort, and all Germans in general, was the main cause of the pernicious design; for to such a degree has nature made most Muscovites barbarians that they cannot bear virtue to be imported by foreigners.[100]

All this conveys Korb's and others' idea that in his struggle for reform, enlightenment and the common good of the Russian people, Peter I could only count on the faithful assistance of his foreign servitors. The representatives of his immediate Russian entourage were either unreliable, or even supported a recalcitrant people, whose stubborn resistance to any novelties questioning their inherited barbarism, egoism and indecency needed to be countered with resolute and, if necessary, brutal measures.

DIPLOMATIC SCANDAL: A SHIFT IN THE TSARS' INFORMATION POLICY AND ITS IMPACT ON WESTERN COVERAGE OF RUSSIAN REVOLTS

As a whole, Korb's book provides an enthusiastic description of tsar Peter's actions and initiatives – and it contrasts his luminous image with the dark reality of his country. In fact, the Russian population had hardly ever been described differently. Apart from that, the antagonism between the Tsar and his country legitimated Peter's occasional cruelty as necessary recourse to the stick. Why then did the publication of Korb's book in 1700/1 result in such a huge diplomatic scandal?

But I have to start with a very short summary on what the Russian government's reaction actually was. At the beginning of 1701, Russian Ambassador Prince P.A. Golitsyn learned in Vienna about Korb's diary. Immediately he wrote a furious letter to inform Peter I about the deed of "culprit Guarient", the Imperial Ambassador and chief of the 1698 delegation to Moscow. Although the diary was published by Korb under his name, Golitsyn took Guarient for the author and deemed him responsible for the publication – politically and personally.[101] Golitsyn had the diary quickly translated into Russian and sent it to Peter, together with the

---

100 Korb, Diary of an Austrian secretary, 201 (Entry of October 6 and 7, 1698).
101 In fact, Korb definitely was the author. This can be clearly determined from Korb's personal documents in the Amberg district archive. The similarities between the diary and Guarient's accounts sent to Kaiser Leopold, is due to the fact that Korb was also responsible for the correspondence with Leopold I. See Haus-, Hof- und Staatsarchiv, Staatsabteilung Rußland I, 18 (1698). I am particularly grateful to Aleksandr Lavrov, who provided me with his copies from the Amberg archives.

Latin original. Golitsyn's personal translator seemed to have had some difficulty with the Latin text. Normally, he translated between from Russian into German and vice versa, maybe Dutch as well, as did most translators at Muscovite foreign office. The translation was inexact, full of mistakes. At the same time the translator deliberately left out the most delicate passages that might have offended the Tsar, such as paragraphs about his active participation in the executions.[102] Thus Peter received a truncated version. However, he still set a whole machinery against the book and its alleged author in motion.

Moscow demanded that Guarient should be relieved of his functions and never again sent to Moscow. And what was even more important, it claimed that the book should be forbidden and withdrawn from the market. But the Emperor refused to put Korb's book on the Index, for he had given the publication his blessing in form of the imperial seal. In response Russian diplomats bought all copies they could get a hold of and burnt them (which is why the original Latin edition is a rarity to this day). Concerning Guarient, the situation was not that different. To dismiss him would have meant a loss of face for the Emperor. In his letter to Peter, Golitsyn complained about the protection the ambassador enjoyed from high-ranking nobles, namely from the earl of Kaunitz. In the end it was Guarient himself who yielded to the pressure and refrained from further missions to Russia. Muscovite diplomacy was not unsuccessful, but its victories were Pyrrhic in central aspects. The auto-da-fé did not extinguish public interest in the book, on the contrary. In educated circles, the few surviving copies were passed around, and the content was widely debated.

But again: why such a harsh reaction altogether? What was the bone of contention for Peter and his court? Why did they attack this book at that particular time? In the historical literature, the objections to blunt descriptions of the executions have been put forward as the main motive. But the executions were staged in public, and in the presence of foreign delegates. Apparently Peter even aimed at Western reception of these brutal events. As we have seen, Leibniz even supposed (and he did so well before the publication of Korb's diary) that Peter wanted to boast of his absolutist power over his subjects in front of the Emperor.[103] Another argument focuses on the representation of Peter's personal participation in the executions: Korb was the only contemporary who referred to these scenes. This alone, goes a current argument in historiography, would have undermined the Tsar's dignity and have been enough for him to do anything he could in order to

---

102 Dukmeyer, Korbs Diarium itineris, 1: 10-13. Dukmeyer has consulted the translation in Moscow.

103 See above.

prevent the circulation of the book.[104] But on the other hand, even after the scandal over Korb's diary Peter would still not refrain from referring to his direct implication in such bloody events. More than a decade later, in 1711 he would tell the Danish envoy Just Juel about his scientific observations during the course of decapitations. He described in detail the execution procedure against one rebel. His case had been exceptional, for, after having been beheaded, his corpse straightened up and remained erect for a minute or so. This account "is credible", notes Juel:

I heard it from the lips of the Tsar himself, and the Tsar is not prone to inventions. To conclude, the Tsar, who judges soundly on everything, expressed the idea that this criminal undoubtedly had narrow veins – a circumstance that slows down the hemorrhaging and thus longer conserves vitality in the body. Similar phenomena, occurring for the same reason, can be observed with birds, and particularly with hens, that sometimes continue to run for quite a while after their heads have been chopped off.[105]

Given such vivid accounts, it seems unlikely that Korb's descriptions of the executions provoked the strong reaction against his book. Peter was rather concerned to propagate his mercilessness abroad – and he relied to a considerable extent on foreigners' accounts to purport his fame. Both at home and through his trip abroad, when supposedly incognito, he invested a lot into disseminating the image of himself as a Tsar who literally took into his hands the destiny of the country. This activity was probably the main novelty he embodied; and it earned him greatest reverence among European enlighteners.[106] Even his cutting off of "five rebel heads" fitted into this model. Active and vigorous initiative included "over-due tasks", such as punishing those who remained stubbornly opposed to the

---

104 On Peter I.s active participation in the execution see Ibid., 2: 101–163. Dukmeyer gives detailed appreciation of the different views expressed in historiography until the end oft he 19th century. For more recent treatments of the matter see Reinhard Wittram, Peter I. Czar und Kaiser; zur Geschichte Peters des Großen in seiner Zeit (Göttingen, 1964), 1: 178; and Brockmann, Der Bruch Peters mit Alt-Moskau, 501-503.

105 See Juel's diary entry of January 30, 1711, Zapiski Iulia Iusta, datskogo poslannika pri Petre Velikom (1709-1711)', in Lavry Poltavy, ed. V. P. Naumov (Moskva 2001), 235. However, it has to be said that Juel refrained from publishing his diary. See below. If Peter I boasted of his cold-bloodedness in front of the Danish diplomat, this latter might have suspected that the Tsar wanted such stories to be circulated through rumors, but not in print. Like anybody else, Juel seems to have been alarmed by the Korb scandal.

106 So Leibniz was particularly impressed when he learned that Peter carpentered himself in the Netherlands. In a letter from 1697 he wrote admiringly to Sparvenfeld: "il travaille de sa propre main". Keller, Wegbereiter der Aufklärung, 400.

country's common good and future development. It was the amputation of rotten limbs designed to save the organism from degeneration. Beyond that, Peter did so for pedagogical reasons. According to Korb's narrative, Peter had to teach and discipline his disloyal and anti-reformatory boyars. Obliging them to emulate him in performing the strel'tsy's executions was a most effective means of putting them into their place.

Visual Representation as the Bone of Contention?

In view of the fact that the cruelties in Russia had been described in newspapers well before the publication of Korb's diary, I would argue that the scandal over Korb's book was provoked mainly not by textual, but by visual portrayals. The book contains quite a detailed copperplate engraving of the galleys with the hanged strel'tsy all around the town wall. Perspective is awkward and the engraving artistically poor. But everything is presented in a very orderly and graphic manner: collective galleys each for ten persons are placed neatly in a row, and smaller galleys for two persons each are pointing out of the embrasures in the town wall. In the background, one can see another huge collective galley built in a rectangle and placed close to the fence of the New Virgin Monastery court. In the garden immediately in front of the walls of the monastery, a smaller galley with three more victims is placed – apparently those who were hanged near the window of the monastery, where Sofiia was taken into custody. In another fenced-in area within the town walls people are shown being tortured and others executed with axes. In the foreground, apart from crying wives and a group of men that apparently welcoming an arriving high dignitary in a carriage pulled by six horses (the Tsar?), two women (probably Sofiia's ladies-in-waiting) are depicted as buried alive with only their heads showing up out of the ground. The illustration represents more or less what was described in the Diary (and in several German newspapers of 1698 and 1699), although some characteristic aspects of the cruelties seem to be missing, for instance the innumerable fires, on which the strel'tsy were roasted to make them confess their crimes.

"So what?" one might ask. Visual representation of the like was widespread in European books, broadsheets, newspapers and other publications at that time. It was common to illustrate punishments of such crimes of lese majesty, much more than illustrating the revolt itself. This was part of the practice of *damnatio memoriae*. The defamation aimed at obliteration of mass-crime and treason.[107] Punishment was visualized as deterrence, which was supposed to have a more immediate impact

---

107 Cf. Angela Rustemeyer, Dissens und Ehre. Majestätsverbrechen in Rußand (1600-1800) (Wiesbaden 2006): 253-254.

than written texts in an age of essentially oral communication. Also, illiterate persons clearly understood – and literally saw – what had happened to the traitors. When preparing the copperplate engravings for his book (or when ordering them), Korb conformed to standards of visual representation he knew from his own cultural background. The picture resembles many other visual representations of executions in the aftermath of 17th-century revolts, often commissioned works created by professionals on the basis of a written text alone.[108]

However, Russian standards of visual representation differed fundamentally from those of its Western neighbours. Neugebauer, former tutor of Peter's son Aleksei who had been recently fired, wrote a pasquinade, in which he pointed up Peter's anger at Korb's book and noted in particular the "clean copper where his Majesty the Tsar is standing with axe and sword slaughtering [one of the rebels]."[109] In fact, on the copperplate there are people with axes chopping off heads, but it is not at all clear that Peter I is supposed to be one of these executioners. This can only be deduced from the text. Be that as it may, even without the portrayal of the Tsar as executioner the picture was perceived as an enormous offense. Visual tradition in Russia was dominated by hagiographic representation of saints in icons and by panegyric portrayals of the sovereign, which also closely followed the hagiographic model. Acts of secular violence were an extraordinary object for engravings, and pictures of punishment scenes were practically unknown.[110] Punishments were staged in public, as had been done in the reprisals for the strel'tsy uprising, similar to many cases of punishments for former revolts in Muscovy. These were vivid and appalling examples that spoke a clear language. The scenes continued to live in the spectators' memories – and certainly they spread rapidly in whispering campaigns: nonetheless they were not visually fixed once and forever and could not be re-regarded.

One innovation is noteworthy in this context: the erection of pillars of shame, i.e. a symbolical representation of punishment. Apparently, these pillars were meant

---

108 See Karl Härter's contribution to this volume. At our workshop André Krischer has shown similar pictures for England.

109 At the same time Neugebauer referred to the depictions of the princesses that would have disgusted Peter. His judgment is interesting, but it would be highly problematic to take Neugebauer for an objective informant, for he apparently tried to revenge himself for the treatment he had suffered. In this sense he also predicted further publications that would present Peter and the Russians in a still less favorable light. Dukmeyer, Korbs Diarium itineris, 2: 17-18.

110 On the visual representations of the Tsar see Frank Kämpfer, Das russische Herrscherbild. Von den Anfängen bis zu Peter dem Großen; Studien zur Entwicklung politischer Ikonographie im byzantinischen Kulturkreis (Recklinghausen, 1978).

as a belated response to columns the strel'tsy had built in 1682 on what is now Red Square, when they had held power for a few months. The columns of 1682 were actually intended to justify the insurgents' actions against a range of high-ranking boyars. The names of these "traitor-boyars" [*vory-boyary*] were engraved on the columns, thus presenting them as traitors to the Tsar(s) and the common good. Thus the previous killings by the strel'tsy were qualified as righteous *executions*, i.e. as legitimate *juridical* measures.[111] In function these columns resembled the pillars of shame in Western and middle-European countries in early modern times, where they were erected at the places of the culprits' razed houses and sometimes lasted for centuries.[112] However, in Russia before 1682, pillars of shame were unprecedented. In 1698 Peter apparently ordered them to be built in order to stress the indictment of the strel'tsy for ongoing criminal activity and high-treason. But they failed to become a regular institution and were not followed up in the further course of the 18th century.[113]

However ephemeral they in the long run, Peter's pillars stood for a fixation and perennization of memory, in some way analogous to pictures. However, since the representation was abstract and rather symbolic than concrete, the pillars were apparently not regarded as equivalent to a drawing, as found in Korb's publication. Pictures had an immediate sensual and emotional appeal, especially in a largely oral culture with an overwhelming majority of illiterates. In medieval and early modern Russia, pictures were expected to be an *iconography* in the most literal sense. They belonged to the domain of worship. Conversely, church and worship, matters of religion were to be kept away from fundamentally secular concerns such as the punishment of traitors. This could be seen from Peter's reaction to the patriarch's attempt to calm his fury with the icon of the Holy Virgin:

[The patriarch] thought the best thing was to take an image of the Most Blessed Virgin, the sight of which might remind him [the Tsar] of the common lot of man, and bring back the common feelings of pity to a mind that was almost degenerating into savagery. But the weights of real justice with which his Majesty the Czar measured the magnitude of this heinous crime were not to be altered by this exhibition of sham pity. For it had come to that pass that Muscovy was only to be saved by cruelty, not by pity. Yet is this severity of

---

111 Volksaufstände in Rußland, passim.
112 In the case of the Frankfurt Fettmilch uprising (1612-16) the pillars of shame remained until the 19th century. See Rudolf Frank, Vincenz Fettmilch: Eine historische Erzählung aus der Geschichte der freien Stadt Frankfurt am Mein (Leipzig, 1861): 1.
113 A. V. Lavrent'ev, "Moskovskoe 'stolbotvorenie' kontsa XVII veka. Pervye grazhdanskie pamiatniki v Rossii i politicheskaia bor'ba v ėpokhu Petra I.", Arkhiv russkoi istorii 2 (1992); Rustemeyer, Dissens und Ehre, 254.

chastisement falsely called tyranny; for sometimes even equity and severity are one and the same: more particularly when disease or obstinate gangrene has taken such firm hold of the members that there remains no other remedy for the general health of the body politic than iron and fire to cut them off. Thus the Czar's invective against the Patriarch was not unworthy of his sovereign office: 'What wilt thou with thy image? Or what business is it of thine to come here? Hence forthwith, and put back that image in the place where it should be venerated. Know, that I reverence God and his Most Holy Mother more earnestly perhaps than thou dost. It is the duty of my sovereign office, and a duty that I owe to God, to save my people from harm, and to prosecute with public vengeance crimes that tend to the common ruin.'[114]

The Tsar urged the Patriarch to bring the icon immediately back to its place, the church. He thus made a clear distinction between ecclesiastical and worldly matters. Taking the icon away from its place of worship seemed an undue intrusion into secular space, a sacrilege, an abuse of a sacred object exclusively used for worship. In his reflection on the necessity of cruelty Korb tried to clear Peter of the reproach of tyranny. At the same time his interpretation of the confrontation between the Patriarch and the Tsar demonstrates that the diarist was completely unaware of the significance of pictures in Orthodox culture. Icons were not mere symbols, but the depicted persons and events were deemed to be really present.[115]

The execution of priests was probably one of the most unprecedented undertakings in Peter's orgy of repression. The extraordinary measures have also to be seen as a response to an abusive use of *pictures* to arouse rioters, since the beheaded priests were accused of having led the insurgents *with icons*. Peter's court regarded the illustrations depicting the executions and torture scenes in Korb's book as a similar encroachment of iconography into the secular sphere. Apart from the explicit authorship that linked the book to the imperial embassy (and made it easier to intervene than with regard to anonymous news correspondents) it was the visual

---

114 Korb, Diary of an Austrian secretary, 199-200 (Entry October 6, 7, 1698).

115 In fact, there had been earlier attempts to curtail the flow of information through diplomatic channels. We know about Moscow's attempts to take action against Swedish "hack writers" who were accused of having spread the rumour of an alliance between Razin and Nikon in 1670/71. See S. M. Shamin, "'Klevety mnogie' o Rossii (o pervykh popytkakh russkogo pravitel'stva borot'sia protiv rasprostraneniia v evropeiskikh informatsionnykh izdaniiakh negativnykh i lozhnykh svedenii o Moskovskom gosudarstve)", XXV Pushkinskie chteniia. A. S. Pushkin i Rossiia. Sektsiia 4: Sovremennaia kul'turologiia i mezhkul'turnaia kommunikatsiia (Moskva, 2006). This attempted intervention had taken place on a smaller scale, but probably it is not a coincidence that it was a representative of the church who was concerned.

representation of the secular act of punishment that distinguished Korb's publication from standard accounts in newspapers that the court had subscribed to and that generally did not contain illustrations.[116] Visual representation was undoubtedly an extremely delicate issue in the medieval and early modern Russian tradition. When Peter saw the illustrations in Korb's book, he reacted, similar to his diplomats, with an instant defensive reflex. In the longer perspective this reflex action was not counter-balanced by a sober reconsideration.

A Revaluation of Public Opinion?
Guarient's Unsuccessful Quest for Justification

While the iconographic dimension of the scandal over Korb's book hints at deep-rooted traditions and expectations that were unwittingly offended, we can see aspects of change in Tsarist government's positions on publicity and to the public sphere. These changes can be seen from Guarient's correspondence with Muscovite officials. Like everything else, the letters remain vague about the actual bone of contention, but Guarient's strategies of defence and justification reveal a lot about the shifting paradigms.

First of all the ambassador denied his authorship. In a letter to Peter's prime minister, Fedor Golovin, he dissociated himself from Korb and took a more or less juridical stance. He refused responsibility for a work that was not written by a subject of the Emperors crown lands (Korb came from Neumarkt in Lower Bavaria):

---

116 An objection against my emphasis on the importance of visual representation could be made with regard to two other publications. Paul Rycaut, Giovanni Battista Donado, Michele Foscarini and Berengano, Der Neu-eröffneten Ottomannischen Pforten Fortsetzung. Oder: Continuirter Historischer Bericht ... Beydes aus deß Herrn Ricaut, Donado, Foscarini, Berengano, &c. Und andern glaubwürdigen Schrifften und Uhrkunden, aus dem Frantzösischen, Italienischen und Holländischen in das Hoch-Teutsche übersetzt und zusammen getragen; Zugleich mit kunstreichen Kupffern und wahrhafften Conterfaiten ... außgezieret (Augspurg, 1700) contains an engraving representing Sofiia's monastery with the gallows around. And another description of the Muscovite state, a small brochure that was published about a year after Korb's diary, Der Moszkowitische Staat Unserer Zeit. Worinnen unpartheyisch beschrieben Dieses grossen Reichs Beschaffenheit und weitläufftigen Gräntzen...; Insonderheit, Was bey dem Liefflindischen Kriege zeithero zwischen Moßkau und Schweden... vorgegangen sey (Cölln, 1702) reproduced Korb's illustration even on the cover; See also Dukmeyer, Korbs Diarium itineris, 1: 17. I can only presume that the brochures, published in Augspurg and Cölln (Brandenburg), went unnoticed by Russian diplomats.

I beg you not to accuse me of an affair that is not mine: I have no part in that, neither by my words, nor by my deeds. It is the story of my secretary and it would have been impossible to forbid him to print anything even without my knowledge, because he is not born here, but in another region of the Reich.[117]

In a letter of the same day (24.12.1701) to P. P. Shafirov, the chief translator of the Tsar's foreign office [*posol'skij prikaz*] and one of Peter I's leading diplomats, Guarient repeated his argument, but the ambiguity of his further reasoning deserves closer attention:

Since in this book there is not a single letter from my quill, and since I have *reported to His Imperial Majesty in a completely different key* in regards to the Tsar's grace [than Korb has done in his book] and the imperial ministers are also informed differently, I hope that in Moscow *you will laugh about such an account* and will not accuse me of it [the account]. [...] On the other hand, in my opinion, the book contains many laudable things, apart from some ridiculous and untrue descriptions.[118]

Guarient's defence has to be situated at the threshold of a new era in imperial diplomatic relations with Russia. This does not mean that *the ambassador's argumentation* was new. It rather appealed to old and well-tried patterns in bilateral relations with Russia. What was new is that *it did not work anymore* for the Russian court. Guarient basically downplayed the significance of Korb's book: why did the Tsar and his diplomats care about this diary? Even if the book was full of lies,[119] the essential thing was that he, the imperial Ambassador, had informed the Emperor and his ministers correctly. This was what counted and what prevented imperial diplomats from getting a faulty negative image of the Muscovite court. If Leopold I had ever read this book, he wouldn't have paid attention to it, said Guarient, as the Emperor relied on the information he got through his diplomatic channels. Consequently his attitude towards the Tsar remained unspoilt and absolutely positive. Relevant in Guarient's reckoning was the Emperor, his court and diplomatic corps, i.e. *the policy-makers*. This position did not necessarily reflect

---

117 Quoted from Ibid., 1: 12.
118 Quoted from Ibid., 1: 13. Guarient waited for this laughter in vain. A few months later he wrote directly to Peter I. to give up and announce his decision to resign from his position as ambassador.
119 Guarient does not entirely condemn the book. If his foremost concern towards Shafirov is to repudiate the accusation against him by renouncing the authorship of the book that has caused such a scandal, he nevertheless tries to rehabilitate Korb's book through a loophole, saying that it contained "many laudable things", see above.

Guarient's personal opinion, but an adopted strategy reflecting what he anticipated to be his interlocutors' point of view.

Guarient's strategic choice was not ungrounded; it was based on experience with Muscovite diplomats and their behaviour in the past. Western newspapers (*kuranty*) were translated at the Tsar's court in order to learn what Western *politicians* knew and thought (including their views about events in Russia). To the Tsar publicity had been important only insofar as it reflected the policy-makers' extent of knowledge. In the 1660s the imperial diplomat Meyerberg, one of Guarient's predecessors, mocked his Muscovite colleagues for referring to Western newspapers as to the Delphian oracle.[120] Accounts in the press only mattered as a source of information for diplomats and politicians. But Guarient claimed that through his secret bulletins the Emperor was much better informed than through newspapers or a book like Korb's. The ambassador was convinced that the Muscovite court did not consider public opinion and public debate to be an independent force that had to be reckoned with.[121] In the European imagination the Tsar was the incarnation of unlimited autocracy, who would not (and did not need to) care about his own population's opinions: there were not even newspapers in Muscovy. Why then should the Tsar care about public opinion abroad? In this sense, Guarient thought or hoped that he only had to clear up a misunderstanding: he assured his correspondents in Moscow that Korb's book did *not* reflect the reports he, Guarient, had sent to the imperial court in Vienna during the Embassy (hence the dissociation from his secretary Korb) and that the contents of the book were far from being a source of the Emperor's view of Russia and its monarch.

But this reasoning no longer cut any ice with the Tsar. Guarient was not listened to and in 1702 he gave up. Once again he wrote directly to Peter I. Reaffirming his innocence, he concluded "I have finally renounced the position of ambassador to your court that was offered to me, in order not to meet your discontented eye and not to harm affairs."[122] Guarient's defence was based on a miscalculation. It turned out that for the Muscovite court, public opinion had become a force to reckon with; this was new. But did it mean that the old way of policy-making over the

---

120 Quoted in Vesti-kuranty, 1: 9.
121 David Hume was not even born and if governments already realized that they rested to a certain extent "on opinion", as the Scottish philosopher would later claim it in his path-breaking Treatise on the Human Nature (1739/40), this was principally a question of domestic policy. The state-run Gazette in France, founded still in the 1630s, was a manifestation of the state's attempts to influence his citizens' opinions through propaganda. Nobody would have tried to bridle public opinion abroad (only in cases of personal insult it was a question of honour to intervene).
122 Quoted from Dukmeyer, Korbs Diarium itineris, 13.

population's heads was abandoned? To answer in the affirmative would be jumping to conclusions. For what we can observe is a concern with public opinion *abroad*.

One reason for this shift in the priorities of Muscovite diplomacy was certainly Peter's recruitment policy. The increased efforts to attract foreign specialists to Russia to work indeed addressed a Western public well beyond the field of political decision-makers. Peter's government was afraid of dissuading foreign specialists from coming to Russia. But it was not mainly the brutal reality of punishment that was deemed prone to repel the candidates; it was the visual representations of such scenes of state violence. This was definitely a wrong assessment: a picture as it was printed in Korb's book was absolutely familiar to occidental Europeans. It would hardly bias him exceedingly against Muscovy.

Although much of the scandal had probably been provoked by cultural differences and ensuing misunderstandings, the affair entailed a more general confrontation concerning the idea of publicity and the public sphere. In the immediate aftermath of the scandal Russian media policy made a quantitative and qualitative leap that would greatly affect foreign relations for generations.

A NEW RUSSIAN MEDIA POLICY

In the Korb case, the intervention was purely to prohibit: Muscovite diplomats demanded that the book should be forbidden and destroyed. In the short term this strategy remained unsuccessful.[123] In addition to the intransigence of the imperial court in Vienna that would not allow a loss of face by giving in Russian demands, the affair stirred up curiosity in European educated circles. The scandal attracted interest in the diary, rather than keeping potential readers away, however difficult it was to get access to the few remaining copies. An episode reported in 1705 by the English ambassador in Muscovy Charles Whitworth shows that Peter did not give up. Whitworth wrote to his compatriot Wich in Hamburg about the Tsar's fury when learning of a recent article published abroad, whose author asserted "that great numbers of people had been put to death by strange Torturers for a Rebellion" in Smolensk. Peter raged: the accounts of "both the Execution and the Rebellion were entirely false, nor was there ony the least Ground for such a scandalous

---

123 The Europäische Fama asserted that, thanks to his persistence, Golitsyn had worked a prohibition of the book. But this is quite doubtful and seems to be rather a piece of Russian propaganda, for Huyssen, who apparently had a function analogous to Böttiger's, was particularly influential in this journal and prescribed what had to be written on Russia.

report."[124] The message for the ambassador was clear: Peter was not willing to tolerate such interference into the representation of his country.

Such restrictive interventions were not entirely new. But from there on they were increasingly accompanied by *proactive* measures to create images and to shape public opinion. This was an innovation. At first glance the new policy only aimed at internal Russian representation. At the end of 1702, less than two years after the Korb affair, the first newspaper was issued in Russia, the *Vedomosti* [Gazette, Bulletin]. If reforms of dress and ceremonial largely copied what Peter had seen in Western Europe, his *Vedomosti* (Gazette) were far away from German or Dutch counterparts that had to assert themselves into the pluralism of the printing market. Maybe the paper rather followed the French model of the state-run *Gazette*, founded in the 1630s by Théophrast Renaudot under the auspices of Richelieu and Louis XIII.[125] Even more so, during the first years of the *Vedomosti's* existence, the Tsar wrote most accounts himself. He apparently attached great importance to this matter. Printed in Moscow and in the new capital (St. Petersburg), the paper had very limited circulation (wavering between fewer than 100 and 4000 copies in 1702-1728).[126]

For instance, in July 1708 contemporaries could read a report on the current revolt of the Don Cossacks under Bulavin in the *Vedomosti*. The chief rebel was presented as an apostate (*bogootstupnik*) and traitor (*vor*) who

planned an uprising in the Ukrainian towns and among the Don-Cossacks. He assembled several traitors [*vory*] and accomplices and sent 'letters of enticement' [*prelestnye pis'ma*] into many towns and villages to summon [the people] to become his treacherous accomplices [*vorovskomu edinomyshleniiu*]. And many such traitors and all the Don-Cossacks rallied to him, some out of need, some because they were under a spell [*prelesti*]. And in a throng the assembled went on to many towns and villages – for ravage and in order to urge still more people to join them.

But the Tsar sent his troops under the command of Prince Ya.F. Dolgorukii, in order to "catch Bulavin and to destroy his evil treacherous council." Then the report

---

124 The letter is dated May 13/2, 1705. Quoted from Astrid Blome, Das deutsche Rußlandbild im frühen 18. Jahrhundert. Untersuchungen zur zeitgenössischen Presseberichterstattung über Rußland unter Peter I (Wiesbaden, 2000), 44-45. We know neither the article nor what it refers to and if something comparable did or did not take place.

125 For the history of the French Gazette see Gilles Feyel, L'annonce et la nouvelle. La presse d'information en France sous l'Ancien Régime, 1630-1788 (Oxford, 2000).

126 Ingrid Maier, "Pervaja russkaja pechatnaja gazeta i ee inostrannye obrazcy", in La Russie et les modèles étrangers, ed. Serge Rolet (Villeneuve d'Ascq, 2010).

enumerated the successes of the Tsar's force, stressing how many rebels were beaten or killed. But probably *the* decisive message of the account was that Bulavin, in a militarily hopeless situation, committed suicide. Today the story of Bulavin's suicide on July 7 is considered a rumour.[127] But it is important to note that this rumour was apparently launched *by the Russian government* – via its newspaper. The chief rebel's alleged suicide was a suitable means of discrediting him and with him the remnants of the rebellion not yet extinguished in some places.

In Russia it was a novelty to write about revolts that were still going on. Formerly, the population not immediately in danger of being won over to the rebels' side had been provided with official information on current revolts only by priests in their sermons.[128] Written secular accounts had been rare and the medieval-style chronicles had only emerged many years after the events. Abandoning former taboos, Peter's new media policy seemed, at first glance, to adopt European standards: similar to Western governments it tried to assert an interpretative monopoly, in order to forestall the propagation of alternative narratives through whispering campaigns.[129] But due to widespread illiteracy and the low print run the pillars of shame were more likely to reach the population.

This makes it likely that Peter's account on Bulavin in the *Vedomosti* aimed not least, and maybe even primarily, at a foreign public. Concomitant measures were taken in order to influence public opinion abroad. Peter's government opened a proverbial second front and started to install "watchdogs" at critical spots that were particularly prone to disseminating news on Russia. We know that shortly after the Bulavin events and the subsequent Russian victory against the Swedes at Poltava (1709), Johann Friedrich Böttiger was put into action in Hamburg. He was resident in Hamburg and paid by the Russian court. He was a key figure in observing and eventually curtailing the German press on anything related to Russian themes. His tasks seem to have been multiple. Of course, he issued official disclaimers, when a newspaper had touched upon a subject that was deemed delicate by the Russian government. But in these cases, the damage had already been done. His main

---

127 Vedomost' no. 8. Moskva [Pechatnyi dvor], July 20, 1708. The paper was issued in 300 copies. Cf. http://imwerden.de/cat/modules.php?name=books&pa=showbook&pid=2154, consulted 12.11.2009. For the classification of the suicide story as a rumour see Blome, Das deutsche Rußlandbild, 256; Heinz-Dietrich Löwe, "Der Aufstand der Don-Kosaken unter Kondratij Bulavin, 1707-1708", in Volksaufstände in Rußland, 255.

128 This was namely the condemnation of the insurgents and particularly the pronunciation of the anathema against the leaders in liturgy. See Rustemeyer, Dissens und Ehre, 254-255. As to the war of information within the realm of revolt see André Berelowitch's contribution.

129 Würgler, Unruhen und Öffentlichkeit.

activity consisted in preventive measures. These were both reactive and proactive. On the one hand he tried to prevent unwelcome news about Tsarist Russia from spreading; on the other hand, he increasingly fed newspapers with "proper" news from the Russian court. In this sense he and his colleagues in other places can be seen as the extended arm of the press policy pursued by the *Vedomosti*. Often publishers did not even realize being provided with "information" from representatives of the Tsar's court.[130]

Apparently Böttiger did not only focus on the press. Even a German baroque composer like Johann Mattheson (1681-1764) in Hamburg seems to have come into trouble. In 1710 he wrote his opera *Boris Goudenow* about the prelude to the Muscovite Time of Troubles (Godunov's reign was 1598-1605). Mattheson's libretto followed the typical intrigue-, love- and power-pattern and did not even include the story of the first False Demetrius, who had conquered the throne from the Godunov family. But the very subject was suspect. It might have included social upheaval and the challenge to dynastic legitimacy, which was particularly dreadful when staged in an *audio-visual* representation. Mattheson was in contact with Russian circles in Hamburg. He had met Böttiger, who must have given him to understand that the Russian government did not approve the production of the opera. We don't know exactly what happened, but in the end Mattheson refrained from putting the work on stage. The premiere would not take place until 2005 (!) in Hamburg. In his autobiography the composer referred only vaguely to "certain circumstances" that had made him withdraw the opera.[131]

---

130 Blome, Das deutsche Rußlandbild, 20-21. Residents with similar tasks seem to have been working in England and France. See ibid., 46.

131 Johann Mattheson, Grundlage einer Ehren-Pforte, woran der Tüchtigsten Capellmeister, Componisten, Musikgelehrten, Tonkünstler etc. Leben, Wercke, Verdienste etc. erscheinen sollen (Hamburg, 1740), 197, quoted from Stephen Stubbs, "Johann Mattheson - the Russian connection. The rediscovery of Boris Goudenow and his other lost operas", Early Music 33, 2 (2005): 283-292, 286. Cf. also Dorothea Schröder, Zeitgeschichte auf der Opernbühne. Barockes Musiktheater in Hamburg im Dienst von Politik und Diplomatie (1690 - 1745) (Göttingen, 1998), 38, 80, who supposes that "Russian tradition" forbade the portrayal of tsars living or dead on the theatrical stage. But this seems unlikely, if we consider that Lope de Vega's El Gran Duque de Moscovia y Emperador Perseguido on the Demetrius topic had been staged already a hundred years earlier. Not only appeared the False Demetrius on stage (whom Lope considered as the true Tsar!), but also Boris Godunov and Vasilii Shuiskii. On Lope de Vega's piece cf. Ervin C. Brody, The Demetrius legend and its literary treatment in the age of the baroque (Rutherford, 1972). See also Maureen Perrie's contribution to this volume. For pictures of the Muscovite sovereign see Kämpfer, Das russische Herrscherbild. We rather have to as-

Korb's account itself was remembered for a long time in Europe,[132] which seems to have been traumatic for the Russian government. Peter's administration made any effort to correct this supposedly negative image by "proactive" representational measures. The main strategy consisted in attributing petty motives of revenge to the author, which would explain his nasty "lies". Still, even before the installation of the Russian emissary in Hamburg, the protestant and pro-Petrine *Europäische Fama* tried to discredit Korb's book. The journal claimed that both, Korb and Guarient, had denied their authorship, but that Guarient had at least financed the publication in his Catholic overzealousness. In reality it would have been "the papal missionaries in Moscow, Dr. Carbonarius and Dr. Pleyer" who had

scrawled it [the book] and filled it with so many unfounded things and untruths, for they were jealous that the Protestant religion enjoyed so many privileges in Moscow, almost more than theirs [the catholic religion], of what the connoisseurs of the Muscovite state can give the best account.[133]

Shortly after Peter's death (1725), at the beginning of Catherine's I reign, a mysterious treatise in form of a *Conversation between Three Friends who come together in one Town, Namely between Menard, Talander and Varemund* delivered such an explanation of the diary's malevolence. Apparently the treatise was commissioned by the Russian government, probably still under Peter I,[134] in order to refute a whole range of allegedly slanderous rumours supposedly circulating abroad. The dialogical form and even the protagonists' grecophile names were characteristic of European Enlightenment discourse. Not only form and content, but also the language, suggest that the pamphlet might have been first published abroad

---

sume that the sensibility of Russian authorities has augmented considerably, especially in the times of Peter I., who was particularly concerned with image building.
132 Dukmeyer, Korbs Diarium itineris, 1: 17-33.
133 Europäische Fama, 51. Theil, 1706, reprinted in 1710. Quoted from Ibid., I, p.19-20.
134 Could this have been a reaction to David Fassmann's very popular Conversations in the realm of the dead ("Gespräche in dem Reiche der Todten")? Fassmann started to issue this regular publication in 1725, just after Peter's death and gave fictive conversations, generally between Ivan IV and Peter I. He drew much of his information on Peter from Korb's Diary and was thus an important disseminator of Korb's representations on Russia, especially because he successfully addressed to a larger public. Cf. Eckard Matthes, "Das veränderte Rußland und die unveränderten Züge des Russenbilds", in West-östliche Spiegelungen, 109-135.

and only then translated into Russian (probably from German).[135] In the tale one Varemund,[136] a lieutenant, who left his home country (which remains unspecified) for service in Russia, where he eventually became a major general, then "enlightens" his compatriots. Influenced by anti-Russian pasquinades his two friends are full of prejudice about his host country. Talander refers to:

a book published in Latin under the name of the secretary of the imperial inter-nuncio Gvarnent's [sic!] Embassy, in which all occurrences that have taken place at court during their stay in Moscow, are described at length in day-to-day entries. Among them turn up several very strange ones, many full of bloodshed, from which the reader gets insight into the extraordinary behaviour of this court and into the cruelty of this government[137] [... particularly] the brutal execution of several regiments of the former Russian infantry, called strel'tsy.

In contrast to all the other foreign slanderers of the Russian Empire, whose pasquinades turn out to be acts of vengeance by people, who came to Russia as specialists (often military) and have been punished or simply degraded for misdeeds and committed crimes, Menard claims "that such a stranger [like Korb] had no reason to write anything but the truth in his diary."[138]

In response, Varemund maintains that Korb's book was written "with malicious fervour" and was full of "exaggerations and lies". Varemund justifies at length the brutal repressions against the insurgent strel'tsy who at any occasion had

---

135 "Razgovor mezhdu trekh priiatelei soshedshikhsia v odnom gorode, a imenno Menarda, Talandra, Varemunda", Russkii vestnik T.4, no. 12 (1841). I am referring to the 19th century reprint of the pamphlet. To judge from the context the pamphlet must have been written between May 1726 and March 1727. Cf. the arguments on http://gorchev.lib.ru/ik/Predystoriya%20SPb_1703god/B2_Razdel_2/2_2_07.html, consulted March 27, 2010. Unfortunately I could not find the original publication, neither foreign nor Russian. The editors do not indicate their source: they only note that it "has probably been composed on the initiative of the government that wanted to refute unofficially the calumnies and false rumours on Russia that were circulated by malicious people abroad". But the complementary information they provide, namely that "a part of it has been published, a long time ago, in one of the Muscovite journals, but here it is printed in its entirety" strengthens my hypothesis that the original text was published abroad in a foreign language, most probably German to judge from the numerous (completely un-Russian) foreign words.
136 Varemund, German: wahre Mund, "true mouth", i.e. the one, who tells the truth.
137 Ibid., 320-321.
138 Ibid., 336-337.

manifested their "wilfulness and insubordination" through dangerous rebellions. The fervent defender of Peter's policies picks up the rumours that had circulated during the 1682 uprising when he asserts that the strel'tsy had attempted the life of the sovereign, not only in Peter's reign, but earlier during his father's (Tsar Aleksei) and brother's (Tsar Fedor) reigns. Although Peter had declared an amnesty in the strel'tsy's favour after previous revolts, they had abused his goodwill with malicious aforethought. In view of the extraordinary threat they presented, Peter had been forced to proceed in an extraordinary way, "to set an appalling example." He would not be able to relieve the country "from these rebellious strel'tsy [*ot tekh rebeliatnikov Strel'tsov*], until the very name of the strel'tsy infantry was abolished." Furthermore,

subsequent uprisings in Astrakhan[139] and elsewhere showed clearly that even the cruelty, with which [the regime] had proceeded against them at that time, did not heal them of their *inborn* wilfulness and insubordination [*ot vkorennogo v nikh svoevol'stva i neposlushaniia*] and would not retain them

from their evil deeds. Varemund remains vague about what Korb's lies precisely were, but in response to his interlocutor's question about the *reasons* for the dairy author's "malice" he explains: "it was said in Moscow that the commission [i.e. Guarient's Embassy] had not been successful at the Russian Court." As the peace of Karlowitz (1699) had been "made without Russian participation", the Tsar had "concluded a two-year armistice with the Turks" separately. In Varemund's opinion this armistice ran counter to the Emperor's interests: "maybe the envoy wanted to take revenge for the failure of his commission."[140]

How did publishers abroad react to these attempts of intervention by Peter I and his successors? Did they comply with Russian lobbyists' interventions? One has to

---

139 The Astrakhan uprising (1705-06) was mainly a matter of the townspeople, merchants, commoners, but indeed, as the main military guard of the town, the strel'tsy played an important role again. However, the strel'tsy of the South probably had not that much in common with the Moscow strel'tsy, who had not been admitted to their homes and families. On the Astrakhan uprising see Nina Borisovna Golikova, Astrakhanskoe vosstanie. 1705-1706 gg. (Moskva, 1975).

140 Razgovor mezhdu trekh priiatelei, 336-338. From Varemund's explanation it does neither become clear why he regarded Guarient's Embassy as a failure nor in what respect the Russian separate armistice with the Ottoman Empire was such a problem for the Roman Emperor and his delegation. On Russian foreign policy with regard to the peace of Karlowitz see Handbuch der Geschichte Rußlands, 257-259 with further bibliographical references.

take into account that ideas about public opinion on parts of the Russian government differed quite fundamentally from those of publishers in the Reich. Guarient's half-hearted efforts to protect his secretary had not impressed his Russian addressees: in spite of some "untrue description" Korb's book "contained many laudable things."[141] This implied that since errors were almost inevitable, they were pardonable. The reader would judge for himself about the value of the accounts. The argument corresponded to the position adopted by the publishers of several German newspapers when defending themselves against disclaimers issued by Russian emissaries like Böttiger, who accused the papers of distorting facts. Due to the curtailed flow of information, claimed many publishers, arriving news accounts from Russia were often contradictory. Under these circumstances, they would print what they received, even contradictory information, in order to leave it for readers to judge on their own. Short introductory comments informed readers about both, the scarcity and contradictoriness of available information, and about the pluralist approach the newspaper adopted to cope with those constraints.[142] In contrast to that the Russian government held that there was only one (its own) "truth" and that everything else had to be rigorously suppressed.

We have seen that Guarient's justifications showed willingness to compromise. In contrast to him, some newspaper agents resisted and tried to keep to their pluralism, at least initially. But pluralism was not a matter of principle; it was a matter of commercial interest. Boring and monotonous articles would not sell and readers were curious to read about Russia. But at the same time, among the readers were merchants engaged in long-distance trade with Russia. They became particularly prone to compromise, once they realized that Peter's government was not kidding. Readiness to yield to Russian pressure in the field of censorship extended well into the political sphere, for the whole commercial community profited from trade activity. Facing increasing complaints from the Russian government that threatened to sanction their commercial privileges, the merchants of Hamburg who traded in Russia did not refrain from petitioning to the Senate and from demanding the arrest of the news printer in order to "satisfy His Majesty the Tsar".[143] And they were heard. At the beginning of the 1720s, the Hamburg Senate even issued a general law interdicting publishers from printing news items on Russian affairs that were not preapproved by the Russian resident-censor. Without the Russian government's approbation nothing could be published any more. This

---

141 Dukmeyer, Korbs Diarium itineris, 1: 13.
142 For examples of such introductory remarks see Blome, Das deutsche Rußlandbild, 40-52.
143 Quoted in ibid., 45.

had far-reaching consequences for the media coverage on Russia, apparently not only in Hamburg.[144]

However, it would be too easy to interpret this confrontation in terms of the proverbial East-West dichotomy. It was rather a clash of the emerging state-Arcanum with a market of unbridled public opinion, which was closely entangled with commercial interests. The numerous newspapers in the Reich published extensively on all sorts of seditions, but tellingly not on those taking place within their own principality or town. Public interest in these events was enormous and rulers proved to be simply incapable of muzzling publishers outside their realm, although they might have wished to do so. During seditions both sides, authorities and rebels alike, therefore tried to win over newspapers and other disseminators of information in neighbouring principalities. The search for legitimacy took thus place under conditions of competition, and sometimes in a veritable war of information.[145] As a matter of fact, the rugged political landscape of the Reich imposed conditions that differed from the informational monopoly (or the monopoly of silence) in Russia.[146]

---

144 See ibid., 50-51.

145 This was not so much different in Russia, but the use of the written word was more limited and both sides recurred to prohibitive measures. Reading the appeals of the other side, and sometimes even talking about the very fact of its issuing of appeals was frequently punished severely during the Razin revolt. See André Berelowitch's contribution to this volume. On the concept of a "war of information" see the ongoing PhD of the sociologist Dario Chi at the Ecole des hautes études en sciences sociales (EHESS).

146 Dutch newspapers were similarly commercialized. In the United Provinces, diplomatic records were even considered public documents: throughout the 16th and 17th centuries every member had access to them. Since 1651 financial questions had been excluded from publication and only at the end of the century secrecy became obligatory. See Belov, Pis'ma Ioanna fan Kellera, 377-378. Elsewhere, diplomatic records made their way into the press as well during the 17th century: residents sent reports not only to their sovereign, but also to newspapers that published them often without specifying their source of information. A major change thus occurred around the turn of the century, roughly at the same time when Peter started his media-political campaigns in the context of Korb's publication.

CONSEQUENCES FOR FOREIGN COVERAGE OF SOCIAL UNREST IN RUSSIA

What were the consequences of this new media policy? To what an extent did it have an impact on the coverage of social conflict in Russia abroad?
Foreign accounts of 17th-century revolts had been numerous and substantial, to the extent that scholars use them to the present day as first-rate sources. For the revolts of the 18th century, the accounts dried out and almost disappeared. The boundary between arcane and public information became more clear-cut. The Danish envoy Just Juel is a case in point. He stayed in Petersburg from 1709 to 1711, and like most diplomats, he kept a diary in which we can find Peter's I abovementioned "scientific" observations on hens' and humans' (i.e. executed rebels') behaviour immediately after decapitation. But while predecessors like Butenant had published their accounts as a matter of course, Juel wrote a little preface to the King Frederic IV stating that his notes were definitely *not* designed for the public: "If I wanted to make them generally accessible through the press, of course I would take precautions and remove all paragraphs in which the Tsar and his subjects are painted in a not too attractive light." He was even convinced that, if the Tsar took notice of the diary, he would complain to the Danish king and accuse him of "deliberately disgracing the Russian nation."[147]

The effect was already palpable during the Astrakhan (1705-06) and the Bulavin (1707-08) uprising. For German readers, the nature of the Astrakhan uprising remained vague: the regime's application of both carrot and stick were presented in a quite schematic way. In 1706 German newspapers stressed the government's clemency. The *Hamburger Relations-Courier* reported that "the Astrakhan rebels have finally submitted, and a part of them has been pardoned and released from punishment". There was no comment on "the other part". The accounts in the *Europäische Fama* were virtually panegyrics to the Tsar. According to its editor Sinold von Schütz, one of the first publishers who absolutely toed Peter's line, news about a huge rebellion in Muscovy in 1706 could not be anything but false rumours (*"Spargamente"*). In one editorial he played down the scope of the events and asserted that the Russian subjects "were too much devoted to their sovereign and understood too well that his fatherly sorrow aimed only at the prosperity and cultivation of the great Muscovite Empire for such to occur." Nevertheless. he could not deny that something had happened; so he praised "his Majesty the Tsar's unrivalled mercy, with which he pardoned the accomplices", with the effect that "the said Astrakhan rebels were ashamed of their own vice. So they reaffirmed their submission and promised to compensate for the 'eyesore of

---

147 Zapiski Julja Justa, 417.

rebellion' by more braveness and unswerving fidelity, declaring their readiness to joyfully sacrifice their lives for the sovereign's glory"[148] Only after considerable delay, when the town rebellion on the Volga had already been over for almost two years and the Bulavin uprising already in full swing, did the *Hamburger Relations-Courier* mention the "stick" that has been applied to (another group of?) the rebels. It stated the execution of "300 of the Astrakhan and Azov rebels", whose "hanged corpses were exposed in the most exclusive streets."[149]

The German coverage of the Bulavin revolt (1707-08) had even less to do with the actual events in the huge region of the Don Cossacks. The *Hamburger Relations-Courier* and the *Kern-Chronik* unanimously reported a *peasant* rebellion. The miseries that generally drove peasants into revolt were much more familiar to Western authors and readers than the situation of the Cossack hosts, from which the movement actually emerged. The factually wrong assertion about the peasants' role as instigators and principal actors of the uprising led to observations on the flight to the peripheries of the empire, a centrifugal movement that was indeed characteristic of peasants' reactions to serfdom and encroachment of the state. The Russian peasants, so goes the account, "had fled to the Don and wanted to live like the Cossacks". Then the Cossacks refused to accept them and even served instead as the principal tools of repression,[150] in one account even in cooperation with Tartars. Consequently the peasants could be subdued and "brought back to their obligations." In reality the Don-Cossacks were the main instigators and actors of the rebellion. Cossack unrest was mentioned, but vaguely and, strangely enough, only for the years preceding the actual Bulavin uprising. The long-lasting Bashkir uprising in the Urals region (1704-11) occurred as well.[151] But Bulavin's name was mentioned neither in relation to the "rebellious peasants" or insurgent Cossacks, nor to the Cossack repressive force that was said to have defeated the peasants. Bulavin was quoted as the leader of "rebellious Tartars" (apparently others than those who allegedly supported the subjection of the rebellious peasants). They would have

---

148 Europäische Fama, 50. Theil (1706): 133. A shortened version is reprinted in ibid., 55. Theil (1706): 505.

149 Hamburger Relations-Courier 19 (2.2.1708), quoted from Blome, Das deutsche Rußlandbild, 255.

150 This is grist to the mill of Soviet historiography and the hypothesis of class-struggle, peasant war and clear-cut social division between the peasant refugees that had recently arrived and the upper class of the well-established and prosperous Cossacks. Cf. Viktor I. Buganov, Bulavin (Moskva, 1988). Nevertheless, even though this fitted well the interpretative framework of Marxist historiography, Soviet historians were serious enough not to rely on such sources.

151 Hamburger Relations-Courier (16.3.1708).

tried to rally support from the Ottoman Empire. And in the end Bulavin, their leader, was said to have committed suicide.[152] This was purported months before he actually died and before his "suicide" was propagated in the *Vedomosti*. We do not know if this rumour was launched by the Russian government already at that time in order to downplay the significance of the movement. Anyway, most of these Western representations of Russian revolts after the Korb scandal were vague and painted a confusing and contradictory picture. Many different resisting groups were mentioned: peasants, Cossacks, Tartars and Bashkirs. But as reported in Germany their actions seemed to have been completely chaotic, uncoordinated and rather senseless. The different groups often struggled internally against each other. Nothing concrete was said about their motives, grievances or claims – a notable difference from the accounts of the 17th century.

In contrast to the profoundly evil image of the strel'tsy that was held up by Peter's government, many foreign representations, when depicting the very existence or potential for revolt in Russia, increasingly referred to a civilization-backwardness pattern. Peter was the incarnation of the enlightened sovereign. Resistance to his efforts at modernizing the country was presented as a manifestation of profound backwardness. If persuasion turned out to be fruitless, the struggle against backward resistance justified the use of violence, especially if the larger project of modernization was endangered. The following reflections in the *Europäische Fama* on prejudice, justice and violence are paradigmatic, especially for how they relate these questions to the character of particular peoples and nations:

The *stubbornness* of the human heart, the obstinacy and the *foolish love of old habits* often tempt the subjects into *ignorant disobedience*, into secret and irresponsible attacks and into a dangerous rebelliousness. The greatest monarchs could never be sure, *if justice had not given them the sword*, with which they could punish and eliminate the troublemakers who *disdain general order and peace and good institutions*. Frequently violent means are more necessary for one *nation* than for another: this has to be taken into account. For a good government one does not only need clemency, but sometimes one has to be severe and resort to force. Some peoples are *so deeply submerged in prejudice*, that [this prejudice] can*not be removed by rational reasoning*; all the more if those who think they are conserving religion, i.e. the clergymen, try to win over the spirits of the credulous with all sorts of teachings that are adverse to the state [my emphases, M.G.].[153]

---

152   Hamburger Relations-Courier (2.2.1708).
153   Europäische Fama 212. Theil (1718), 628-29. Quoted from Blome, Das deutsche Rußlandbild, 262.

Peoples (*Völcker*) and nations (*Nationen*) are distinguished on the basis of their developmental level. Prejudice, ascribed to some peoples more than to others, is partly related to religion, whose adepts are presented here almost as the preachers of backwardness, in contrast to the state that appears as the promoter of reason and rationality. This view would fit into claims about the priests' alleged key role in the strel'tsy uprising (as they were said to have led the rebels with icons). The accusation of the clergy as the exponent of backwardness also justified the enhancement of state power to the detriment of the Orthodox Church, insofar as the Patriarchate was replaced by the Holy Synod and the administration of church property handed over to the Monastical Prikaz, i.e. to a state office.[154] But while curtailing the clergy's powers in the Orthodox centre, Peter allowed missionaries to act freely in the periphery among the Islamic and pagan tribes. If they had hardly been touched by Peter's predecessors,[155] the Church now launched huge campaigns of forced Christianization, for instance among the Muslim Bashkirs, a major provocation that fuelled their revolt of 1704-1711. Western representations, normally not particularly favourable towards the Orthodox Church, then seemed to justify its missionary activity in the light of a *civilizational gradient* between more or less backward peoples of the Russian Empire. In the centre the influence of the Orthodox Church was already considered backward and therefore harmful: for this reason, Peter was thought to be right when curbing the clergy's power there. But in the more backward periphery the influence of the Church was still the harbinger of progress. In this light, to quote just one example, Swedish officer Johann Bernhard Müller[156] described the Ostyaks and Voguls, nomad pagan tribes roaming between the Urals and the Enisei, almost as animals, which was not an entirely new slant: "They lick their wounds like dogs." According to his account there would be no hope "that they will ever be *civilized*",

---

154 For a survey of Peter's church policy see Handbuch der Geschichte Rußlands, 333–40. For a more detailed account see James Cracraft, The church reform of Peter the Great (London, 1971).

155 This imperial practice of expansion and rule with a rather tolerant religious policy was inherited from the Mongolian system of rule. The imperial centre contented itself with co-opting the elites of the conquered peoples and did not interfere into the internal socio-economic, cultural and religious structures of the newly incorporated territories. Such an allowance of heterogeneity seems to have been an alternative to the Western model of homogenization in early modern times. See Andreas Kappeler, Russland als Vielvölkerreich. Entstehung, Geschichte, Zerfall (München, 2001).

156 Müller had been captured after the battle of Poltava, sent to Tobol'sk, and in 1712 charged by Peter to travel to the Siberian North along the Ob'.

unless it be by embracing the Principles of Christianity, and submitting to these Regulations which the Metropolitan is now endeavouring to introduce among them in order to bring them to *a more regular way of Life* than they have led hitherto. If this laudable Attempt takes Effect, there is no doubt it will at the same time considerably *alleviate their extreme Poverty and Misery, which is in great measure owing to their irregular Life.*[157]

This perspective that development should relieve them of an animal-like existence was a new dimension, characteristic of Enlightenment projections. Only Christianity could bring these savages from ignorance and push them from the darkness and obscurity of their brutish nature towards the light of civilization. And for nomad heathens it seemed not to make a difference that the promoter of Christianity was the Orthodox Church. However, those Ostyaks were not ready to voluntarily give up "the Vanity of the idolatrous Worship of wooden Images", in order "to adore the true living God":

[T]hose People, prepossessed with the Antiquity of that Service, *opposed* all the Metropolitan's Endeavors, alledging, that their Ancestors had, Time out of Mind, maintained the Worship of their Sheitans [idols], and fared well by it; that as for themselves, they were from their Childhood brought up to it, and were *unwilling* to change it for another, which would make them believe the Souls of their Ancestors to be in a State of Damnation, or at best in a very dubious Condition: So that at first they seemed resolved rather *to venture upon the last Extremities*, than to renounce the Religion and Customs of their Fore-fathers. [...]
Those who lived *in more remote Parts*, shewed *still greater Obstinacy* in forsaking their Idolatry. Some Priests of their Sheitans were very active in countenancing the Sticklers for the ancient Worship, by making them believe, that the Idol had foretold what would happen, eight Days before the Metropolitan's Arrival, and warned them to withstand the Attempts of the Christians, which he [the idol] would certainly baffle and disappoint by his powerful Protection.

Müller would not specify exactly what it meant when these peoples stood up to "all Extremities in maintaining their Religion". We can only guess about the extent of violence the Orthodox missionaries resorted to in order to break the resistance of the population. To judge from foreign accounts the aim of the civilizing project

---

157 I quote from the English translation of Weber's account that reproduces large sections of Müller's descriptions of Russian Christianization efforts. Friedrich Christian Weber, The present state of Russia. In two volumes. Being an account of the government of that country, both civil and ecclesiastical; of the Czar's forces by sea and land, ... The whole being the journal of a foreign minister who resided in Russia at that time. With A description of Petersbourg... (London, 1722-23), 2:70.

justified all means, even if, in the end, "the pious Zeal and convincing Arguments" of the metropolitan "were of such Weight with those People, that they also consented to the burning of their Idol."[158] In confrontations with idolaters, the Orthodox missionaries were viewed as champions of progress and of a civilizing mission. The greater the opponents' backwardness, the more crucial were their ringleaders. Only the "priests of the Sheitans" could transform that stubborn backwardness of the nomad population into a dangerous rebellious force. They thus had to be neutralized, no matter by which means. Using violence for that purpose was far from being taboo, although non-violent methods were preferable.

In similar key the Danish envoy Just Juel depicted Peter's cordial treatment of "a Siberian prince, who was called tsarevich like the Tsar's son", because "his ancestors had been Tsars of Siberia, before they came under Russian dominion". This Siberian prince often accompanied the Tsar or his ministers on their travels – all this at the expense of the court. According to Juel, Peter did so "partly out of pity, and partly [out of fear] that [the tsarevich] might make his way back home, stir up a rebellion and try to regain the status and power of his ancestors."[159] Such illegitimate lust for power had to be nipped in the bud and potential ringleaders had to be contained and neutralized. But the breeding ground that made them so dangerous was ignorance and backwardness. In order to foment uproar and revolts shamans, the tsarevich and others could rely on a backward and credulous population, who did not understand that they were only being exploited by evil villains, whereas the enlightened Tsar and his missionaries were fighting for their bright future. This made it a paramount task to civilize the local population.

Epilogue

Such interpretations by foreigners seemed to be acceptable to Peter's and his successors' governments, especially when the observers wrote about potential rather than actual upheaval. Benign methods of education were to be highlighted, while a scenario of looming backward revolt constantly threatening the government's civilizing efforts pre-emptively legitimated harsh measures of repression.

Peter I was actually perceived as the first enlightened monarch in Europe, well before Frederic II of Prussia or Joseph II of Austria and Catherine II of Russia. This image was fostered by Russia's stereotypical barbarism which was gradually transformed into backwardness. From the vantage point of Western perceptions of

---

158 Ibid., 2: 89-91.
159 Zapiski Iulia Iusta, 58-59.

Russian revolts we have seen that this shift announced itself already before Peter's actual reign. But Peter's personality became the main focus that helped to crystallize the crucial dichotomy of a backward population and an enlightened ruler, who would be able to launch an effective *mission civilisatrice*. The ferocity of repression might have been a temporary irritating factor for some – and Leibniz showed slight irritation in his correspondence –, but in comparison to other European countries this sort of reprisal was not exceptional at all: just at the same time "domestic state violence" reached a climax in Louis XIV's France with the repression of the Huguenot Camisards in the Cevennes[160] – and France was rather seen as a model of absolutist progress. No doubt, Peter's active participation in the executions that Korb referred to in his Diary was extraordinary. But Peter was generally perceived as an extraordinary monarch. His reputation as a sovereign who took into *his own hands* the destiny of his country was largely supported by his own self-representation. To a certain extent, Western, especially German, perception of Peter I helped to bring about Enlightenment thinking and the very idea of *aufgeklärter Absolutismus* (enlightened absolutism). The current English (*enlightened despotism*) and French terms (*despotisme éclairé*) sound even more paradoxical to our ears. But they mirror what leading enlighteners deemed necessary towards a "backward" population such as the Russians, and even more so the savage non-Russian peoples further to the East. The image of Peter's government and policy thus had a cathartic effect to the emergence of such notions.[161]

The Russian government's attempts to monopolize representation of revolt or, more precisely, to obliterate memory and put the very event of revolt under taboo, remained dominant throughout the Enlightenment period, while contacts to the West significantly intensified. This policy of taboo culminated in Catherine II's reaction to the Pugachev uprising (1773-75). Immediately after the repression of this last and biggest revolt since the Time of Troubles that again started from the Cossack periphery and temporarily took hold of huge territories, including vast peasant-dominated black-earth lands – Catherine II forbade any mention of these events for half a century, to the effect that Pushkin would be the first Russian to write on this major social upheaval. But such a practice was not exceptional, neither. All over Europe governments tried to impose *damnatio memoriae*,

---

160 Howard G. Brown, "Domestic State Violence. Repression from the Croquants to the Commune", The Historical Journal 42, 3 (1999), 597-622.

161 Grosso modo this is the line of the argument in Astrid Blome and Volker Depkat, Von der 'Civilisirung' Rußlands und dem 'Aufblühen' Nordamerikas im 18. Jahrhundert. Leitmotive der Aufklärung am Beispiel deutscher Rußland- und Amerikabilder (Bremen, 2002), referring simultaneously to the Wild West and the Wild East.

generally by an exclusive representation of public punishment and executions, in order to supersede anything related to the rebels' very actions and (maybe even, to a certain extent, legitimate) motives. Like in Russia, success was limited. Dissident narratives of the events, including panegyrics of revolt-leaders were bequeathed orally, often in folklore.[162] But it was extraordinary that a government tried to manipulate and control foreign representations of domestic revolts. And for this reason the Russian diplomacy's harsh reaction to the publication of Korb's diary aroused much curiosity all over Europe. Again there had been precedents in the second half of the 17th century. But in the Korb case the consecutive measures of establishing Russian resident-agents such as Bötticher in Hamburg who were in charge of muzzling foreign representations made clear that Peter was not kidding. And this foreign-press policy seemed to have a long-lasting impact throughout the whole 18th century, when foreign accounts of Russian revolts became almost insignificant, sometimes merely inexistent. Of course, the Pugachev-revolt of 1773-75 was a major event that could not be ignored in Europe. But Catherine's commemorational prohibition definitely scared European commentators. The few accounts of the events were published anonymously.[163]

The case of Korb's Diary played an important part for this shift of paradigms in foreign coverage of Russian revolts. Of course, the Russian government's foreign-press-policy was still amplified by the experience of the great Northern war, when both sides tightened their propaganda measures, bot restrictive and proactive. Nevertheless, I would argue that the Korb scandal was due to a considerable extent

---

162 This clandestine commemoration has been studied by Suter on the example of the Swiss peasant war (1653). Suter, Der schweizerische Bauernkrieg von 1653. To be sure, for Russia we know of such narratives, poems and songs, for the big Cossack revolts, see Aleksandra Nikolaevna Lozanova, Pesni i skazaniia o Razine i Pugacheve (Moskva, Leningrad, 1935), but not for the strel'tsy uprising of 1698. Often popular commemoration centered on the officially defamed leaders. For 1698, such outstanding leaders seem to be lacking, at least in official memory.

163 Apart from newspaper reports there seem to have been only two detailed accounts of the events, one in French, sort of a historical novel published immediately after the end of the revolt, one in German, probably written by the famous geographer Gerhard Friedrich Müller, who worked in Russian. His friend Anton Friedrich Büsching waited until Müller's death, and even then he published the account only anonymously. "Zuverläßige Nachrichten von dem Aufrührer Jemeljan Pugatschew und der von demselben angestifteten Empörung", in Magazin für die neue Historie und Geographie. angelegt von D. Anton Friedrich Büsching, Königlich-Preusischen Oberconsistorialrath, Director des Gymnasiums im grauen Kloster zu Berlin, und der davon abhängigen beyden Schulen. Achtzehnter Theil (Halle, 1784): 3-70.

to cultural misunderstanding, notably the incompatibility of visual cultures. The first thing Russian diplomats and Peter himself could see in Korb's Latin work was the copperplate with the panorama of Moscow entirely dominated by gallows, execution and torture scenes. For European spectators this was a completely usual form of representation. For Russians it was not. For them such pictures were shocking, since they did not correspond at all to their own visual culture that remained largely dominated by iconography and ecclesiastical representation, where even the suffering of the Christ was depicted only in very veiled symbolical forms. In this domain further research will be necessary, especially focusing on zones of contact between Western and Orthodox visual cultures. A focus on contact zones: clashes and conflicts on the one hand, rapprochement and syncretism on the other, would be particularly promising strategy in order to decipher the particularities of the early modern visual languages that are far from disclosing themselves easily to 21st century observers.

Revolts as Political Crime: Legal Concepts and Public Representation

Quietis publicae perturbatio: Revolts in the Political and Legal Treatises of the sixteenth and seventeenth Centuries

FABRIZIO DAL VERA

1. CRIMINALIZATION OF THE COLLECTIVE VIOLENCE: AN OVERVIEW

The evolution of penal law during the early modern age in Europe shows that from the beginning of the sixteenth century there was an extensive use of *crimen laesae maiestatis* in order to punish and repress many kinds of crime.[1] Even minor crimes, previously not seen as a problem by the authorities, began to be considered as an offence against the State and a threat to political order. As has been clearly proven by legal historians, there was a shift in the penal relevance of actions from the level of damage to the level of disobedience. In this way, the repressive procedure of political crimes was used to deal with any kind of penal infraction perceived as a danger to public order.[2]

Revolts and insurrections became the focus of attention for jurists concerned with problems of public order and with the legal instruments to defend inner stability and repress any form of criticism of authority. There was increased interest in collective episodes of violation of *maiestas*, which were punished by *crimen seditionis* and understood as a concrete manifestation of the broader *crimen maiestatis*.

---

1 For an analysis of the development of political crimes in the early modern age see: Mario Sbriccoli, *Crimen laesae maiestatis. Il problema del reato politico alle soglie della scienza penalistica moderna* (Milano, 1974).
2 See Mario Sbriccoli, "Giustizia criminale", in *Lo Stato moderno in Europa. Istituzioni e diritto*, ed. Maurizio Fioravanti (Roma, 2002) 178-182.

The use of *crimen seditionis* to cope with all episodes of collective violence must to be understood as a reaction to the increase in peasant insurrections, characterising the beginning of the sixteenth century. Peter Blickle underlined that "in the late medieval society peasant resistance was accepted. This can be seen in the fifteenth and early sixteenth centuries, on the one hand, in the increasingly numerous refusals to pay homage and, on the other, in the many agreements reached in territories and principalities to settle peasant complaints".[3] The ongoing rise of peasant protests during the first quarter of the sixteenth century produced a general and uninterrupted situation of conflict, with a consequent destabilization of the political orders. The epidemic of peasant resistance spread and its increasingly focused demands led to the revolution of the common man of 1525.[4] In reaction to that uncontrolled movement of uprisings, the authorities changed their strategy. Where they had formerly searched for compromise with the protesting peasants, they now shifted to vigorous repression and criminalization. This change led to the penal ordinance of 1532 of Emperor Charles V (the *Constitutio Criminalis Carolina*), which stated in article 127: "Whoever incites dangerous, illegal, and malicious rebellion of the common people against authorities in a territory or city shall, according to the circumstances of his misdoings, be punished with decapitation or flogging and shall, in all cases, be exiled from the territory or city in which he incited rebellion".[5]

2. LEGAL SOURCES:
TRACTATI, DISSERTATIONES, DISPUTATIONES

This process of criminalization is reflected in the development of penal doctrine. By analysing the legal understanding of the term *seditio* – the way in which the crime was defined – it is possible to reconstruct the development of the legal argumentations, which led the jurists to legitimate severe repression of peasant protests. During the late Middle Ages the problem of political crime, namely the theory of *crimen maiestatis*, had been continuously analysed by glossators, commentators and jurists heavily involved in the praxis. Carlo Ghisalberti

---

3   Peter Blickle, "The Criminalization of Peasant Resistance in the Holy Roman Empire: Toward a History of the Emergence of High Treason in Germany", *Journal of Modern History* 58, suppl. (1986), 88-89.
4   See Horst Buszello et al., ed., *Der Deutsche Bauernkrieg* (Paderborn, 1995); Peter Blickle, *Die Revolution von 1525* (München, 2004).
5   "Die peinliche Gerichtsordnung Kaiser Karls V. Contitutio Criminalis Carolina", in *Die Caroline und ihre Vorgängerinnen*, ed. Josef Kohler, vol. 1 (Halle, 1900), 65.

underlined that this process of interpretation came to a close in the fifteenth and sixteenth centuries, when a series of treatises entitled *de crimine laesae maiestatis* and *de seditionis* was published.[6] These treatises, later collected and published together in the eleventh volume, first part, of the *Tractatus Universi Iuris*,[7] represent the first attempt to offer a systematic analysis of the doctrine on crimes against the security of the State. In this volume we find two treatises on sedition, the *Tractatus de seditiosis* by Nicolas Bohier[8] (1469-1539) and the treatise *De seditionisbus libri sex* by Konrad Braun[9] (ca. 1495-1563), which became a common reference in the following legal debate.

The treatises published in the *Tractatus Universi Iuris* brought order to the problem of political crimes, but the legal and political analysis on sedition kept evolving for more than a century. The two treatises already mentioned were followed by the treatise *De seditiosis. Liber singularis* by Claude Mondain[10] (d. 1594), the *Tractatus de seditione* by Andreas Dalner[11] (d. 1618), *De Seditionibus, Seu Discordiis domesticis* by Martin Schoock[12] (1614-1669) and *Tractatus iuridico-politicus de rebuspublicis turbidis in tranquillum statum reducendis* by Philipp Andreas Oldenburger[13] (d. 1678).

In addition to these works, there are other sources which must be considered in order to follow the legal debate on sedition. The problem of collective political

---

6 See Carlo Ghisalberti, "Sulla teoria dei delitti di lesa maestà nel diritto commune", in *Archivio giuridico* 149 (1955), 100-177, 101.

7 *Tractatus Universi Iuris*, XI, pars I (Venetiis, 1584).

8 Nicolas Bohier, "Praeclarus et elegans tractatus de seditionis omnibus civitatum villarum vel castrorum dominis scabinis seu consulibus ac ceteris reipublicae administratoribus utilis, quotidianus ac necessaries", in *Rerum Criminalium praxes, et tractatus omnium nobiliorum qui ad hunc diem exiverunt iureconsultorum, in quibus processus publicorum iudiciorum, maleficiorumque et supliciorum omnium, quae in usum cadere possunt, ratio non minus succincte quam docte traditur* (Francofurti, 1588), 1. ed. 1515, 104-133.

9 Konrad Braun, *De seditionibus libri sex, rationibus et exemplis ex omni doctrinarum et authorum* (Moguntiae, 1550).

10 Claude Mondain, *De seditiosis. Liber singularis, ad interpretationem Iuris* (Lutetiae, 1567).

11 Andreas Dalner, Tractatus de seditione cum ex sacra et profana historia, tum ex iure, eiusque interpretibus desumtus (Viennae Austriae, 1599).

12 Martin Schoock, *De Seditionibus, Seu Discordiis domesticis: Libri Tres; Quibus omnia, huc pertinentia, distincte proponuntur: non modo per præcepta, verum etiam exempla; tum antiqua, tum recentia* (Groningæ,1664).

13 Philipp Andreas Oldenburger, *Tractatus iuridico-politicus de rebuspublicis turbidis in tranquillum statum reducendis, in eoque conservandis* (Genevae, 1678).

crimes was also analysed in general works on penal law, like the treatises written by Tiberio Deciani and Pierre Gregoire[14]. Moreover, from the beginning of the seventeenth century, within the literature analysing the *Politica* by Aristotle, it is possible to find chapters dedicated to the problem of the *mutatio reipublicae*, where the reasons for sedition are analysed in different constitutional contexts[15]. Lastly, this topic is also addressed by several *dissertationes* and *disputationes* on this topic, which are short works produced in German universities in order to achieve the doctoral title.[16] This kind of source is particularly relevant for the study of the debate's development: their authors had to prove they knew the legal debate on the topic, but at the same time they also had the chance to contribute to debate by integrating new perspectives offered by contemporary political theory.[17]

Focusing on treatises, *dissertations* and *disputationes* in order to study the development of legal and political wisdom on sedition is justified by the fact that these texts aimed, as aforementioned, to summarize the former doctrinal tradition

---

14 See Tiberio Deciani, *Tractatus criminalis*, Tomus Primus, liber 7, cap. 7 (Francofurti, 1613), 143-147 and Pierre Gregoire, *Syntagmatis iuris universi*, Pars Tertia, liber 35, cap. 6 (Venetiis, 1593), 362-364.

15 See Frideric Tilemann, De eversionibus rerum publicarum politica dissertatio (Wittenberg, 1597); Henning Arnisaeus, Doctrina politica in genuinam methodum, quae est Aristotelis, reducta (Lugduni Batavorum, 1606); Bartholomaeus Keckermann, Systema disciplinae politicae publicis praelectionibus anno MDCVI. propositum in gymnasio Dantiscano [...]. Seorsim accessit Synopsis disciplinae oeconomicae, dispositionem eius breviter adumbrans [...] (Hanoviae, 1608); Bernhardus Zieritz, Dissertatio de conversionibus et eversionibus rerumpublicarum (Lipsiae, 1609); Hermann Conring, Disputatio politica de Mutationibus Rerumpublicarum (Helmestadt, 1635); Hermann Conring, Dissertatio politica de morbis ac mutationibus rerumpublicarum (Helmestadt, 1640).

16 See Christianus Taubmann, Disputationem hanc inauguralem de turbatoribus pacis publicae, ex iure publico & practicorum observationibus desumptam [...], (Wittebergae, 1640); Georgius Gulielmus Zapf, De origine, progressu ac remediis seditionum (Ienae, 1659); Georg Friedrich Glandorff, Dissertationem historico-politicam de rebellibus (Wittenberg, 1675); Johann Balthasar Mylius, Disputatio juridica de seditione (Leipzig, 1682); Achilles August von Lersner, Disputatio politico-juridica de seditionibus, occasione tit. 30 lib. 9 C. de seditiosis (Basileae, 1688); Johann Christian Schmids, Dissertatio politico-juridica De tumultibus (Jena, 1714); Georg Heinrich Ayrer, De multitudine seditiosa (Gottingae, 1747).

17 On legal *dissertationes* in the early modern time see Karl Härter, "Ius publicum und Reichsrecht in den juristischen Dissertationen mitteleuropäischer Universitäten der Frühen Neuzeit", in *Juristische Zeitschriften in Europa*, ed. Michael Stolleis and Thomas Simon (Frankfurt/Main, 2006), 485-528.

and to bring order into the understanding of the phenomenon. The jurists involved in this debate were educated in the system of common-law (*ius commune*) and naturally looked back to that tradition in order to find legal concepts to describe the collective protests they witnessed and, at the same time, to control and repress them.

The treatises mentioned, and the other shorter works produced within the universities, can be considered as a homogeneous *corpus* of sources, not only because of their topic, but also because of the way in which the topic was analysed. Indeed, it is also possible to look at the development of political thought by analysing the form of the political languages used, namely how the themes and problems are grouped, systematized and communicated. Moreover, the context of production should be considered, as well as the use and circulation of the sources. Who were the authors? Where were they working and for whom were they writing?[18] While acting in different countries, the jurists were part of the same 'community of discourse' that investigated collective forms of protest. This community was clearly the result of the common-law tradition as a shared background; nevertheless, these jurists were also personally connected because almost all of them were working at university and facing, in different times and in different contexts, the same problems related to the control of public order: their works were well-known within their circle and later authors quoted their predecessors extensively, often without regard to confessional borders.

As aforementioned, the *ius commune* was a shared background that ensured a cross-border diffusion of treatises. The jurists referred to the same legal tradition and therefore used the same language and the same concepts. Investigating episodes of collective revolts they were interested in collecting historical examples mostly from ancient history, but also from contemporary chronicles. Indeed, all the treatises refer to revolts that affected communities and cities of the whole European continent.

Moreover, the genre *tractatus* follows a formal pattern, a shared and accepted model to organize the content and present argumentations. First of all, these sources on sedition are concerned with the problem of the legal understanding of the phenomenon, namely with the definition of the *crimen seditionis* according to the tradition of *ius commune*. The jurists used a very rich lexicon to describe the different forms of collective rebellion. *Seditio, congregatio armatorum, concitatio*

---

18 See Merio Scattola, *Dalla virtù alla scienza. La fondazione e la trasformazione della disciolina politica nell'età moderna* (Roma, 2003); id., "Zur einer europäischen Wissenschaftsgeschichte der Politik", in *Werkstatt Politische Kommunikation. Netzwerke, Orte und Sprachen des Politischen*, ed. Christina Antenhofer et. al. (Göttingen, 2010), 23-54.

populi, tumultus, factiones, partialitates, facinus, rixa were the concepts borrowed from Roman law and from medieval glosses and commentaries.[19] Secondly, they analysed the causes of insurrections and used historical knowledge extensively to investigate past incidents of unrest. All the treatises quoted a multitude of sources, from the Bible to secular chronicles, in order to provide examples of the various factors provoking inner discord and consequently producing violent and organized protests against the authorities. Finally, the investigation of the causes of inner discord was always used to elaborate political strategies in order to repress or to intervene preventively. The jurists were indeed trying to provide public officers with adequate knowledge to avoid conflicts within society or at least to control all the situations characterised by diffuse discord (*discordia civilis*). All the treatises considered are characterised by this recursive structure, with no particular variations.

The opportunity to consider these sources as a *corpus* also depends on the fact that the jurists were moved by concrete problems related to the maintenance of public order. They had to face questions such as: how to repress insurrections? How to legitimize the use of violence in repressing them? How to prevent inner discord? How to act within the political community in order to control political commotions? The increase of social and political conflict from the end of the fifteenth century forced the authorities to elaborate the necessary political concepts to cope with unquiet political situations. In writing these treatises the jurists moved from their immediate experience of conflict to conceiving political strategies of intervention to deal with the development of protests and uprisings. They focused on concrete instruments to repress ongoing rebellions by force and, at the same time, on the elaboration of preventive policies to avoid the formation of discord and dissent. As Winfried Schulze has pointed out, the authorities' reaction to peasant resistance and subsequent criminalization gave rise to the substantial literature on the problem, which is characterised by a practical approach to social conflicts. Schulze suggests that these treatises should be considered as a "praktisch orientierte Politikwissenschaft"[20]: they concentrated on the definition of the crime, namely on the legal concepts used to repress uprisings, but at the same time they also

---

19 See Sbriccoli, *Crimen laesae maiestatis*, 283-305.
20 Winfried Schulze, "Die veränderte Bedeutung sozialer Konflikte im 16. und 17. Jahrhundert", in *Europäische Bauernrevolten der frühen Neuzeit*, ed. id. (Frankfurt/Main, 1982), 287; see also id., "Geben Aufruhr und Aufstand Anlass zu neuen heilsamen Gesetzen. Beobachtungen über die Wirkungen bäuerlichen Widerstands in der Frühen Neuzeit", in *Aufstände, Revolten, Prozesse. Beiträge zu bäuerlichen Widerstandsbewegungen im frühneuzeitlichen Europa*, ed. id. (Stuttgart, 1983), 261-285.

elaborated strategies to prevent and control such crime, producing what can be labelled as a doctrine of prevention.

These developments in the doctrine on sedition can be studied by analysing how different categories of crime were applied to different forms of protest and how these attributions changed over time. Following the methodological approach of conceptual history, as it has been defined and applied by Reinhart Koselleck, the term *seditio* can be considered as a central concept, dense in social and political meaning. First of all, it is necessary to analyse how the term has been defined and used within a specific context, by jurists working in a concrete troubled situation. Therefore, the treatises will be analysed using the method of historical and lexical semantics: the semantic field of the concept of *seditio* will be studied in order to understand the relationship between the changes in the doctrine, based on the historical interpretation of the legal tradition, and the broader social context. Then, the changes within the crimes will be compared over a broader period of time in order to trace the development of the processes of criminalization.[21]

Sedition is indeed an inherently political offence, encompassing all behaviour threatening the government or political authorities in general. In the early modern period *crimen seditionis* was aimed at punishing a wide range of unlawful actions. It was therefore flexible and open to extensive interpretations. Following an underlying interpretative hypothesis to explain development and changes in the doctrine of sedition, I assume that there is a direct interdependence between the definition of *crimen seditionis* and the broader political context that needs to be explained for each treatise. An overview of the development of the doctrine reveals that in times of endemic conflict and political crisis the jurists were interested in harshly repressing any acts directed at overthrowing the established order. Due to this will to react strongly to dissent, they tended to extend offences against *maiestas* to include any episodes of violence, even against minor magistrates. This extensive definition of the crime provided legal resources for inflicting capital punishment even for minor unrest. This interpretative development of the doctrine was characteristic of the sixteenth century and is particularly salient in the treatises written by jurists directly involved in rebellions – not as participants, of course, but as witnesses or persecutors.

The doctrine developed partially in a different way during the seventeenth century, when jurists were no longer working in a "state of emergency" – although

---

21 See Reinhart Koselleck, "Begriffsgeschichte und Sozialgeschichte", in *Vergangene Zukunft: zur Semantik geschichtlicher Zeiten*, ed. id. (Frankfurt/Main, 1995), 107-129. For an example of the application of lexical semantics to the study of the political languages see Pietro Costa, *Iurisdictio: semantica del potere politico nella pubblicistica medievale: 1100-1433* (Milano, 1969).

incidents of unrest remained highly problematic. The doctrine of sedition reached a new stage at the beginning of the seventeenth century, when jurists dealing with the problem were all working at university and writing for an academic audience. They therefore had the possibility to reconsider previous doctrine – with less pressure coming from the external political situation – in order to define a sharper conceptual instrument that was able to differentiate between various forms of collective violence.

3. THE FOUNDATION OF *CRIMEN SEDITIONIS* IN THE ROMAN LEGAL TRADITION

In its more general meaning and without further connotations, the idea of sedition in the early modern period was used to describe a general perturbation of the public order, which meant an infraction of public peace (*quietis publicae perturbatio*) and a subsequent state of confusion. As Mario Sbriccoli clearly summarises, the notion of *seditio* defined a collective revolt, which usually arose in an urban setting, but could also occur in other contexts, wherever there was a concentration of people. Generally it was preceded by a minimum of preparation and organization and led to a series of lootings and devastation that sometimes culminated in murders and massacres.[22] Since this first attempt to define the crime, we can see that sedition was a very flexible concept that could refer to a variety of acts, ranging from the first steps of the perturbation of public order to much more dangerous and serious behaviours, which could also lead to a veritable civil war.[23]

The term *seditio* emerged in the Roman republic and developed well into the Roman Principate.[24] In the early modern age it was rediscovered by jurists looking for a legal understanding of endemic violent movements against the authorities. In the context of *ius commune*, the description of what can be considered as sedition started from the reference to the *Codex Iustiniani* (promulgated for the first time in 529), according to which *seditio* was indeed defined as general perturbation of the public peace.[25]

---

22 Sbriccoli, *Crimen laesae maiestatis*, 274.
23 See Reinhart Koselleck, "Revolution. Rebellion, Aufruhr, Bürgerkrieg", in *Geschichtliche Grundbegriffe. Historisches Lexikon zur politisch-sozialen Sprache in Deutschland*, ed. Otto Brunner et al., vol. 5 (Stuttgart, 1984), 653-685.
24 See Gerard Osthoff, "Tumultus – Seditio. Untersuchungen zum römischen Staatsrecht und zur politischen Terminologie der Römer" (Ph.D. diss., Universität Köln, 1953), 102-150. This study is unfortunately not available in print.
25 C. 9. 30: De seditiosi et his qui plebem audent contra publicam quietem colligere.

In Roman law, namely in the *lex Iulia maiestatis* (about 48 B.C.) one can identify "the historical and legal foundation of the dogmatic construction of *crimen laesae maiestatis*",[26] which remained in use for all the centuries of *ius commune*. Consequently, the *lex Iulia* represents the doctrinal and theoretical model for the definition of the concept of *seditio*.[27] However, the Roman legal tradition took two approaches to criminalising episodes of public violence. Resisting authorities with recours to violence could thus be punished either as *crimen laesae maiestatis* or as *crimen vis*.

Since the titles in the *Codex Theodosiani* (promulgated in 439) and later in the *Codex Iustiniani*, the behaviour disturbing the public order of the political community was always related to the *crimen laesae maiestatis*. This becomes evident from the commentaries of the titles of the *Codex* concerning attacks against the *maiestas*. Indeed, the criminal behaviour punished on the basis of *crimen maiestatis* referred to any action designed to provoke inner discord and civil wars, namely to all behaviour relating to the idea of sedition. According to the definition of the *crimen* offered by the Roman jurist Ulpianus (170-228) and lately collected in the Justianian's Digest (promulgated in 533):

D. 48. 4. 1pr. (Ulp. 7 de off. proc.): Proximum sacrilegio crimen est, quod maiestatis dicitur. § 1 Maiestatis autem crimen illud est, quod adversus populum Romanum vel adversus securitatem eius committitur. Quo tenetur is, cuius opera dolo malo consilium initum erit, quo obsides iniussu principis interciderent: quo armati homines cum telis lapidibusve in urbe sint conveniantve adversus rem publicam, locave occupentur vel templa, quove coetus conventusve fiat hominesve ad seditionem convocentur: cuiusve opera consilio malo consilium initum erit, quo quis magistratus populi Romani quive imperium potestatemve habet occidatur: quove quis contra rem publicam arma ferat: quive hostibus populi Romani nuntium litterasve miserit signumve dederit feceritve dolo malo, quo hostes populi romani consilio iuventur adversus rem publicam: quive milites sollicitaverit concitaveritve, quo seditio tumultusve adversus rem publicam fiat.[28]

---

26 Ghisalberti, Sulla teoria dei delitti di lesa maestà nel diritto comune, 146. For the history of the development of the title *Ad legem Iuliam Maiestatis* see Richard A. Bauman, *The Crimen Maiestatis in the Roman Republic and Augustian Principate* (Johannesburg, 1970), 266-292.
27 See Theodor Mommsen, *Römisches Strafrecht* (Leipzig, 1899), 562-565.
28 "The crime of lese majesty may closely resemble that of sacrilege. § 1 The crime of lese majesty is committed against the Roman people, or against their safety, and he is guilty of it by whose agency measures are maliciously taken for the death of hostages, without the order of the Emperor; or when men armed with weapons or stones appear in the city, or are assembled against the State, and occupy public places or temples; or where assem-

This broad definition provided all the basic elements of the concept of *seditio*, which were used in early modern doctrine to discipline the use of collective violence. Indeed, the *crimen maiestatis* was meant to punish all the behaviour and actions against the *populus romanus*[29] and its security; among those actions Ulpianus also included the congregation of armed men, moved by the conscious will to fight against the *res publica* and the common good. Killing a public officer (*magistratus*), carrying arms in order to occupy public spaces, encouraging sedition or tumult and inciting violence were all actions that could be punished by the *crimen maiestatis*. Such a commentary made available a legal argument to sustain that the infraction of the public order represented an attack against the security of the Roman people: all forms of collective violence were potentially perceived as a threat to the stability and continuity of the political community and, for this reason, they could be criminalized as *crimen maiestas* and consequently punished with death.

As has been mentioned before, Roman law also provided a more general *crimen vis* to punish the unlawful use of violence in public spaces. The *lex Iulia de vi publica* (17 B.C)[30] was used to repress violent acts against public officers, anything disturbing their political functions, or, more generally, any action aiming to interrupt the normal course of political life. Although the kind of behaviour criminalized by the *crimen vis* could be recognised as a form of perturbation of public peace, it was not stigmatised as a politically structured attack against the Roman people and, therefore, not perceived as a threat to the entire political community. Consequently, the punishment for this crime consisted of the confiscation of goods and forced exile. As can easily be seen, the Roman law offered different ways of reacting to public violence, according to the dangerousness attributed to the different types of behaviour.

---

blies have been called together, or men convoked for sedition; or where, by the malicious aid and advice of anyone, plans have been formed by which the magistrates of the Roman people, or other officials invested with command or authority may be killed; or where anyone bears arms against the government, or sends a messenger or letter to the enemies of the Roman people, or communicates to them any password; or commits any act with malicious intent by means of which the enemies of the Roman people may be assisted in their designs against the government; or where anyone solicits or inflames soldiers, in order that a sedition or a tumult may be excited against the State".

29 The notion of *maiestas* refered to the *dignitas* attributed to the *populus romanus*, which originally held it; during principate time *maiestas* shifted from *populus* to *princeps*, becoming a personal attribute of emperor.

30 C. 9. 12.

The *crimen vis* was an alternative option to criminalize and repress violence: it aimed at protecting minor magistrates and, as such, was a flexible instrument to control violent behaviour in everyday political life. In contrast to that, the *crime maiestatis* covered only attacks against the top figures of the political hierarchy and left the intermediate levels of power without legal protection. For the jurist of the early modern age, who accepted the *lex Iulia maiestatis* as a doctrinal model for the definition of political crimes, this feature represented a problematic aspect to be reconsidered and integrated based on contemporary needs.[31] Indeed, they had to provide legal defence for all the intermediate public officers – members of local government, tax collectors, representatives of central authorities – which were not protected by *crimen maiestatis* as it was defined in the Roman law.

The process of adaptation of the titles of the *Codex* and the Digest related to the changed political context led to an extensive application of the *crimen maiestatis* in order to punish all manifestations of resistance against the authorities. This extension was based on the idea that all members of the power's hierarchy, even minor magistrates holding only a derivate *maiestas*, had to be protected by it. This led to a considerable increase of occasions and possibilities to oppose an authority invested with *maiestas* and therefore to commit the crime. Importantly, a proper and exhaustive definition of the *crimen maiestatis* was missing in the juridical doctrine: rather than elaborating a definition, jurists compiled extensive lists answering the question *crimen laesae maiestatis quid sit*. Due to this, instead of a theoretical understanding of the *qualitas rei* of the crime they indicated concrete ways in which it was committed; therefore, starting with the cases specified in the Roman law, they extended the behaviour which was punishable as *crimen maiestatis*. Finally, during the development of the early modern penal law, the doctrine started to consider behaviour with a minimal political connotation as political crimes; this behaviour was previously not considered as a threat to the authority and consequently not yet assimilated to the *crimen maiestatis*.[32]

These three developments led to an extensive interpretation of the concepts of *rebellio* and *seditio*, which were the two crimes subsumed under the broader *crimen laesae maiestatis*, namely the two concrete manifestations of the crime.[33] The

---

31 Ghisalberti, Sulla teoria dei delitti di lesa maestà nel diritto comune, 146-150.

32 Sbriccoli, Crimen laesae maiestatis, 258-266.

33 In order to define the notion of *rebellio*, the early modern doctrine constantly referred to the comment by Bartolus de Saxoferrato to the Imperial Constitution *Quis sit rebellis* (1313) promulgated by Henricus VII. According to Bartolus, rebelling was like resisting and resisting meant to do something against, to refuse to do something or to disobey. See Bartolus de Saxoferrato, "Tractatus super Constitutione Extravaganti, Ad Reprimendum",

process of extension that has been briefly described, involved indeed both notions: on the one hand, during the sixteenth century penal doctrine started to increasingly equalise *crimen maiestatis* and *crimen rebellionis*, thereby abandoning the differentiations made by previous doctrine.[34] For political conflicts this meant that one could be accused of rebellion more often and, at the same time, a clear and indubitable subsumption of that accusation under the *crimen maiestatis*. On the other hand, the enlargement of the concept of *seditio* was based on the idea that every form of perturbation of the public order, even minor episodes of violence, must be recognized as a direct strike against the authority.

4. DEFINITION OF *SEDITIO* IN THE SIXTEENTH CENTURY

a) Nicolas Bohier

In 1515 Nicolas Bohier,[35] a French jurist, member of the *Grand Conseil* and President of the *Parlement de Bordeaux*, wrote his aforementioned treatise *De seditiosis*. Just one year before he had been sent to repress an insurrection in Agen and was directly involved in the organisation of the trial against the insurgents. The experience gained on that occasion represented the starting point to reconsider the former legal tradition dealing with collective forms of discord and to elaborate a first systematic attempt to bring order to the topic. The first part of the treatise is dedicated to a general analysis of the causes of civil discord. This is followed by a depiction of the revolt he had recently repressed.[36]

The revolt in Agen in July 1514 was provoked by a new impost on wine and other goods for consumption. The town consuls had levied the tax in order to pay back a municipal debt. The burghers perceived this as unfair and unjust. After initial murmurings people met to discuss a common reaction and some minor

---

gl. Tenore, in *Consilia, Quaestiones et Tractatus* (Venetiis, 1585), 104r: "...rebellare idem est quod resistere, secundum Hug. C. de seder. L. 2. Lib. 12, et hoc resistere potest fieri faciendo aliquid contra, vel non faciendo, et non obediendo [...]". On Bartolus' comment on the Imperial Constitution see Diego Quaglioni, "Rebellare idem est quam resistere". Obéissance et résistance dans les gloses de Bartolo à la constitution "Quoniam nuper" d'Henry VII (1355), in *Le Droit de résistance XIIe-XXe siècle*, ed. J.-C. Zancarini (Lyon, 2001), 35-46.

34 Ibid., 263 f.
35 On Bohier see G.D. Guyon, "Bohier (Boyer, Boerius), Nicolas", in *Dictionnaire historique des juristes français (XIIe-XXe siècle)*, ed. P. Arabeyre et al. (Paris, 2007), 95-97.
36 Bohier, De seditiosis, § 1, pp. 104-114.

incidents followed; the revolt began with the ringing of the bells which summoned the crowd to gather in the main square, who then besieged the town hall and captured some members of the local elite. Attacks against the town consuls continued for days, while the widespread violence led to the destruction of several buildings and parts of the city wall. The insurrection lasted for two weeks until it was brutally repressed.

According to Giovanni Procacci, the uprising should be understood within the framework of a broader conflict: the protest was the result of the growing burden of taxes and a direct act against the local oligarchy and rich families, who were accused of monopolizing offices, pursuing their particular interests in running public affairs and profiting from the unequal distribution of taxation.[37]

After his description of the unrest, Bohier used the words *seditio* and *discordia civilis* indifferently, implying a convergence between the two concepts.[38] It is only in the passages that follow, that two terms are explained separately: sedition is described as a form of violent and degenerated discord, while *discordia* is defined as a precondition to the explosion of a widespread conflict, which could also lead to armed insurrection. This introduction to the topic and the narration of the revolt in Agen are functional to the following definition of the crime, insofar as sedition is presented not as a unique violent act against the authority, but rather as a series of related behaviour aiming to plot against the *res publica*. *Seditio*, according to the formula offered by the Roman law is a form of perturbation of the public peace.[39] Bohier, referring to the medieval glosses and commentaries, tries to explain the etymological origin of the term:"seditio dicitur quasi seorsum itio, quia in diversum vadunt aliosque trahunt: vel dicitur a sedo per contrarium, plerumque populo

---

37 See Giovanni Procacci, *Classi sociali e monarchia assoluta nella Francia della prima metà del secolo XVI* (Torino, 1955), 161-173. See also David F. Burg, *A world history of tax rebellions. An encyclopedia of tax rebels, revolts and riots from antiquity to the present* (New York, 2004), 144; Perez Zagorin, *Rebels and rulers 1500-1660, Society, states and early modern revolution, agrarian and urban rebellions*, vol. 1 (Cambridge, 1982), 237 ff.

38 On the concept of *seditio* in Bohier and Braun see David von Mayenburg, "Ubi est incolumitas obedientiae, ibi sana est forma doctrinae – Aufruhr und Revolte im kanonischen Recht", in *Der Einfluss der Kanonistik auf die europäische Rechtskultur*, vol. 2: *Öffentliches Recht*, ed. Franck Roumy (Köln, 2011) 217-266.

39 Bohier, De seditiosis, § 2, n. 1, 114: "seditio est quietis publicae perturbatio"/"sedition is a perturbation of public order"; the reference to the Roman law is C. 9. 30.

discordante itur ad manus".⁴⁰ As well as an unsuccessful attempt to link the term to the Latin verb *sedare*, meaning the opposite of sedition, the term is explained as referring to a movement that divides the people and splits them up.

In order to better understand the meaning of the concept and to clarify the relationship between *seditio* and *discordia*, Bohier quotes three authorities: Antoninus Florentinus, Thomas Aquinas and Isidore of Seville. They are central to an understanding of the medieval representation of sedition. According to Antonius Florentinus' *Summa Theologica*, *seditio* is a particular form of discord, namely the discord that arises within the multitude.⁴¹ Florentinus referred to the *Summa theologiae* by Thomas Aquinas, where the *seditiosus* was described as

qui seditionem excitat. Et quia seditio quandam discordiam importat, ideo seditiosus est qui discordiam facit non quamcumque, sed inter partes alicuius multitudinis. Peccatum autem seditionis non solum est in eo qui discordiam seminat, sed etiam in eis qui inordinate ab invicem dissentiunt.⁴²

The discord produced by a seditious man was in this way characterised as of public nature: not just a disagreement between two private parties, but discord triggered by political reasons and involving the "multitude". The understanding of what should be considered as *seditiosus* was based on what Isidore of Seville had already written in his encyclopaedic work *Etymologiae*. According to Isidore, "qui dissensionem animorum facit et discordias gignit"⁴³ can be accused as the author of sedition. Starting from this definition, Thomas Aquinas claimed that fomenting civil discord in general or committing sedition could be considered as the same sin. By referring to these definitions, Bohier presents an extensive interpretation of the crime, which allowed him to criminalize several types of behaviour which cause dissension

---

40 Ibid.: "sedition derives from going a part, because they go away and bring others with them, or it derives from the verb squash (as its contrary) and generally it comes from the idea of the people fighting among themselves".

41 Antonius Florentinus, *secunda pars summae*, tit. 4, c. 8, § 1 (Basilee, 1511): "seditio importat discordiam, non quancunque sed inter partes alicuius multitudinis"/"sedition does not refer to every discord, but to discord developing among parts of a multitude".

42 Thomas Aquinas, *Summa Theologiae*, IIᵃ-IIae q. 42 a. 1 ad 1: "A seditious man is one who incites others to sedition, and since sedition denotes a kind of discord, it follows that a seditious man is one who creates discord, not of any kind, but between the parts of a multitude. And the sin of sedition is not only in him who sows discord, but also in those who dissent from one another inordinately".

43 Isidore of Seville, "Seditiosus", in *Etymologiae sive origines*, X, 250: "a seditious man is who sows dissent among minds and begets discord".

within the political community, from the first murmuring against members of the government up to more explicit appeals to resist the authorities. This position was far from unique in the debate. On the contrary, it was the standard argumentation used by several jurists; the authorities quoted by Bohier were indeed a shared reference for all jurists dealing with collective forms of protest, insofar as their definitions were always the background for further analysis of the phenomenon.

In this preliminary attempt to retrace a definition of *seditio* in Bohier, we see that its core concepts were *dissensio* and *discordia* and that a sedition was understood as a form of division of or within the multitude, although the word *multitudo* was not yet specified and therefore used in a general way. A further effort to clarify the crime was the distinction between sedition and the other forms of division and opposition, which were not to be confused.

Thomas Aquinas, in a passage quoted later by all the jurists, wrote that a *seditio* was different from a war, which was a conflict against foreign people, namely against people not bound to the same political obligations and loyalty. *Seditio* was thus described as a clash or division taking place within a singular people, i.e. when one part of it stood against the other. Moreover, since a multitude referred to a large number of persons, *seditio* was different from a simple strife (*rixa*) between two or a few individuals.[44] Private strife was not perceived as a political problem and was therefore considered as different from sedition, which was strongly connected to the idea of a multitude in action. Indeed, sedition could happen in different contexts – and Bohier specified "*in exercitu, in classe, in campo, in schola*"[45] –, but a large number of people always had to be involved.

War and strife were also different from sedition for another reason, which had considerable consequences on the possibility of intervention and repression. Again

---

44 Aquinas, *Summa Theologiae*, II²-IIae q. 42 a. 1 co.: "Secundo differunt, quia bellum proprie est contra extraneos et hostes, quasi multitudinis ad multitudinem; rixa autem est unius ad unum, vel paucorum ad paucos; seditio autem proprie est inter partes unius multitudinis inter se dissentientes, puta cum una pars civitatis excitatur in tumultum contra aliam. Et ideo seditio, quia habet speciale bonum cui opponitur, scilicet unitatem et pacem multitudinis, ideo est speciale peccatum"/"Secondly, they differ in that war is, properly speaking, carried on against external foes, being as it were between one people and another, whereas strife is between one individual and another, or between few people on one side and few on the other side, while sedition, in its proper sense, is between mutually dissentient parts of one people, as when one part of the state rises in tumult against another part. Wherefore, since sedition is opposed to a special kind of good, namely the unity and peace of a people, it is a special kind of sin"; Bohier, De seditiosis, § 2, n. 2, 114.

45 Bohier, De seditiosis, § 2, n. 4, 115.

Bohier quotes Thomas Aquinas, who wrote that "bellum et rixa important mutuam impugnationem in actu, sed seditio potest dici sive fiat huiusmodi impugnatio in actu, sive sit praeparatio ad talem impugnationem".[46] Following this interpretation, the term war is applied only to an open conflict, whereas the concept of sedition is rather different: it refers indeed to unrest and insurrections, but also to all the activities that usually precede them, such as murmuring against authorities, gathering people or plotting. This position is sustained by the gloss to Paulus' Second Epistle to the Corinthians[47] that has already been quoted by Aquinas and was now taken up by Bohier. Aquinas, according to the gloss, wrote that "seditiones sunt tumultus ad pugnam, cum scilicet aliqui se praeparant et intendunt pugnare".[48] Therefore, sedition was defined as the will of plotting against authorities and the term could also be applied to describe all the unlawful behaviour preceding an insurrection.

This is a core passage that helps to comprehend how the process of criminalization of collective forms of protest was connected to the enlargement of the semantic field of *crimen seditionis*. Not only concrete violent actions were to be considered as a crime, but also types of behaviour, which could be interpreted by the authorities as a form of organised malcontent and a way to prepare a protest.

Such an effort to produce an extensive idea of sedition is the result of the practical approach assumed by the jurists. Bohier, as well as other authors of treatises on sedition, had been directly involved in the repression of insurrections. He was well aware of the different steps producing a collective disagreement and wanted to develop legal instruments to nip sedition in the bud. We can see here how the legal doctrine was forced to serve political needs and how it was used to define strategies to control public spaces and to repress political protest. Indeed, by classifying the initiation of disagreement and discord within the political community as part of the *crimen seditionis*, Bohier wanted to legitimize preventive action taken by the *magistratus*. The jurists embraced the idea that it was necessary to consider a seditious man as not only one who actively took part in sedition, but also anybody involved in its preparation. This was aimed to criminalise the very intention to disturb public order as well as all behaviour perceived as a threat to established authority. It emerges here that the will of plotting was recognised as a core element in defining the crime. Jurists implied that any possible criticism of the

---

46 Aquinas, *Summa Theologiae*, II^a-IIae q. 42 a. 1 co.: "war and strife denote actual aggression on either side, whereas sedition may be said to denote either actual aggression, or the preparation for such aggression".

47 2 Corinthians 12.

48 Aquinas, *Summa Theologiae*, II^a-IIae q. 42 a. 1 co.: "seditions are tumults tending to fight, when a number of people make preparations with the intention of fighting".

authorities should be characterised as a plot to consciously damage them. At the same time, they perceived any episode of collective violence as a concrete manifestation of a more or less shared will to destabilise the public order. Therefore, not only violent acts were unlawful, but also all behaviour producing discord and considered as a preliminary phase of unrest.

As we can see, the extensive interpretation of the term *seditio* was grounded in a broad definition of *seditiosus*. Bohier quoted a long extract from the *Tractatus de maleficiis* by Bonifazio Vitalini:

Seditiosus autem dicitur ille, qui seditionem vel proditionem tractat de aliqua civitate vel castro habendo, vel dando causam faciendi guerram contra publicam utilitatem, vel tractat facere novitatem in civitatem, vel novitatem contra publicum et bonum statum civitatis, vel tractat se fieri dominum terre, vel loci alterius ad turbam populi, vel similia contra publicam utilitatem.[49]

The seditious man was defined as whoever was involved in sedition or treason (*proditio*), whoever waged war against the common good or tried to introduce something new into the political body; in general, a person who produced discord among the people and acted against public unity was considered as *seditiosus*. This extensive definition offers several points to be analysed and clarified. For the first time in Bohier the convergence between sedition and treason was made explicit and clear and, in this way, the crime was connected to the *crimen laesae maiestatis*. Political treason is evidently something different from public disorder produced by the public use of violence. By introducing the concept of treason jurists considerably changed the crime and assigned new meaning to all the activities preceding unrest. Murmuring against authorities or the meeting of people were considered as evidence of a will to plot. Disorder produced by violence, and the consequent damage of the *bonus publicum*, were not collateral effects, but the real aim conceived by insurgents.[50]

---

49 Bonifazio Vitalini, Tractatus de maleficiis, tit. De seditiosis, 396r: "A seditious man is defined whoever manages to set a sedition or treason within a city or stronghold by waging war against common good or by giving reason for it; he is whoever wants to introduce changes in the city or against the government or wants to take domain and control of a territory in order to bring discord among the people and against the common good".

50 Bohier, De seditiosis, § 1, 104-114.

b) Konrad Braun

The treatise of Bohier was well known to the Catholic German jurist Konrad Braun,[51] who, in 1550 wrote his *De seditionibus libri sex*.[52] In a first attempt to answer the question *quid sit seditio*, the jurist referred to the ancient classics. According to Cicero, who considered the phenomenon in several passages in his works, sedition occurs when there is a division within the people, because of an inner disagreement or a conflict with the authorities.[53] This first definition also introduces the leading theme of discord within the people. Referring to classical political thought, the jurist had the possibility to list several terms used to circumscribe the concept of *seditio*. Sedition was the result of a violent movement of the people and could be defined as *impetus, motus, incursio, concitatio plebis, vis multitudinis*. This movement of the multitude was associated with the idea of uncontrolled violence and illustrated with violent images designed to appal the reader. Many metaphors were used to describe movements of protest. Apart from Cicero, Braun referred to the works of Sallust, Cyprian, Pindar, Livy and Virgil, where the movement of the people was described as a disease, a fire and as a storm. All these metaphors were based on antonymous conceptual couples such as order/disorder, stillness/movement, unity/division and health/illness.[54]

---

51 See Theobald Freudenberger, "Braun, Konrad", in *Neue Deutsche Biographie* 2 (1955), 556; Maria Barbara Rößner, *Konrad Braun (ca. 1495-1563) - ein katholischer Jurist, Politischer, Kontroverstheologe und Kirchenreformer im konfessionellen Zeitalter*, (Münster, 1991).

52 On the concept of *seditio* in Braun see Jörn Johannsen-Reichert, *Das Thema "Aufruhr" aus religiöser, juristischer und politischer Sicht im deutschen Raum wärend des konfessionellen Zeitalters (1517-1617)* (Aachen, 1996), 32-56.

53 Braun, De seditionibus, 1: "Seditio à seorsim eundo dicta est, ut Ciceroni placet, quod plebis vel inter se, vel cum magistratibus dissentiens, seorsim secedat"/"Sedition derives from the idea of coming asunder, as Cicero wrote; this occurs when the people disagree among themselves or with public officers".

54 Ibid.: "[…] seditio, nunc vehementiori morbo, nunc incendio, turbini, et à Pindaro tempestati maris comparatur: Quam et tempestatem aliquoties appellat Livius. Ad quam comparationem, etiam Poeta noster allusisse videtur, qui Aeolum ventos oratione sua placare fingens, eos seditioso populo comparatur. Ac veluti (inquit) magno in populo cum saepe coorta est,/Seditio, saevitque animis ignobile vulgus,/Iamque faces et saxa volant, ac meritis si forte virum quem,/conspexere, silent, arrectisque auribus adstant,/Ille regit dictis animos, et pectora mulcet./Sic cunctus pelagi cecidit fragor, aequora postquam/Prospiciens genitor, coeloque invectus aperto./Flectit equos, curruque volans dat lora secundo (Virgil, Aeneid, 1, vv. 147-154). Hinc etiam concitari, incendi, flagrare,

At the end of his brief historical overview Braun discusses and criticizes the definition offered by Bohier. As it has been stressed, the French jurist, with his background of education in Roman law, identified sedition as a perturbation of the public peace. According to Braun, this was not acceptable as a definition, but simply as a description of the phenomenon. Moreover, if sedition produces a perturbation of the internal order of the *respublica*, it is also true that not every disorder could be related to it. It was therefore necessary to provide a legal definition of the phenomenon, able to suit different situations. For that, Braun proposes a complex explanation of the concept, composed by a series of elements that need to be clearly defined. He wrote that:

verius itaque definitur seditio, ut fit motus populi et subditorum, eorumque qui eiusdem multitudinis partes sunt, vel in eadem multitudine versantur, quo vel plures inter se, vel unus pluresve adversus eos, quibus fidelitate astricti sunt, utilitatis alicuius consequendae, vel damni alijs aut iniuriae inferendae causa, scientes et volentes in detrimentum et damnum Reipublicae, ad dissensionem concitatur.[55]

Sedition is presented as a movement of the people, namely of those who were part of a multitude. This movement could take place within the multitude itself or against the authority, to which the subjects were bound by political obligation. Such a movement consciously and willingly produced discord in order to take advantage of it or to damage the *respublica*. The jurist's attempt to define *seditio* exceeded the simple description of the phenomenon we have seen in Bohier's writings. For Braun the definition had to be sufficiently abstract and formal, in order to be valid

---

aestuare, saevire seditiones apud autores dicuntur: ab incendio videlicet, et morbo sumpta metaphora: et seditiosi ipsi turbolenti, et tumultuosi appellantur"/"sedition is sometimes compared to the most violent illness, sometimes to a whirlwind and by Pindar to a storm. Livy as well calls it storm. We see that also our Poet, Virgil, alluded to that similarity: "And when – he wrote – seditions rise among great people, and low people enrage, and flames and rocks fly, then if the people see a serious and virtuous man, they calm down and listen, he soothes their anger, thus the storm's commotion quietens: the father squashes the horses and drives the coach". Therefore, other authors also refer to sedition as the act of instigating, inflaming, burning, enraging; the metaphors come from blaze and illness and seditious men are called turbulent and tumultuous".

55 Ibid., 2: "sedition is more correctly defined as a movement (commotion) of the people and subjects, namely of whoever is or becomes part of a multitude; this movement takes place among the people or against those, to whom the people are tied by a fidelity bond; finally, this movement is provoked in order to provoke dissension and to willingly achieve an advantage or to damage the political community".

for different conflicting contexts. Therefore, he offered a flexible model for a general theory of sedition.

The semantic field of the concept defined by Braun was partially different from the one elaborated by Bohier and responded to different needs. Specification was achieved through the combination of the term with other concepts. At the base of sedition there was the idea of a movement, which was not to be understood as just an ordinary change in the political order. The Latin word he used was *motus*, but according to Braun, to understand the meaning of this movement, it was necessary to link it to the words *studium* and *conatus*.

Motum in hac definitione pro genere ponimus, non quidam ut generaliter mutationem in Republica designet, ut generationem, corruptionem et similia: nec ut quemlibet etiam animi motum denotet, ut in illo Iureconsulti [Callistratus : D. 1. 18. 19]. [...] Item in illo Ciceronis [Cicero, De claris oratoribus] [...]. Nunquam animus agitatione et motu vacuus esse potest. Sed ut studium et conatum ardentius aliquid machinandi significet.[56]

The notion of a sudden movement, representing the violent action of the insurgents, was combined with the idea of an effort to change the political order or to plot against authority. The *motus* was a conscious motion aimed at changing the political order. It should be understood as a passion, a desire to conspire. The given description conveys the idea of purposeful and deliberate participation in the protest, not only a generic malcontent, but also a will to intervene and to achieve a specific result.

The crowd (*hominum multitudo*) was the collective subject of this movement. Braun, as well as Bohier, wrote that sedition was always associated with a multitude of people assembled. If it was possible to simply list situations in which people gathered, it was difficult to specify a number that would define a congregation, or other more rigorous definitions of such a collective subject. Braun was sure that it was not possible to establish a general rule and left it to the magistrate to decide case by case.[57]

---

56 Ibid.: "The term movement does not indicate a general change in the political community, like generation or corruption, or a general commotion like in Callistratus (D. 1. 18. 19) or in Cicero (De claris oratoribus). This movement cannot be without an aim, but, on the contrary, it is a passion and an effort to plot".

57 Ibid.: "Addidimus in definitione: Populi, Cuius appellatione hoc loco omnis hominum multitudo venit. Nam seditio esse potest, ubicunque est hominum multitudo, ut in populo, in gente, in collegio, in exercitu, in classe, in schola, et in quolibet coetu et congregatione [...]. Caeterum, quot homines multitudinnem, quot populum, quot collegium, quot gentem, quot exercitum, quot caetum et congregationem faciant: certa quidam regula dari

The core of the definition is the infraction of political loyalty, to which all subjects are bound. The basic element of the crime thus consisted of the resistance of authority. This allowed the jurist to directly link the concept of *seditio* to rebellion. Braun wrote that it was not even important to determine the number of the people taking part in the action: the relevant point was the rebels' behaviour towards legitimate superiors.[58]

Braun further discussed the problem of conscious and willing participation in sedition. In order to sustain that the phenomenon had to be subsumed under the broader idea of high treason he kept arguing that all sedition was aimed at achieving an established advantage or damaging the political body. Every violent action against authority potentially weakened the whole community and thus had to be considered as a threat to the *respublica*. The injury inflicted to the community was the result of civil discord, which was understood at the same time as a means to perturb the inner equilibrium and as the outcome of sedition:

vel Utilitatis consequendae, vel damni alijs, aut iniuriae inferendae causa: Haec verba finem seditionis denotant. Omnis enim seditio fit aut ob utilitatem aliquam consequendam, aut damnum iniuriamue a nobis repellendam, alijsue inferendam. Inter se ad dissensionem scientes et volentes in detrimentum et damnum Reipublicae concitantur: His verbis forma seditionis explicatur: Quippe à discordia seditio et nomen et formam accipit. Nam quid aliud est seorsum ire, quàm cum alij dissentire. Nec omnis discordia seditionem parit, set ea

---

non potest. [...] Est igitur in arbitrio Iudicis, et boni viri positum, ut ipse, quot homines multi sint vel pauci, quot populus, turba, gens, caetus, congregatio et c. interpretetur: eamque rem ita arbitretur, ut materie subiectae convenire existimabit"/"We add to the definition: people, this term comes from the idea of a multitude of men. Indeed, sedition can occur wherever there is a multitude of men, like among the people, in an assembly, in the army, in a battlefield, inside a union and in any congregation. It is not possible to give a rule in order to determine how many men make a multitude, a people, an assembly, an army or a congregation. Therefore, the judge has to interpret it and decide how many men make a multitude or a congregation".

58 Ibid.: "Sed et propter rebelles, additur verbum Subditorum. Rebellio siquidem subditorum est erga Dominos suos, nec ad numerum vel multitudinem hoc casu respicitur: Sive enim multi sunt, sive pauci, Si obedientiam dominis suis subtrahunt, seditiosi et rebelles appellantur"/"In order to explain the term "rebels" we add the term "subjects". Indeed rebellion against authorities does not depend on the number of men taking part in it. Even if they are many or few, if they deny obedience to the authorities, they have to be considered rebels and seditious men".

tantum, quae Reipublicae detrimentum, et damnum affert, et quietem illius et tranquillitatem perturbat.[59]

Moreover, Braun specified that not all kinds of discord should be criminalized and repressed, only those aimed at damaging the community.[60]

The general theory proposed by Braun was a flexible instrument to criminalize different forms of unrest. The perturbation of the public order could develop indeed in both horizontal and vertical direction.[61] On the one hand, the concept could be used to criminalize all the horizontal forms of disagreement within the people, namely any division produced by inner discord such as, for instance, the existence of factions. The crime associated with sedition could be applied to political discord within the people even without any direct attack against the authority. Disorders and violence within the community were enough to perturb the public order and, consequently, to be considered as a threat. On the other hand, *seditio* was also a concept suitable to describe attacks against the vertical structure of power, namely when the multitude moved against the established government. Despite these two possibilities, the *crimen seditionis* was always considered as an act of rebellion against the legitimate authority and therefore likened to the *crimen rebellionis*. The core of the crime was indeed, according to Braun, subtraction from the political obligation to which all the subjects were bound. The convergence between *seditio* and *rebellio* was functional to legitimise the repression of every form of collective dissent.

---

59 Ibid., 4: "Achieving advantages, provoking damages or injuries: these words indicate the aim of sedition. Indeed, any sedition is made in order to achieve an advantage, to avoid damages or to inflict them to others. Willingly provoking dissension in order to create damages to the political community: these words explain the form of sedition. Certainly, sedition derives its name and form from disagreement. Moreover, dividing and disagreeing are different: not every kind of dissent produces seditions, but just the one aimed at inflicting damages to the political community and at perturbing the public order".

60 There were indeed also forms of positive competition between the people, which have to be tolerated and even encouraged by the authority: ibid.: "Sic nec mutua inter civesa aemulatio et dissensio, qua alter alterum prudentia, consilio, et rebus gerendis, superare intendit, seditio est: Nam et ipsa Reipublicae, non solum non noxia est, sed etiam utilis"/"So, competition and discord among people, aimed at improving prudence and judgment, are not sedition: indeed, these kinds of competitions not only are not noxious for the political community, but in fact are useful".

61 Johannsen-Reichert, Das Thema "Aufruhr", 41-43.

5. DEVELOPMENT OF *CRIMEN SEDITIONIS* IN THE SEVENTEENTH CENTURY

During the seventeenth century the legal debate on sedition revealed increasing attention on the forms of collective violence that did not immediately aim to oppose or criticise the top level of the political hierarchy. The treatises dealt with the emergence of dissent within the crowd and attempted to provide the public officer with the necessary wisdom to cope with all unlawful uses of violence that might incite disorder within the community, from minor riots to more structured and organized rebellions. Jurists like Bohier and Braun were mostly interested in defining a crime that was suitable for brutal repression of any forms of protest against authority. Apart from this aspect, subsequent authors rather concentrated on conflicts among the people that were threatening to result in a generalized state of violence. They were particularly concerned with violence itself and focused on all kinds of infraction of public peace. Therefore, they elaborated a concept of *seditio* that was appropriate to provide a more adequate punitive reaction to a wider range of violent behaviours.

From outside the legal debate, in 1589 in his *Politicorum sive civilis doctrinae libri sex* Justus Lipsius briefly defined sedition as a "multitudinis in Principem aut magistratus, subitus et violentus motus",[62] describing therefore the crime as a violent assault on the authorities. This definition synthesized former doctrinal elaborations, focusing on violence as a core element of the crime and indicated that sedition could be directed against both the top level of the political hierarchy, or against a public officer of a lower rank. A more nuanced distinction between strikes against the *princeps* and offences against a public officer received more attention in the ensuing debate in which jurists tried to achieve a more refined calibration of the authorities' reactions.

A few years later, in 1599, Andreas Dalner, who like Bohier was a direct witness of peasant protests,[63] wrote in his *tractatus* that "seditio nihil aliud est,

---

62 Justus Lipsius, *Politicorum sive civilis doctrinae libri sex* (Antversiae, 1598), 210.
63 Dalner was a councillor in Lower Austria and witnessed the peasant uprising of 1597. He was deeply impressed by the violence of that event and wrote his treatise under the influence of his immediate experiences. Two years after its first edition in Latin, the treatise was published in German translation under the title *Ein Tractat: Von Aufruhr und Empörung auß geistlichen und weltlichen Historien* (Ingolstadt, 1601). See Roth, Kollektive Gewalt, 125 and Schulze, Die veränderte Bedeutung sozialer Konflikte, 299. On the peasant uprising of 1597 in Lower Austria see Otto Kainz, "Das Kriegsgerichtsprotokoll im niederösterreichischen Bauernaufstand aus dem Jahre 1597" (Ph.D. diss., University of Wien, 2008).

quam in provincia, territorio, urbe, castro, vel alio aliquo loco, contra publicam quietem et disciplinam, consulto animo, facta populi suis legibus uniti concitatio".[64] Dalner, distinguished between sedition committed against the *respublica* or the Emperor and sedition committed against a minor part of the political body that might produce some sort of inner disorder.[65] This second case was not subsumed under *the crimen maiestatis*, but it was punished according to the law concerning public use of violence, namely the *lex Iulia de vi publica*.[66]

In his work *De Seditionibus seu discordiis domesticis*, published in 1664, Martin Schoock[67] made great efforts to analyse the genesis and development of inner discord. According to him the best definition of a state of sedition was the one offered by the rhetorician Libanius (ca. 314- ca. 394), who wrote, in his *Oration pro*

---

64 Dalner, Tractatus de seditione, 5: "sedition is nothing else than a commotion in a region, a city, a, stronghold against public order and established rules; this commotion is based on a deliberate union among the people".
65 Ibid., 7-8: "Seditio autem duplex est; una adversus Rempublicam vel Imperatorem committitur: altera eiusdem membra fit. Illa quidem [...] est, quando quis opera sua, fraudolentove consilio, non modo paganos, verum etiam milites, [...] solicitat, concitatve, quo telis et armis instructi seditionem seu tumultum in Reipublicae seu Imperatoris exitium moturi conveniant. [...] Item si quis per seditionem Reipublicae seu Imperatoris subjectam civitatem oppugnet, occupetque; nam et ipse crimen laesae majestatis incurrit [...]. Haec vero est, quando quis opera, seu malo consilio suo, homines concitat, quo telis et armis convenientes, adversus Reipublicae seu Imperatoris membra, seditionem moveant, civitatesve ad Imperatore non pertinentes oppugnent, vel bona rapiant: quo pertinet l. in eadem causa. 3. in princ. et §. in eadem causa, his verbis: in eadem causa sunt, qui pessimo exemplo, convocta seditione villas expugnaverint, et cum telis et armis bona rapuerint. ff. ad legem Iuliam de vi publica [D. 48. 6]"/"Sedition is double: one I committed against political community and emperor, the other against political body's parts. The first one occurs when people, armed with weapons and spears, organise seditions and tumults against political community and emperor, or when the people occupy or assault a city that is subject to the emperor. This is a case of lese majesty. The second one occurs when the armed people organise seditions and tumults against a part of the political community or against a city that is not subject to emperor. This sedition is covered by the Julian law on public violence".
66 C. 9. 12; D. 48. 6.
67 Schoock was born in Utrecht in 1614. He had a very "cross-disciplinary" education and became professor of Classic Literature, Oratory, History and Logic in Deventer and Groningen. After 1664 he became the official historian of the prince-elector of Brandenburg and worked as professor in Frankfurt (Oder) until his death. See Jacob Cornelis van Slee, "Schoock, Martin", in *Allgemeine Deutsche Biographie* 32 (1891), 324-325.

Thalassio of 388, that "seditio est, quando diversitas cupiditatis perturbato inter se committit: quando scinditur incerti in studia contraria: ut hi arces occupent, alii portus detineant: quando muniunt se muris et propugnaculis: quando in se invicem auxilia vocant: quando civitas non una manet".[68] Schoock understood sedition as an intermediate step between *factio* and *bellum civile*, which he perceived as the last and most dangerous stage of the disruption of political unity.

In order to better understand what sedition meant for the political community, the jurist compared it with *rebellio* and *perduellio*. Starting from the explanation of *rebellio* provided by Henricus VII in the Imperial Constitution *Quis sit rebellis*[69] (1313) and from Ulpianus' comment on the *lex Iulia de maiestate*,[70] Schoock emphasised the convergence of the two terms and concluded that

qui perduellionis reus est, hostili animo adversarius rempublicam vel principem animatus. Ex quibus patet, seditiosos, quatenus tumultuantur illegitime contra legitimum suum

---

68 Schoock, De Seditionibus, Seu Discordiis domesticis, 63.The passage quoted is Libanius, *Libanii Opera. Orationes XXVI-L*, vol. 3, ed R. Foerster (Lipsiae, 1906), 308-333.

69 Heinrich VII, "Declaratio Quis sit rebellis", a. 1313, in *Monumenta Germaniae Historia. Legum sectio IV. Constitutiones et acta publica imperatotum et regnum*, Tomi IV. Pars II., ed. Jakob Schwalm (Hannoverae/Lipsiae, 1909-11), n. 931, 967: "...quod illi omnes et singuli sunt rebelles et infideles nostri et imperii, qui quomodocunque publice vel occulte contra nostrum honorem infidelitatis vel rebellionis opera faciunt et in nostramseu imperii prosperitatem aliquid machinantur contra nos sive nostros officiales in hiis, que ad commissum eis offitium pertinent..."/"...are rebel and unfaithful to us and the empire all those that organise publicly or secretly rebel or unfaithful activities against our honour, or plot against our prosperity, against us or our public officers...".

70 D. 48. 4. 11: "Is, qui in reatu decedit, integri status decedit: extinguitur enim crimen mortalitate. nisi forte quis maiestatis reus fuit: nam hoc crimine nisi a successoribus purgetur, hereditas fisco vindicatur. plane non quisque legis iuliae maiestatis reus est, in eadem condicione est, sed qui perduellionis reus est, hostili animo adversus rem publicam vel principem animatus: ceterum si quis ex alia causa legis iuliae maiestatis reus sit, morte crimine liberatur"/" He who dies while an accusation against him is pending retains his civil status unimpaired, for the crime is extinguished by death, unless he was accused of lese majesty; for if he is not cleared of this offence by his successors, his estate will be forfeited to the Treasury. It is evident that not everyone accused of lese majesty under the Julian Law is in this position, but only he who is guilty of high treason, and is animated by hostile intent against the State or the Emperor. For if anyone is accused under any other section of the Julian Law on lese majesty, he will be released from the charge by death".

Magistratum, habendos quoque esse Rebelles et perduelles. Licet aliquis, imo plures quoque crimen perduellionis incurre possint citra seditionem.[71]

Despite this statement, he underlined that the Roman jurist Modestinus – a student of Ulpianus – in the Digest defined episodes of sedition subsumed under rebellion as *atrox seditio*[72], implying that it was different from simple sedition. Although Schoock did not develop this argument, this quotation reveals a breach with the former understanding of *crimen seditionis* that was always thought to be a concrete manifestation of the broader *crimen maiestatis*. Modestinus suggested dividing the concept of *seditio* into two subcategories: *atrox seditio*, which is properly a case of rebellion, and *simplex seditio*, which is an episode of collective violence but not necessarily an offence against *maiestas*. Embracing this specification of the crime, Schoock seems to be interested in describing sedition as a form of civil discord that did not always lead to *crimen maiestatis*.

This distinction was made clear and more explicit by Achilles Augustus Lersner (1662-1732)[73] in his *Disputatio politico-juridica de seditionibus*,[74] published in 1688. In order to understand the doctrine of sedition, the jurist explains the meaning of concepts used in the legal debate that, according to him, were often confused, producing an inaccurate idea of *crimen seditionis*. *Tumultus civilis*, *turba* or *discordia domestica* were used as synonyms of *seditio*, although they indicated previous stages of inner discord, that usually occurred before the explosion of the real sedition. Lersner states a lack of accuracy in how the perturbation of the public order was expressed: he sustained that often the term *seditio* was confused with *conjuratio* and *rebellio*, which were not necessarily the same offences.

According to Lersner, sedition is different from a plot (*conjuratio*) and therefore should not be confused with treason. People taking part in a sedition do not necessarily share the will to damage the government or strive for a common purpose. The argumentation here is the opposite of what we have seen in Bohier:

---

71 Schoock, De Seditionibus, Seu Discordiis domesticis, 79-80: "Whoever is guilty of treason is moved by hostile will against the political community or against the *princeps*. Among them, those who take part to sedition rebelling against lawful officers have to be considered rebels and betrayers. Though, it is also possible to commit treason without taking part to sedition".

72 D. 49. 16. 3. 19: "Qui seditionem atrocem militum concitavit, capite punitur"/"Whoever excites a violent sedition among the soldiers is punished with death".

73 Lersner was born in Frankfurt am Main and worked there as a chronicler. We do not know much about his life. See W. Stricker, "Lersner, Achilles August", in *Allgemeine Deutsche Biographie* 18 (1883), 432-433.

74 See footnote 16.

while the French jurist sustains that gathering together was already to be understood as evidence of an agreement between people, Lersner considers the possibility of spontaneous unrest, which is therefore not the result of a planned action. The two jurists are moved by different scopes: Bohier wants to assimilate any sedition to *crimen maiestatis*, sustaining that there is a shared will in any collective form of dissent. On the contrary, Lersner is interested in showing that it is also possible to have spontaneous sedition, which should not be punished as *crimen maiestatis*.

At the same time, also the term *rebellio* was often incorrectly used to criminalise sedition. Indeed rebellion did not simply refer to the refusal of respect and fidelity to the magistrates: rebelling meant literally to wage war against the legitimate authority and against the entire political community. Lersner states that sedition is not always a collective case of rebellion. The term *rebellio*, he keeps arguing, is similar to *perduellio*, namely to high treason, and therefore *seditio* and *rebellio* should not simply be used as synonymous. Similarly to Schoock, Lersner wants to differentiate the concept of *seditio* into two subcategories, which correspond to different levels of sedition. He believes that sedition can be the result of a spontaneous commotion of the people without the conscious will to subvert the established authority and, in that case, he argues that the *crimen maiestatis* cannot be applied. Secondly, we have seditions that can be considered as collective rebellion and is characterised by the intention to plot against the government. Only an insurrection against the top level of the hierarchy, or aimed at damaging the entire community, should be considered, according to Modestinus and Schoock, an *atrox seditio*.

As Lersner specifies

est igitur seditio Commotio populi, qua pars civitatis vel exercitus adversus eos insurgit, qui rebus praesunt. Per eos qui rebus praesunt, tam principes summos, quam magistratus intellectos volo. Et quidem si commotio illa tendat adversus principem, vel directa sit in perniciem reipublicae incidit in crimen laesae Majestatis: si vero adversus inferiorem solum Magistratum sit esorta, et in eo subsistat, crimen Majestatis non est.[75]

The jurist introduced again the distinction, known to the Roman law, between assaults against the *princeps*, namely the top of the hierarchy, and against minor

---

75 Ibid., 2-3: "Therefore sedition is a commotion of the people; with this commotion part of the political body or of the army rises against the government. Using the term government I mean both the top level of the hierarchy (*princeps*) and lower officers. If the commotion is against the *princeps* or produces damages to the political community it is a case of crimen maiestatis; otherwise, if it is only directed against lower officers it cannot be considered a case of lese majesty".

magistrates. Offences against minor magistrates should not be punished by the *crimen maiestatis*. Sedition could be considered a case of high treason (*perduellio*) – and therefore treated as a breach of *maiestas* – only when it was aimed towards ruinining or damaging the *res publica* or when it was an attempt to subvert or destabilise the political order.[76]

To allow the application of the punishments provided by the *crimen maiestatis*, the sedition had to be motivated by the will to injure the political order. If the unrest was the result of private discord and the people involved did not intend to damage the authorities or break the political order, then the punishments to be applied were the ones provided by the *lex Iuliam de vi publica et privata*. Therefore, death was not the only punishment available and the magistrate was free to evaluate case by case, taking into account the state (*dignitas*) of the person accused.[77]

---

76 Lersner, Disputatio politico-juridica de seditionibus, 32: "Dicendum itaque eam demum seditionem in perduellionis crimen incurrere, quae tendit ad exitium principis aut senatorum ejus, vel subversionem ac immutationem reipublicae: non quae ad exitium privatorum, ut post alios docet Antonius Matthaeus, De criminibus. *Commentarius ad Lib. XLVII et XLVIII Digesti*, tit. 2, cap. 2, Vesaliae, 1679, Prospero Farinacci, *Variae quaestiones*, quaest. 113. num. 183. et 192, Venetiis, 1584, ubi quod dictum est poena laesae Majestatis teneri qui tumultum concitat, ita declaratur, si ille tumultus tendat in damnum principis: sin vero concitetur absque animo offendendi aut laedendi principem, locum esse poenae arbitrariae. Ita si quis privato ductus odio plebem colligat, et excitato tumultu ad arma vocat, ad creandam adversario suo molestiam, licet in crimen Majestatis non incidat, pro qualitate tamen dignitatis aut in furcam tollendus, aut bestiis objiciendus, aut in insulam deportandus est"/"Therefore, seditions that tend to ruin the *princeps* and his senators, or tend to subvert the political community, are considered high treason; but seditions that tend to ruin private subjects are not considered high treason, as it is taught in Antonius Matthaeus and Prospero Farinacci, where it is said that whoever incites tumults, if they are aimed at damaging the *princeps*, is punished by *crimen maiestatis*. Otherwise, if they do not injure or damage the *princeps*, the punishments can be arbitrary. Therefore, if tumults are produced by private disagreements, it is lawful not to apply the *crimen maiestatis*: in this case, according to the *status* and honour of the people involved, they can be hanged, thrown to wild beasts or deported in an island".

77 Ibid., 33: "Nec dissentiunt ab hac sententia illi, qui tumultum in privatorum hominum perniciem et damnum concitatum in poenam legis Juliae de vi publica vel privata incidere censent, in quibus est Menochio, *De arbitrariis iudicum quaestiones et causis*, lib. 2. cas. 394. n. 78, Venetiis, 1578, Antonius Matthaeus, De criminibus. *Commentarius ad Lib. XLVII et XLVIII Digesti*, tit. 2, cap. 2, Vesaliae, hujus enim criminis poena, quae olim fuit deportatio et publicatio bonorum, vel si privata fuerit, hodie aritraria est, et ad mortem quoque extendi potest"/"This position is also sustained by who, like Menochio and Mat-

Lersner was concerned with an evaluation of the *gradus* of sedition, namely with the possibility to distinguish between different levels of dangerousness for the stability of the political community.

(Seditiones) vero gradus quidam sunt: vel enim intra solam fidei et obsequii denegationem subsistit, moxque iterum sopitur: vel ulterius ad caedem puta magistratus vel ducis aliorumque ac rapinas progreditur: vel denique in bellum intestinum erumpit, quae omnium maxima et atrocissima species est seditionis et vere lerna malorum.[78]

These passages show how the jurist tried to distinguish different forms of sedition, depending on how they were affecting the public order. Instead of reducing several different categories of collective protest to the *crimen maiestatis*, by considering every violent strike as a rebellion, he suggested that minor forms of discord be considered separately from violent assaults which threaten the security of the entire political order. The aim of this argumentation was to provide a better understanding of social conflict and consequently to calibrate the authorities' repressive measures.

6. UNLAWFUL VIOLENCE AND *RESISTENTIA LICITA*

A further element of the concept of *seditio*, which did not enter the definitions offered by the jurists, but emerged from their political analysis of the causes of concrete insurrections, is the idea that sedition is usually provoked by the perception of an injustice committed by the authorities.[79] The jurists criminalized any form of collective protest that was perceived as a threat by the authorities. As we can see from the treatises of Bohier and Braun, they classified revolts, seditions and rebellions indiscriminately as unlawful forms of violence against the authority that had to be severely criminalized and repressed. At the same time, they tried to limit the application of the crime and analysed situations in which it was even

---

thaeus, claim that tumults provoked to damage private people have to be punished by the Juliam law on public violence. The punishment for this offence, with earlier was deportation and confiscation, is now arbitrary and can be also extended to death".

78 Ibid., 3: "Seditions differ in their degree: they can consist just in the refusal of fidelity and deference and can be quickly settled; they can proceed from this degree to murders of officers and robberies and they can finally become civil wars, which are the worst kinds of sedition".

79 On the problem of justice practices as reason of revolts see Andrea Zorzi, "Politiche giudiziarie e ordine pubblico", in *Rivolte urbane e rivolte contadine nell'Europa del Trecento: un confronto*, ed. Monique Bourin et al. (Firenze, 2008), 381-419.

lawful to resist the authority. What was not possible to punish as a *crimen seditionis* had to be recognised as *resistentia licita*.[80]

While defining what violent actions led to the crime, the jurists also pointed out which behaviours should be considered as lawful. Indeed, the definition of the crime and the effort to understand the processes of organisation of dissent also took into consideration violent reactions that could not be legitimately punished. However, jurists were mostly concerned with the protection of the public order and left only little scope for the people to react lawfully to the government. As jurists, they were part of the intellectual elites legitimating the political authorities and defending them from strikes and criticism. Defining the *crimen seditionis* and providing strategies to intervene into problems of public order were part of the process of affirmation and consolidation of governmental policies towards different conflicting contexts. Therefore, all these authors were not interested in arguing to

---

80 On the right of resistance see Robert von Friedeburg, *Widerstandsrecht und Konfessionskonflikt: Notwehr und Gemeiner Mann im deutschen-britischen Vergleich 1530-1669* (Berlin, 1999); id. (ed.), *Widerstandsrecht in der frühen Neuzeit: Erträge und Perspektiven der Forschung im deutschen-britischen Vergleich* (Berlin, 2001); Angela De Benedictis, "Supplicare, capitolare, resistere. Politica come comunicazione", in *Suppliche e "gravamina". Politica, amministrazione, giustizia in Europa (secoli XIV-XVIII)*, ed. Cecilia Nubola and Andreas Würgler (Bologna, 2002), 455-472; id., "Resistere: nello Stato di diritto, secondo il diritto 'antico', nell'Europa del 'diritto al presente'", *Quaderni fiorentini per la storia del pensiero giuridico moderno* 31 (2003): 273-321; id., "Il diritto di resistere. Una città della prima età moderna tra accusa di ribellione e legittima difesa (Bologna, 1506)", in *Ordnung und Aufruhr im Mittelalter. Historische und juristische Studien zur Rebellion*, ed. Marie Theres Fögen (Frankfurt/Main, 1995); id., "Sapere, coscienza e scienza nel diritto di resistenza. Le ragioni di un seminario e del suo titolo", in *Wissen, Gewissen und Wissenschaft im Widerstandsrecht (16.-18. Jahrhundert)*, ed. Angela De Benedictis and Karl-Heinz Lingens (Frankfurt/Main, 2003), 1-47; Luise Schorn-Schütte, "Obrigkeitskritik und Widerstandsrecht. Die politica christiana als Legitimitätsgrundlage", in *Aspekte der politischen Kommunikation im Europa des 16. und 17. Jahrhunderts. Politische Theologie – Res Publica – Verständnis – Konsensgestützte Herrschaft*, ed. id. (München, 2004), 195-232; Angela De Benedictis, *Una guerra d'Italia, una resistenza di popolo. Bologna 1506* (Bologna, 2004); id., "Narrare storie, difendere diritti: ancora su "tumulto" o "resistenza"", in *Praktiken des Widerstandes: Suppliken, Gravamina und Revolten in Europa (15.-19. Jahrhundert)*, ed. Cecilia Nubola and Andreas Würgler (Berlin, 2006), 29-50; id., "Resisting Public Violence: Actions, Law, and Emotions", in *Finding Europe. Discourses on Margins, Communities, Images ca. 13th - ca. 18th centuries*, ed. Anthony Molho et al. (Oxford-New York, 2007), 273-290.

sustain the people's resistance – nor were they allowed to do so – and mantained a very detached perspective when considering the problem.

I would like to summarize the argumentations of three of these authors in order to present only a few examples from the very rich and broad debate on resistance that unfolded during the sixteenth century, mainly in the wake of the Protestant Reformation.

Bohier analysed this problem referring to the congregations within the political community. It was necessary to define criteria in order to evaluate the different kinds of congregations and to decide in which cases the people were entitled to assemble. The jurists started from a definition of *congregatio*, which was the generic term for any organised group bound together by an agreement. Such congregations among the people were subdivided into different categories, implying different degrees of legitimacy or illegitimacy: *unio, confederatio, secta, conventicula* or *coniuratio*.[81]

Bohier dedicated several pages to answer the question "populus quando posit se congregare sine superioris, aut suorum iudicum auctoritate".[82] The analysis of the problem started from the clear prohibition of any congregation, which was sustained by several authoritative quotes: from 1 Maccabees 14, where it was said that the people have no right to make an assembly without the authority's permission, to the reference to the *Codex Iustiniani*, namely to the *lex Denuntiamus vobis* and the *lex Conventicula*.[83]

---

81 Bohier, De seditiosis, § 2, n. 5, 115: "Item etiam de congregatione in qua aliqui pactionibus vel statutus firmatur quae habent diversa nomina secundum quod congregati eis nomen imponunt, vel secundum quos ius imponit. iam aliquando vocatur unio, aliquando confoederatio, aliquando secta, aliquando conventicula, aliquando coniuratio".

82 Ibid., 116: "...whenever people are allowed to lawfully assemble without permission of authorities".

83 Law *Denuntiamus vobis omnibus*, Codex, *De his qui ad ecclesias confugiunt vel ibi exclamant* (C. 1. 12. 5): "Denuntiamus vobis omnibus, ut in sacrosanctis ecclesiis et in aliis quidem venerabilibus locis, in quibus cum pace et quiete vota competit celebrari, abstineatis omni seditione. nemo conclamationibus utatur, nemo moveat tumultum aut impetum committat vel conventicula collecta multitudine in qualibet parte civitatis vel vici vel cuiuscumque loci colligere aut celebrare conetur. nam si quis aliquid contra leges a quibusdam sibi existimet perpetrari, liceat ei adire iudicem et legitimum postulare praesidium. sciant sane omnes, quod, si quis contra huius edicti normam aut agere aliquid aut seditionem movere temptaverit, ultimo supplicio subiacebit"/" We notify all of you to abstain from every kind of sedition in the Holy Churches, and in all other venerated places, in which it is proper for you to offer your prayers in decent tranquillity, and let no one make use of loud cries, cause any tumult, commit any attack, or collect or hold any nu-

According to Bohier, assemblies and congregations did not necessarily have to be considered as a negative phenomenon, but they had negative influences on the people and led them to discord.[84] Any agreement between the people was perceived as a danger to the public order, insofar as it was always followed by fights, violence and, in general, discord among the people. From the perspective of the defence of public peace, every discussion or organisation was considered as a potential threat to authority. According to this, a congregation could be considered lawful depending on its scope and therefore all organised activity of the people aimed at weakening the authority or damaging the common good had to be banned.[85]

Only against a tyrannical government the people had the right to assemble in order to resist. Bohier, quoting Aquinas, sustained that a tyrannical government is not lawful because it is not aimed at achieving the common good, but private interests. Therefore, the perturbation of this government must not be criminalized as sedition, unless this perturbation produces a worse situation for the people than the tyrannical government.[86] Bohier thus claimed that in some cases resistance was

---

merous assemblies in any part of a city or village, or in any other place whatsoever. For, if anyone thinks that the laws have been violated to his prejudice, he can go into court and demand the protection of the law; and all persons are hereby notified that if anyone disobeys, or contravenes the provisions of this Edict, or attempts to excite sedition, he shall be subjected to the extreme penalty"; law *Conventicula*, Codex, *De episcopis et clericis* (C. 1. 3. 15): "Conventicula illicita extra ecclesiam in privatis aedibus celebrari prohibemus, proscriptionis domus periculo imminente, si dominus eius in ea clericos nova ac tumultuosa conventicula extra ecclesiam celebrantes susceperit"/"We forbid holding religious assemblies in private houses, even outside the Church, under the penalty of confiscation of the house, if the owner of the same permitted ecclesiastics to hold new and tumultuous meetings therein outside the church".

84 Bohier, De seditiosis, § 5, n. 2, 117: "...quia istae conventions illiciunt subditos ad peccandum, et ad iurgia, quae licet per se non sint malae, temen quia malum ex eis sequi potest reprovantur a iure...".

85 Ibid., § 5, n. 4, 117: "...per finem licitum, licita cognoscitur congregatio, et contra, per finem illicitum quod sit illicita..."/"...assemblies are considered lawful if aimed at lawful purposes; on the contrary, they are considered unlawful if aimed at unlawful purposes".

86 Bohier quoted Aquinas, *Summa Theologiae*, II^a-IIae q. 42 a. 2 ad 3: "...quod cum regimen tyrannicum non sit iustum, quia non ordinatur ad bonum commune, sed ad bonum privatum regentis [...]. Ideo perturbatio huhiusmodi regiminis non habet rationem seditionis, nisi forte quando sic perturbatur inordinate tyranny regimen, quod multitudo subiecta maius detrimentum patitur ex perturbatione sequenti, quam tyranny regimine"/"A tyrannical government is not just, because it is directed, not to the common good, but to the private good of the ruler. Consequently there is no sedition in disturbing a government of

lawful, but he also put strict limitation to that possibility. Neither did he explain how the damage caused by a tyrant should be concretely evaluated and by whom, nor would he determine at what point it was legitimate for the crowd to intervene.

In Braun, the possibility of lawful association of the people is analysed when he considers the problem of factions within the political body. The faction represented an organized form of discord, which was lawful or unlawful depending on its aim.[87] All factions aimed at defending the political body and private goods are considered lawful and useful for the entire community. Braun wrote that

si enim ad defensionem rerum nostrarum amicos congregare possumus, quanto magis pro defensione Reipublicae, bonis inter se societatem inire, et adversus improbos cives Rempublicam tueri licebit: Sicut et iusta est factio, quae ob id inter bonos cives coalita est, ut Tyranni e republica eiiciantur, qui nulla alioqui ratione commode expelli possunt.[88]

All alliances among people aimed at the defence of life and properties were considered *coniurationes licitae* and were tolerated and even desired. However, even in the case of a tyrant perturbing the community, the possibility for the people to organise themselves is presented as the *extrema ratio*, not as part of normal political life.

In order to understand Braun's analysis of the possibility to resist an illegitimate tyrannical government, it is necessary to consider how political hierarchy was legitimized in the treatise. According to Braun, all the subjects had to obey secular powers, which were subordinated to God. Indeed, "potestatibus quoque humanis obediendum est, Paulo Apostolo ita praecipiente. Omnis anima, inquit, potestatibus sublimioribus subdita sit. Non est enim potestas nisi a Deo: quae autem a Deo sunt,

---

this kind, unless indeed the tyrant's rule is disturbed so inordinately, that his subjects suffer greater harm from the consequent disturbance than from the tyrant's government".

87 Braun, De seditionibus, 64: "Factio est divisio multitudinis alicuius per aemulationem, in diversa studia, cum inter ipso alii aliis priores esse volunt. Quod et honestis ex causis, et ex inhonestis fieri potest. Unde et faction in bonam et in malam partem accipitur, ac inizio quidem factio honestum vocabulum erat"/"Faction is a division among the multitude, produced by competition to prevail on others. Factions can be divided in lawful and unlawful according to their reasons. Therefore we have good and bad factions, although at the beginning the term had a positive meaning".

88 Ibid., 64-65: "if we can assemble to defend friends' properties, then we can even more assemble to defend the political community; we can create unions among people and protect the political community against plotters. For the same reason, a faction is right and lawful when it assembles good subjects in order to expel tyranny from the community – if there is no other more suitable way to do it".

ordinata sunt. Itaque qui protestati resistit, ordinationi Dei resistit".[89] Quoting Saint Paul, Braun sustained that resisting secular authority was similar to resisting God.[90]

This strong rejection of any resistance was partially outbalanced by another quote from the Bible, namely from the Acts of the Apostles, which states "we must obey God rather than men".[91] According to this passage, it was possible to conceive lawful resistance to an order that is unjust and against God. Combining these two passages, the Letter to the Romans and the Acts of the Apostles, Braun refers to the traditional Christian discourse on resistance: every man has to obey, but when the orders are against God he has to resist and accept to be persecuted for that.[92] The possibility to resist was therefore presented by the jurist as a very abstract one and left to individual choice. Braun devoted comparably little attention to the problem: although he was referring to the Christian discourse on resistance, he actually did not conceive of any concrete and lawful opposition to power and did not quote any historical fact to illustrate how that doctrine could actually be applied.

In 1678 Philipp Andreas Oldenburger[93] published his *Tractatus iuridico-politicus de rebuspublicis turbidis in tranquillum statum reducendis*,[94] which in some respects can be considered a comprehensive synthesis of the entire debate (although it was not the last treatise on sedition). Analysing the causes of sedition, Oldenburger indicated two cases of lawful resistance. The violation of the subjects' liberties and rights was considered an illegitimate government practice that provoked malcontent and discord among the people. Unrest aimed at protecting such liberties and rights was therefore considered lawful and labelled as legitimate defence.[95] Tyranny was another cause of legitimate resistance. Violence against

---

89 Ibid., 13: "We have to obey also to secular authorities, as Saint Paul prescribes. Every person is to be in subjection to the governing authorities. There is no authority except from God, and those, which exist, are established by God. Therefore whoever resists authority opposes the ordinance of God".
90 Epistle to the Romans, 13.
91 Ibid., 17: "Oportet Deo magis obedire, quam hominibus". See Acts of the Apostles, 5.
92 Wolfgang Reinhard, *Geschichte der Staatsgewalt: Eine vergleichende Verfassungsgeschichte Europas von den Anfängen bis zur Gegenwart* (München, 1999), 227-235.
93 Oldenburger was a student of Hermann Conring and worked as professor of law in Geneva. He was known as an "enfant terrible" of his time for his polemical writings and for his disputes with Conring and von Pufendorf. See Goldschlag, "Oldenburger, Philipp Andreas", in Allgemeine Deutsche Biographie 24 (1887), 261-263.
94 See footnote 13.
95 Ibid., 37: "[...] quando in Rebuspublicis mistis Procerum libertas iura et privilegia violantur atque atteruntur: Sed eo in casu non est vera seditio, sed justa defensio"/" [...] when in the mixed government the rights and privileges of the aristocratic people are vio-

tyrannical government or against the brutalities inflicted by magistrates was often the starting point for commotions and unrest. Responding to illegitimate violence with violence was not a crime: the subjects had the right to fight an illegitimate government whenever their lives were endangered. Any attempt to protect their lives was a case of *defensio licita*.[96]

7. CONCLUSIONS

The study of the development of legal and political concepts used to define collective forms of violence allows a better understanding of how the practices of control changed over time. During the sixteenth century the legal doctrine elaborated a concept of *seditio* based on the strong convergence of *proditio*, *rebellio* and collective violence. Any form of violent reaction to the authorities was understood as a threat to the entire political body and therefore labelled as *crimen laesae maiestatis*. Investigating offences perturbing the public order, jurists advanced an extensive definition of *crimen seditionis*, covering a wide range of collective forms of protest. All violent assaults on the government were attributed to a political will to damage the entire community: this allowed the jurists to relate every organised disagreement to *proditio* and *perduellio* and therefore to consider it as a rebellion against the authority. Moreover, even minor forms of violence, producing inner disorders, were considered episodes of sedition.

In the early modern age the development of political crimes was characterised by the extensive use of *crimen laesea maiestatis* in order to repress any episode of dissent and any form of opposition to the authority. The legal perception of the collective forms of protests changed within this broader development of the penal law and produced a concept of *seditio* functional to the control of public order.

The literature on sedition was characterised by a considerable effort to understand the reasons of inner dissension and political conflict. The jurists were

---

lated and reduced, that is not a case of proper sedition, but it is a case of right and lawful defence".

96 Ibid., 44-47: "Sunt autem graviores et frequentiores rebellandi causae ex parte rectorum sive imperantium sequents; et quidem prima ac potissima Principum et Magistratum crudelitas [...]. Adeo verum est illud: Violenta nemo imperia continuit diu; magisque acerba quam diuturna existunt. Et quidni defensio vitae humanae, qua nihil est carius in ejusmodi casu esset licita et favorabilis"/"There are also serious and common reasons of rebellion created by authorities; the main one is cruelty. It is true that violent governments do not last long. In this case the defence of life – nothing is more valuable than life – is lawful".

interested in studying all the phenomena related to collective forms of discord and protest, in order to provide the conceptual instruments for repressing and preventing unrest. This attempt to elaborate legal means of controlling insurrections influenced the development of the doctrine and led jurists to define, during the second half of the seventeenth century, a more articulated concept of *seditio*. They distinguished between different grades of sedition, depending on the dangerousness of the violent behaviour for the political order. In doing so, they provided the magistrate with the legal possibility to classify a concrete sedition at their own discretion either as a *crimen maiestatis*, or as a minor violent unrest, which could be punished in different ways, depending on circumstances. This change in the definition of *crimen seditionis* must be understood in relation to the development of a preventive perspective based on the analysis of the concrete political context. The preference for a preventive approach, instead of a merely repressive legal response to unrest, obliged the jurists to examine the processes of development of dissent and made it necessary to have a concept of *seditio* that was suitable for different situations.

The treatises on sedition integrated two closely related levels: the legal doctrine and the political wisdom aimed at controlling public order. The earlier doctrine was always directed at giving concrete answers to contemporary conflicting situations, but was also influenced by the development of political theory. The study of the concept of *seditio* traces the development of legal and political strategies applied to control public order and to neutralise political dissent.

Early Modern Revolts as Political Crimes in the Popular Media of Illustrated Broadsheets

KARL HÄRTER

The fruitful research on revolts in early modern Europe is still primarily characterised by a social historical approach, focussing on the socio-economic causes of social upheaval – especially in rural areas – as well as on the motives and activities of the disadvantaged groups or rebels.[1] Recent studies also addressed the issue of how revolts and similar forms of social unrest were represented in public media, taking into account how the authorities as well as the rebels used the public sphere for their respective interests.[2] However, only few studies paid thorough attention to the responses of the legal systems to revolt and similar phenomena – ranging from rural and urban revolts to rebellions and conspiracies of the nobility – and their long-term impact on the legal systems and the associated legal discourses in early modern Europe. Winfried Schulze argued that the harsh military suppression of the German Peasant War and other peasant revolts was followed and accompanied by preventative mechanisms of juridification ("*Verrechtlichung*"). This meant that throughout the early modern period conflicts between peasants and authorities did not only foster legislation, but were more and more dealt with or

---

1 For an overview see: Peter Blickle, *Das Alte Europa. Vom Hochmittelalter bis zur Moderne* (München 2008), 186-206; Peter Zagorin, *Society, states, and early modern revolution. Agrarian and urban rebellions*, Rebels and rulers, 1500 – 1660, Vol. 1 (Cambridge 1982); Peter Zagorin, *Provincial rebellion. Revolutionary civil wars, 1560 – 1660*, Rebels and rulers, 1500 – 1660, Vol. 2 (Cambridge 1982).

2 Andreas Würgler, *Unruhen und Öffentlichkeit. Städtische und ländliche Protestbewegungen im 18. Jahrhundert* (Tübingen 1995); Andreas Würgler, "Revolts in Print: Media and Communication in Early Modern Urban Conflicts", in *Urban Elections and Decision-Making in Early Modern Europe, 1500-1800*, ed. Rudolf Schlögl (Newcastle-upon-Tyne 2009), 257-275.

even solved via the imperial courts and other legal mechanisms like supplication.[3] In addition, Peter Blickle has referred to the increasing legislation after the German Peasant War, pointing out the criminalisation of social protest, resistance and peasant revolts as "treason", and therefore as political crimes which were not clearly legally defined and allowed arbitrary justice.[4] Moreover, recent case studies by legal historians analysed the legal consequences of the German Peasant War and the trials and punishment of the ringleaders in the Bavarian uprising against the Austrian occupation in 1705.[5] However, crime, law and justice do not achieve a prominent role in research on early modern revolts, and comparative studies on the different reactions and strategies of the legal systems in Europe to all kinds of revolts are almost non-existing.

In this respect the following analysis decidedly follows the approach of legal and especially penal history, regarding revolts from the perspective of political crimes,[6] which was not only a central viewpoint of the early modern authorities, but served also as a main representation of revolts in popular media such as pamphlets or illustrated broadsheets. Recent studies on the representation of crime and punishment in popular media, and notably in early modern illustrated broadsheets, proved the strong and complex interconnection between penal law, the actual

---

3   Winfried Schulze, *Bäuerlicher Widerstand und feudale Herrschaft in der frühen Neuzeit* (Stuttgart-Bad Cannstadt 1980); Winfried Schulze, "Geben Aufruhr und Aufstand Anlaß zu neuen heilsamen Gesetzen. Beobachtungen über die Wirkungen bäuerlichen Widerstands in der Frühen Neuzeit", in *Aufstände, Revolten und Prozesse. Beiträge zu bäuerlichen Widerstandsbewegungen im frühneuzeitlichen Europa*, ed. Winfried Schulze (Stuttgart 1983), 261-285.

4   Peter Blickle, "The Criminalization of Peasant Resistance in the Holy Roman Empire: Toward a History of the Emergence of High Treason in Germany", *Journal of Modern History* 58 (1986), 88-97.

5   Malte Hohn, *Die rechtlichen Folgen des Bauernkrieges von 1525. Sanktionen, Ersatzleistungen und Normsetzung nach dem Aufstand* (Berlin 2004); Christian Strasser, *Der Aufstand im bayerischen Oberland 1705 - Majestätsverbrechen oder Heldentat? Eine Untersuchung der Strafprozesse gegen die Anführer der in der "Mordweihnacht von Sendling" gescheiterten Erhebung* (Münster 2005).

6   B. L. Ingraham, *Political crime in Europe. A comparative study of France, Germany, and England* (Berkeley 1979). See also the postulation for a more intense interchange between "Revoltenforschung" and "Kriminalitätsforschung" by Andreas Würgler, "Diffamierung und Kriminalisierung von "Devianz" in frühneuzeitlichen Konflikten. Für einen Dialog zwischen Protestforschung und Kriminalitätsgeschichte", in *Devianz, Widerstand und Herrschaftspraxis in der Vormoderne. Studien zu Konflikten im südwestdeutschen Raum (15.-18. Jahrhundert)*, ed. Mark Häberlein (Konstanz 1999), 317-347.

practices of criminal justice and the images of the legal responses in popular media.[7] The latter did not solely mirror the intentions and purposes of the authorities, but, moreover, reflects common attitudes and perceptions of crime and order. The image of crime and punishment in illustrated broadsheets could evoke ambiguous effects: augmenting the legal construction of crimes and the authoritarian purposes of punishment, as well as reflecting on and influencing the common perception of order and security, furthermore satisfying the curiosity of the public as well as intensifying the public memorisation of crimes or revolts.[8] Thus, interrelated analyses of revolts as political crimes in both legal discourses as well as in popular media could yield new insights into the representation of revolts in a European context and implicates a cross-border approach. Since early modern penal law was not restricted to any "national" law, it can be characterised as a European phenomenon, based on the "common law" (*Gemeines Recht*) and the writings of hundreds of jurists from different countries. And, likewise, the illustrated broadsheet can be considered as a European mass-medium, distributed sometimes multilingually in different European countries, and referring to events, crimes and revolts in other countries.[9] For this analysis, I have chosen illustrated broadsheets

---

7   Karl Härter/Gerhard Sälter/Eva Wiebel (ed.), *Repräsentationen von Kriminalität und öffentlicher Sicherheit. Bilder, Vorstellungen und Diskurse vom 16. bis zum 20. Jahrhundert* (Frankfurt am Main 2010).

8   Dietmar Peil, "Strafe und Ritual. Zur Darstellung von Straftaten und Bestrafungen im illustrierten Flugblatt", in *Wahrnehmungsgeschichte und Wissensdiskurs im illustrierten Flugblatt der Frühen Neuzeit (1450-1700)*, ed. Wolfgang Harms and Alfred Messerli (Basel 2002), 465-486; Harriet Rudolph, "Warhafftige Abcontrafactur? Die Evidenz des Verbrechens und die Effizienz der Strafjustiz in illustrierten Einblattdrucken (1550-1650)", in *Evidentia. Reichweiten visueller Wahrnehmung in der Frühen Neuzeit*, ed. Gabriele Wimböck, Karin Leonhard and Markus Friedrich (Münster 2007), 161-183; Gerd Schwerhoff, "Kriminalitätsgeschichte - Kriminalgeschichten: Verbrechen und Strafen im Medienverbund des 16. und 17. Jahrhunderts", in: *Verbrechen im Blick: Perspektiven der neuzeitlichen Kriminalitätsgeschichte*, ed. Rebekka Habermas and Gerd Schwerhoff (Frankfurt am Main, New York 2009), 295-322; Karl Härter, "Criminalbildergeschichten: Verbrechen, Justiz und Strafe in illustrierten Einblattdrucken der Frühen Neuzeit", in *Repräsentationen von Kriminalität, ed.* Härter, Sälter and Wiebel, 25-88.

9   David Kunzle, *The Early Comic Strip. Narrative Strips and Picture Stories in the European Broadsheet from c. 1450 to 1825* (Berkeley et al. 1973); Wolfgang Cilleßen (ed.), *Krieg der Bilder. Druckgraphik als Medium politischer Auseinandersetzung im Europa des Absolutismus* (Berlin 1997); Wolfgang Harms and Michael Schilling (ed.), *Das illustrierte Flugblatt in der Kultur der Frühen Neuzeit. Wolfenbütteler Arbeitsgespräch 1997* (Frankfurt am Main et al. 1998).

which were primarily published in Central Europe, but refer to revolts in the Holy Roman Empire of the German Nation as well as in other countries, selecting exemplary types and cases such as the "Fettmilch-riot" in Frankfurt (1612-1616) as a typical urban revolt, the "magnate-conspiracy" in Hungary (1670/71) as a typical revolt spearheaded by members of the nobility, and "Horea's uprising" in Transylvania (1785) as a "late" peasant's revolt.

The selection is based on a sample of almost 100 illustrated broadsheets and pamphlets covering nearly 30 different revolts and political crimes in Europe between 1567 and 1785[10] as well as on a comprehensive study on the representation of ordinary crimes in early modern illustrated broadsheets.[11] The three revolts alone, which I will be analysing in the following, evoked a strong media-response and were covered in 23 more or less different illustrated pamphlets and broadsheets. This was accompanied by other, non-illustrated, more voluminous publications, especially polemic pamphlets, "popular descriptions", semi-official documents such as collections of court-records and authoritarian ordinances and laws. As far as possible, I have incorporated them into this study to demonstrate interconnections between popular media, public/official media policy and legal discourses.

---

10 The main sources are: Wolfgang Harms (ed.), *Deutsche illustrierte Flugblätter des 16. und 17. Jahrhunderts, Vol. I-III, IV, VII* (Tübingen 1985-1997); John Roger Paas, *The German political broadsheet 1600-1700, Vol. 1-9* (Wiesbaden 1985-2007); Digitale Bibliothek Spezial: *Deutsche Einblattholzschnitte* (Berlin 2003) (CD-ROM: Directmedia Publishing GmbH), with 3400 woodcuts from: Max Geisberg, *The German single-leaf woodcut: 1500-1550*; ed. Walter L. Strauss, Vol. 1-4 (New York 1974); Walter L. Strauss, *The German single-leaf woodcut: 1550-1600*. Vol. 1-3 (New York 1975); Dorothy Alexander, *The German single-leaf woodcut: 1600-1700*, in collaboration with Walter L. Strauss, Vol. 1-2 (New York 1977). Many broadsheets are available on the internet: Bildarchiv Foto Marburg [http://www.fotomarburg.de/index_html]; Einblattdrucke der frühen Neuzeit: Bayerische Staatsbibliothek [http://www.muenchener-digitalisierungszentrum.de]; Verzeichnis der im deutschen Sprachraum erschienenen Drucke des 17. Jahrhunderts [http://www.vd17.de].
11 Härter, Criminalbildergeschichten.

Political crimes and revolts in early modern illustrated broadsheets	
1567/1568 Treason / conspiracy, Count Egmont and Horn, Netherlands	3
1575 Treason, Brandenburgischer Hofjude Lippold, Holy Roman Empire	2
1579 Assassination, Vizier Mohammed Sokullu, Ottoman Empire	1
1584 Assassination, William of Orange, Netherlands	3
1589 Assassination / regicide, Heinrich III, France	3
1595 Treason / conspiracy, Count Hardach (Hardegg), Holy Roman Empire	3
1601 Treason / conspiracy, Chancellor Nikolaus Krell, Holy Roman Empire	2
1605 Gunpowder-plot, England	5
1610 Assassination / regicide, Henry IV, France	8
1616 Women's-riot, Republic of the Netherlands	1
1612-1616 Fettmilch-riot, Holy Roman Empire	14
1617 Treason / conspiracy, Count Concini, France	1
1621 Rebellion, Bohemian Nobility, Bohemia / Holy Roman Empire	8
1626 Peasant's revolt, Austria / Holy Roman Empire	2
1637 Treason, Wallenstein, Holy Roman Empire	3
1637 Assassination, Mayor of Liège, Holy Roman Empire	2
1650/51 Rebellion of the Fronde, France	1
1653 Swiss Peasants' War, Swiss Confederation	2
1671 Rebellion of Razin, Russia	4
1670/71 Magnate-rebellion, Hungary	7
1672 Pika-revolt /Tököly, Hungary	1
1672 Riot / treason, Johann and Cornelis de Witt, Netherlands	5
1683 Assassination, Vizier Cara Mustapha, Ottoman Empire	3
1705/06 Bavarian revolt against Austrian occupation, Holy Roman Empire	6
1757 Assassination of Louis XV, Damiens, France	3
1758/59 Assassination / regicide, Joseph I, Portugal	4
1785 Peasants' revolt of Horea and Kloska, Hungary	2

Fig. 1: Illustrated broadsheets dealing with revolts and political crimes

LEGAL DEFINITIONS AND ELEMENTS

It should be understood that a constricted perspective on the media representation of revolts as political crimes has to cross crucial and well researched issues such as the causes and motives of revolts or the subsequent actions undertaken. As a result, it can make little use of such models like social protest or resistance.¹² Despite the fact that many serious social or political conflicts, which could be or were considered as "revolts", were dealt with or even solved by negotiation, mediation or via the mechanism of *"Verrechtlichung"*, early modern authorities or states reacted also within the legal framework of penal law, criminal justice and punishment. In this respect "revolts" and similar phenomena were mainly regarded as crimes such as rebellion, sedition, breach of peace (*Landfriedensbruch*), treason, *perduellio*, conspiracy, or lèse-majesty. This concise list of possible legal interpretations of revolts as different crimes already shows that at the end of the late middle ages no uniform or even clearly defined legal conception of political crimes and revolts existed in Europe. Only from the 16th century onwards did the legal systems in Europe – that is, the state based legislation and the actual practice of criminal justice, as well as the writings of the common law-jurists – gradually, often in reaction to social or political unrest, develop a more concise legal concept of political crimes.¹³

Nevertheless, not before the beginning of the 19th century did these different efforts result in a juridically stringent "modern" legal codification of political crimes, implemented by the French code pénal of 1810, evolving into a model for European penal legislation in the 19th century and the "modern" legal definition of political crimes in particular.¹⁴ Thus, the early modern era can be seen as an incubation period of the legal implementation and differentiation of political crimes including the criminalisation and punishment of revolts. However, different and wide-ranging legal constructions were still used, influenced also by traditional conceptions and laws: the *crimen laesae maiestatis* and the *perduellio* in Roman

---

12 On resistance and Widerstandsrecht see: Angela De Benedictis and Karl-Heinz Lingens (ed.), *Wissen, Gewissen und Wissenschaft im Widerstandsrecht (16.- 18. Jh.) / Sapere, coscienza e scienza nel diritto di resistenza (XVI-XVIII sec.)* (Frankfurt am Main 2003).

13 Friedrich-Christian Schroeder, *Der Schutz von Staat und Verfassung im Strafrecht* (Munich 1970); with regard to the concept of mass-delicts: Andreas Roth, *Kollektive Gewalt und Strafrecht. Die Geschichte der Massedelikte in Deutschland* (Berlin 1989).

14 Dirk Blasius, *Geschichte der politischen Kriminalität in Deutschland (1800 - 1980). Eine Studie zu Justiz und Staatsverbrechen* (Frankfurt am Main 1983); Karl Härter, "Asyl, Auslieferung und politisches Verbrechen in Europa während der "Sattelzeit": Modernität und Kontinuität im Strafrechtssystem", in *Dimensionen der Moderne. Festschrift für Christof Dipper*, ed. Ute Schneider and Lutz Raphael (Frankfurt am Main u. a. 2008), 481-502; Karl Härter, "Die Entwicklung des Strafrechts in Mitteleuropa 1770-1848: Defensive Modernisierung, Kontinuitäten und Wandel der Rahmenbedingungen", in *Verbrechen im Blick. Perspektiven der neuzeitlichen Kriminalitätsgeschichte*, ed. Rebekka Habermas and Gerd Schwerhoff, (Frankfurt am Main and New York 2009), 71-107.

Law, the more English and Germanic *treason*, the *crimen fractae pacis publicae* (breach / violation of the peace: *Landfriedensbruch*), and *seditio* / sedition (*Aufruhr*). Because of their different social and political contexts – rural, urban, aristocratic – their various manifestations and their diverse aims, revolts could be and were subsumed legally under suchlike crimes or concepts, taking also in account the purposes of punishment the concerned states or authorities pursued. The *crimen laesae maiestatis* put the ruler in the centre of the definition of the crime; thus, every activity aiming at the violation of his person, honour or rule could be classified as lèse-majesty, ranging therefore from verbal insults and pamphlets to violent action, assassination and regicide.[15] One of most serious crimes in the concept of the *crimen laesae maiestatis* was that of *perduellio*: high treason and violent action against the ruler committed with *animus hostilis*. Because the sacred body of the ruler represented the divine and secular order, the concept of *crimen laesae maiestatis* could easily be expanded to the state, its officials and all forms of upheaval and revolt against the ruling elite or the state.

In the English and German legal traditions, the crime of treason was distinguished from that of *crimen laesae maiestatis*, putting the emphasis on such elements as conspiracy, plots, conjurations or collaboration with foreign powers and focussing stronger on the ruling elites.[16] In this respect, revolts and rebellions of the nobility or towns against "their" ruler were often also considered as treason. Initially, the commitment of treason was restricted more or less to the elite, the office holders and military officers, but was extended in the 16th century in England and the Holy Roman Empire to political crimes and dissidents in the whole. A crucial element in the conceptualisation of the crime was the breach of loyalty (*Treuebruch*), which easily could be extended to every conspiracy, rebellion or any other dissident activity in which the nobility or office holders were involved. With the emergence of a more modern system of international relations between states, as well as the development of a professional military system, particularly revolts and

---

15 Mario Sbriccoli, *Crimen laesae maiestatis. Il problema del reato politico alle soglie della scienza penalistica moderna* (Milano 1974); Helga Schnabel-Schüle, "Das Majestätsverbrechen als Herrschaftsschutz und Herrschaftskritik", in *Staatsschutz* (= Aufklärung 2 (1992)), ed. Dietmar Willoweit (Hamburg 1994), 29-47; Angela Rustemeyer, *Dissens und Ehre. Majestätsverbrechen in Russland (1600-1800)* (Wiesbaden 2006).

16 Kenneth R. Minogue, "Treason and the early modern state: Scenes from a mesalliance", in: *Die Rolle der Juristen bei der Entstehung des modernen Staates*, ed. Roman Schnur (Berlin 1986), 421-435; John G. Bellamy, *The Tudor law of treason. An introd.* (London 1979); Simon H. Cuttler, *The law of treason and treason trials in later medieval France* (Cambridge u. a. 1981).

rebellions with a foreign element like the cooperation of rebels with rivalling states were considered as military treason (*Landesverrat*), thus adding a new "criminal" element to the legal definition of revolts as political crimes.

Further developments and differentiation of political crimes resulted from social conflicts – especially peasant revolts – and the emergence of public security as a primary aim of the early modern state with regard to public law, internal politics, policing and the penal policy. In the late Middle Ages, the Holy Roman Empire established the *crimen fractae pacis publicae* – the crime of *Landfriedensbruch* – in several laws and public treaties (*Landfriedensordnungen* and *Landfrieden*). Initially aiming at the feuds of the nobility, the legislation and penal practice of the 15th and 16th centuries much more emphasised the criminal activities of dangerous groups and bandits (*landfriedensschädliche Leute*) and social protest / upheaval of peasants as central elements of the crime. Therefore, public security superseded the older idea of common peace as the main intention of penal legislation and the purpose of punishment.[17] Moreover, the legal concept of the crime's definition allowed its application to social revolts and facilitated a broader range of flexible legal reactions, respectively the purposes of punishment: Not retaliation with respect to the sacred ruler but the restitution of the state's order, deterrence and prevention gradually became more important. This resulted in a somewhat new legal definition of such mass-crimes or crimes against the state as sedition, appearing for the first time in the Holy Roman Empire in the imperial penal code of 1532 as "*Aufruhr des Volkes*" and in England in the middle of the 16th century.[18] In first half of 16th century the English parliament passed over 60 treason statutes and riot acts, defining riots and revolts as treason and sedition, threatening capital punishment, but also milder penalties like fines to be imposed on so-called followers (*Mitläufer*), and therefore aiming at a flexible response to "mass-crimes". Similarly, the penal law of the Old Reich and its members (the imperial estates and cities) did comprise in parallel the crimes of treason (*Verräterei*), revolt (*Aufruhr*), breach of peace

---

17 Karl Härter, "Von der Friedenswahrung zur "öffentlichen Sicherheit": Konzepte und Maßnahmen frühneuzeitlicher Sicherheitspolicey in rheinländischen Territorien", *Rheinische Vierteljahresblätter* 67 (2003), 162-190; Karl Härter, "Sicherheit und Frieden im frühneuzeitlichen Alten Reich: Zur Funktion der Reichsverfassung als Sicherheits- und Friedensordnung 1648-1806", *Zeitschrift für historische Forschung* 30 (2003), 413-431.

18 *Die Peinliche Gerichtsordnung Kaiser Karls V. von 1532 (Carolina)*, 6th edition, ed. Arthur Kaumann (Stuttgart 1975), Art. 127; compare also Art. 124 (*Verrat*/treason) and 129 (*Fehde*/feud). On England see Andy Wood, *Riot, rebellion and popular politics in early modern England* (Basingstoke 2002), 32-42.

(*Landfriedensbruch*), sedition and lèse-majesty.[19] The German as well as the English example shows that the criminalisation of revolts took place in penal codes and the writings of the jurists – the "common law". However, it was also developed in a growing body of single ordinances and public laws, as well as in the trials and practises of courts with respect to the actual punishment of revolts and political crimes.[20] Flexible legislation and a flexible reaction of the penal systems in Europe originated not least from the intensification of "revolts" since the 16th century, which were to be quelled not only by military force, but by legal public action on part of the state, thus demonstrating the illegitimate causes of revolts as well as the reasonable and just reaction of the state in maintaining public order and security. With regard to these intentions and the necessity of flexible legal reactions, neither did the single laws and penal codes nor the common law jurists establish a clear and stringent legal definition of revolts or other social / political mass-crimes (upheaval, uprising, insurrection, riot, rebellion etc.). Instead, they provided a mixture of different elements and possible reactions / penalties corresponding with the different forms, manifestations and motivations of political crimes and revolts, respectively.

The crucial elements or features of the legal conceptualisation and criminalisation of revolts as political crimes in early modern Europe also influenced the "legal representation" or "criminal image" of revolts.[21] In principle, rebels from all social groups – subjects / peasants, burghers / citizens and members of the elite / nobility could be considered as political criminals and treated nearly equally with regard to trial and punishment. Not the social status, but the character of the "criminal group" and the role of the participants of a mass-crime lead to legal differentiation. Collectiveness and the formation of a "criminal dissident group" of a sufficient number of three or more members was considered a precondition of a mass-crime or mass-tort, whether form of gatherings of larger groups and public tumult or the subversive activities of secret groups, conjurations, cabals, or "criminal" sects. The necessity of flexible legal reaction and punishment lead to the legal differentiation of the participants and their roles in such groups or mass-de-

---

19 Compare for instance *Constitutio criminalis Theresiana oder der [...] Mariä Theresiä [...] peinliche Gerichtsordnung*, (Vienna 1769), Art. 61 (crimen laesae maiestatis) and Art. 62 (sedition).

20 On the function of police ordinances (*Policeyordnungen*) with regard to the development of criminal law see: Karl Härter, *Policey und Strafjustiz in Kurmainz. Gesetzgebung, Normdurchsetzung und Sozialkontrolle im frühneuzeitlichen Territorialstaat* (Frankfurt am Main 2005).

21 On the legal definition see: Ingraham, political crime, 19-36; Schroeder, Schutz; Roth, kollektive Gewalt.

licts / revolts, basically distinguishing ringleaders, riot leaders and instigators on the one, and the followers / satellites on the other hand, using also the concept of a seducer and the seduced.

With regard to the activities of a criminal or revolting group, public actions were distinguished from the more secretive political activities. The former included a broad range of different punishable acts (offences) comprising symbolic and ritualistic actions such as the distribution of pamphlets, protest gatherings, assembling in public and submitting complaints or gathering and swearing an oath as well as more violent forms of open, dangerous tumult and armed revolt with excessive use of violence and weapons, or even military force in the case of military riot and mutiny. The symbolic, ritualistic and public dimension of the legal representation of revolts was complemented by the more "secretive" punishable activities, most commonly conceptualised as plots or conspiracies, especially of the nobility or dissident religious groups.[22] The legal definition implied an appointment to commit a political crime and to instigate or spark a revolt, and therefore extended the punishment of revolts from the actual deed to their planning and preparation – even the intention – of a political crime. In this respect, regicide and attempted assassination of the ruler or a state official committed by a single person could also be considered as part of a conspiracy and the beacon to start a rebellion.[23] This resulted in a preventative criminal law which allowed flexible arbitrary criminalisation and the punishment of political crimes or attempted revolt as anticipatory crimes (the so-called *"Vorverlagerung der Strafbarkeit"*).[24] Moreover, conspiracy added a foreign dimension to revolts: hostile states and powers instigating, participating or supporting a conspiracy and a revolt with the aim of destabilising a state or taking over the rule. In this respect, participants of a conspiracy or revolt could be charged as traitors to their country (*Landesverrat*). The interconnection between conspiracy and revolt and the involvement of hostile foreign powers in its planning and preparation strongly influenced the legal representation and public image of revolts as political crimes.

---

22 Yves-Marie Bercé and Elena Fasano Guarini (ed.), *Complots et conjurations dans l'Europe moderne. Actes du colloque international* [...] (Rome 1996); Barry Coward and Julian Swann (ed.), *Conspiracies and Conspiracy Theory in Early Modern Europe From the Waldensians to the French Revolution* (Ashgate 2004).

23 Compare for example the case of Damien who's assassination of Louis XV was considered as part of a conspiracy and an attempted coup d'état: Dale K. Van Kley, *The Damiens affair and the unravelling of the Ancien Régime, 1750–1770* (Princeton, N.J. 1984).

24 See the pre-modern English concept of "imaging the King's death" and the context of treason and revolt: Wood, Riot, 33; Bellamy, law of treason, 10-12; Schroeder, Schutz, 238.

In contrast, the motivation of political crimes and revolts played only a marginal role in the legal conceptualisation and representation. They had to be considered as "political" in the sense that they threatened the monarch / ruler, the state or the existing order in general. As has been pointed out, in the early modern period we can observe a shift in the object of protection through penal law from the ruler / monarch to the state and the overall order. In this respect all kind of revolts – from social upheaval to rebellions of the nobility – were primarily considered as political crimes aiming at the state and its order.

The different legal crimes did not result in fundamentally different concepts of punishment. Based on Roman Law, nearly all early modern penal laws and codes in Europe comprised the threat of capital and corporal punishment to be executed in public – the theatre of public punishment (*Theater des Endlichen Rechtstags*). This included strong symbolic elements and rituals, in particular additional and dishonourable forms of punishment such as hanging (from the *arbor infelix*), quartering, dismemberment, the confiscation of property, the razing of the houses of the delinquents and banishment of their families.[25] In this respect the penalties not only mirrored the deed, as, for instance, with the dismembering of the "oath-finger" in the case of treason (breach of the oath of fealty). Moreover, they aimed at the elimination of the physical and social body of the rebel, i.e. his honour, property, social reputation, family and supporters, and intended to obliterate that the crime – or the revolt – possessed any legitimate reasons or aims. The death penalty could be extended by confiscation of property / real estate, the expulsion of relatives / families as well as the obliteration of the family-name. The punishment of revolt and rebellion aimed at infamy and defamation, and because of the special quality of a political crime – revolt as a public mass-tort or mass-crime – the *damnatio memoriae* achieved a crucial role in penal practice as well as in juristic and legal discourses. In short, a main purpose of punishing political crimes and rebels in a public context was the *damnatio memoriae*: the defamation and obliteration of the revolt, as well as the commemoration of just legal punishment.

From the 16th century onwards we can observe a shift to harsher and more severe punishment of political crimes and revolts in penal law as well as in penal practice. However, this was paralleled by a more flexible application of penalties with regard to the role of a criminal or rebel (ringleader or follower), preliminary actions (conspiracy), the involvement of foreign powers, the actual performance

---

25 On the early modern "theater of punishment" and the penalties in case of political crimes see Richard van Dülmen, *Theater des Schreckens. Gerichtspraxis und Strafrituale in der frühen Neuzeit*, third edition (München 1988); Richard J. Evans, *Rituals of Retribution. Capital punishment in Germany 1600-1987* (Oxford 1996); Ingraham, political crime, 39-59; Strasser, Aufstand, 232-264.

and the use of violence etc. In this respect, punishment was executed as a public ritual and possessed a highly symbolic communicative function. Especially the public application of capital punishment obtained an exemplary and symbolic function with regard to ringleaders, conspirators and seducers, conveying retaliation, deterrence and general prevention as its main intentions (*Strafzwecke*), particularly with regard to the public, potential rebels and actual followers. The latter – the followers and those seduced – were often merely punished leniently or even pardoned if they renounced the "rebellion" and acknowledged the authorities. In using such strategies of flexible punishment, the state could communicate the message that it had the power to re-establish the rightful order and that it responded with equitable and just punishment to political crimes and revolts within a legal framework.

However, the punishment of political crimes, revolts and rebels was characterised by ambiguities and problems, especially as concerns collectiveness and the role of the public, for both punishment as well as revolt depended on collectiveness and publicity. Concerning the problem of collectiveness, mass-crime and the punishment of rebels, it was often hard to distinguish between the ringleaders and the seduced in legal categories and to mete out proper punishment. Moreover, the public execution of ringleaders would mean that the vast majority of followers, who were only leniently punished, could or could be forced to watch at least to deter or "convert" (convince) them. But assembling a larger crowd in the theatre of public punishment could cause further tumult, as it provided the rebel with the last opportunity to speak to an audience, or it could help make the rebel leaders martyrs. In this regard, public punishment could augment the symbolic public dimension of a revolt and help communicate or memorise the "political" message or even the "just causes" of a revolt to followers or the public. Furthermore, political crimes and revolts aroused the curiosity of the public and therefore obtained a growing importance as a prominent topic in popular media. Broadsheets, newspapers, books and collections reported and depicted revolts and political crimes following commercial intentions, but also communicating and influencing a peculiar image of such occurrences.

The authorities themselves also made use of the public, enhancing the legal responses to revolts and public punishment by using additional public rituals and media to communicate and co-memorise the just punishment of revolts. Sometimes public memorials, like the pillar of shame (*Schandsäule*) in the case of the Fettmilch-revolt in Frankfurt, were erected. In the 17th and 18th centuries, states and officials issued declarations, laws, collections of court records, as well as semi-official reports, pamphlets and broadsheets which communicated and justified the legal responses to revolts and political crimes. In responding to political crimes or revolts, the authorities developed a distinct media policy, controlling public media and printings via censorship on the one hand, but, moreover, also communicating their view of political dissent and order, effectively transmitting their image of just legal responses to political crimes and revolts. Because revolts implied a public challenge of the order, the state was not only dependent on symbolic public penal justice, but had to legitimate its reactions via different popular media. The suppression of a revolt and the punishment of the rebels had to be communicated to the public as a just reaction – and was supposed to be preserved in public memory as a means of re-establishing the order and the legitimate system of rule. On the other hand, the challenge of the revolt as well as the rebels needed to be defamed and possibly obliterated from public memory. Especially the illustrated broadsheets reflect these ambivalent intentions and the problem of the opinion leadership and interpretation – *Deutungsherrschaft* and *Sinndeutung* – of revolts as political crimes.

IMAGES IN ILLUSTRATED BROADSHEETS

Illustrated broadsheets with their typical "comic-strip"-like combination of illustrations and text on one sheet emerged as a new type of mass-media in the first half of the 16th century. They were produced by professional "printing shops", which were normally located in an imperial city, often manufacturing 1-2000 copies of a single broadsheet. Authors and painters / engravers are often unknown or identical with the printer. Sold at more or less low prices, they were distributed widely. Though the rate of alphabetisation was very low, they reached a broader public because everyone could read the illustrations, and in addition, literate consumers and professional distributors read them to a wider public, for example in public houses, places or at festivities. The illustrations played a prominent role: often one to six large-sized pictures were placed in the centre or upper range of the sheet, telling a basic story which everybody was able to understand. Even if only one picture was used, it sometimes contained different illustrations (picture in picture) telling a story. Many broadsheets used a bold headline with typical key-words and basic information (locations, date, involved persons) on the crime / revolt and the legal reactions. For instance a broadsheet dealing with the execution of the "rebellious" Bohemian nobles in 1621 was titled: *Extract auß Prag. Warhafftige Zeitung/ welcher gestalt auff der Röm. Keys. Maj. gnädigsten befelch/ die Böhemischen Rebellen/ von Grafen/ Herrn Ritter: und Burgerstandts Personen/ auff einer am Altstätter Ring auffgerichten/ und mit schwartzem Tuch uberzognen Bühnen/ den 21. Junij dises schwebenden 1621. Jahrs zu Prag/ Iustificirt und hingericht worden* (Fig. 2).[26]

---

26 Reprinted in: Harms, Flugblätter, Vol. II, 306; Paas, Broadsheet, Vol. 3, 362.

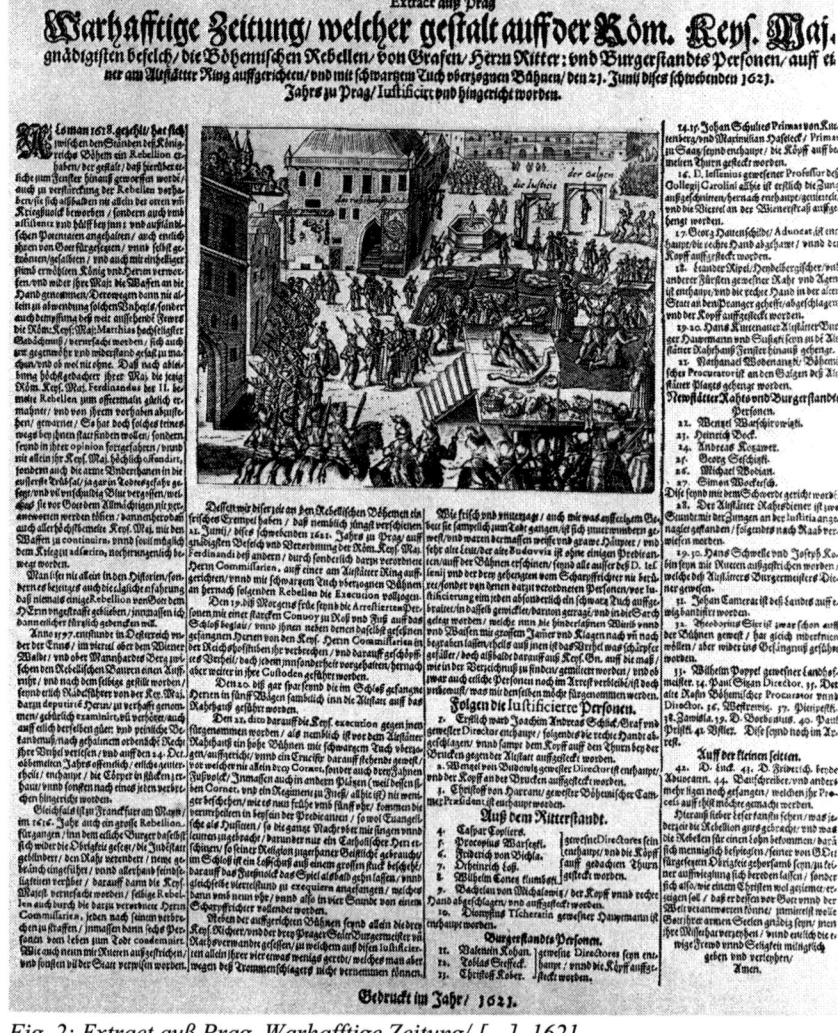

Fig. 2: Extract auß Prag. Warhafftige Zeitung/ [...], 1621

Attributes like "true" and "newspaper" gave them an objective and official complexion, thus augmenting the official appeal of the broadsheet. Besides the difficult problem of discerning the "real" author, the contents and messages are clearly influenced by the interests of the authorities who could exercise control via censorship, or directly commissioned the printing. However, topics, messages, images and appeal were not only influenced by state but also by commercial interests and the curiosity or communicative needs (*Kommunikationsbedürfnisse*) of their consumers. Accordingly, besides religious and political "propaganda" (in the Reformation or the Thirty-Years War) the broadsheets covered increasingly popular topics such as "marvels", catastrophes, wars, news and crimes from all over Europe.[27]

Among the common topics of early modern illustrated broadsheets, which were produced in the Holy Roman Empire (and therefore written in German), crime and punishment – especially serious ones – obtained a considerable proportion of 10 to 15 percent with a certain continuity during the early modern period.[28] One third of them can be classified as political crimes or crimes with an explicit political context: treason, conspiracy, assassination, regicide, and revolts; on the whole, 27 political crimes are depicted in 99 broadsheets (see figure 1), many of them connected with revolt, riot, upheaval or rebellion. With regard to their legal representation and the elements of political crimes, all types of revolts are covered: peasants' revolts, communal upheaval and rebellions of the elites / nobility, albeit the latter ones seemed to be over-represented in comparison with their actual emergency in early modern Europe. Though the broadsheets analysed were produced and mainly distributed in the Holy Roman Empire, they dealt with revolts and political crimes from different countries or regions: the Netherlands, the Swiss Confederation, France, Hungary, Russia and the Ottoman Empire; many of these events possessed a certain public significance and a "European" dimension.

The texts as well as the illustrations mainly focus on the reactions of the state or the authorities and on the public punishment of the criminals / rebels. The actual performance of a revolt or the actions of the rebels are seldom depicted and only sometimes described. Violent actions of the masses ("the revolt itself") are displayed only in the case of the Women's-riot in Delft 1614 (Republic of Netherlands), the Fettmilch-riot in Frankfurt (1612-1616), the peasants' revolt in Austria 1626, the assassination of the *Bürgermeister* of Liège in 1637, and the riot in which the De Witt Brothers were executed as traitors (or lynched). One broadsheet dealing with the Swiss peasants' revolt in 1653 depicts solely the clubs and bludgeons of the rebels, thus representing the violent image of the revolt as well as symbolising the savageness and backwardness of the rebels, who were using

---

27 Incidentally it is not possible to give a more comprehensive analyses on early modern broadsheets as mass-media; compare instead: Kunzle, Early Comic Strip; Michael Schilling, *Bildpublizistik der frühen Neuzeit. Aufgaben und Leistungen des illustrierten Flugblatts in Deutschland bis um 1700* (Tübingen 1990); Kristina Pfarr, *Die Neue Zeitung. Empirische Untersuchung eines Informationsmediums der frühen Neuzeit unter besonderer Berücksichtigung von Gewaltdarstellungen* (Mainz 1994).

28 For a comprehensive analyses see: Härter, Criminalbildergeschichten.

only archaic weapons.²⁹ Only a few broadsheets illustrate the combat between armed rebel groups and military forces like, for example, the Austrian peasants' revolt in 1626 (this however only in the background and using mockery), thus depicting and referring to the military suppression of revolt. Although this happened to be a frequent reaction of the early modern authorities to revolts, the image of military suppression – for instance dominating the few pictures of the German Peasants' War – was superseded in the illustrated broadsheets by the image of crime and punishment within the legal space of the criminal justice system. In this respect, the development of the illustrated broadsheets as an early modern mass media reflected the legal differentiation and representation of revolts as political crimes by using crucial elements of the conceptualisation of revolts as crimes as well as the punishment of rebels. The following examples will verify this in more detail.

COMMUNAL REVOLTS: 1612-1616

Though the production as well as the readership of broadsheets was located mainly in towns and cities, which were often confronted with social unrest, protest, and upheaval, only a few illustrated broadsheets dealt with communal revolts. One prominent example that had a considerable political and public impact in the Holy Roman Empire was the so called Fettmilch-revolt (or riot / uprising) in the imperial city of Frankfurt am Main on the eve of the Thirty-Years War, starting in 1612 and ending with the punishment of the rebels in 1616.³⁰ In many respects the Fettmilch-revolt provides an outstanding, albeit typical example of an early modern urban uprising, distinctive legal responses of the involved authorities – especially the emperor of the Holy Roman Empire – and a broad resonance in the print-media. This ranged from official statements and documents to semi-official pamphlets, reports, and popular broadsheets, spreading the news in the whole of the Old Empire, as well as in other European countries like, for instance, France: "there was

---

29 Andreas Suter, *Der schweizerische Bauernkrieg von 1653. Politische Sozialgeschichte - Sozialgeschichte eines politischen Ereignisses* (Tübingen 1997), 155 f.
30 On these events see: Christopher R. Friedrichs, "Politics or Pogrom? The Fettmilch Uprising in German and Jewish History", *Central European History* 2 (1986), 186-228; Matthias Meyn, *Die Reichsstadt Frankfurt vor dem Bürgeraufstand von 1612 bis 1614. Struktur u. Krise* (Frankfurt am Main 1980); Rivka Ulmer (ed.), *Turmoil, trauma, and triumph. The Fettmilch uprising in Frankfurt am Main (1612 - 1616) according to the Megillas Vintz: a critical edition of the Yiddish and Hebrew text including an English translation* (Frankfurt am Main et al. 2001).

certainly an appetite for news about Frankfurt that extended far beyond the city itself", emphasises Christopher R. Friedrichs.[31]

The revolt broke out in 1612 because a large group of citizens (members of the guilds, craftsmen and merchants) was disaffected with the rule of the patrician families, the council's administration, high taxes, the handling of the city's privileges and especially with the presence of the large Jewish community. A committee was formed, complaints and supplications were submitted to the emperor and the city council. An imperial commission tried to mediate between the conflict parties, and eventually, a compromise settlement was negotiated but failed. In 1614, the upheaval took a turn to violent revolt with an attack on the city hall, the forced resignation of the magistrates and the establishment of a new council as well as the plundering of the Jewish ghetto and the violent expulsion of the Jews carried out by a group of citizens led, amongst others, by Vincenz Fettmilch, all of them craftsmen and merchants. The revolt was not only "simultaneously anti-Jewish and anti-patrician in character",[32] but also affected the emperor, who was not only formally the *Stadtherr* of Frankfurt but also the protector and legal guarantor of the Jews (or their imperial privileges). From this perspective, the basically urban revolt infringed the legal system of the Old Reich: the so called *Reichsverfassung*. The emperor reacted immediately, the imperial aulic court (*Reichshofrat*) declared the *Reichsacht* (imperial ban) on the rebels, and troops were mobilised, but it was the citizens themselves who re-established the old council, arrested Fettmilch and his comrades and handed them over to the imperial commission. The commission, on behalf of the emperor and the imperial aulic court, held an inquisitorial trial that ended with verdicts against seven ringleaders and 31 of their associates. They were found guilty for committing a *crimen laesae maiestatis* against the emperor as well as committing sedition, treason and conspiracy with regard to the city council and the Jews; the ringleaders were sentenced to death, their families and associates to flogging and banishment.

The Fettmilch-revolt evoked a strong echo in the contemporary print media, with the involved groups also making use of popular media themselves.[33] The

---

31 Friedrichs, Fettmilch Uprising, 195; see also the comprehensive survey and analyses by Würgler, Revolts in Print.
32 Friedrichs, Fettmilch Uprising, 188.
33 Robert Brandt and Olaf Cunitz (ed.), *Der Fettmilch-Aufstand. Bürgerunruhen und Judenfeindschaft in Frankfurt am Main 1612–1616*. Ein Ausstellungsprojekt des Historischen Museums Frankfurt in Zusammenarbeit mit dem Historischen Seminar der Johann-Wolfgang-Goethe-Universität (Frankfurt am Main 1996); Bernd Herbert Wanger, *Kaiserwahl und Krönung im Frankfurt des 17. Jahrhunderts. Darstellung anhand der zeitge-*

rebels printed pamphlets, supplications and petitions, and the authorities distributed printings of the imperial ban, their decrees and mandates, court records and the final verdict.[34] Besides some newspaper reports several popular relations and pamphlets were printed between 1614 and 1617, some of them illustrated and explicitly naming the events a revolt or rebellion, like: *Gründlicher Bericht Von dem Aufflauff unnd Tumult/* [...]; *Newe Zeittung: Warhafftiger Bericht/ was massen die Judengassen* [...] *von den Handwercks Gesellen angeloffen/ gestürmet/ geplündert*; or the Cursus Francofurdianus: *Außbruch der Franckfurtischen Rebellion/ und Anfang der newen Empörung daselbst* [...]; and the *Appendix* [...] *Darinnen vermeldet wird, der Anfang und Verlauff der Empörung zu Franckfurt am Meyen* as well as the comprehensive *Diarium Historicum: Darinnen* [...] *gefährlicher auffstandt/ und das schwürige Unwesen* [...] *verzeichnet ist*, published in two editions in 1615 and 1617.[35]

---

nössischen Bild- und Schriftquellen und unter besonderer Berücksichtigung der Erhebung des Jahres 1612 (Frankfurt am Main 1994); Würgler, Revolts in Print.

34 Copia Der Kays. Achts-Erklärung/ so in deß heiligen Reichs Statt Franckfurt am Mayn/ Mittwochs den 28. Septembr. Anno 1614. Durch einen Kays. Herolden/ wider darin benandte Personen publicirt worden (Frankfurt am Main 1615); Peinlich Urtheil wider die Franckfurtische Rebellen Vincenz Fettmilchen, Conrad Gerngroß, Conrad Schoppen und Consorten ergangen, exequirt und vollstreckt (Frankfurt am Main 1616).

35 Gründlicher Bericht Von dem Aufflauff unnd Tumult/ welcher in der Stadt Franckfurt am Mayn geschehen/ und sich darinnen begeben und zugetragen hat. Wie allda die ledige Bursch oder HandwercksGesellen [...] die Jüdengasse [...] angelauffen/ mit Gewalt in die Jüdenhäuser gefallen [...] und zum Theil etliche Jüden am Leibe beschädiget worden. Anno 1614 [...] (Frankfurt am Main 1614); Newe Zeitung/ Warhafftiger Bericht auß der Statt Franckfurt am Mayn: was sich mit Bürgern .. auch mit den Juden verlauffen und zugetragen hat wie der Tumult und Lermen angangen/ auch wie sie die Juden gestürmet haben [...] (Frankfurt am Main 1614); Cursus Francofurdianus: Außbruch der Franckfurtischen Rebellion/ und Anfang der newen Empörung daselbst. Das ist/ Hochbetrübter zustand der Statt Franckfurt am Mayn/ unnd weiterer Verlauff/ wie/ an wem/ an wie vilen Personen .. das peinliche Urtheil an denselben exequirt unnd volstreckt werden soll [...] (Frankfurt am Main 1616); Appendix, Der Historischen Relativen Gregorij Wintermonats, Darinnen vermeldet wird, der Anfang und Verlauff der Empörung zu Franckfurt am Meyen, Auch wie die Aechter den 28. Februarij dieses 1616 jahrs sind justificirt worden, ordentlich und kürtzlich nackelnander beschrieben [...], (Frankfurt am Main 1616); Diarium Historicum: Darinnen Deß Heyligen Reichs Statt Franckfort an dem Meyn gefährlicher auffstandt/ und das schwürige Unwesen [...] ordentlich verzeichnet ist [...] (Frankfurt am Main 1615 und 1617).

In sheer quantity the illustrated broadsheets outnumbered all other printings; more than 20 different were distributed, covering essential events and stages of the revolt, as well as the responses of the authorities, from the outbreak in 1612, the violent plundering of the Jewish ghetto in 1614, and the severe punishment in 1616. Most of them were produced in Frankfurt itself; however there are also examples of broadsheets printed in Darmstadt and Augsburg. They were distributed all over the Holy Roman Empire; one was even written in Dutch and produced for the Netherlands. At least three broadsheets dealt with the revolt itself, the violent actions and the plundering of the Jewish community, but more than ten covered the punishment of the rebels and therefore focused on the legal reaction to the revolt as a political crime.[36]

One of the first broadsheets appearing in 1614 was the *Zeytung des verlauffs zu Franckfurt am Meyn von der blünderung der Juden Gasse*, produced by the printer and painter Johann Ludwig Schimmel.[37] The two sheets with two large pictures and a rhyming text dealt only with the violent plundering of the Jewish ghetto (the *Judengasse*) and the expulsion of the Jews. The text draws a clear relationship between the Jews and the authorities (emperor and city council), describing them as protectors of the Jews: "*Niemandt dörfft ihn [the Jews] halt ein krumb wort/ Zu reden/ sie lieffen zu der Obrigkeit fort/ Da wahren sie beschützt als fromme Kindt/ Daher der Neyder viel kommen sindt.*" In this respect, the Jews were blamed as a cause of the revolt and the violence against them received the character of a rebellious political action aiming at the authorities. In the first sheet the plundering is described as a violent fight between burghers and Jews, the latter defending their houses and the *Judengasse* and wounding one of the aggressors. The attacking burghers are illustrated as a tumultuous, rioting group, using weapons and firebrands as well as carrying away several objects and goods.

---

36 Some of them reprinted in: Daniel Dornhofer, "Matthias 1612-1616: Vertreibung und Rückkehr", in *Die Kaisermacher. Frankfurt am Main und die Goldene Bulle 1356-1806. Katalog*, ed. Evelyn Brockhoff et al. (Frankfurt am Main 2006), 476-499, 490-492; Brandt/Cunitz, Fettmilch-Aufstand. There are at least 23 broadsheets reported, however, I did not have the opportunity to examine them all and therefore restricted the analyses to 13 different broadsheets.

37 Zeytung des verlauffs zu Franckfurt am Meyn von der blünderung der Juden Gasse, geschehen im Jahr Christi 1614 den XXII. und XXIII. Augustus (Frankfurt am Main 1614).

Fig. 3 and 4: Zeytung des verlauffs zu Franckfurt am Meyn von der blünderung der Juden Gasse

The second illustration shows a different scenario: armed men controlling the flight and expulsion of the Jews, who are leaving the city by boat; some burghers are watching from a bridge and their windows. Order is re-established – underlines the text – because the soldiers of the imperial commission as well as many burghers themselves kept the rebels at bay, calmed them down and resolved the cause for violent escalation of the revolt by expelling the Jews in an orderly manner. However, the broadsheet depicts and names grief and harm of the Jews and claims that some burghers gave them shelter and protection.

A second broadsheet from 1615 – depicting and describing 16 stages of the revolt in 12 pictures and additional text – consolidated the image that the violent revolt was the fault of a minority of rioting burghers – the *gemeine Pöbel* (mob) – lead by a few ringleaders, whereas the majority made use of mass meetings and complaints only to negotiate a new constitutional arrangement. Its failure, the unruly *Pöbel* and the agitation of the ringleaders led to violence and the plundering of the Jews, but also to a new government via customary public vow. After the publication of the imperial ban and several mandates, one of the ringleaders as well as the majority of the burghers realised their error, arrested the ringleaders and handed them over to the imperial commission. This broadside also emphasises that the burghers re-established order together with the authorities, which had been endangered by an opposition under the control of power-hungry leaders making use of mass meetings and stinging an unruly mob, which then resulted in an illegitimate revolt. Though there is no decisive statement that the events altogether constituted a serious political crime, the criminal elements – mass-tort, violence, conjuration, disregard of imperial authority – are present and depicted.[38]

In 1616, after the verdict and the actual punishment of the rebels, all following broadsides are dominated by the image of the Fettmilch-upheaval as a criminal revolt and a political crime. Every woodcut depicts nearly the same scenario: the punishment of the rebels and their ringleaders, using a large picture showing the different penalties and additional scenes. The one of Johann Ludwig Schimmel (Fig. 5) comprises crucial elements and icons symbolising the political crime, the punishment and the response of the authorities to the revolt, also to be found in other broadsides.[39]

---

38 Wahrhafftige vnd eigendliche Abbildung deß gantzen Handels/ so sich in der Keyserl. Reichstatt Franckfurt am Mayn vnd Sachsenhausen zwischen dem Raht vnd Bürgerschafft von 1612. biß ins 1615. Jahr zugetragen vnd verlauffen hat (Frankfurt am Main 1615).

39 Kurtzer Abriß vnd Bericht der Keyserlichen Execution vnd Verfahrung mit den Aechtern/ vnd dero anhenger/ sampt einführung der Jüdenschafft [...] (Frankfurt am Main 1616).

Fig. 5: Kurtzer Abriß vnd Bericht der Keyserlichen Execution vnd Verfahrung

In the middle of the picture we see the scaffold set up at the market place of Frankfurt cordoned by heavily armed soldiers and railings with posts showing the imperial eagle: The punishment of the rebels is taking place within the separated legal space of the empire, where only the delinquent, the executioner, the judge and several officials (representative of the imperial commission) and the soldiers appear. The city council and the representatives of the guilds on the two platforms in the centre of the background as well as the burghers of Frankfurt surround that space, watching from the outside. The executioner decapitates one of the delinquents, the recently severed finger of whom can be seen in front of him. The dismembering of the finger – the *Schwurfinger* – clearly points at the illegal conjuration or conspiracy in terms of penal law. Two more decapitated corpses of ringleaders are positioned on the scaffold. In the background on the left, outside the city three gallows are set up; one with a corpse hanged at the feet and another exposing part of quartered corpse. Both death penalties – reverse hanging and quartering – are typical of the aggravated and infamous punishment of treason. In the case of the Fettmilch-revolt, the four main ringleaders were dismembered, decapitated, quartered and parts of their corpses were exposed at the gallows outside of town. Furthermore, their heads were impaled and exposed on the gate tower on the Rhine side, which was the main entrance to the city, depicted with the four decapitated heads and a super-sized imperial eagle in the left background of the broadsheet. The symbolic implication, communicated and enhanced by the broadsheet, is quite obvious: The ringleaders and the revolt are to be commemorated as a serious political crime. This was emphasized by the total demolition of Fettmilch's house shown in the foreground of the illustration on the right and the infamous shaving, flogging and banning of his family depicted in the background on the right: the total social disintegration and exclusion of the main ringleader – comprising his family, his name, his house – for eternal memory (*"zum ewigen Gedächtnuß"*). Apart from the ringleaders and their families, the punishment of other rebels (17 associates and followers) by flogging and banning, shown in the background on the left, seems almost lenient. In addition to the punishment of the rebels, the restitution of the legal and imperial order is represented by the re-entry of the Jewish community in form of a procession, just passing the scaffold.

All other broadsides dealing with the punishment of the rebels depict the same scene and make use of similar iconic elements: scaffold, armed soldiers, imperial posts and eagle, the dismembering of the *Schwurfinger* and decapitation, the tower with the heads, the gallows with the quartered corpses, whipping and expulsion, the demolition of the house, the re-entry of the Jews etc. However, there are slight differences. The *Wahre und eigentliche Contrafactur der Kayserlichen Execution* printed 1616 in Augsburg by Krebs shows a much larger number of imperial soldiers surrounding the scaffold as well as accompanying and protecting the Jews on their re-entry into the city, in a similar manner to the entry of the emperor and the estates of the Empire (*Reichsstände*) on the occasion of the imperial election in

Frankfurt.[40] Another broadside entitled *Eine gewisse/ warhaffte/ doch trawrig und erbärmliche Newezeittung/ Von dem betrübten Zustandt/ welcher zu Franckfurt am Mayn/ den 9. Martji dß schwebenden 1616. Jahrs geschen,* printed by Balthasar Hoffmann in Darmstadt 1616 (fig. 6), gives a slightly different image and valuation of the revolt.[41] The woodcut shows portraits of the four main ringleaders, albeit depicted as respectable burghers, whereas the demolition of the house is not shown. Their crimes are not explicitly quoted and the revolt is characterised as a quarrel (*Streit*) among the burghers. The delinquents are not presented as ringleaders conducting a revolt against the imperial order but as faithful, remorseful sinners arousing the compassion of the burghers: "*viel leuth hatten groß mitleyden*". In consequence the revolt is characterised rather as a religious upheaval of the Christian *Bürgergemeinschaft* against the Jews who achieved imperial punishment of the Christian sinners with harsh penalties: "*daß soviel unschuldig Christen Blut/ vergossen ist durch der Jüden Muth/ darüber geschen groß Wunderzeichen*". Though the broadsheet did not explicitly raise doubts about imperial punishment, the revolt is presented subtly as a lapse or sin of Christians reacting to the Jews, whereas their punishment remains a divine miracle and the secret of the authorities ("*der Obrigkeit Geheimniß*"). In this respect, the broadside demonstrates that other representations of revolts – in this case religious, anti-Jewish and with certain sympathy for the rebels – existed which at least could help to commemorate the revolt not as a political crime, but as failure and sin which could be exculpated. Nevertheless, the *Darmstädter* broadside constitutes an exception, possibly influenced by one of the ringleaders, Konrad Gerngroß, who prior to his arrest had fled to nearby Darmstadt, the residence of the Lutheran Landgraviate of Hesse.

---

40 Wahre und eigentliche Contrafactur der Kayserlichen Execution so den 28. Febr. Anno 1616 zu Franckfurt am Mayn an etlichen Aechtern und Handwercksgesellen volnzogen werden (Augsburg 1616).

41 Eine gewisse/ warhaffte/ doch trawrig und erbärmliche Newezeittung/ Von dem betrübten Zustandt/ welcher zu Franckfurt am Mayn/ den 9. Martji dß schwebenden 1616. Jahrs geschen [...] (Darmstadt 1616).

Fig. 6: *Eine gewisse/ warhaffte/ doch trawrig und erbärmliche Newezeittung*

On the whole, the public interpretation and popular memorisation of the revolt was dominated by the authoritarian view of the imperial punishment of a political crime to be commemorated through the erecting of a *Schandsäule* – a "pillar of shame" or "infamy monument" – at the devastated place of Fettmilch's house. Two more illustrated broadsheets, printed in Frankfurt by Conrad Corthoys and again Johann

Ludwig Schimmel, depict the *Schandsäule*; one in combination with the tower showing the impaled heads and the imperial eagle, as well as depicting the burghers reading the engraved message (in German and Latin): *"Sempiternae Rebellionis memoriae"* (fig. 7).

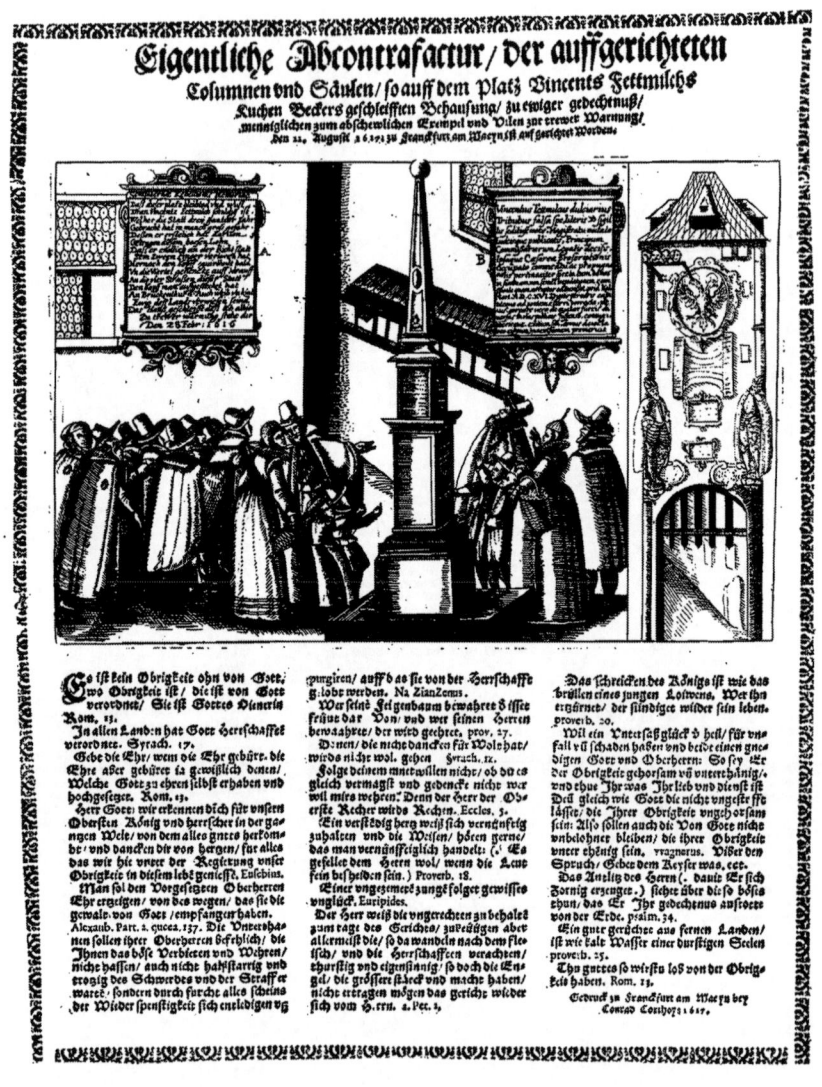

Fig. 7: Eigentliche Abcontrafactur/ der auffgerichteten Columnen vnd Säulen [...].

Both broadsides state deterrence and eternal memorisation as the purposes of the punishment and the pillar: *"zur ewigen Gedächtnuß der Rebellion und jedermann zur höchsten Warnung"* – *"zu ewiger gedechtnuß/ menniglichen zum abschewlichen Exempel/ und Vilen zur trewer Warnung".*[42]

The actual punishment as well as its representation in the broadsheets conveys a distinct image of an urban revolt as the political crimes of *crimen laesae maiestatis*, treason, sedition and conspiracy, instigated through the conspiratorial machinations of the ringleaders. Although the image of revolt in the first broadsides was formed by the tumultuous actions of the mob and the violent plundering of the Jewish ghetto, the later and more numerous broadsheets represented the revolt mainly as a crime of ringleaders against the emperor and the legal order of the empire. This, in turn, reacts and punishes the ringleaders as *"Ächter"* (defiers) of the secular and divine order, which is re-established not only through imperial punishment of the ringleaders, but also by the renewal of the imperial legal protection of the Jews.

REBELLIONS OF THE NOBILITY

Images and the elements of the punishment of the Fettmilch-revolt are to be found in many other broadsheets covering not only urban, but also rural revolts and rebellions of the nobility. The upheaval or resistance of the Bohemian nobility against the Emperor is covered in eight illustrated pamphlets, six of them dealing only with the punishment of the nobles in Prague in 1621. Though the revolt had strong religious motivations, the nobles as well as some of their burgher-associates were punished as rebels for the political crime of *crimen laesae maiestatis*, and the woodcuts use the corresponding iconographic elements: the scaffold surrounded by the soldiers and a crowd of nobles and citizens watching the punishment of more than 40 delinquents, many of them dismembered (at the hand), decapitated, quartered and hanged, with some followers and relatives flogged and expelled. The heads of the twelve ringleaders are impaled at the gate tower and the quartered corpses are exposed outside of town on pillars and gallows. The *Eigentliche Abbildung deß Process der Pragerischen Execution* adds some pictures showing the

---

42 Eigentliche Abcontrafactur/ der auffgerichteten Columnen vnd Säulen: so auff dem Platz Vincents Fettmilchs Kuchen Beckers geschleifften Behausung/ zu ewiger gedechtnuß/ menniglichen zum abschewlichen Exempel/ und Vilen zur trewer Warnung/ den 22. Augusti 1617 zu Franckfurt am Mayn ist aufgerichtet Worden, Conrad Corthoys (Frankfurt am Main 1617); Eigentliche Abconterfyung Vincentz Fetmilch Kuchen-beckers Seullen: Welche auffgericht ist worden/ den 22. Augusti. im Jahr 1617. Auff den Platz seiner geschleifften Behausung/ zur ewigen Gedächtnuß der Rebellion und jedermann zur höchsten Warnung für Augen gestelt, Johann Ludwig Schimmel (Frankfurt am Main 1617).

trial and the families begging for pardon.[43] The message is clearly depicted and stated: *"Hieraus liebe Leser kanstu sehen/ was jederzeit die Rebellion guts gebracht/ und was die Rebellen für einen Lohn bekommen/ daran sich menniglich bespiegeln/ seiner von Gott fürgesetzten Obrigkeit gehorsamb seyn/ zu keiner auffwiegelung sich bereden lassen"*, as the *Extract auß Prag. Wahrhafftige Zeitung* concludes, referring also to the Austrian peasants' revolt in 1597 and the Fettmilch-upheaval.[44]

Using similar arguments, the broadside *Eigentliche und warhaffte/ und nach dem Leben gestalte Bildnussen/ Der ehedessen höchstberühmten Ungarischen Grafen/ Nunmehro aber wegen abscheulicher Conspiration wieder Unser Allerdurchlauchtigstes und Unüberwindlichstes Römisches Oberhaupt Justificirten Rebellen/ Nadasti/ Serini/ Franchipani und Bonis* justifies the punishment of the magnate-rebels in 1671: *"Wer sich Gottes Ordnung hier frevelmütig wiedersetzet/ Wieder den Justitia ihr Schwerd ganz rechtmässig wetzet."* It belongs to no less than seven broadsheets and illustrated pamphlets dealing with the rebellion of the Hungarian nobility (or magnates) in 1670/71. In the second half of the 17th century we can observe a slight increase in the popular media dealing with revolts. Broadsides on pamphlets (sometimes illustrated) appeared covering the Swiss Peasants' War in 1653,[45] the rebellion of the Fronde in France, the Rebellion of Stenka Razin in Russia in 1671,[46] the rebellion of the Hungarian magnates in 1671, followed by the Kurucs- or Tököly-revolt in the 1670s and 1680s, the riot in Grafenhaag 1672, in which an organised mob hanged (or executed) the de Witt brothers at a "shame-gallows" for alleged conspiracy and treason, the peasants

---

43 Eigentliche Abbildung der Pragerischen Execution Welcher massen uff befelch der Röm: Key: Maytt: die hieunden beschriebenen, Grafen, Herrn, Ritter und Burgerstadts Personen den 11. (21.) Junii diß 1621 Jahrs zu Praag Iustificirt, und hingericht worden [1621].
44 Extract auß Prag. Wahrhafftige Zeitung.
45 Suter, schweizerische Bauernkrieg, 155 f., 313.
46 Umständlicher Bericht Von deß grossen Rebellen wider Moßkau Stephan Razins Hinrichtung. Geschehen in der Stadt Moßkau den 6. Junij st. v. 1671; Kurtze doch Wahrhafftige Erzehlung von der Blutigen Rebellion in der Moscau/ Angerichtet durch den großen Verräther und Betrieger Stenko Razin Donischen Cosaken: Wie er wider seinen Käyser [...] Alexe Michaloiwits [...] Anno 1667. auffgestanden/ Und seine Rebellion continuiret biß Anno 1671./ da er gefangen/ und [...] am 2. Iunii in die Stadt Moscau eingeführet und am 6. drauff offentlich allda gerichtet worden. Enthält außerdem: Copie Des Urtheils/ Welchs Dem Stenko Rasin auff dem Richt-Platze in der Stadt Moscau Am 6. Junii Anno M.DC.LXXI. Vorgelesen worden, Emden 1671.

upheaval in Brussels 1678,[47] the rebellion of the Streltsy in Moscow 1682,[48] the tumultuous assassination of Vizier Cara Mustapha in1683[49] as well as the urban upheavals in Bremen in 1654, in Cologne in 1686 and in Hamburg in 1687.[50] Moreover, some comprehensive popular books on revolts and treason in European countries were published, such as, for instance, the Continuirende Rebellion in 1650, dealing with France and England, or the *Europäische- Schand- un[d] Laster-*

---

47 Unvermutheter Brüsselischer Land- und Bauern-Auffstand: Mit Eigentlichen Bericht derselben Furiösen Eiffers/ samt des Auffstands Ursach/ hitzigen Verlauff/ und vernünfftigen Wieder-Begütigung/ Vermittelst Des Herrn Herzogs von Villa Hermosa Excellenz, Printzen Vaudemont, und anderer Herren hochreifflichen Zusprechens. Herausgegeben Vom 17. (27.) Junij, 1678.

48 Eigentlicher Bericht wegen des in der Stadt Moßkau Am 15/16 und 17 May Anno 1682 entstandenen greulichen Tumults/ und grausahmen Massacre. Wie auch; Der augenscheinlichen Lebens-Gefahr/ in welche der daselbst befindliche Könichliche Dänische Resident/ mittelst dieses Auffstandes/ verfallen [...] (Hamburg 1682).

49 Eigentliche Abbildung derjenigen Execution, welche aus Befehl des jetzt-regierenden Türkischen Kaysers, Mahumets des Vierdten, an dessen Groß-Vezier Kara Mustapha [et]c. In diesem zu End-lauffenden 1683. Jahr ausgeübet worden, 1683; Wahrhaffte Beschreibung/ Was sich seith der entstandenen grossen Empöhrung im Türckischen Läger und zu Constantinopel vom 7. Octobr. biß 2. Decembr. 1687. zugetragen (Regensburg 1688).

50 Wahrer/ kurtzer Bericht/ Deß in der Stadt Bremen gefärlich entstandenen Tumults und Auffstandes/ Am 6. Septembr. Anno 1654 [...], 1654; Iusta Divae Themidis Ultio, Oder: Gerechte Rach-Vergeltung der H. Gerechtigkeit und wohl-verdiente Belohnung/ Bürgerlicher Untreu und Aufruhrs/ wieder die vorgesetzte hohe Obrigkeit: Zu einem abscheulichen Bey-Spiel/ und billichen Straff-Exempel/ höchst-vermeidlichen Ungehorsams/ und auffständlicher Empörung/ verstockter und Halsstarriger Gemüther. Vorgestellet An den Cölnischen Executions-Proceß/ Dreyer boßhafftigen Aufwickler und Ertz-Rebellen. Nicolaui Gulichs. Abraham Saxens/ und Anthonii Mesthovii. Wie solche .. jüngsthin zu Mühlheim den 23 Februarii/ dieses mit Gott tragenden 1686sten Jahrs/ exemplarisch abgestrafft und Executirt worden, 1686; Wahrhafftig-Abbildender Auffruhr- und Empörungs-Spiegel: In welchem Alle unruhige und verwegene Köpffe gahr leicht und eigentlich zu erkennen seyn/ beydes Ihnen selbst zu nöthiger Betrachtung/ und allen [...] bedenckenden Gemüthern zu nützlichem Gebrauche vorgestellet. Worbey Eine kurtze Erzehlung dessen/ was in Hamburg etliche Jahre hero durch die beyde hingerichtete Haupt-Redelsführer/ Jastram und Schnitger/ verübet worden (Friedberg 1687).

Cronic/ Der vornembsten Stadt- un[d] Lands-Verräthern/ Rebellen/ Meer-Räubern/ Ertz-Mördern/ Mord-brennern/ Falsch-Müntzern/ Gottslesterern in 1674.[51]

Many broadsheets focussed on rebellions and conspiracies of the nobility, and most notably the Magnate-revolt of 1670/71 evoked a strong echo in the popular print media all across Europe.[52] Newspapers reported, reports and treatises on the revolt and the trial appeared, court records and the verdict on the rebels were printed, and several illustrated broadsheets covered the revolt. This media-attention had different reasons: first of all it was an anti-Habsburg revolt against the Emperor Leopold I, led by the prominent Hungarian and Croatian nobles Zrinyi, Frangepan, Nádasdy, Rákóczi, Bonis, Nagy and Tattenbach, five of whom were sentenced to capital punishment. Secondly, the "confessional", "national" and "international" elements, the involvement of France and the Ottoman Empire, the motives of the rebels and its controversial character – a treacherous conspiracy and rebellion or a legal uprising and legitimate resistance-movement – did not only arouse the interest of the European public, but urged the involved parties to make use of public media to demonstrate their positions and legitimate their actions. In this regard, the illustrated broadsheets covering the magnate-revolt are an appropriate example of the public contention on the media representation of revolts, which again was dominated by the responses of the authorities, the trial and the punishment of the rebels and the interpretation of the revolt as a political crime. Leaving single newspaper reports aside, neither the actual preparation of the upheaval nor the short-time outbreak of the armed rebellion in 1670 was covered in popular media. The illustrated broadsheets as well as other popular and the semi-official

---

51 Continuirende Rebellion: Das ist: Gründlicher Bericht/ und kurtze Außführung/ so wol der anjetzo newen in Franckreich erweckten Rebellion/ deren Ursachen/ und nochwährenden Mißverstände/ zwischen etlich Parlamenten/ und dem Cardinal Mazarini: Erster/ und Ander Theil. Als auch deß Newen Parlaments in Engelland/ nach Hinrichtung ihres Königs [...], 1650; Johann Georg Schiele, Europäische- Schand- un[d] Laster-Cronic/ Der vornembsten Stadt- un[d] Lands-Verräthern/ Rebellen/ Meer-Räubern/ Ertz-Mördern/ Mord-brennern/ Falsch-Müntzern/ Gottslesterern/ [et]c. wie auch der Weltbeschräiten Schandhuren/ Zauberin/ etc. etc. Sampt Deroselben Gerichtlich ergangenem Urtel und Proceß. Vom Jahr 1614. biß 1674 (Ulm 1674).

52 On the revolt and the trial see: Franz Theuer, *Tragödie der Magnaten. Die Verschwörung von Muray bis zum Ödenburger Reichstag. Ein historischer Bericht* (Wien u.a. 1979), especially 258-337; Jean Bérenger, "La conjuration des Magnats hongrois (1664-1671)", in *Complots et conjurations, ed.* Bercé and Fasano Guarini, 317-345. On the echo in popular media and the Habsburgian media policy: Jutta Schumann, *Die andere Sonne: Kaiserbild und Medienstrategien im Zeitalter Leopolds I.* (Berlin 2003), 118-128.

publications rather focused on the trial, the punishment and the rebels as "individuals". At least five broadsheets and some illustrations in the relations display large individual portraits of the rebels: The *Eigentliche und warhaffte/ und nach dem Leben gestalte Bildnussen/ Der ehedessen höchstberühmten Ungarischen Grafen/ Nunmehro aber wegen abscheulicher Conspiration wieder Unser Allerdurchlauchtigstes und Unüberwindlichstes Römisches Oberhaupt Justificirten Rebellen* showed the four main leaders, counts Nadasti, Serini, Frangipani and Bonis. The *Warhaffte Contrafactur und Abbildung, deren ehmals Vornehm-Berühmten drey Ungarischen Grafen/ Nachmals aber an Ihrer Römischen Kays erl. Mayst. höchst-vergriffenen Rebellen, Nadasti, Serini und Frangipani, mit beygefügter ausführlicher Beschreibung, was massen selbige, dem billich-ergangenem Urtheil gemäß zur Execution gezogen* as well as the *Eigentliche und warhaffte/ und nach dem Leben gestalte Bildnussen/ Der ehedessen höchstberühmten Ungarischen Grafen/ Nunmehro aber wegen abscheulicher Conspiration wieder Unser Allerdurchlauchtigstes und Unüberwindlichstes Römisches Oberhaupt Justificirten Rebellen/ Nadasti/ Serini/ Franchipani und Bonis* (fig. 8) displayed portraits of Nadasti, Frangipani and Serini.[53] In addition, three more broadsheets or illustrations were published, displaying only Serini and Frangipani or single portraits of Nadasti and Count Tattenbach. Beyond this, all broadsheets show smaller illustrations of the capital punishment of each of the delinquents.[54]

---

53 Warhaffte Contrafactur und Abbildung, deren ehmals Vornehm-Berühmten drey Ungarischen Grafen/ nachmals aber an Ihrer Römischen Kays erl. Mayst. höchst-vergriffenen Rebellen, Nadasti, Serini und Frangipani, mit beygefügter ausführlicher Beschreibung, was massen selbige, dem billich-ergangenem Urtheil gemäß zur Execution gezogen, und den 30. April dieses 1671. Jahrs vom Leben zum Tod gebracht worden [1671]; Eigentliche und warhaffte/ und nach dem Leben gestalte Bildnussen/ Der ehedessen höchstberühmten Ungarischen Grafen/ Nunmehro aber wegen abscheulicher Conspiration wieder Unser Allerdurchlauchtigstes und Unüberwindlichstes Römisches Oberhaupt Justificirten Rebellen/ Nadasti/ Serini/ Franchipani und Bonis, Geschehen im Monat April 1671 [1671].

54 Wahre Abbildung beeder Rebellen Peter Serini und Francisci Frangepan, welche zur Neustadt in Österreich im Zeughaus enthaubtet worden [1671]; Warhaffte Bildnuß Francisci Nadasti welcher wegen Aufrührischen Meineyds in den Rahthaus Zu Wienn enthaubt worden, den 30. April, vormittag zwischen 8. und 9 Uhr im Jahr 1671 [1671]; Eigentliche Conterfactur und Bildniß deß Rebelle Hannß Erasmi gewesenen Grafen von Tättenbach. Welcher im Rahthauß zu Grätz in Steuermarck den 1. Decembris dieses zu End lauffende 1671. Jahrs mit de Schwerdt von Lebe zum Todt gerichtet [...], [1671].

In comparison to former popular images of revolts, we can observe a change in the illustrations: The punishment itself faded into the background and the individual rebels came to the fore, albeit depicted as a conspiratorial group. Especially the broadsheet *Eigentliche und warhaffte/ und nach dem Leben gestalte Bildnussen* and a very similar illustration in the pamphlet *Warhafftige und ausführliche Relation, Wie die Ungarischen Rebellen Zu Wien in Oesterreich [...] Zur verdienten Straffe gezogen worden* (fig. 9) use a characteristic iconic visualisation.[55] The four portraits of the conspirers are entwined by two large dragon-like serpents, assaulting the enthroned imperial eagle, which holds them off at sword-point. The serpents are knotted together by smaller serpents whose tails reach down to the spectators of the punishment. The symbolic meaning is quite clear: The revolt was instigated and performed by the treacherous ringleaders, forming a viperous conspiracy which, on the one hand, was based on the masses (or Hungarian society itself) and, on the other hand, strengthened by foreign powers (France and the Ottoman Empire), symbolised by the smaller serpents. The emperor reacts by utilising the sword of justice, and insofar moves within the ranks of the legal system. To strengthen the legality of the imperial reaction and to answer assumptions of unjust persecution of legitimate opposition and protestant dissidents, the broadsheets contained lengthy remarks on the confessions of the rebels, the verdicts and the execution. Moreover, they recapitulated the conviction of the *"Räthleinführer"* on the ground of *"Crimen laesae Majestatis & perduellionis"*, especially for setting up a *"höchstgefährliche und weitaussehende Conspiration"*, and trying to subjugate Hungary to foreign powers by setting up a treacherous alliance. The texts emphasise that the delinquents voluntarily confessed and regretted their crimes at the public execution, some of them even converting from Calvinism to Catholicism. Thus, the detailed depiction of severe public punishment, which included the delinquents' decapitation, dishonourable hanging, dismemberment of the right hand, the confiscation of their property, the deletion of their titles and the shaming exposition of their corpses, was not only just and equitable, but accepted by them: *"ich habe es sehr wohl verdienet"*, the *Warhaffte Contrafactur und Abbildung* cites Count Zrinyi. Justice, the deterrence of supporters and followers (*"dem Volck zum Abschreck"*) as well as the obliteration of each rebel whose memory was to be utterly destroyed (*"dessen Gedächntnis von der Welt ausgetilget"*) are the clearly stated and depicted authoritarian messages.

---

55 Warhafftige und ausführliche Relation, Wie die Ungarischen Rebellen Zu Wien in Oesterreich/ Als auch Zur Wienischen Neu-Stadt Und zu Preßburg Am 30. Aprilis Anno 1671. Zur verdienten Straffe gezogen worden. Nebst dem Nadastischen/ Serinisch- und Frangypanischen Urtheil, 1671.

Fig. 8: *Eigentliche und warhaffte/ und nach dem Leben gestalte Bildnussen*

Fig. 9: *Frontispiece and title page of the Warhafftige und ausführliche Relation*

Although all broadsheets and most popular media propagated this interpretation of the imperial court in Vienna, the imperial media policy as well as the purposes of the actual punishment partially failed. Some members of the noble families involved continued their opposition and resistance against Habsburg rule, and more revolts such as the Kuruc uprisings were to come, answered again with punishment and covered in corresponding illustrated broadsheets.[56] A few pamphlets (but no illustrated broadside) were published which tried to delegitimise the harsh punishments as the repression of legitimate political opposition and the protestant religion. Moreover, the broadsides and pamphlets of the magnate-revolt were used in Hungary and Croatia to commemorate unjust punishment of "patriotic martyrs". With regard to the European public, the representation of the revolt as the treacherous magnate-conspiracy and a serious political crime was largely dominant.[57]

PEASANTS' REVOLTS AND RESISTANCE IN THE 18TH CENTURY

Authoritarian media policies and the representation of revolts as political crimes also dominated the few illustrated broadsheets dealing with social upheaval in the 18th century, especially in the case of the Bavarian upheaval in 1705/06 and the peasants' revolt of Horea and Kloska in Hungary in 1785. However, these two revolts occurred under specific circumstances, as both of them could also be regarded as "resistance movements" against the "foreign" occupation and domination by the Habsburgs. Concerning early modern peasant's revolts, historians have stressed that after the military repression of the Peasants War in 1525, conflicts were increasingly dealt with within a legal framework and by using legal procedures.[58] The previous remarks have demonstrated that such legal responses also included the further criminalisation of social protest, as well as criminal justice procedures and subsequent punishment against rioting peasants and their ringleaders. In addition, we can observe that in the 18th century, authorities and states alike increasingly used military force in matters of "inner security", the prosecution of criminals (especially bandits and gangs) and the execution of severe penalties. The illustrated broadsheets dealing with crime, punishment and revolt are

---

56 Abbildung, welcher Gestalt der Hungarische Haupt-Rebell Picaii, neben 19 andern seiner Gehülffen, zur wolverdienten Straff gezogen und hingerichtet worden/ zu Arva den 28. Novembr. Anno 1672 [1672].
57 Schumann, Kaiserbild und Medienstrategien, 127-128.
58 Blickle, Criminalization; Schulze, Beobachtungen.

in part representative of these trends, most notably in the pamphlets and broadsides dealing with the Bavarian revolt against the Habsburg occupation in 1705/06.[59] Several illustrations use the familiar iconic programme in depicting capital punishment with quartering and the exposition of the quartered corpses at the gallows, and showing portraits of the ringleader Kraus.[60] Two broadsheets add a new media strategy, enhancing the representations of revolts and the reactions of the authorities in popular media with mockery. The illustration depicting the arresting of the *"Bauernrebell Krauss"* shows a peasant hiding fearfully in a hay barrel excusing himself to the approaching soldiers with the words: *"ich bin ein arm verführtes Bäuerlein"*.[61]

A second broadsheet entitled *Das rebellische Bayrn Parlament zu Braunau*, shows the assembly of the Bavarian peasants and burghers at Braunau in 1705 (the so called *Landesdefesionskongreß* or *Braunauer Parlament*) as a collection of ridiculous figures and animals (dogs and boars), who nevertheless are easy to perceive as a conjuration with the Gallic cock in the background window, instigating the revolt.[62] Though the revolt was bloodily crushed by Austrian military forces, killing hundreds of peasants and burghers (the so called *Sendlinger Mordweihnacht*), the following broadsheets depict only the capital punishment of the ringleaders for crimes such as the *crimen laesae maiestatis, perduellio* and treason. Furthermore, the emperor published additional reports and pamphlets to propagate, *"daß der wider die Röm. Kayserl. Majestät und dero höchstlöbl. Administration der Chur-Bayerischen Lande von den Unterthanen darinnen vorgenommene Auffstand unrechtmäßig, Gewissen-loß und hochstraffbar sey"*.[63]

---

59 Many of them reprinted in: Christian Probst, *Lieber bayrisch sterben. Der bayrische Volksaufstand der Jahre 1705 und 1706* (Munich 1978), 313, 336, 392, 403, 407; Henric L. Wuermeling, *1705. Der bayerische Volksaufstand und die Sendlinger Mordweihnacht. Mit einem Prolog von Winston S. Churchill*, 5th edition (Munich 2005), 63, 285.

60 Der Bayrischen Rebellen Rädelsführer Erste Execution Lohn und Warnung, 1706; Wahrhaffte Abbildung des bayrischen Rebellen Matth. Kraußen Hinrichtung in Kehlheim [1706], both reprinted in: Probst, Volksaufstand, 403, 407.

61 Einer von den verwegensten rebellischen Bauren in Bayern Krauss oder schwartzer Jockel genannt [...] (Nürnberg).

62 Das rebellische Bayrn Parlament zu Braunau, Probst, Volksaufstand, 392 f.

63 Gründliche Vorstellung, daß der wider die Röm. Kayserl. Majestät und dero höchstlöbl. Administration der Chur-Bayerischen Lande von den Unterthanen darinnen vorgenommene Auffstand unrechtmäßig, Gewissen-loß und hochstraffbar sey, 1706. Compare the comprehensive study of Strasser, Aufstand im bayerischen Oberland.

Fig. 10: Das rebellische Bayrn Parlament zu Braunau

Fig. 11 & 12: Two different representations of revolt: the execution of the ringleader Kraus (Wahrhaffte Abbildung), and Khlarwein as a Bavarian patriot (Rechtfertigung Plinganser, in: Probst, Volksaufstand, 313)

Though the Habsburg media policy spread the image of the upheaval as a criminal revolt, at least one pamphlet seemed to support the perspective of the "resistance fighters" and martyrs for their country.[64] Despite the option to use popular media for an affirmative representation of revolts, the Bavarian example on the whole solidifies that the emperor and the authorities did not only control the public media, but used them to communicate the authoritarian representation of revolts as political crimes.

In the course of 18th century, the ambiguous or even "dangerous" options for an affirmative representation of revolts and political opposition in popular media gained more importance. Social protest movements and revolts made increasing use of print media. Likewise, enlightened discourses criticised censorship, political oppression and capital punishment. In this respect, the European authorities had to deal with a sensitised public that could react differently to the severe public punishment of rebels and an authoritarian media policy aiming at the representation of revolts as political crimes. The example of the Peasants' revolt in Hungary (Transylvania) against serfdom and the Habsburg regime lead by Horea and Kloska, who were executed in 1785, may serve to finally prove this. Habsburg suppressed the revolt of the Romanian peasants at the end of 1784 with military force, and an imperial commission sentenced more than 30 rebels to death. Joseph II pardoned all rebels who renounced the revolt and acknowledged the authorities or mitigated the death penalties, with the exception of the three "ringleaders" Horea, Kloska and Crisan (the latter one committing suicide prior to the execution). They were executed by using the conventional punishment for high treason and lèse-majesty: Horea and Kloska were broken on the wheel, disembowelled, decapitated and quartered in front of a large crowd of peasants, cordoned off by the imperial army; afterwards the quartered corpses and the heads were exposed on pillars. The punishment was clearly aimed at retaliation, deterrence and general prevention with regard to the assembled peasants and the still ongoing social unrest in the Habsburg territories.

The revolt as well as the capital punishment of its leaders evoked a strong echo in the European press and other print media, not least because Joseph II – the "enlightened reformer" – was involved, and reforms such as the abolishment of serfdom and social unrest constituted prime issues of the enlightened discourses. The reactions in the public media were mixed: Many followed the official interpretation of the revolt as a political crime that was rightfully suppressed. Others – especially newspapers – tried to give more or less "objective information" on the upheaval, and some publications showed favour for the causes of the revolt

---

64 The so called "Rechtfertigung Plinganser": Probst, Volksaufstand, 313.

or dismissed the "barbaric" punishment of its leaders.[65] The public dispute on the interpretation of the revolts is discernible in the two broadsides, respectively illustrations, depicting the punishment of Horea and Kloska.

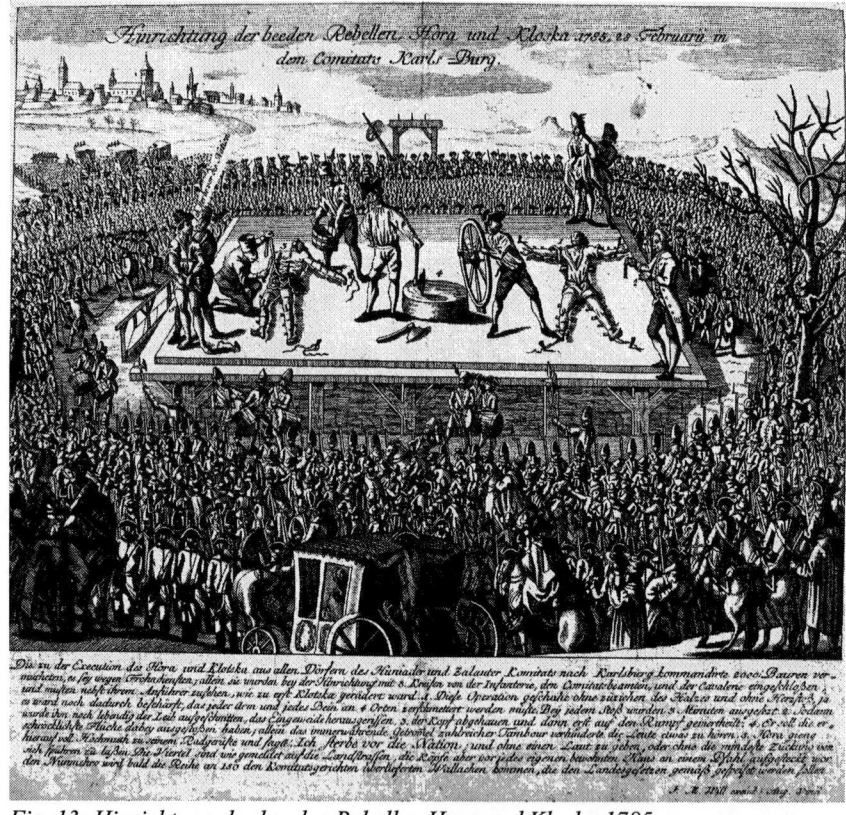

Fig. 13: *Hinrichtung der beeden Rebellen Hora und Kloska 1785*

The broadsheet *Hinrichtung der beeden Rebellen Hora und Kloska 1785, 28. Februar, in dem Comitats Karls-Burg*, printed in Vienna and published 1785, shows the typical scenery of the execution with the wheel, the disembowelment, the executioner with the axe ready for decapitation, the pillars and gallows in the background to expose the quartered corpses etc.[66] Though actually a vast crowd of peasants was present (the text says 2000), the illustration over-emphasises the

---

65 See the thorough (but biased) study of Nicolae Edroiu, *Horea's uprising: European echoes* (Bukarest 1984).

66 *Hinrichtung der beeden Rebellen Hora und Kloska 1785, 28. Februar, in dem Comitats Karls-Burg* (Vienna 1785).

presence of the well-ordered military forces, among them several coaches with higher clerics or other officials, depicting the authorities as attending the punishment of the rebels in person. The execution platform is surrounded by military music (drummers), drowning out the last speech of one of the rebels, who shouts: *"ich sterbe vor die Nation"*. Insofar, the state not only dominates the scenery, but is in full control of the peasants as well as demonstrating its power and ability to suppress a revolt by using the traditional public punishment of the *Endliche Rechtstag*. The "seduced", but pardoned "followers" are allowed to attend the execution of the ringleaders, who are punished as traitors, but the state prevents the rebels from making a last speech to communicate "their" message of the revolt: the liberation of the nation. On the other hand, the image is ambivalent: The state needs exceptional means like loud music and has to rely on vast military forces as well as on "barbaric" punishments to deal with social unrest and upheaval.[67]

A second broadside entitled *"Vorstellung der Execution"*, probably produced by the printer Johann David Donnhäuser from Frankfurt am Main, gives a slightly different view: peasants trying to enter the platform, a larger crowd of peasants, but a smaller number of soldiers and only one drummer in the background.[68]

Fig. 14: *Vorstellung der Execution*

---

[67] Compare the reaction of Brissot to the capital punishment of the rebels: Leonore Loft, "The Transylvanian Peasant Uprising of 1784, Brissot and the Right to Revolt: A Research Note", *French Historical Studies* 1 (1991), 209-218.

[68] Vorstellung der Execution, welche an den beyden Wallachischen Rebellen, Horia und Klotska, zu Karlsburg vollzogen worden / I. D. D. [d.i. wahrscheinl. Johann David Donnhäuser] (Frankfurt 1785).

Concluding Remarks

The early modern illustrated broadsheets are an important popular media of a cross-border, Europe-wide representation of revolts, communicating the image of revolts as political crimes and the reactions of the authorities within the legal framework of penal justice and punishment. In this respect, the representation of revolts in broadsheets and popular media follow the patterns of *"Verrechtlichung"*. In addition, the state and its legal system are placed at the centre of the popular representation of revolts, thus communicating that revolts were increasingly considered – particularly in penal law and the juristic discourses – as crimes against the state (or its representatives), and that the state had to be protected against such political crimes. From this point of view, the broadsides and pamphlets reflect the development of *"Staatsschutz"*. I do not suggest that this was a linear development or even a process of modernisation, but I would like to stress that the representation of revolts in criminal law and public media was closely linked and formed a more or less prevailing pattern of perception and reaction within the legal system and the legal construction of political crimes.

Therefore, all types of revolts in different European countries were covered, though we can observe a slight preference for the rebellions of the nobility and political crimes aiming at the ruler and the state. It seems that peasants' revolts – by sheer quantity – are somehow underrepresented because either the authorities did not perceive them as main threats to the order, or could rely on the combination of legal process (*Rechtsweg*) and criminal justice, whereas the revolts of the nobility were considered as the more dangerous threat to the state or the system of government. On the other hand, it could also be argued that crimes in the sphere of the nobility were of higher interest to the public and made a better topic for selling broadsheets. Nevertheless, the broadsheets and pamphlets convey no substantial difference between the revolts of peasants, burghers or nobles: All of them are represented as political crimes with the focus on the legal reactions of the authorities, especially on the harsh public punishment of the rebels, depicted as ringleaders, traitors and conspirers. Here, the representation of revolts as political crimes in popular print media corresponds with the developments in penal law and the juristic discourses, using similar elements and symbols: the revolt as *crimen laesae maiestatis*, treason, sedition and conspiracy; the differentiation between ringleaders and followers and the public capital punishment of the former with quartering, dismemberment, decapitation, the exposition of corpses and heads and the appearance of shame pillars.

Concerning the overall images, symbols and icons, one may discern no substantial difference to the representation of ordinary crimes in illustrated broadsheets, albeit there are slight variations. The broadsides dealing with ordinary crimes often depict the crime itself or the motifs of the criminals, whereas the causes of a revolt or the motivations of the rebels are almost ignored and the actual performance of a revolt is very seldomly depicted. In the case of ordinary crimes, no authority feared that the public could appreciate the motifs of the criminal, but with regard to revolts, popular media could harbour ambivalent effects and help spread oppositional ideas or even legitimate causes of social unrest and protest. For political crimes, respectively revolts, the legal responses of the authorities are related to different *Öffentlichkeiten* (public stages): The rebels themselves used the public and print media and, likewise, penal punishment depended on the public theatre of the *Endliche Rechtstag*. Beyond that, it also required the authorities' public media to distribute the image of a just legal reaction to crime and to enhance the desired impact of public punishment: the *damnatio memoriae* of the rebels and the obliteration of political dissidence, as well as deterrence and general prevention with regard to followers.

In this respect, the illustrated broadsheets were clearly influenced by the media policy of the authorities and their view on revolts. However, one should not forget the commercial interests of the printers and the curiosity of a growing public for sensational news: Broadsheets and pamphlets were to be sold to distribute a message. Accordingly, they offered limited space for slightly different images and representations of revolts. Some broadsheets furnished a revolt with an "individual" face in portraits of "ringleaders" who looked like honourable burghers or nobles. Rebels could appear as seduced or errant sinners with a righteous cause who had pursued the wrong path of violence and insurrection against the authority. Even a distinct representation of rebels as criminals who had to be punished with harsh penalties could promote their perception as martyrs.

Thus, the authorities not only needed to control the popular media dealing with political crimes by censorship, but, moreover, also had to develop a media policy of their own to influence public opinion. This first of all included the publishing of "own" pamphlets or their commission and the placing of the legal response and public capital punishment at the centre of the message and the image they were to disseminate: The suppression of a revolt and the punishment of the rebels as a legitimate and just reaction of the state within the legal framework of penal law. Viewed in this light, the broadsheets contain and depict crucial symbols and icons of penal justice or cite confessions and verdicts as well as emphasising the presence of a well-ordered and powerful state. In contrast, the rebels are depicted and characterised as traitors and conspirers collaborating with foreign enemies. Especially the image of traitors and conspirators – shaped in the public media as well as in penal law – seemed to influence the perception and representation of political crimes on the whole: Attempted assassination as well as the formation of secret "conspirative" groups were regarded as the preliminary stage or the start of a revolt against the state. On the other hand, the authorities developed an additional media strategy with regard to the representation of peasants' revolts: the mocking of the rebels and the revolt, however, still using the image of severe penal punishment.

In conclusion, the effect and function of the broadsheets and pamphlets was to disseminate the theatre of public punishment to a wider public and to commemorate just legal punishment, thus enhancing the flexible legal responses to revolt: the defamation of the ringleaders as traitors and conspirers and their total social exclusion and disintegration; the deterrence of seduced or potential followers, as well as their reconciliation with the legal and political order, which they accepted especially by attending public punishment; the *damnatio memoriae* and obliteration of the revolt particularly with regard to its causes, which were now labelled as being purely "criminal", so that not the slightest reminiscence that the revolt occurred under any legitimate reasons or aims remained.

However, these were mainly the effects the authorities affiliated and desired, and it is hardly valid to conclude that illustrated broadsheets and popular media dealing with revolts fully obtained such an impact and successfully influenced public opinions and attitudes in Europe according to the described representation of revolts. For the media, representation of revolts could cause ambiguous effects and the broadsheet helped to keep the memory of the revolts themselves alive, as they demonstrated that "political crimes", unrest, dissent and protest had, in fact, existed and that the state had to use severe remedies to cope with them. Ongoing unrest and potential rebels could make use of broadsheets to memorise "martyrs" of a just cause and to demonstrate the "cruel" suppression of resistance and opposition. Furthermore, the representation of revolts and political crimes could help spread the news of revolt to a wider European public, across the borders, in foreign countries with a more sceptical public or even to competing powers. There is still very little research on the "productive use" of popular media by contemporaries, as it is even more difficult (or perhaps even impossible) to measure the impact of popular media dealing with crime for the early modern period than for the present. Still, early modern legal as well as public discourses certainly formed a persisting "cross-border" representation of pre-modern revolts as political crimes against the state and its order, planned and committed by conspiracies and criminal groups to which the state responded within a legal framework, albeit using all the options of the criminal justice system as well as the opportunities of the public media.

Authors

Yves-Marie Bercé studies early-modern France and Europe. Since his doctoral thesis *Histoire des Croquants: étude des soulèvements populaires au XVIIe siècle dans le sud-ouest de la France* (Genève/Paris, 1974) popular revolts are among his major research interests. He is author of *Le roi caché* (Paris 1990), of *Revolt and Revolution in Early Modern Europe*, transl. J. Bergin, (Manchester, 1985), and of *The Birth of Absolutism. A History of France, 1598-1661* (Palgrave, 1996). In 1998 he has been awarded with the prize Madeleine Laurain Portener for the entirety of his work. He is member of the *Institut de France*.

André Berelowitch is Associate researcher at the *Centre d'études des Mondes Russe, Caucasien et Centre-Européen*, EHESS (Ecole des hautes études en sciences sociales) in Paris. He is specializing in Russian social and intellectual history of the 16th and 18th centuries. Among his numerous publications are *La hiérarchie des égaux. La noblesse russe d'ancien régime, XVIe-XVIIe siècles* (Seuil, 2001), an annotated Russian edition (with P. Uvarov and V. Nazarov) of Jacques Margeret's account of the Time of troubles in early 17th century Muscovy: Žak Maržeret, *Sostoyanie Rossiiskoi imperii* (Moscow 2007), as well as theoretical considerations on more general trends in historiography such as "Limites et portée du comparatisme", *Cahiers du monde russe* 46/1-2 (2005): 13-17.

Bettina Bommersbach has studied History and Literature in Bielefeld and Paris and is preparing a PhD thesis on the Jacquerie and the movement of Etienne Marcel in 1358. In her research she has focused on French revolts of the 14th and 15th centuries. She has been research assistant in the Bielefeld Collaborative Research Centre working on a project called "Violence as Means and Subject of Pre-Modern Political Communication – Protest Movements and their Repression in Late Medieval France and England", which was supervised by Prof. Dr. Neithard Bulst. Her publications include "Gewalt in der Jacquerie von 1358", in *Gewalt im politischen Raum. Fallanalysen vom Spätmittelalter bis ins 20. Jahrhundert*, ed.

Neithard Bulst, Ingrid Gilcher-Holtey & Heinz-Gerhard Haupt (Frankfurt, 2008), 46-81 and "Violence dans la Jacquerie de 1356. 'Faire couler à plaisir le sang'", in: P. Rigault, P. Toussaint (eds.), La Jacquerie. Entre mémoire et oubli 1358-1958-2008. Actes du colloque de Clermont, Amiens 2012, 73-88.

Fabrizio Dal Vera studied Communication Studies and Early Modern History at Bologna University. His research interests include political languages and theories, with a particular focus on political crimes and terrorism. In his PhD Dal Vera dealt with legal and political treatises on seditions. Among his publications is the article "Seditio: Aufruhr im politisch-rechtlichen Denken Konrad Brauns (1491-1563)", in: George K. Hasselhoff, David von Mayenburg (eds.): *Die Zwölf Artikel von 1525 und das "Göttliche Recht" der Bauern – rechtshistorische und theologische Dimensionen*. Würzburg, Ergon-Verlag, 2012. In his forthcoming book "*Seditio: la tutela dell'ordine pubblico nella trattatistica giuridico-politica tra XVI e XVII secolo*" he shows how collective episodes of violence against the authorities were gradually criminalized in 16th-17th century France and Germany.

Malte Griesse studied history in Cologne, Volgograd, Moscow and Paris. Part of his PhD, defended at the *Ecole des hautes études en sciences sociales* (Paris), has been published under the title *Communiquer, juger et agir sous Staline: la personne prise entre ses liens avec les proches et son rapport au système politico-idéologique* (Frankfurt, Bern et al., 2011). He has taught mainly in Paris, Bielefeld and Konstanz, where he leads a research group on "Early-Modern Revolts as Communicative Events" at the Cluster of Excellence "Cultural Foundations of Social Integration". Currently he is holding a one-year research-fellowship at the Mahindra Humanities Center (Harvard University, Cambridge).

Karl Härter is Research Group Leader and Senior Research Scientist at the Max-Planck-Institute for European Legal History, Frankfurt/M. and Professor for Early Modern and Modern History at the University of Darmstadt. His major research interests are legal and constitutional history of Early Modern Europe, notably the history of crime and penal law. Current projects concern the history of political crime and the formation of trasnational crimnial law regimes. He has published monographs on the Imperial Diet in the Age of the French Revolution and *Policey und Strafjustiz in Kurmainz*, several collected volumes on *Repräsentationen von Kriminalität und öffentlicher Sicherheit, Grazia e giustizia fra tardo medioevo ed età contemporanea, Politische Kriminalität, Recht, Justiz und Polizei zwischen Früher Neuzeit und 20. Jahrhundert*, and *Revolts and Political Crime from the 12th to the 19th Century*, and more than 90 Articles in collected volumes and journals.

Helmut Hinck has studied History and English Literature in Bielefeld and written a MA thesis on the representation of the English rebels of 1381 in contemporary sources. He has been research assistant in the Bielefeld Collaborative Research Centre working on a project called "Violence as Means and Subject of Pre-Modern Political Communication – Protest Movements and their Repression in Late Medieval France and England", which was supervised by Prof. Dr. Neithard Bulst. He is preparing a doctoral dissertation on popular protest and its repression in late medieval England. His publications include "Obrigkeitliche Gewalt bei der Niederschlagung der englischen Erhebung von 1381", in *Gewalt im politischen Raum. Fallanalysen vom Spätmittelalter bis ins 20. Jahrhundert*, ed. Neithard Bulst, Ingrid Gilcher-Holtey & Heinz-Gerhard Haupt (Frankfurt, 2008), 82-133 and "The Rising of 1381 in Winchester", *English Historical Review* 125 (2010), 112-131.

Ingrid Maier works as a Professor of Russian at the Department of Modern Languages (Uppsala University). She has published extensively on 17th-century newspaper translations into Russian ('Vesti-Kuranty'), focusing on the cultural and historical background of this text corpus and on the individual translations from Dutch, Latin, Polish, German, and English sources. She is an international consultant of the Russian State Archives of Ancient Documents (RGADA), Moscow; a member of the advisory board of the German research institute Deutsche Presseforschung (Bremen); and a member of the editorial board of the on-going *Dictionary of the Russian language ($11^{th} - 17^{th}$ centuries)*. At present (2013–2017), Maier is leading a major research project, financed by *Riksbankens jubileumsfond* (Bank of Sweden Tercentenary Foundation).

Maureen Perrie is Emeritus Professor of Russian History in the Centre for Russian and East European Studies, University of Birmingham, U.K. She has published extensively on Russian history from the 16th to the 20th centuries: her monographs include *Pretenders and Popular Monarchism in Early Modern Russia: the False Tsars of the Time of Troubles* (Cambridge University Press, 1995), and she edited the first (pre-Petrine) volume of *The Cambridge History of Russia* (2006). In 2001-2004 she served as President of the *British Association for Slavonic and East European Studies* (BASEES). Her current research is on the concept of the 'true tsar' in 17th-century Russia.

Angela Rustemeyer (1965) is Universitätsdozentin of Eastern European history at Vienna University. She has also taught at Cologne University, Heidelberg University, and the University of Halle-Wittenberg. She wrote her doctoral thesis about domestic servants in Petersburg and Moscow, 1861–1917 (1994) and her Habilitationsschrift about lèse-majesté in early modern Russia (2004). Her research interests include crime and law in Russia and France, 1500–1930, economy and culture in early modern Eastern Europe, and the history of ethnography and historiography. Since 2009 Angela Rustemeyer has been running projects for the development of adult literacy at the *German Adult Education Association*.

Stepan Mikhailovich Shamin holds a PhD in History and is Senior Researcher at the Institute of Russian History of the Russian Academy of Sciences. He is the author of many publications on Russian 17th century history and culture, among them *Kuranty XVII stoletiia. Evropeiskaia pressa v Rossii i vozniknovenie russkoi periodicheskoi pechati* [17th-century news digests: The European press in Russia and the genesis of Russian periodical publications] (Moscow, St. Petersburg, 2011).

Frank Sysyn is director of the Peter Jacyk Centre for Ukrainian Historical Research at the Canadian Institute of Ukrainian Studies, professor in the Department of History and Classics at the University of Alberta, and editor in chief of the Hrushevsky Translation Project, the English translation of the multi-volume History of Ukraine-Rus'. A specialist in Ukrainian and Polish history, he is the author of Between Poland and the Ukraine: The Dilemma of Adam Kysil, 1600-1653 (1985), Mykhailo Hrushevsky: Historian and National Awakener (2001), and studies on the Khmelnytsky Uprising, Ukrainian historiography, and early modern Ukrainian political culture. He is also coauthor, with Serhii Plokhy, of Religion and Nation in Modern Ukraine (2003).